Transnational Spaces
and Identities in the
Francophone World

FRANCE OVERSEAS: Studies in Empire and Decolonization

Series Editors
Philip Boucher, A. J. B. Johnston, James D. Le Sueur, and Tyler Stovall

Transnational Spaces and Identities in the Francophone World

Edited by

HAFID GAFAÏTI,

PATRICIA M. E. LORCIN,

and DAVID G. TROYANSKY

University of Nebraska Press   Lincoln & London

Much of chapter 2, "The Uncomfortable Inhabitants of French Colonial
Modernity: Mandate Syria's Communities of Collaboration (1920–1946)" by
Keith David Watenpaugh, is drawn from *Being Modern in the Middle East:
Revolution, Nationalism, Colonialism, and the Arab Middle Class* (Princeton
NJ: Princeton University Press, 2006) and is used here with permission. Much
of chapter 5, "Excluding the *Harkis* from Repatriate Status, Excluding Muslim Algerians from French Identity" by Todd Shepard, is drawn from chapter
9 of his book, *The Invention of Decolonization: The Algerian War and the
Remaking of France* (Ithaca NY: Cornell University Press, 2006), and is used
here with permission. A version of chapter 19, "Displaying World Culture
in Provincial France: *Francophonie* in Limoges" by David Troyansky, was
presented at the 2003 meeting of the Society for French Historical Studies
in Milwaukee, Wisconsin. Research was funded by a grant from Texas Tech
University.

⊗

Library of Congress Cataloging-in-Publication Data

Transnational spaces and identities in the francophone world / edited by
Hafid Gafaïti, Patricia M. E. Lorcin, and David G. Troyansky.
    p. cm. — (France overseas : studies in empire and decolonization)
Includes bibliographical references and index.
ISBN 978-0-8032-4452-8 (paper : alk. paper)
1. France—Ethnic relations. 2. Minorities—France—Social conditions.
3. Immigrants—France—Social conditions. 4. France—Emigration and
immigration—Social aspects. 5. Postcolonialism—Social aspects—France.
6. France—Colonies—Social conditions. 7. French-speaking countries—
Social conditions. 8. Postcolonialism—Social aspects—France. 9. Transna-
tionalism. 10. French literature—France—Colonies—History and criticism.
I. Gafaïti, Hafid. II. Lorcin, Patricia M. E. III. Troyansky, David G.
DC34.T73 2009
305.8009171′244—dc22
2009003405

Set in Sabon by Bob Reitz.

Contents

Editors' Preface

Migratory movements throughout the Francophone world and within France itself have led to the formation of diasporas and immigrant cultures that continue to transform both French society and immigrants themselves while contributing to global or transnational identities and cultures. Social scientists have studied these migrations. More culturally oriented scholars have begun to explore how literary and historical texts account for these movements by not only rewriting cultures and producing migratory and immigrant identities but also by redefining the very notion of national literature, culture, and history. The contributors to this volume examine how these phenomena have led to the constitution of national and transnational cultures and how diasporas contribute to the construction of new identities that defy traditional ways of thinking about identity, culture, nation, and history.

Simply put, historians and literary scholars of France and *Francophonie* have gained a more profound recognition of the complicated nature of relations between the "Hexagon" and the wider world. It is not just a matter of relating different geographic spaces or observing a clash of clearly defined identities. Spaces themselves are related in very complicated ways, with people migrating in various directions and gaining multiple identities, particularly with the emergence of a second and third generation following the mid-twentieth-century migrations associated with decolonization. To be sure, there has been a long tradition of French colonial studies tracing the spread of French power and expertise to the wider world as well as describing French withdrawal and the development of new national identities. But whereas older historical methodologies tended to emphasize the economic and the political, postcolonial studies emphasize culture and discourse. Historians and literary scholars have more to say to one another.

Awareness of the importance of immigration has complicated historians' conceptions of the Hexagon, and a wave of studies followed Gérard Noiriel's *Le creuset français*.[1] Those early studies explored themes of assimilation and integration. But just as studies of American immigration evolved from the melting pot to multiculturalism, French studies now call into question the universalism of the old Jacobin tradition itself.[2] And in both countries the historical literature has shifted from the social to the cultural. Immigrants bear cultural traditions with them, transform "host" communities, and are in turn transformed. French historical studies reveal a fragmented narrative, and in a very influential series of historical works, France itself has been presented in the plural as *les France*.[3] But those representations of French history and identity may not have been sufficiently plural. Steven Englund rightly remarks that for all their creativity many of the studies that make up Pierre Nora's *Les lieux de mémoire* seek to restore a unified French identity, and Hue-Tam Ho Tai notes the absence of colonial and postcolonial sites of memory in Nora's project.[4]

In literary studies francophone sites of memory have certainly asserted themselves, as writers in French describe migrations between vastly different territories and lives lived between cultures. Francophonie itself has both African and French origins. It can be associated with the *négritude* movement of Senghor or the cultural politics of Bourguiba, but it also has late-nineteenth-century roots in the French cultural geography of Onésime Reclus and a great variety of international institutional manifestations in the late twentieth century.[5] A way of describing literature, cultural politics, and identity, Francophonie has become a site of multiple memories.

Recognition of this complication and of the usefulness of juxtaposing historical and literary approaches provided the germ for a conference held at Texas Tech University in March 2002, the university's thirty-fifth annual comparative literature symposium. Sixty-five writers, literary scholars, and historians gathered to discuss transnational cultures, diasporas, and immigrant identities in France and the francophone world. The gathering included readings of fiction, reflections on narrating diasporic experiences, and a North American premiere of a play, but most contributions were scholarly papers.[6] A selection of the French-language papers has appeared in *Migrances, Diasporas et Transculturalités Francophones: Littératures et cultures d'Afrique, des Caraïbes, d'Europe et du Québec* (Paris: L'Harmattan, 2005). The present volume gathers a selection of the English-language contributions, reworked and reordered into a representative and coherent whole, along with two papers presented elsewhere by two conference participants (Aldrich and Troyansky).

One of the discoveries of the conference was the importance of cross-disciplinary work. Social scientists and literary scholars often employ different languages, but they can communicate common concerns about social conditions and ways of representing them. Participants moved relatively easily from one disciplinary world to

another. In his own career, for example, one of the Lubbock conference participants, Azouz Begag, wrote as a sociologist on immigrant
youth and made a literary splash with a fictionalized memoir of the
beur experience of *banlieue* youth in Lyon, which reached a wide
French public in a film version.[7] In 2005 he became French minister
for equal opportunities, a post he quit at the height of the 2007
presidential campaign in order to publish a strong critique of government reaction to conditions and events in the immigrant suburbs
and of French public policy and rhetoric more generally. Clearly the
issues raised here are of contemporary political import.

Begag's career is not quite typical, but the interdisciplinary impulse
that prompted the Lubbock conference and this book continues
to manifest itself in several ways. In one dimension historians and
littéraires join forces. Thus, for example, literary scholar and contributor to this volume Georges Van Den Abbeele collaborates with
historian Tyler Stovall in examining matters of colonialism and race,
and conference participant Seth Graebner combines historical and
literary insights in a study of representations of the Algerian city.[8]
In another dimension it becomes increasingly difficult to separate
French history from French colonial history. Thus Gary Wilder's
book on négritude joins francophone literary history to the history
of the French state while transcending old geographical divisions,
and Todd Shepard's study of decolonization wins the American
Historical Association's J. Russell Major Award for best book in
French history.[9] Even the topic of Franco-French conflict in the Vichy
period finds a more global context in books by Eric Jennings and
Ruth Ginio, and James Le Sueur's important work on intellectuals
and Algerian decolonization treats French and Algerian intellectuals together.[10] At an institutional level French departments develop
programs in French studies, often with strong social-scientific content; and graduate students in French history almost routinely study

the wider francophone world. On a practical level the events in the working-class suburbs of French cities in 2005 called for interdisciplinary responses, including such artistic ones as found in *The French Evolution: Race, Politics and the 2005 Riots,* an exhibition that brought works of Alexis Peskine to the Museum of Contemporary African Diasporan Arts in Brooklyn, New York, in 2007.

Colonialism and Immigration

It would be wrong to imagine the world of the banlieue as something emerging suddenly and with no prior history. It was a result of much longer-term historical forces and movements between France and colonial and postcolonial territories. Part 1 of this book looks back from the predicament of multiculturalism to its sources in France's global empire, which extended to the Americas and the Caribbean to East Asia, the Middle East, and Africa. French expansion reaches back to the early modern period, but the section on "colonialism and immigration" concentrates on twentieth-century examples situated in North Africa, the Middle East, and France itself.

Philip Dine's chapter explores a powerful myth that continued to justify French control of Algeria well into the struggle over independence. "The French Colonial Myth of a Pan-Mediterranean Civilization" offers a particular variant of the more general idea of a "*mission civilisatrice*" that had operated globally in the nineteenth century.[11] Not only did that myth justify colonial domination, but it functioned as a formative element among people of European origin, the *pieds-noirs*, who so complicated the history of French-Algerian relations. Literary claims of a Mediterranean melting pot or Mediterranean humanism went back to the 1930s and were activated anew during the Algerian War (1954–62). Dine follows it into the writing of Albert Camus, whose *Le Premier Homme* appeared posthumously only in 1994. The play of history and memory kept the myth alive into the contemporary period with its debate over the status of Camus as French/Algerian/francophone writer.

Algeria may be the most traumatic case, but French colonialism and colonial immigration extended well beyond that one country. Keith Watenpaugh's chapter, "The Uncomfortable Inhabitants of French Colonial Modernity: Mandate Syria's Communities of Collaboration (1920–1946)," on French "*civilisation*" and the various communities of Syria extends the analysis of colonial legacies and integration of non-French populations to the Middle East. He pays attention to religion and class in his treatment of the Greek Catholic and Armenian communities of Aleppo from the immediate aftermath of the Armenian genocide to the 1940s. He demonstrates the attraction non-Western middle classes felt for French culture and its particular institutional manifestation in the *Scouts de France*. Thus he offers a look at a francophone form of socialization for youth in the late colonial world.

The first section of the book ends with Elisa Camiscioli's "Race Making and Race Mixing in the Early Twentieth-Century Immigration Debate," a look at French fears of degeneration resulting from immigration of nonwhites. The emergence of pronatalist pressure groups and fear mongering among the new practitioners of demography, who were alarmed at the falling French birthrate, has already drawn historians' attention.[12] Camiscioli sees in that phenomenon the construction of new racial categories. Political rhetoric packaged in social-scientific studies declared French "whiteness" to be in danger. She calls into question old claims of the color blindness of French colonial assimilation. While her analysis focuses on the interwar period, the controversy over race-consciousness continues to rage in French representations of themselves and comparisons between France and the United States.

Immigrant Spaces and Identities

Part 2 offers the most concrete or literal treatments of immigrant spaces and identities. Neil MacMaster in "Shantytown Republics: Algerian Migrants and the Culture of Space in the *Bidonville*" explores the use of space by residents of shantytowns that sprang up around French cities in the era of immigration of populations from the Maghreb after the Second World War. Building upon a classic study by Pierre Bourdieu, MacMaster explores the shape of these sprawling neighborhoods and their uses both at the macro and micro levels. Instead of his essay becoming a study of official repression and indoctrination, it becomes an appreciation of how cultural borrowings from North African cities and French policies of urbanism and control and the appropriations of space by the immigrants themselves become ways of adapting to challenging circumstances and making a new environment their own.

Immigrants in France found themselves adapting not only to particular physical environments but also to particular demographic and politically defined categories. From this perspective, in "Excluding the *Harkis* from Repatriate Status, Excluding Muslim Algerians from French Identity," Todd Shepard examines problems of identity in the precise context of *harki* migration to France in the wake of the Algerian War of Independence. Harkis were Algerian collaborators with French colonial authorities who faced Algerian retribution and sociopolitical exclusion at the hands of French authorities in the metropole. Shepard explores the details of political categories that sought to impose a particular identity on a community that faced not only a double exclusion but also a shadow existence, as French and Algerian historical memory imposed a kind of erasure until the very recent past.

In the 1980s the French public began to pay attention to the challenge of multiculturalism. Not only did the far right use the "other" as a hobgoblin representing all that was discomfiting in France,[13] but the left also expressed fears of social fragmentation, and immigrant children and grandchildren made their presence felt in some of the most perceptive fictional and nonfictional writing of the period. Some of that awareness struck the public most forcefully in the arts of the 1990s. And the form that traveled most rapidly and broadly was the cinema.

The international public became aware of French multicultural-ism through the films of Mathieu Kassovitz, and we conclude part 2 with a study of their reception in France. Kassovitz's second and most famous film, *La Haine* (1995), shocked the majority French audience and viewers in the immigrant and working-class banlieue. It used techniques familiar from American cinema to reflect developments in the French urban landscape to provoke diverse responses. Alain Gabon's chapter, "The Transformation of French Identity in Mathieu Kassovitz's Films *Métisse* (1993) and *La Haine* (1995)," juxtaposes the more "documentary" *La Haine* with the earlier and lighter *Métisse* to explore their reception. Gabon concentrates on the diversity of responses and the particularities of 1990s French politics and culture.

Writing Algerian Identities

Harkis constituted one group of Algerians seeking to forge a collective identity, and they represent an artifact of the history of colonialism. Part 3 examines other groups and individuals attempting to form identities in independent Algeria and in immigrant communities in France. It includes both historical and literary investigations into the problems of migration and identity and adds the issues of gender and sexuality.

In "A Poet's Politics: Jean Sénac's Writings during the Algerian War," Robert Aldrich examines the paradox of "a pied-noir supporter of Algerian independence who was murdered in independent Algeria." We are far from the typical pied-noir community but still in the world of negotiations over relationships between European and Algerian in a period of crisis. Sénac represents a case of European identification with Algerian independence, an attempt to convince pieds-noirs of their error, and a critique of the famous position taken by Albert Camus. Aldrich explores the complicating factor of Sénac's sexual marginality and its legacy for both France and Algeria.

Trudy Agar-Mendousse's "Counterviolence and the Ethics of Nomadism: Malika Mokeddem's Reconstruction of Algerian Identity" extends the chronology from independence to the 1990s and reveals an Algerian woman writing in French of violence, counterviolence, and nomadism. By taking a synoptic view of Algerian history, Mokeddem can trace a variety of representations and contexts for the development of Algerian female identity in a world of French violence and appropriations of French culture. Traces of history and echoes of a longer-term past permit what Agar calls a "creative counterviolence."

Mary McCullough's chapter, "Interpretation, Representation, and Belonging in the Works of Leïla Sebbar," shifts our attention from the Algerian setting of war and resistance to French territory and the world of *Beur* literature. She examines Leïla Sebbar's interpretation in the 1990s of key events from the period of the Algerian War of Independence. McCullough explores the appropriateness of treating Sebbar, herself an immigrant writing about children of immigrants, as a "Beur" writer. She points out how Sebbar is expected to offer a sociological realism but actually engages in a more literary enterprise that represents France as richly multicultural.

Jewish Migrations and Identities

The next section of the book comprises three chapters on a relatively neglected aspect of francophone studies, the Jewish experience on both sides of the Mediterranean. The three essays also represent divergent disciplinary approaches, ranging from the social historical to the literary and philosophical. Yet they all address themes of identity.

Sarah Sussman's study, "Jews from Algeria and French Jewish Identity," explores a very complicated set of characteristics. Algerian Jews in France "were Jewish *and* Sephardi on the one hand, French *and* pied-noir *and* Maghrebi *and* Algerian, on the other." In short they were "*frontaliers.*" Their existence in Algeria predated French arrival in 1830, and their status as French citizens resulting from the Crémieux Decree of 1870 set them apart from other Algerians, but they then became seen as a subgroup among the pieds-noirs, a group with a strong attachment to the French language and French identity. Yet language also separated them from the French, as they shared much with their Arab and Berber neighbors, and in France they found themselves alienated from their Ashkenazic coreligionists. Sussman describes themes of loss, displacement, nostalgia, and an attempt to create identity through communal institutions, religious practice, and folkways, most especially cuisine. Her work derives both from published sources and interviews.

Johann Sadock pushes further the analysis of francophone Jewish identity, but his sources are essentially literary. In "Anti-Arab and Anti-French Tendencies in Post-1948 Oriental Jewish Literature Written in French," he explores how "Oriental" Jewish literature combines anti-Arab and anti-French tendencies but at the same time finds commonalities. Jews and Arabs could both view the French as colonizers, and Jews could express nostalgia for preindependence Arab Muslim countries or alternatively integrate into French society. He takes us on a tour of the work of Albert Memmi, Paula Jacques, Hélène Cixous, Claude Brami, Annie Cohen, Gisèle Halimi, Amram El Maleh, Marco Koskas, and others. Sadock describes a wide range of discourses but isolates a bitterness toward Arabs mitigated by individual friendships and sympathies "and by the sense of belonging to a common Oriental sphere of influence."

Sadock's corpus is literary, but his goal is to understand a group's mentality. Brigitte Weltman-Aron in "The Figure of the Jew in North Africa: Memmi, Derrida, Cixous" also discusses Cixous and Memmi, but her concerns are less sociocultural than philosophical as she also brings Derrida, Blanchot, Lévinas, Heidegger, and Sartre into the picture. While Weltman-Aron relies heavily on Memmi, her approach owes much to Sartre's reflections immediately after the Second World War. "Does the Jew exist? And if he exists, what is he?" The answer in this philosophical tradition is complex, uncertain, and indeterminate. The language seems to resist a clear sense of time and place, but in fact the whole discussion derives from the obsessions of two philosophical generations running from the Shoah and Jewish migration from the Maghreb to the present.

Francophone Spaces and Multiple Identities

Part 5 takes us to much wider geographic and literary spaces. The chapters explore literary and personal relationships across a francophone world stretching from Lebanon, West Africa, and the Caribbean to Vietnam. They represent French as a global language resulting from the history of colonialism and demonstrate various solutions to the problem of multiple identities.

Antony Johae's "Transnational Identities in the Novels of Amin Maalouf" examines questions of identity in the work of a writer who fled the Lebanese civil war to settle in France. In answer to the question whether he feels himself to be more French or Lebanese, Maalouf's answer is *"l'un et l'autre."* Indeed he was raised as an Arabic-speaking Christian and schooled in French. And Johae traces Maalouf's treatment of identity in literary works set in the worlds of Omar Khayyam, of the sixteenth-century voyager Leo Africanus, and of nineteenth- and twentieth-century Lebanon. Otherness becomes the norm.

The French language is a key to identity in Joseph Militello's chapter, "Madwoman in the Senegalese Muslim Attic: Reading Myriam Warner-Vieyra's *Juletane* and Mariama Bâ's *Un chant écarlate*." The 1982 novel *Juletane* bridges the worlds of the francophone West Indies and West Africa. It is set in the early 1960s, when Pan-Africanism and négritude tried to transcend the differences of the two worlds. Indeed the character of Juletane permits an exploration of the problem of "the assimilation of a francophone Antillean woman into a francophone West African society, differences so insuperable that the two parties regard one another with a profound sense of alterity." Militello reads the novel against works of Jean Rhys and Mariama Bâ, blending literary, psychological, and sociological concerns.

The other two chapters in the section explore the world of Vietnamese literature in French. Georges Van Den Abbeele's "Gender, Exile, and Return in Viêt-Kiêu Literature" focuses on the "overseas Vietnamese," including not only exiles from the end of the American war but also exiles from a century of Chinese, French, and Japanese rule. And the resulting literature uses a background of two millennia of history and memory, a long experience of dealing with exile and return.

Ali Yédes uses that long-term background to explore francophone literary treatments of Vietnamese history. In "Vietnamese Relationships: Confucian or Francophone Model," he examines Buddhist and Confucian traditions in Vietnamese culture and their survival well beyond the period of direct Western influence. He criticizes previous scholars who have presented French colonialism as introducing modernity, and he claims that themes of individualism and freedom are already present in the early-nineteenth-century work of Nguyễn Du. For Yédes Vietnam's subsequent literary history reveals its affinity for French ideas picked up in French colonial schools and expressed in Vietnamese francophone literature.

Postmodern Sites and Identities

Part 6 attempts to go beyond themes of modernity. The first two chapters look at traditional elements and postmodernity in the Muslim and Arab worlds and focus upon representations of women. One looks at the problem of thinking only in terms of traditional and feminist alternatives. The other describes a particular artistic way of "revisioning the 'east.'" The final chapter explores the emergence of an institution of Francophonie in provincial France.

Habiba Deming in "Feminism and Neocolonialism: Discursive Practices" expresses dissatisfaction with the simple binary opposition between colonialism and postcolonialism. For her "Muslim femininity" was a basic element of colonial discourse, but she resists the idea that postcolonialism would result in a complete abandonment of the past and an adoption of a feminism modeled on the West's. Deming uses two novels from the early 1990s that achieved a privileged status as representations of women's condition in Algeria. She sees in the work of Nina Bouraoui and Malika Mokeddem a clinging to colonial stereotypes of a misogynistic Islam and to Western ideas of feminist emancipation.

David Prochaska in "The Self as Other: Yasmina Bouziane" discusses a very different take on Orientalism and the female self. He observes the presence in the 1990s of Middle Eastern and North African artists in the West, and he examines the particular case of Yasmina Bouziane, a filmmaker and photographer of Moroccan and French origin, who works in the United States. Bouziane plays in a postmodern way with the traditions of Orientalism, especially in the nineteenth-century's production of postcards of Arab women for consumption by Western men. She photographs herself in poses reminiscent of the Orientalist past but expresses the power of the female character over the male voyeur or represents herself as a cross-dressing photographer. This challenge to the colonialist male gaze is neither a return to precolonial ideals or a simple modernist opting for feminism. It is a manipulation of a colonialist tradition as a way of overcoming it and of playing with multiple identities in a global culture.

Colonialism, postcolonialism, and multiplicity of identities even in *la France profonde* are among the key concerns of David Troyansky's "Displaying World Culture in Provincial France: *Francophonie* in Limoges." The chapter explores the institutionalization of francophone culture in an area of France that was simultaneously experiencing some nostalgia for its own regional identity. The Limousin, and particularly the city of Limoges, sought to establish itself as a major center on the landscape of Francophonie. Local leaders attempted to establish a new vocation in a multicultural world, involving high-cultural exchange, entertainment, and practical pedagogy for the region's population.

Conclusion

This volume displays the vitality of Francophone studies in a range of disciplines, periods, and settings. It includes ventures by literary scholars and historians into one another's territories and reminds us that Francophonie as a historico-cultural fact and as a concept is not just a late-twentieth-century phenomenon but something that grows out of much longer-term interactions between colonizer and colonized, between peoples of different nationalities, ethnicities, and religions. And it examines a multiplicity of places where cultural confrontations *à la française* (*à la francophone?*) have occurred.

Running through the book are the key ideas of transnational spaces and identities, and its six parts sort the chapters according to fairly obvious categories. Thus we have sections on colonialism, Algeria, francophone Jews, and so forth. But quite appropriately for examination of multiple and hybrid identities, the chapters' themes reach beyond the individual parts in which they are situated, and "spaces" refer to local, national, transnational, and theoretical contexts. They include physical space as in McMaster's chapter on housing, folkways as in Sussman's on dietary and religious practices, and mythic cultural space as in Dine's on the Mediterranean. They may emphasize aesthetic values as in McCullough's or focus overtly on the political. Thus Aldrich explores political writings, and both Camiscioli and Shepard discuss policy and citizenship, much more explicitly than the other contributors. Collectively we are balancing literary, historical, and sociological contexts. We all point to transnational concerns and demonstrate how Francophonie links France to a wider world even as we urge appreciation of particular terrains.

Notes

1. Gérard Noiriel, *Le creuset français: histoire de l'immigration, xixe–xxe siècle* (Paris: Seuil, 1988), which appeared in English translation in 1996, *The French Melting Pot: Immigration, Citizenship, and National Identity*, trans. Geoffroy de Laforcade (Minneapolis: University of Minnesota Press).

2. See, for example, Dominique Schnapper, "Making Citizens in an Increasingly Complex Society: Jacobinism Revisited," in *The Jacobin Legacy in Modern France*, ed. Sudhir Hazareesingh (Oxford: Oxford University Press, 2002), 196–216.

3. Such was the subtitle (after *république* and *nation*) of the last volumes of Pierre Nora's seven-volume *Les lieux de mémoire* (Paris: Gallimard, 1984–93).

4. Steven Englund, "The Ghost of Nation Past," *Journal of Modern History* 64 (1992): 299–320 and Hue-Tam Ho Tai, "Remembered Realms: Pierre Nora and French National Memory," *American Historical Review* 106, no. 3 (2001): 906–22.

5. Xavier Denian, *La francophonie*, 5th ed. (Paris: PUF, 2001); Jacques Barrat, *Géopolitique de la Francophonie* (Paris: PUF, 1997); see also the website of the Agence

Intergouvernementale de la Francophonie: *www.agence.francophonie.org*. For a more strictly literary approach, see Michel Beniamino, *La francophonie littéraire: essai pour une théorie* (Paris: L'Harmattan, 1999).

6. "Transnational Cultures, Diasporas, and Immigrant Identities in France and the Francophone World." The 35th Annual Texas Tech University Comparative Literature Symposium. A writers' roundtable included the following participants: Azouz Begag, Réda Bensmaïa, Kébir Ammi, Régine Robin, and Alek Baylee Toumi. The theatrical première was of Toumi's *Albert Camus: Entre la mère et l'injustice*.

7. Among Azouz Begag's sociological works, see *L'immigré et sa ville* (Lyon: Presses Universitaires de Lyon, 1984); his most famous novel, which was filmed, is *Le gone du Chaâba* (Paris: Seuil, 1986). A conference in Lubbock even makes an appearance in his 2004 novel, *Le Marteau Pique-Coeur* (Paris: Seuil).

8. Tyler Stovall and Georges Van Den Abbeele, *French Civilization and Its Discontents: Nationalism, Colonialism, Race* (Lanham MD: Lexington, Books, 2003) and Seth Graebner, *History's Place: Nostalgia and the City in French Algerian Literature* (Lanham MD: Lexington Books, 2007).

9. Gary Wilder, *The French Imperial Nation-State: Negritude and Colonial Humanism between the Two World Wars* (Chicago: University of Chicago Press, 2005) and Todd Shepard, *The Invention of Decolonization: The Algerian War and the Remaking of France* (Ithaca NY: Cornell University Press, 2006).

10. Eric T. Jennings, *Vichy in the Tropics: Pétain's National Revolution in Madagascar, Guadeloupe, and Indochina, 1940–1944* (Stanford CA: Stanford University Press, 2001); Ruth Ginio, *French Colonialism Unmasked: The Vichy Years in French West Africa* (Lincoln: University of Nebraska Press, 2006); and James Le Sueur, *Uncivil War: Intellectuals and Identity Politics During the Decolonization of Algeria*, 2nd ed. (Lincoln: University of Nebraska Press, 2005).

11. See also Patricia Lorcin, "Rome and France in Africa: Recovering Colonial Algeria's Latin Past," *French Historical Studies* 25, no. 2 (2002): 295–329 and Peter Dunwoodie, *Writing French Algeria* (Oxford: Clarendon Press, 1998).

12. One of the best treatments of the political nature of early French demography and its expression of anxiety at the falling birthrate can be found in chapter 4, "Le vieillissement héritier de la dénatalité," in Patrice Bourdelais, *Le nouvel âge de la vieillesse: Histoire du vieillissement de la population* (Paris: Odile Jacob, 1993), 117–54.

13. See, for example, Françoise Gaspard, *Une petite ville en France* (Paris: Gallimard, 1990), which appeared in English translation in 1995, *A Small City in France,* trans. Arthur Goldhammer (Cambridge MA: Harvard University Press).

Acknowledgments

Most of the chapters in this book are revised versions of papers delivered in March 2002 at the 35th Annual Texas Tech University Comparative Literature Symposium, which we organized while we were all on the faculty of that university. We would like to acknowledge the sponsors of the event: the College of Arts and Sciences, the Department of Classical and Modern Languages and Literatures, the Department of History, and the Department of English. Generous support came from the university administration, colleagues, and friends. In particular, we thank David Schmidly, John Montford, David Smith, John Burns, Jim Brink, Jane Winer, Robert Stewart, Peder Christiansen, Bruce Daniels, Madonne Miner, Idris Traylor, Don Dyal, Jim Reckner, Fred Suppe, Gwen Sorell, Alberto Julian Pérez, Sharon Diane Nell, Phade Orion Vader, Fran Lorin, Esther Lichti, Sandra River, Jon Hufford, and Cate Logan.

In 2005 we published a collection of French-language papers in a volume entitled *Migrances, Diasporas et Transculturalités Francophones: Littératures et cultures d'Afrique, des Caraïbes, d'Europe et du Québec* (Paris: L'Harmattan, 2005). By then two of us had left TTU, and we have continued to collaborate at a distance. We are grateful to Heather Lundine, editor in chief and history acquisitions editor at the University of Nebraska Press, for her belief in the project, to copyeditor Brian King, for catching errors and infelicities, and to the anonymous readers for the press, for helping us think about turning a broad collection of papers into a coherent volume.

I

Colonialism and Immigration

I

The French Colonial Myth of a Pan-Mediterranean Civilization

PHILIP DINE

Officially France's colonial history came to an end with the accession to independence of Algeria, the country's most cherished and most fiercely defended overseas territory, on 5 July 1962, some 132 years after French forces first landed on the beach at Sidi Ferruch near Algiers. For while France would maintain its hold on isolated imperial outposts that often predated Algeria such as Guadeloupe and Martinique in the Caribbean, which became full "overseas departments" of the Republic, Algeria was undoubtedly the jewel in the French imperial crown, and its loss marked the end of empire in its entirety. Yet nearly half a century after that traumatic withdrawal, the historiography of France's imperial adventures—and, crucially, misadventures—remains a deeply divisive and regularly contested issue. The polemic prompted in 2005 by the conservative government's legislation to make obligatory the teaching in French schools of the positive contribution made by the country's "presence overseas"[1] is merely the most recent manifestation of an ongoing debate surrounding the French colonial experience. Within this hotly contested field, the most strongly competing readings of the nation's colonial past invariably concern Algeria and particularly the war of national liberation that brought to an end the most sustained and most developed colonial settlement to be found anywhere in the French empire.

This chapter focuses attention on both the complex reality and the multiple representations of that most ambitious of French colonial constructions: Algérie française or French Algeria. Central to the discussion is a particularly powerful and durable fiction that the literary critic Jean Déjeux was among the first to identify as the French colonial myth of a pan-Mediterranean civilization.[2] More particularly this essay argues that the creation, consolidation, and continued existence of Algérie française was at least as much the product of mindsets or *mentalités* as it was of material realities (to the extent that these formal categories may in fact be legitimately separated for the purpose of historical analysis).[3] Indeed, following Tony Smith, the present discussion contends that, at least as far as the French colonial presence in Algeria was concerned, history was primarily understandable not in terms of rational economic or strategic interests, nor yet as a result of the shortcomings of a political system, but rather as a function of ideology.[4] Central to the French colonial project in Algeria were of course the million or so settlers of various European origins who made their homes in the territory. Their continued and apparently immutable, economic, political, and cultural ascendancy in the territory after the Second World War—in spite of the decolonizing "Winds of Change" then sweeping through many other parts of the European colonial empires—led directly to the Algerian war. For the *pieds-noirs* (literally "black feet" as the settlers were known) were both the most visible and the most essential component of French Algeria, and their determination to resist at all costs the increasingly urgent calls for radical social and political change first provoked and then prolonged the Algerian nationalists' armed struggle for the territory's independence.

From an ideological point of view, the settler community's subsequent entrenchment reflected a continuation of established systems of interpretation rather than any serious questioning of the communal world-view that had rendered inevitable the 1954–62 conflict. On the contrary there was if anything a hardening of the most fundamental beliefs of the pieds-noirs as expressed by the colony's political representatives as well as by its many and various literary defenders, whether in Algeria or in "metropolitan" France. Central to the articulation of these beliefs was a network of overlapping myths of origin, place, identity, and mastery.[5] The settler community developed, and its metropolitan defenders repeated, this myth system in a continued but inherently vain attempt to legitimize European minority control of the increasingly disputed territory. The challenge of the ultimately triumphant Algerian uprising was thus integrated into a much older interpretative grid. This explanatory system had begun to emerge in response to the large-scale European immigration that followed the Franco-Prussian War of 1870 and by the turn of the century enabled the nascent settler community to respond ever more confidently to the most basic questions posed by its presence in a manifestly foreign land. As Jean Déjeux memorably puts it: "Who are we? How can we prove that this land belongs to us and that we are at home here?"[6]

A number of key ideological themes provided reassuring answers to these profoundly troubling questions but none more so than the myth of the eternal Mediterranean. Indeed such is its attraction that it continues to be evoked by the exiled European settler population of Algeria to this day. Perhaps the most obvious marker of its durability is the number of *cercles algérianistes*, or pied-noir cultural groups, currently active in France. In addition to the Cercle Algérianiste National, which is based in Narbonne and publishes the periodical *L'Algérianiste*—"Revue d'expression de la culture des Français d'Afrique du Nord" (a journal presenting the culture of the [now exiled] French population of North Africa)—there are currently over thirty *cercles* active across France. They are mainly but not exclusively located in southern France and the Paris region, thus reflecting the patterns of settlement that followed the pieds-noirs' "repatriation" in 1962–63.[7] There is also a Chair of Algerianist Studies at the Centre Universitaire Méditerranéen in Nice. Operating under the joint auspices of the University of Nice and the celebrated Collège de France, this institution was from its foundation in 1933 until 1965 a prestigious intellectual and cultural center under its eminent administrator Paul Valéry. It was then incorporated into the local university before being reestablished in recent years as a research institute organizing conferences and public lectures on what might conveniently be summarized as pied-noir culture.[8]

The specific contribution made by various theories of Mediterraneanism to this shared symbolic store—pied-noir culture—emerges from one of the many press investigations of the settler diaspora included in the historiographical *ouverture* prompted by the thirtieth anniversary of the Evian peace agreement in 1962. In an article revealingly entitled "Pour que nos enfants cessent d'avoir honte de nous" (In order that our children will no longer be ashamed of us), Philippe Eliakim, a reporter for the popular news magazine *L'Evénement du Jeudi*, interviewed the organizers of several cercles algérianistes and received the following response from one of the group:

> "After all," he asks, "why does no one ever talk about 'Algerianist' [i.e. settler] culture?" Proudly, the organizers work their way through the list of their famous writers, Emmanuel Roblès, Louis Bertrand, Jean Pommier, not forgetting Albert Camus, of course;

they mention the composer Camille Saint-Saëns, together with the painters of the "Algiers School," who were based for half a century at the Villa Abd el-Tif, and whose paintings shine with a unique light. All children of French Algeria. "Algerianism is not a pseudo-equivalent of your metropolitan civilization," insists Alain Martin, one of the organizers of the circles, "but rather a culture in its own right: a mixture of Arab, Berber, Maltese, Sicilian, Spanish, and French influences."[9]

This impassioned representation of the cultural autonomy of Algérie française requires some critical unpacking, both chronological and thematic, if we are to situate it convincingly against the historical backdrop of colonial Algeria. However, the particular contribution made here by the Mediterraneanist vision of the territory as a culturally inclusive *creuset* or melting pot should be immediately apparent.

Before moving on to consider the components of the Mediterraneanist myth system(s) in more detail, we ought to note that in the wave of commemorations that accompanied the thirtieth anniversary of the ending of the Franco-Algerian conflict, the exiled settlers and their descendants who looked to the Mediterranean as a means of linking the hitherto conflictual relations of France and Algeria to a brighter future of mutual cooperation were hardly alone. Thus, for instance, in an important series of articles published in *Le Monde* entitled "L'Algérie de la deuxième mémoire" (approximately, "Remembering Algeria"), French readers were encouraged by a variety of commentators to "Retrouver la Méditerranée" (Relocate the Mediterranean). To take only one example, Thierry Mandon, the then socialist deputy for the Essonne *département* in the Île-de-France (the densely populated central region that includes greater Paris), contrasted the artificial community generated by the postwar project of Europeanization with a deeper, more organic, and characteristically southern variety of kinship:

> The Twelve [then existing European Union member states] do possess a certain cultural unity. . . . However, we have at least as much in common with the Mediterranean peoples: it's a question of a different rhythm of existence; of a form of rural life that is tending to disappear, in France at least, while we still have real need of it; and of strong spiritual values, which are not only to do with religion. We need a concerted policy for the south of Europe. This is something that is not currently taken seriously.[10]

In a rather different register but covering very similar ideological ground, a contributor to a 1992 volume entitled *La Méditerranée réinventée: Réalités et espoirs de la coopération* (Reinventing the Mediterranean: the reality of and prospects for cooperation) drew attention to the positive contribution that sporting relations could make to Franco-Algerian understanding:

> Thanks to Olympia, the Mediterranean became the cradle of Olympic sport, both ancient and modern. Renewed, rethought, readapted, readjusted, and newly conceived according to the norms of twentieth-century society, by that strange little French nobleman, Baron Pierre de Coubertin, the "Games" were born again, in 1896, in their homeland, Greece, where the very first Olympiad had taken place in 776 BC. . . .
>
> Thus, since the days of the classical games, several countries share and claim as their own the same heroes and the same sporting idols, who are seen as Mediterranean cousins even if they are not brothers in the same nation. . . . Soccer, because it has conquered the most popular social strata, is the most dependable catalyst of mutual appreciation. . . . It may thus bring together in a shared passion the most diverse constituencies, establishing

emotionally charged sporting links between North Africans and Latin peoples.[11]

The concrete achievements of the Mediterranean Games, launched in Alexandria, Egypt, in 1955 and held in Algiers in 1975 and in the French Languedoc-Roussillon region in 1993 bear out this perceived sporting linkage as does the very visible contribution made by soccer in the writings of Albert Camus and others to the Mediterranean-ist conception of colonial Algeria.[12] The December 1995 edition of *L'Algérianiste*, which contains a detailed and celebratory account of colonial Algeria's classical sporting "heritage" in an article entitled "Les jeux et les spectacles de l'Afrique romaine" (The games and spectacles of Roman Africa), highlights the abiding appeal of this sports-inflected variation on the theme of the eternal Mediterranean.[13]

Let us return now to this mythical schema's properly literary origins, for the main conceptual and thematic strands from which the politically charged myth of a pan-Mediterranean civilization was woven were produced initially by the literary ideologues of colonial Algeria. To this end I shall draw particularly on the critical insights of Peter Dunwoodie, Azzedine Haddour, Lucienne Martini, and David Schalk, as well as on what is arguably the single most significant pied-noir literary text to have emerged since 1962, Albert Camus's posthumously published *Le Premier Homme* (The first man). Peter Dunwoodie's *Writing French Algeria* (1998) is a reliable guide to both of the principal varieties of Mediterranean myth proposed by the literary spokesmen of French Algeria; that is to say, the Latin myth of Louis Bertrand and the Algerianists on the one hand and the Hellenist myth of Albert Camus and the Ecole d'Alger (School of Algiers) on the other. While Camus himself needs little introduc-tion, the Algiers-based group of liberal humanist intellectuals that he represented to French and international audiences alike may be less familiar to a modern reader and consequently merits discussion below. Also worthy of note is their literary ancestor and ideological rival, Louis Bertrand (1866–1941). Born in the eastern French department of the Meuse in what would in the wake of 1870 become the lost provinces of Alsace-Lorraine, Bertrand took up a teaching post at the Lycée Bugeaud in Algiers from 1891 to 1900. There in 1897 Bertrand's wholly positive experiences in "Latin" North Africa prompted him to begin writing a series of novels celebrating the colonial enterprise, a propagandist endeavor epitomized by his literary commemoration of the centenary of the French invasion of Algeria, *Le Roman de la conquête 1830* (The romance of the 1830 conquest) (1930).[14]

Dunwoodie's own title—*Writing French Algeria*—has clear echoes of David Prochaska's important work, *Making Algeria French* (1990), and indeed these two studies have a similar objective in that they each seek to explore the historical formation of a qualitatively new settler society in the territory.[15] Moreover, as a counterpoint to the attention given elsewhere in his work to the physical infrastructures and networks of power relations of the emergent settler colony, Prochaska's study includes some valuable reflections on the creation of a distinctively colonial culture in Algeria. This leads him to consider particularly the roles played by language and literature, alongside street names and picture postcards, in the settler community's processes of identity construction.[16] Dunwoodie, in turn, focuses sustained and persuasive critical attention upon the very specific contribution of a variety of literary texts to the imaginative construction of Algérie française. While it is impossible to do justice here to the subtleties of Dunwoodie's analysis, we may trace its main conclusions with regard to the Mediterraneanist component of settler myth making in the colony.

Dunwoodie's point of departure for a study of the properly

colonial fiction of French Algeria—as opposed to the variously exotic and erotic metropolitan productions that had preceded it, the so-called *littérature d'escale* (stopover or tourist writing)—is conventional enough in that he identifies Louis Bertrand's *Le Sang des races* (The blood of the races) (1899)[17] as representing a radical break in the depiction of the territory and both its European and Arabo-Berber inhabitants. For our purposes here, what is central to Bertrand's ideological project is the depiction of the settlers of Algeria as a *peuple neuf* in the making: a distinct and distinctive settler race entitled to dominate the colonized territory now and in future years because of its privileged status as the "natural" heirs to the glory that was Rome. Through the notion of the Mediterranean man, a racial archetype that Bertrand claims to have (re)discovered in the mixed southern European ancestry and community of the settlers of French Algeria, the writer offers his preferred reading of Algeria's past. This foregrounds and valorizes the Roman heritage of Algeria, while simultaneously denigrating and even denying the territory's Arabo-Berber past and present alike. Dunwoodie explains the enormous justificatory potential of this doubly partial reading of Algeria's history for the territory's emergent colonial ascendancy:

> While justifying the French occupation pragmatically by highlight-
> ing the hard work and sacrifices required to make the supposedly
> empty, unworked land fertile, Bertrand also uncovers a moral
> justification in the fact that "Latin" peoples (i.e. neighbouring
> nations) occupied the area long before the "Arabs" (i.e. outsiders
> from "Arabia") who introduced only a religion. . . . The proof, for
> Bertrand, lies in the Roman archaeological vestiges throughout
> Algeria, in the unrecognized Latinity of a wide range of phenom-
> ena such as couscous, religious architecture, the burnous of rid-
> ers, Turkish baths, the native plough and the irrigation methods

used in the oases, horse-breeding, furniture and jewellery, the
dalmatic and the fan. . . . These cultural traits—both material
effects and social practices—form the so-called concrete proofs
of the fact that Islam had only partially evicted the former Latin
(and Christian) culture.[18]

While Bertrand's myth of *Afrique latine* received a variety of slants
by the generation of "Algerianist" writers that followed him in the
first two decades of the twentieth century and even some criticism
for being obsolete by such resolutely modernizing literary figures
as Robert Randau and Jean Pommier, its retrospective justification
of the 1830 Algiers Expedition and the century of colonization that
had followed it was never seriously threatened before the 1930s.[19]
On the contrary, thanks to the efforts of respected historians and
archaeologists such as Gaston Boissier, Gustave Boissière, and perhaps especially Stéphane Gsell, this tendentious reading of Algeria's
precolonial history became a commonplace of the academic and
political discourses of Algérie française.[20]

In fact the regular appeal made to this theme in the literature
generated during and after the 1954–62 war of national liberation
underscores the mythical construct's power to retain its grip on the
imaginations of the settlers' literary defenders long after this date.
So for instance in Frédéric Valmain's novel *Les Chacals* (The jackals) (1960), a new arrival in Kabylia from "metropolitan" France
is informed that "Nearly all the houses in the village are built from
stone taken from the Roman ruins." This local reliance on the
ancient labors of the territory's Roman occupiers extends even to
that most powerfully symbolic of French public edifices, the local
war memorial or *monument aux morts*. In the case of Tigzirt's particular commemorative monument, we are solemnly informed that
"It is the most beautiful memorial in existence!" for reasons that

Valmain's narrator goes on to explain: "the Tigzirt town council had demonstrated its good taste by using a splendid Roman column in all its strict simplicity. . . . They had no money to pay for a real monument. So the only solution was to help themselves from among the Roman ruins."[21] I have commented elsewhere on Jean Lartéguy's depiction of French paratroopers as the descendants of the Augusta Legion in his bestselling novel *Les Centurions* (1960), together with the exiled *pied-noir* Gabriel Conesa's systematic recourse to the Latin theme in his *Bab-El-Oued* (1970).[22] In these and similar cases, and from Bertrand to Conesa and beyond, we find evidence to support the Fanon-inspired counterreading of the myth of Afrique latine put forward by Azzedine Haddour in his study of *Colonial Myths: History and Narrative* (2000).

Haddour's deconstruction of Bertrand's writings permits a sophisticated critique of the internal contradictions of a representation of Algerian history, which intended to legitimize colonial development and to encourage the progress of the settler community, but which can ultimately result only in a stultifying ideological immobility:

> Louis Bertrand's mythic representation offers at one and the same time an image of the colonized culture as "both present and mummified" and an image fetishizing Roman ruins and reflecting the mummification of the colonizer's society, its closure, its fixity. An analysis of Bertrand's mythic representation confirms [Albert] Memmi's claim [in his *Portrait du colonisé précédé du portrait du colonisateur* (1957)] that colonial society is "frozen," that its social structures are "corseted" and "hardened."[23]

The practical political implications of this inability to give ground conceptually would of course be made only too painfully apparent in the period between 1954 and 1962 and would thus ultimately lead in the most bitter of historical ironies to the definitive physical expulsion of the settler community from its adopted homeland. However, a new generation of French Algerian writers was to emerge in the 1930s that would make strenuous literary efforts to discover strategies for coming to terms with the increasingly conflictual politics of the territory. This was the so-called Ecole d'Alger, and in the "second-generation" Mediterraneanism of this group and especially that voiced by its most celebrated member, Albert Camus, we find further evidence of the settler community's abiding weakness for engaging artistic misrepresentations of harsh colonial realities.

This said, we should not underestimate the extent to which the writings and public pronouncements of Camus and his group of young writers—which included particularly Gabriel Audisio, René-Jean Clot, and Emmanuel Roblès—represented a genuine attempt to break with the culturally and politically debilitating ideology of Latin Africa. Roblès was among the very first European writers in Algeria to reflect seriously on the condition of the colonized population of Algeria and would make indigenous characters important and even central figures in such pioneering novels as *L'Action* (1938) and *Les Hauteurs de la ville* (1948).[24] Camus, for his own part, would in 1939 famously plead the case for a more just treatment of the suffering Berber population of the impoverished region of Kabylia in an important series of articles published in the leading leftist newspaper of the territory, *Alger Républicain*.[25] However, the group's collective challenge to the Algerian colonial establishment, like the liberal humanism that underpinned their analysis of the settler community's ills particularly as regarding its relations with the territory's Arabo-Berber population, was from the outset and throughout undermined by its own internal contradictions. This underlying failure to break with what we might regard as the epistemological orthodoxy of Algérie française has been shrewdly characterized by Neil MacMaster, following Peter Dunwoodie's analysis:

Fundamentally they remained trapped in the same historic/colonial impasse as the Algerianists and what is perhaps more striking is not the supposed break between the Ecole d'Alger and the older, conservative group, but the underlying similarities or continuities. The Ecole remained grounded in a myth of a Mediterranean people but one which shifted away from the Roman/Latin symbolism of the Algerianists, rejected for its identification with colonial militarism as well as the founding myths of Italian fascism, toward an aesthetic denoted by Greece, Odysseus and "open" seafaring communities.[26]

It will not be necessary to dwell here on the Ecole d'Alger's "quasi-racist aesthetic of beautiful, bronzed youth," although we might usefully underline its inherently escapist, obfuscatory, and, indeed, even hallucinatory qualities.[27] However, we do need to consider the representation of the colonized population of Algeria derived from its patent model of Mediterranean humanism. Central to this representation is a vision of colonial Algerian society as the culturally inclusive creuset or melting pot noted earlier in this discussion. While Gabriel Audisio is usually credited with the invention of this mythic trope in the 1930s,[28] it is Albert Camus's continued commitment to this key theme over a period of some thirty years that is worthy of comment here. More specifically, it is in that long-term failure to see through the myth of a common Mediterranean humanity that Camus demonstrates his inability to conceive of an Algeria outside the cultural and political straitjacket of continued French colonial rule. For ultimately, as Azzedine Haddour argues, "Although he [Camus] stressed the unity of the Mediterranean world he was incapable of thinking in terms other than those of a French colonizer."[29] A brief examination of two very different texts by Camus will suffice to make this point.

The first of these texts is an article published by Camus in *L'Express* on 9 July 1955 in which he wrote, "If I feel myself to be closer, for instance, to an Arab peasant, or a Kabyle shepherd, than to a shop-keeper in one of our northern French towns, then that is because a shared sky, an imperious nature, and a common destiny have proved stronger, for many of us, than natural barriers or the artificial divisions maintained by colonization."[30] Neither Camus's good faith nor his goodwill are in question here. However, nor can there be much doubt that such comments almost a year into the Algerian war reveal the great writer to be precisely that archetypal liberal humanist *colonisateur de bonne volonté* or colonizer of goodwill famously identified just two years later by Albert Memmi, the now well-known Tunisian Jewish intellectual critic of French colonialism.[31] Having failed to influence the Algerian war directly in 1956 when both the nationalists and especially his own settler community roundly condemned his courageous but futile "Appeal for a Civilian Truce," Camus would be hailed the following year by a worldwide audience when he was awarded the Nobel Prize for literature. However, Camus's infamous declaration while in Sweden—in response to a heckling Algerian student in the course of a university visit—that he preferred his "mother" to "justice"[32] was widely interpreted and almost universally condemned as revealing his underlying fidelity not only to his actual mother still living in Algiers, Catherine Sintès, but also to Algérie française and its obdurate pied-noir community. With Camus's decision in the wake of this outcry to remain silent after the publication of his *Actuelles III: Chroniques algériennes* in 1958, which was followed quickly by the writer's premature death in 1960, little additional evidence existed to chart the evolution of his thinking as the Algerian conflict continued and intensified.[33]

Camus's silence served as background to the huge interest generated in France and internationally by the posthumous publication of *Le Premier Homme* in 1994. Although there is much of value in this unfinished novel, there is also much that inclines this reader at least to situate the text within a tradition of variously epic and heroic fictional accounts of the French colonial project in Algeria. This tradition is arguably at its best (and certainly at its most developed) in Jules Roy's six-volume novel cycle *Les Chevaux du soleil* (The horses of the sun) (1967–75). It is more typically (and thus less impressively) represented by *Le 13e convoi* (The thirteenth convoy) (1987) and *Le 113e été* (The 113th summer) (1991), two halves of a *chronique romanesque* by Jacques Roseau and Jean Fauque that, as the titles suggest, focus respectively on the rise and fall of colonial Algeria.[34] Jules Roy was a former career soldier who had resigned his commission in protest at France's Indo-China war (1946–54) and who went on to write a stinging critique of the Algerian conflict, *La Guerre d'Algérie*, published in 1960, which included a sustained attack on his own community that many of the settlers would never forgive.[35] However, even in the hands of such a clear-sighted and critical member of the pied-noir community, what we might conveniently characterize as the novel of settler possession and dispossession appears to display an apparently inherent tendency to function as an apologia for Algérie française. More particularly, recounting the settler experience of diaspora post-1962 can all too easily turn into an Algerian colonial variation on the theme of Paradise Lost.[36]

However, what is striking in the present context is the ease with which the Nobel Prize–winner was drawn in *Le Premier Homme* into the mythifying mainstream of colonial literary reaction to the Algerian war. Camus's silence from 1958 on was only broken nearly forty years later when the text that he had been working on at the time of his death was finally made public; and that text is in fact a colonialist novel that sits all too easily alongside those *post facto* justifications of the French Algerian project. As Dunwoodie explains:

> Given its status as only partly reworked autobiography and nascent
> fiction, *Le Premier Homme* is clearly the most revealing text in
> which Camus endeavours to rework the issue of the European
> presence in colonial Algeria. It is also the text which most clearly
> articulates Homi Bhabha's notion of the belatedness that marks
> colonial writing, the attempt to map an ever-receding past time/
> space before the collapse of the as yet unsullied European self.
> For critics, the text represents an autobiographical-historical *re-*
> *tour aux sources* and . . . an attempt to rehabilitate the *Français*
> *d'Algérie* in the midst of the Algerian War.[37]

This attempt by French Algeria's most famous son to write his
own and his community's way out of colonial trouble, *in extremis*,
has drawn wide comment and various interpretations.[38] As David
Schalk has pointed out in his own elegant and persuasive reading of this much-debated work, as an inevitable result of the very
particular circumstances of its production and publication, "the
text we have to work with is ambiguous as is all great art, perhaps
especially, incomplete great art."[39]

Yet, for all its unavoidable ambiguity, it was perhaps only to be
expected that Camus's literary reconstruction of personal, familial, and communal origins in colonial Algeria should among other
strategies once again have had recourse to the justificatory myth of
the eternal Mediterranean. The continued mobilization of this rhetorical figure—which dated back at least as far as Gabriel Audisio's
Jeunesse de la Mediterranée (1935)[40]—as late as 1960 and in the
culminating and most overtly Algerian of Camus's literary productions may legitimately strike the modern reader as disappointing. All
too predictably in fact, when Camus evokes the spirit of the settler

colony in this its darkest hour, it is precisely the myth of a distinctive southern identity shared by the pieds-noirs with the Arabo-Berber population of Algeria—and, moreover, with them alone—that is uttered to justify the continued French presence in the territory. As an old, isolated, and increasingly embattled farmer explains to a rare visitor who asks him about his own plans for the future now that so many Europeans are leaving the countryside:

> "Oh, me, I'm staying put, and right to the bitter end. Whatever happens, I'll still be here. I've sent my family to Algiers and I'll croak [*je crèverai*] here. They don't understand that in Paris. Apart from us, do you know who the only ones are that understand it?"
>
> "The Arabs."
>
> "Quite right. We are made to get along. They are just as stupid and as brutal as us, but we share the same human blood. We'll carry on killing each other for a while, cutting off each other's balls, and torturing each other a little. Then we'll go back to living together again, between men. It's the land itself that wants it that way. Do you want an *anisette*?"[41]

All the familiar markers of the eternal Mediterranean man are here in a wartime amalgam of the apparently competing but ultimately complementary myths uttered by Louis Bertrand and the Ecole d'Alger. In this moment of crisis, the simplicity, violence, and sexuality of Bertrand's *peuple neuf* join forces with the utopic vision of a shared Mediterranean humanity. As for the closing reference to the aniseed spirit that constituted the settler community's ritual drink, this serves to underline the talismanic and even totemic function so often attributed to anisette in pied-noir fiction. It is not simply an *apéritif* in fact but a characteristically Mediterraneanist signifier of authenticity and integrity.

To conclude, this chapter has attempted to demonstrate that the French colonial myth of a pan-Mediterranean civilization constitutes a privileged site for the exploration of the ideological and indeed psychological landscape of Algérie française. That such a remarkable intellectual figure as Albert Camus was unable to escape its grip even as the settler colony in Algeria approached extinction serves to underline both the insidiousness and the tenacity of this mythical construct. In the final analysis then, we must surely concur with Peter Dunwoodie's reading of Le Premier Homme as not only an unfinished novel but also an uninterrupted struggle between the great liberal humanist's "nostalgic evocation of a more innocent, less violent past" and his belated, and unwilling, "realization that personal values have been overtaken by events."[42] At the core of those values was Camus's preferred representation of a sea that always divided France and Algeria at least as much as it united them; and it was over that mythic body of water that the literary giant of Algérie française was, like many lesser figures before and after him, ultimately unable to stride.

Notes

1. "Loi du 23 février 2005 sur la reconnaissance dans les programmes scolaires du 'rôle positif de la présence française en outre-mer.'"

2. Jean Déjeux, "De l'éternel méditerranéen à l'éternel Jugurtha," Revue algérienne des sciences juridiques, économiques et politiques 14, no. 4 (December 1977): 658–728.

3. I have made this case at length elsewhere. See Philip Dine, Images of the Algerian War: French Fiction and Film, 1954–1992 (Oxford: Clarendon, 1994), 146–212.

4. Tony Smith, The French Stake in Algeria: 1954–1962 (Ithaca NY: Cornell University Press, 1978), 23–30.

5. Dine, Images of the Algerian War, 146–77.

6. Déjeux, "De l'éternel méditerranéen," 725. All translations from French are my own. See also Hubert Gourdon, et al., "Roman colonial et idéologie coloniale en Algérie," Revue algérienne des sciences juridiques, économiques et politiques 11, no. 1 (special issue on this theme, March 1974).

7. Local *cercles* exist in Aix-en-Provence, Annecy, Avignon, Bagnols/Céze, Béziers, Bordeaux, Carcassonne, Châtillon, Clermont-Ferrand, Draguignan, Grenoble, Hyères, Lons-le-Saulnier, Lyon, Marseille, Mont-de-Marsan, Montauban, Montpellier, Nantes, Narbonne, Neuilly sur Seine, Nice, Paris, Pau, Perpignan, Poitiers, Saint-Etienne, Sète, Toulon, Toulouse, and Valence.

8. The series of conferences and public lectures offered in early 2002 are suggestive of its thematic (and ideological) orientation: 9 January, "Marcello Fabri, un représentant de la culture française d'Algérie"; 21 March, "L'arrière-fond ethnico-religieux de la guerre d'Algérie"; "Albert Camus-Pascal Pia: une amitié"; and "Le Sahara" (Source: http://www.cum-nice.org).

9. Philippe Eliakim, "Pour que nos enfants cessent d'avoir honte de nous," *L'Evénement du Jeudi,* 5–11 March 1992, 62.

10. Patrick Jarreau, "L'Algérie de la deuxième mémoire: II. Un clivage dans l'inconscient des politiques," *Le Monde,* 18 March 1992, 17.

11. Jacques Marchand, "La fête sportive," in *La Méditerranée réinventée: Réalités et espoirs de la coopération,* ed. Paul Balta (Paris: Editions de la Découverte/Fondation René Seydoux, 1992), 303, 312.

12. See Philip Dine, "Un héroïsme problématique—Le sport, la littérature et la guerre d'Algérie," *Europe* 806–7 (June-July 1996): 177–85. See also, by the same author, "France, Algeria, and Sport: From Colonisation to Globalisation," *Modern and Contemporary France* 10, no. 4 (November 2002): 495–505; and "The End of an Idyll? Sport and Society in France, 1998–2002," *Modern and Contemporary France* 11, no. 1 (February 2003): 33–43.

13. Maurice Cretot, "Les jeux et les spectacles de l'Afrique romaine," *L'Algérianiste* 72 (December 1995): 37–42.

14. Louis Bertrand, *Le Roman de la conquête 1830* (Paris: Fayard, 1930). For an incisive analysis of continuities in the use of the Latin theme in the representation of French Algeria from Bertrand to Camus, see Patricia M. E. Lorcin, "Rome and France in Africa: Recovering Colonial Algeria's Latin Past," *French Historical Studies* 25, no. 2 (Spring 2002): 295–329.

15. Peter Dunwoodie, *Writing French Algeria* (Oxford: Clarendon, 1998); and David Prochaska, *Making Algeria French: Colonialism in Bône, 1870–1920* (Cambridge: Cambridge University Press, 1990). See also the review essay by Neil MacMaster, "Writing French Algeria," *French Cultural Studies* 11 (2000): 149–55.

16. Prochaska, *Making Algeria French,* 206–29.

17. Louis Bertrand, *Le Sang des races* (Paris: Ollendorf, 1899).

18. Dunwoodie, *Writing French Algeria,* 100–101.

19. Dunwoodie, *Writing French Algeria,* 156.

20. Dunwoodie, *Writing French Algeria*, 101, 104. See also Alain Calmes, *Le Roman colonial en Algérie avant 1914* (Paris: L'Harmattan, 1984): 13–18. Compare Jean-Claude Vatin, *L'Algérie politique: histoire et société* (Paris: Armand Colin and Fondation Nationale des Sciences Politiques, 1974), 8–56.

21. Frédéric Valmain, *Les Chacals* (Paris: Fayard, 1960), 28.

22. Dine, *Images of the Algerian War*, 37–38, 157–58.

23. Azzedine Haddour, *Colonial Myths: History and Narrative* (Manchester, UK: Manchester University Press, 2000), 25.

24. Emmanuel Roblès, *L'Action* (Algiers: Imprimerie Algérienne / Soubiron, 1938; and *Les Hauteurs de la ville* (Paris: Seuil, 1948, 1960).

25. Albert Camus, "Misère de la Kabylie" (1939), in the same author's *Essais*, 'Pléiade' edition, (Paris: Gallimard/Calmann-Lévy, 1965), 903–38.

26. MacMaster, "Writing French Algeria," 153–54.

27. MacMaster, "Writing French Algeria," 154. Compare to Lucienne Martini, *Racines de papier: Essai sur l'expression littéraire de l'identité des pieds-noirs* (Paris: Editions Publisud, 1997), 259.

28. See, for instance, Claude Liauzu, "Gabriel Audisio, Albert Camus et Jean Sénac: Entre Algérie française et Algérie musulmane," *Confluences Méditerranée* 33 (Spring 2000): 161–71.

29. Haddour, *Colonial Myths*, 29.

30. Cited by Martini, *Racines de papier*, 264–65.

31. Albert Memmi, "Camus ou le colonisateur de bonne volonté," *La Nef* 12 (December 1957): 95–96.

32. Camus, *Essais*, 1881–82.

33. Albert Camus, *Actuelles III: Chroniques algériennes* (Paris: Gallimard, 1958).

34. Jules Roy, *Les Chevaux du soleil* (Paris: Grasset, 1967–75); Jacques Roseau and Jean Fauque, *Le 13e convoi: chronique romanesque (1858–1871)* (Paris: Robert Laffont, 1987); and *Le 113e été: chronique romanesque (1903–1962)* (Paris: Robert Laffont, 1991). Jacques Roseau, a *pied-noir* community activist in France, was murdered by rival militants in Montpellier in 1993.

35. Jules Roy, *La Guerre d'Algérie* (Paris: Julliard, 1960).

36. Dine, *Images of the Algerian War*, 176–77.

37. Dunwoodie, *Writing French Algeria*, 266–67.

38. See especially David L. Schalk's incisive comparison of competing readings of the novel, together with his own characteristically even-handed approach to this contested work: "Was Algeria Camus's Fall?" *Journal of Contemporary European Studies* 12, no. 3 (December 2004): 339–54. Compare (and contrast) Philip Dine, "(Still) A la recherche

de l'Algérie perdue: French Fiction and Film, 1992–2001," *Historical Reflections / Réflexions Historiques* 28, no. 2 (Summer 2002): 255–75.

39. Dine, "A la recherche de l'Algérie perdue," 349.

40. Gabriel Audisio, *Jeunesse de la Méditerranée* (Paris: Gallimard, 1935).

41. Albert Camus, *Le Premier Homme* (Paris: Gallimard, 1994): 168–69. Compare Martini, *Racines de papier*, 265.

42. Dunwoodie, *Writing French Algeria*, 279.

2

The Uncomfortable Inhabitants of French Colonial Modernity

Mandate Syria's Communities of Collaboration
(1920–1946)

KEITH DAVID WATENPAUGH

Est-ce parce que mon père en parlait sans cesse? Tout ce qui concerne le Mandat me fait regretter d'être née un peu trop tard. . . . Le Mandat raconté par mon père m'évoquait le monde fascinant de Casablanca, où Ingrid Bergman et Humphrey Bogart jouent leur éternelle scène d'amour sous les ventilateurs.—Marie Seurat née Ma'marbashi, "Mandat, mon beau Mandat"

Is this because my father spoke about it unceasingly? All that relates to the Mandate makes me regret having been born a little too late. . . . The Mandate as told by my father, evoked for me the fascinating world of *Casablanca,* where Ingrid Bergman and Humphrey Bogart play their eternal love scene under the ventilators.—Marie Seurat, "Mandat, mon beau Mandat"

With the advent of the French occupation of Syria following World War I, the colonial strategy for ruling the cities of the Eastern Mediterranean under France's rule was a part purposeful, part accidental intensification of preexisting categories of religious and ethnic difference.[1] However, less well understood is how that strategy intersected the colonized's comprehension of—or indeed anxiety about—their own modernity. An example of this intersection is to be found in the ideological terms upon which Edmond Rabbath, a Sorbonne-educated Catholic Syrian lawyer and the chief ideologue of the National Bloc, the premier bourgeois nationalist movement in Syria, based his opposition to French rule: an appeal not to Arab nationalism, per se, but rather to the basic tenets of "French civilization."[2]

The inherent ambivalence of Rabbath toward the French, and French culture, language, and political theory in particular, reinforce Homi Bhabha's contention that "Resistance [to colonialism] is not necessarily an oppositional act of political intention, nor is it the simple negation or exclusion of the 'content' of another culture, as a difference once perceived. It is the effect of an ambivalence produced within the rules or recognition of dominating discourse as they articulate the signs of cultural difference and reimplicate them within the deferential relations of colonial power."[3] Moreover, it is easy to imagine how collaboration could be conceptualized along the same lines: it too is not simply a matter of affirming or accepting the culture of the colonizer but carries with it a complex and multilayered engagement with power and cultural difference; it too is not just a mimetic process or the reversal of resistance.

By focusing on a series of discrete moments in the seemingly collaborationist response of two minority communities in Aleppo, the Byzantine-rite Greek Catholics and the Armenians, this chapter moves issues of colonial modernity outside the political narrative and into the spheres of domesticity, education, and communal identity. The encapsulated nature of these communities, especially their middle class, a condition that had grown in intensity by the late 1930s, and the intimacy of their relationship with the French and other foreign communities mark the unique importance of their encounter with the cultural and ideological dimensions of colonialism. Each case highlights the formation of a body of complex social, political, and economic exchanges that constitute a phenomenon I call the "colonial contract." In this context, the contract constituted an exchange of the active or passive support for colonialism by members of these communities for a series of distinct social and communal privileges. For the Armenians the terms of this exchange included French protection of the community as a distinct ethnicity and transformation from abject poverty into an urban protomiddle class; for the Greek Catholics, the exchange guaranteed the francophone Greek Catholic—especially its middle class—seamless integration with the metropole. For that community cooperation with the French and participation in the civilizing mission allowed the community to draw closer and even seek to close completely the "distance" between it and its metropolitan exemplar; likewise it secured their position in a separate sphere within the city's colonial architecture of community. Ultimately as the contours of this contract become visible, so does the realization that neither the Greek Catholics nor the Armenians of Aleppo were passive recipients of French paternalism. Rather they were active agents in the negotiation and reformulation of their role in the colonial encounter.

This realization is crucial to revising the study of French colonialism in the Arab Eastern Mediterranean, which has focused primarily on the theme of resistance, where the kinds of cooperation practiced by these two communities is often characterized as culturally inauthentic and thus not—or at least, less—worthy of study. The more traditional approach creates a binary construction of resistor versus colonial oppressor, which emphasizes the moral superiority of the former; likewise this binarism can admit few categories of hybridity or layers of ambivalence. Such a structure cannot escape the same reductive Manicheanism that underlies and legitimates colonialism itself: European-Syrian, Christian-Muslim, French-Arab is reproduced in any narrative of resistance that emphasizes the dichotomy between the collaborator and the nationalist. The historiography of French Mandate Syria often reflects this same binarism. In this historiography the degree to which linguistic and religious minorities—most especially the middle-class components of these groups—cooperated with the colonial enterprise situates them uncomfortably in the narrative of nationalist resistance and liberation of the inter and postwar periods. Likewise this mode of representation creates a blind spot in our understanding of the period as it leaves large portions of the Syrian colonial population invisible to history, and where these components of society are visible, it is only in a nationalist, anticolonialist narrative's demonology.

The Armenians: Cooperation and the Costs of Survival

The complex relationships between the French colonial authorities in Syria and the Armenian refugee community constitute a vital field within which to begin the interrogation of colonial cooperation. By 1922 as a consequence of a genocidal program undertaken by the Ottoman authorities that exterminated a vast portion of the Armenian population of the empire, a stateless, non-Muslim, non-Arabic–speaking, primarily rural, and disproportionately female group of survivors had been violently uprooted and forced to flee Anatolia and were living on the margins of Syria's major cities. The vast bulk of these displaced individuals—more than fifty thousand—found refuge in and around Aleppo, altering it forever. The mandate authorities estimated that by 1923 approximately two hundred thousand Armenians had passed through Aleppo. Over seventy-five thousand had resettled in the post-Ottoman province of Aleppo, with fifty thousand of these in the city. The remainder settled in camps near Damascus and Beirut; large portions of this

population subsequently emigrated to North and South America.[4]
The community that took shape was caught in a political and social
no man's land: on one side was the memory of the killing fields of
Anatolia and the newly formed ultranationalist Republic of Turkey
that barred a return to their homeland, and on the other side was an
often hostile Syrian population that generally viewed these refugees
as ethnic, linguistic, and religious outsiders. The ambiguous and
vulnerable status of the Armenians in Syria forced community representatives and leaders to mobilize political and cultural resources
and to accept governmental and nongovernmental, paternal, albeit
often-altruistic aid to survive. That strategy for survival took the
form of a complex arrangement that transcended mere collaboration. This relationship first took shape in the immediate context of
the humanitarian and tutelary aspects of the mandate between the
refugee communities and the French authorities and, in a second and
broader way, between the Armenians and the West writ large.

However, questions about motivation and intent—beyond the
basic needs of colonial administration—remain unresolved in such
an analysis. For example, did the Armenians ever imagine themselves as compradors, beholden as it were to the French?[5] Was
the political status of Armenians in Syria mediated solely by the
French, or were other actors involved? In what ways did it matter that this population was neither Muslim nor Arabic-speaking?
Similarly how did the changing relationship between the two groups
of actors contribute to French conceptions of their own *civilizing
mission* at home and abroad, as well as to the evolving concept of
international humanitarianism? How did the Ottoman Armenians,
a community with a history of complex objective institutions, including religious hierarchies, political formations of both the right and
left, middle-class social and philanthropic organizations, and youth
movements like the Boy and Girl Scouts, re-create these institutions

in a transnational diaspora and colonial context? Moreover, does a parallel exist between the way the Armenian community of Syria sought to build a relationship with the French and the modes of communal cooperation between Armenians and the prewar Ottoman state?[6]

As the Armenian community created and structured relationships with power within the framework of the mandate system, it both redefined its members' political and class status and transformed their corporate identity. In so doing they created a space for cooperation with what Elizabeth Thompson in her *Colonial Citizens: Republican Rights, Paternal Privilege, and Gender in French Syria and Lebanon* labels "paternal" colonial authority, thereby preserving the community itself in the wake of a brutal attempt to destroy it by the Ottoman authorities and in the face of a host population that viewed their presence for the most part as a sectarian, political, and economic threat.[7]

This translated distinctly into the movement to "rescue" Armenian orphans and girls from Muslim households and then to integrate them into urban society and the massive building projects that replaced the refugee camps with paved streets and proper middle-class homes. Underlying these movements—and complicating the terms of the contract—was an international humanitarian effort of pro-Armenian groups and the League of Nations' Nansen International Office for Refugees that sought to preserve the Armenian community by developing it in partial isolation from the remainder of an emerging Syrian national community.[8]

An arresting portrayal of the Armenian experience in Syria—the missionary-inspired effort to find and retrieve Armenian women, girls, and boys from Muslim households in rural and urban areas—is a filmed reenactment of the rescue of a pair of young Armenian women from the tent of a Bedouin chieftain made for fund-raising

by a Danish missionary in the late 1930s.[9] The film opens with
the Armenian driver of a Ford Model T owned by a relief agency
drawing water for his overheated radiator from a pond somewhere
in the Syrian portion of Mesopotamia. A woman dressed in Bedouin clothes filling water skins beside him informs him that she is
Armenian and named Lucia and wants to escape. They agree to
meet later at that spot. The scene shifts to a Bedouin's tent, where
another Armenian woman, Astrid, is forced to perform menial
labor and is even beaten. Lucia invites Astrid to leave with her,
and after much hesitation, she agrees. Returning to the pond at the
appointed date, the two find the driver and effect a daring escape.
A chase ensues, but the Bedouins on horseback are no match for
the Armenian in his technologically superior Model T. When the
group reaches Aleppo, the film focuses on Astrid, who, while still
in Bedouin garb, is brought into a building identified as a rescue
house. A few moments later she reemerges with a stylish bob hair-
cut, wearing a dropped-waist calico dress. The use of the clothes
as simulacra of modernity is obvious and functions in way similar
to the deployment of examples of technology.

Meanwhile, Astrid is shown around the rescue home where young
women are being taught to read Armenian, to clean and to cook,
and to crochet lace. They are taught modern housekeeping skills
as well as a craft in anticipation of entering the workforce or, as
was often the case, traveling to the West as mail- order brides for
immigrant American-Armenian men. In a fundamental moment,
Astrid tells her life story to a clerk who writes it down, and thereby
she acquires a written past. A tearful reunion ends the film as an old
woman recognizes Astrid on the basis of a birthmark as her own
long lost granddaughter. Astrid is thus reunited with the remnants
of her biological family and, more importantly, with modern urban
society; to do this she has had to abandon/escape her adopted family

in the desert, coded by the filmmakers as antimodern, brutal, and barbaric.

Mark Sykes, the highest-ranking British diplomat in Syria at the time and architect of the Sykes-Picot Treaty of 1915, estimated in 1918 that between four and five thousand children of both sexes had been sold along the route of the death caravans to Bedouin, *fellahin* and townspeople. In addition to this number, he believed that some two hundred girls had been purchased as de facto slaves for Aleppo's extensive network of brothels.[10] By 1927 as the period of rescue drew to a close, Karen Jeppe, a Danish missionary and the director in Aleppo of the Commission for the Protection of Women and Children in the Near East, estimated that her agency had participated in the rescue of over sixteen hundred people.[11]

Central to the process of rescue were the several rescue homes in the city, similar to the one run by the Near East Relief as described by its chief relief worker E. Stanley Kerr:

> On reaching Aleppo the children were given a warm welcome by members of the NER [Near East Relief] reception staff. . . . At this center the children were checked by NER medical personnel, with special attention to contagious diseases and intestinal parasites, and were then grouped according to sex and age and prepared for transport to orphanages in the districts where they had been born. Girls who had been violated (some, indeed, were pregnant) were placed in "rescue homes" which had the facilities for infant care.[12]

These homes were places wherein, according to Jeppe, the rescued would be "restored . . . to a normal life in their *own* world."[13] The missionaries would define the boundaries of this world in ethnographic, if not racist, terms. Again Jeppe, noting that many of the rescued Armenian boys who had been between the ages of six and twelve in 1915 escaped the rescue home to return to the Bedouin, observed:

> An interesting feature is that many of them, after a short stay with us, returned to the Arabs. It seemed too difficult for them to adapt themselves to Armenian life, which means learning and thinking and in general a good deal of toil, as all civilized life does. The vast steppes and the aimless nomadic life with the cattle lured them back. In the beginning this filled us with despair; but we soon learned that they would be sure to return to us again. After all, they could not forget their people and their faith and the spiritual atmosphere that was their birthright. Sometimes they would stay away a year or two, but finally they came home, this time to settle down among their own people.[14]

Contemporary conceptions of the inherent moral and racial superiority of the Christian Armenians, whose "national purity" should not be sullied by intercourse with, in Jeppe's words, the Bedouin "cattle," obviously shaped this missionary world-view. Also, an underlying paternalistic assumption of the missionary effort was that they knew the "real" wishes of the "rescuees" even if they did not know them themselves. Thus, for racially inflected humanitarian reasons, the Armenians deserved intervention for the restoration of their community. Crucially, it could be argued that this notion of rescuing the community was unprecedented in the Armenian community and only existed as a peculiar feature of missionary paternalism. As might be expected, most nonmissionary rescue efforts were conducted by immediate family members, acting not as representatives of a community, but rather as individuals seeking to locate their surviving relatives. Further, while the large number of potential "rescuees" and the sheer scale of the horror of the genocide with its mass deportations and policy of systematic rape was unparalleled, the abduction and enslavement of girls and young women from settlements by rural nomads was less so. The attempt to rehabilitate women who had been raped or who had entered into common-law relationships or legal marriages with non-Armenian men and had had children with them proved problematic. In these cases the missionaries with the backing of the French authorities broke apart families in the name of community, racial purity, and Christianity. Nevertheless, the rescue movement both reflected and reinforced an international sanction for the idea of distinct and relatively superior—in racial and religious terms—ethnic Armenian community. In the writings of Jeppe and others, this community had attained, or could attain, a national character and possessed a level of civilization not necessarily shared by the broader Muslim society, by definition, and deserved protection from that majority.

The rescue movement was a popular cause in the West. In fiscal year 1926 alone, tens of thousands of pounds from various organizations were sent to the rescue commission in Aleppo. Among these organizations were the (London) Lord Mayor's Fund, the Armenian Ladies Guild, the Friends of Armenia, and the Bible Lands Society. The remaining cost of the enterprise was provided not by the Syrian state but rather by the League of Nations. Consequently, the rescue movement became an unprecedented international cause that far transcended its local context.[15] Rarely were French officials directly involved in the process, though they often lent *gendarmes* to rescue efforts. The conclusion of Jeppe's 1927 report to the League of Nations provides a hint of the utility of French support for the rescue movement and the alignment with the missionaries:

> And now nothing remains but to thank . . . the Mandatory Power for Syria for their enduring sympathy and most valuable aid in the work that has lasted so many years. . . . It has been a light in

the darkness and a source of happiness to many people who have
suffered terribly from those evils which it is the special aim of the
League of Nations to root out or at least to mitigate.[16]

The fiction of the mandate system imposed humanitarian responsibilities on colonial authorities. In this vein, supporting the rescue
movement aided French efforts to define and defend their presence
in the Levant on a broader international stage. This almost gestural
place of the Armenians in the matrix of colonial legitimization was
relatively new, although Great Power politics of the nineteenth-
century "Armenian Question" often justified increased involvement in Ottoman affairs on the basis of the protection of Christian
minorities. In the late 1920s the French pointed to their support
for the refugees as evidence of both a civilizing and humanitarian
dimension to their rule.[17]

The rescue movement also dovetailed neatly into the preexisting
conceptions of an Armenian national community as articulated
by the various Western pro-Armenian groups and Armenian exilic
political parties of the time.[18] However, rarely could they marshal
the resources of organizations like Near East Relief. Indeed, several
of these groups voiced concern that the success of the missionaries
undermined the authority of the Armenian organizations in Aleppo.
An early example of such a conflict is seen in the outrage evidenced
when American missionaries translated the Bible into Turkish—the
spoken language of vast numbers of the refugees—written in the
Armenian script and even began to publish a newspaper, *Maranata*,
using the same format. Conversely the Armenian organizations asserted that the refugees should be taught modern literary Western
Armenian. Regardless, the rescue movement was both a product
of and contributing factor to the drawing of a boundary around
the Armenian community in Aleppo, demarcating it culturally and

politically and assuring its alignment with both European civilization and modernity. The rescue movement, beyond aligning the
community with the West, equally contributed to a cementing of
the distance between Aleppo's Armenians and the Arab Muslim
community of the city. Finally, despite the intervention of the missionaries, an intervention that was supported by Armenian political and cultural organizations in Syria and elsewhere, a tradition
of gratitude toward the Bedouins for saving orphans from death
along the banks of the Euphrates permeates the modern historical
consciousness of Armenians of Aleppo.

The placing of the Armenian community more squarely into
the discursive framework of French colonialism occurred in 1928,
when High Commissioner Henri Ponsot affirmed that the Armenian
refugees residing in Syria had the right to vote in the constituent
assembly elections that year. Armenians in Syria had been granted
Syrian citizenship in the wake of the Treaty of Lausanne, although
their integration into Syrian political structures remained in doubt
in the period prior to those elections. This change, which significantly altered the sectarian demographics of the Syrian electorate,
provoked a great deal of local outrage and points to the changing
nature of citizenship in the post-Ottoman states of the Eastern
Mediterranean.[19] The Armenians like the Syrians had possessed Ottoman citizenship in the period before the war. Indeed, many of the
Armenians in the city of Aleppo were originally from the province of
Aleppo, albeit from the portion that had become part of the Republic
of Turkey, primarily Marash, Urfa, and Ayntab. Nevertheless, with
the drawing of the new boundaries they became stateless and their
status an issue of both local and international politics. Inasmuch
as the granting of citizenship to the Armenians was couched in
humanitarian terms, the techniques of the French intervention in
the shadow public sphere of the Syrian electoral process points to

another motive. The French had concluded that increased levels
of Christian political participation were fundamental to their attempts to suppress the political power of the National Bloc. French
political activism in Syria found and promoted a cross-confessional
constituency within urban society—Muslim, Christian, and Jewish—
to oppose the National Bloc, which at the same time did not resist
the tutelary fiction of the mandate. Conversely the National Bloc
often excluded this part of the electorate from participation with
a combination of boycotts and terror campaigns against potential
voters.[20] Indeed, an anonymous pamphlet appearing in the city at
the time of the elections read: "Not satisfied with these acts of oppression, they [the French] have recently introduced unto our land
100,000 Armenian refugees, of whom many have been raised to
a high rank. . . . All our commerce and finance have gone to these
usurpers";[21] and a later Damascus newspaper headline read: "The
Zionists are better than the Armenians."[22] The effort to align the
Armenian refugee population with the French Mandate authorities
was based on integrating the refugees into modern urban society as
members of what French policymakers identified as the respectable
lower middle class. This process was explained by Ponsot during
a meeting of the Central Committee for Refugee Aid in Beirut, 24
June 1931:

> One must lend support to the real distress which this situation
> [refugeehood] creates. This is what has been done in Syria and
> Lebanon. This [situation] has been brought under control in ma-
> terial terms through loans of money, and in moral terms, by a
> humane welcome which has allowed them to acquire the national
> status [i.e., citizenship] of the country which has opened its doors
> to them. It is necessary to help the refugees primarily to establish
> them permanently. This is what the goal is. With the Armenians,

what one fears is that as soon as they have a little savings, they will wish to go elsewhere. This must be avoided, and to avoid it, we must make of them small-property owners, of a house, of land or of a field. This task is underway: what has been done in the Levant toward this goal does honor to the League of Nations.[23]

More concretely, early 1930s French refugee policy was devised on a four-point plan: (1) the purchase of urban land and the construction of homes and then the transfer of these homes and land to the refugees for sale or rent; (2) the placement of refugees in public and private enterprises; (3) professional apprenticeships; and (4) the organization of a *crédit agricole et la petite industrie* to aid the refugees. In total, these measures were intended to integrate the Armenians by providing them with property, a trade, or a profession in a way that intensified their linkage with the French state, the local economy, and agriculture. The most visible manifestation of this process was the transformation of the refugee camps to the north of Aleppo into urban neighborhoods. The building of these new neighborhoods in the city accompanied similar projects in Beirut and Damascus, as well as agricultural installations, primarily along the Turkish border and in the province of Alexandretta. Indeed, in the self-congratulatory view of the author of the 1936 Nansen Office Report to the League of Nations, the building of these new neighborhoods had transformed "Aleppo and Beyrouth from Oriental into modern cities."[24]

It was estimated that at the beginning of the process of the *installation définitive*, some 4,000 shanties existed in Aleppo, housing approximately 20,000 people. By 1936 2,061 new residential structures had been built, housing some 3,121 families or 15,644 people. In that same year, 356 houses were under construction, leaving only 583 shanties standing and occupied by 2,995 people.[25] The architecture of the homes themselves—multistoried with separate sleeping rooms for different family members—imposed a middle-class lifestyle and notions of privacy. The semidetached or detached structures often had indoor plumbing and running water and were on Aleppo's electrical grid. In addition to the homes, part of the development of the neighborhoods included the establishment of public/civic institutions, primarily intended to ease the transition to urban life.[26]

In addition new churches for Orthodox, Catholic, and Protestant congregations were built, and private organizations started schools, a maternity hospital, a clinic, and a community center for adult orphans.[27] Additionally, the Nansen Office opened settlement/welfare offices in the camps, and the mandate authorities built a municipal police station. By 1930 upward of one thousand workshops had opened for carpet weaving or embroidery, the chief means of support of the female survivors of the genocide.[28]

These were planned communities, the very forms of which reflected the intention of their planners to formulate modern, efficient social spaces that would assure the class ascendance of their inhabitants. In addition, the relative success of the building projects aided the formulation in French bureaucratic culture of an edifice of stereotypical ideas about Armenian industriousness, work ethic, and compliance that accompanied a uniform belief that as a whole the community "always looked to France to help it in its struggle against problems."[29] Or as Charles Godard, municipal counselor of urban affairs of Aleppo in the late 1930s, explained in his description of the new neighborhoods, "the history of the development of these quarters speaks to the qualities of the Armenian people, who, beneath the protection of the Syrian and French flags have recovered a nation. The 'bidons à pétrole' and the shanties of wood and paper have been replaced by houses of fired brick."[30] A visitor to contemporary Aleppo is still struck by the form of suburban Armenian neighborhoods like Midan, known to its inhabitants as Nor Giwgh, the New Town. The district's wide thoroughfares, its rectilinear street plan, the preponderance of signage in the Armenian script, the use of Armenian and Turkish speech, and the relative lack of Muslim religious establishments all mark it as a space different from the rest of the city as well as evidence of the persistence of the distinct nature of the Armenian community in Syria. Ultimately the complex relationship between the French and Armenians in the postwar period shows the difficulty in generalizing the position of non-Muslim minorities during the Mandate period. The French secured their position vis-à-vis the League of Nations with their support of the rescue movement as it couched the occupation of the country within an emerging discourse of humanitarianism. Likewise, it phrased the French Mandate—perhaps for French domestic consumption—in the nationalist-inflected conception of France as the "protector" of the Christians of the Orient. It played into ideas about race and hierarchies of racial distinction, a conception of particular concern to American missionaries like E. Stanley Kerr, who conceived the rescue of young Armenian women in ways that recalled the genre of nineteenth-century American Indian captivity narratives.

In sum the realization in the late 1920s and early 1930s that the Armenians were not going to "go home," a profound and deeply troubling moment for the refugees, was seized by the mandate authorities as a way of reinvigorating the colonial contract. The French, drawing upon the support of international organizations, settled the refugees in separate, distinct communities. The settlement of the refugees in such a way reinforced both the notion of the uniqueness of the Armenians in Syria and a commitment to exchange support of French interests for a commitment to the establishment of this community as both modern and middle class. It also contributed to French efforts to alter the demographics of Syria and Lebanon in a way that aided their political efforts and hindered the possible formation of unified opposition to their rule. When only viewed in this manner, the Armenians emerge as vulgar tools of French policy, placing parochial community self-interest before national exigency. However, when this discursive strategy is pushed aside, a much more textured account emerges that also contributes to broader understanding of issues that continue to haunt other refugee and displaced populations in the Middle East and elsewhere. Viewed from outside a resistance narrative structure, the terms of the colonial contract, the rescue movement, and the creation of these neighborhoods appear emblematic of a formation of separate space for Armenians within the political culture of interwar Syria. This was something more than ghetto politics or colonial strategies; the formation of this new physical and social space for the refugee community bound the Armenians to an idealized middle-class modernity and made a complete break with Ottoman-era structures of political subordination as well as the broader Sunni Muslim Arabic–speaking majority. Had the community been allowed a "natural" process of integration and assimilation, the profile of the Armenian community in the increasingly violent urban politics of Syria would have been significantly reduced. Instead, by navigating the fluid uncertainties of French colonial domination, and later those of the equally perilous independent postwar regimes, the Armenian community *survived*—perhaps the ultimate act of resistance.

The Scouts et Guides de France

Among Maggie Homsy's most prized possessions is a photograph of her at the age of fifteen as a patrol leader in a flag ceremony at the yearly mass meeting of her Scout group, the Scouts et Guides de France circa 1946.

1. Maggie Homsy (*center, with beret*) during a 1946 joint Scout et Guide de France celebration in Aleppo. Reprinted with permission from Keith David Watenpaugh, *Being Modern in the Middle East: Revolution, Nationalism, Colonialism, and the Arab Middle Class* (Princeton NJ: Princeton University Press, 2006).

In the image, the symbols and signs on the uniforms and flags differed little from other scouting movements of the interwar period: *fleurs-de-lys*, shorts and campaign hats for boys and culottes and berets for girls. This remarkable consistency and the fact that thousands of middle-class teenaged Arabs had been part of a French Catholic youth movement is not just a consummate moment of hybridity in the relationship between colonialism and the colonized, but it also evokes the "cultural cringe" that often accompanies moments of seeming undiluted mimicry of the cultural forms of the colonial powers.

The movement was poorly received at the time outside Christian circles and was eventually banned altogether by the independent Syrian state (circa 1950). For Arab nationalists and many in the Sunni elite, it provided evidence of both Christian complicity with the foreign occupiers and a self-conscious distancing of the Christian community, primarily Uniate Catholics, from Syrian society. That conclusion was made more acute by the fact that the Scouts de France of Aleppo vehemently rejected any association with the growing and equally middle-class Arab Scout movement in the Levant. The young people in the movement, however, often remember their years as Scouts or Guides as among the happiest in their lives and moreover as proof of their clear attainment of middle-class status transcending the limits of the Eastern Mediterranean. For them, their parents, and community leaders, it was not an abnegation of their status as Syrians or for that matter Arabs, but rather a natural sign of their membership in a transnational middle class. Nevertheless, the Scouts de France movement, especially as it manifested itself in Aleppo in the 1930s and early 1940s, is a testament to how thoroughly the Greek Catholic middle class of the city relied on the idiom of French cultural practice to assert its modernity. And it also shows how the act of attaining undisputed middle-class status had become contingent on being *seamlessly* European. And while this form of practice—which extended to the realms of education, given names, and fashion—eased this wing of the middle class's entrance into globalized networks of emigration and commerce, it rendered members of the class increasingly irrelevant in the immediate architectures of urban and national community; the price of membership in the transnational middle class—the terms of the colonial contract—would be the ultimate, though gradual, effacement of the community from the city, especially as the French Mandate itself drew to a close. Aleppo's Uniate Christian middle class was far from the only group in the Ottoman and post-Ottoman Eastern Mediterranean to have adopted and adapted Scouting. Indeed, within a decade of its organization in Britain in 1908, ostensibly with the goal of preserving the British Empire,[31] the movement had spread

42

to Istanbul and other Ottoman cities.[32] The movement's seemingly universal appeal as both an educational device and a tool for making citizens in successor states of Syria, Turkey, Lebanon, Egypt, Jordan, Palestine, and Israel and the manifestation of Jewish, Armenian, Orthodox, Catholic, and Muslim groups suggests a viable common denominator with which to understand the way non-Western middle classes sought to be modern.[33] Moreover, the lack of modifications in the adaptation to the basic structure of Scouting and its attendant symbols, signs, and shibboleths complicates our understanding of the emergence of a transnational middle class in the cities of the Eastern Mediterranean, as it unravels the complex knot of anxieties about class status and gender roles as well as notions of history and progress that played such a fundamental role in the experience of members of that stratum. It may seem difficult to take seriously a youth movement like Scouting. The kind of distaste that such movements elicit—with their seeming lack of authenticity and active cooperation with the colonial enterprise—has likewise led many to look past Scouting and other youth groups to focus exclusively on more violent paramilitary and nationalist organizations that drew far fewer adherents. Ultimately this neglect is inconsistent with the value modern middle-class society places upon the need to create and control institutions intended to train, discipline, and socialize its boys and girls and to use such institutions as performative sites in which to be modern.

Scouting was not a simple case of slavish derivation or unreflective collaboration. Diverse middle classes not just in the interwar Middle East but throughout the world self-consciously and actively employed the movement to assert their position in an emerging modern urban order and claim for themselves the kind of distinction and class identity that membership in these organizations signaled in the metropole. And just as middle-class modernity reformulated definitive feminine and masculine identities, it has also constructed the identity of youth; the *sine qua non* of being modern and middle class was and is that one's children have childhoods, or rather that one's children should be teenagers before becoming adults—a luxury not shared by the vast majority of people in the colonial and postcolonial non-West, where young people entered the workforce or agriculture at an early age. Scouting played a part in that construction of youth.

In the Scouts de France movement all the colonial concerns about language, sect, community preservation, and distinction coalesced.[34] Founded by French officers in Aleppo, it grew in the course of the 1920s and 1930s under local leadership until it encompassed twelve boy groups and three girl groups made up almost exclusively of Uniate Catholic children and adolescents by the time the postcolonial Syrian state forcibly disbanded the movement in 1948. Moreover, the memory of the movement has been successfully obliterated from the official history of Syria, and any historical documentation about it is in the hands of former members or in brief notices in the French Mandate archives.[35]

Meeting twice a week, on Sundays and Thursdays, the boys and girls gathered to speak French, work on badges and skills, play games, and read books. Among the books mentioned in oral history interviews are French translations of Kipling's *Kim* and stories about Mowgli from *The Jungle Book* as well as Cooper's *Last of the Mohicans*. Books in Arabic about Scouting were of little interest as, in the words of one respondent, "they reflected a completely different mentality."[36] Members of the units came exclusively from the city's professional and commercial middle class. Attempts to form organizations among poorer Christians, primarily Syrian Orthodox, failed because the boys were expected to earn a living and could not spare the time to participate in group activities—they did not have childhoods.[37] The units sought to create and reinforce patterns of association, promoting the horizontal linkages so fundamental to Aleppo's middle-class society. In the words of one oral history, "Scouting gave us the ability to succeed in society; honest, strong, don't be afraid to be yourself. We were from middle-class families. . . . In politics no one became important; all of us became doctors, pharmacists, engineers, businessmen and bankers."[38]

Public marches were a central feature of Scouts de France activity, and it was through these marches and parades that they inscribed themselves on Aleppo's urban fabric. By the late 1930s these marches had grown to form a central ritual of the city's Christian community, allowing it to have a public persona in the Christian neighborhoods of the city. Such a presence, nevertheless, constituted a transgressive act in a place and time where organized public activity by members of religious minorities had been historically circumscribed and certainly contributed to the sectarian tension underlying Christians' relationship with the Muslim majority. Marching in Aleppo was not reserved only to Scouts de France. The funeral of Saʿdallah Jabiri, who had died in 1947, occasioned a massive parade. Pierre Khoury, a Cub Scout at the time of the funeral, recalled: "All the Boy Scouts of Aleppo marched, even the Jews, Armenians, and Christians. There were Muslim Boy Scouts, their shorts covered their knees just because of a religious prohibition . . . we saw them so few times."[39] Young adult leader Henri Ayyab recalls not being invited by the national authorities and reports: "we imposed ourselves, or else they would have said 'the Christian Scouts do not love their country.'"[40]

It is understandable that the Scouts de France were viewed as outsiders or even traitors in Syria. The use of French and the centrality of Catholicism clearly identified them with the imperial power that had occupied the region. The Scouts de France's symbols—symbols

that identified them with, among other things, the Frankish crusaders of the Middle Ages—were antagonistic, if not inflammatory.[41]
Yet, for the Scouts de France in Aleppo, the use of this language of
symbols connected the Scouts in France with the boys and girls in
Syria. Hence, the boundaries of the community made legible in the
movement indicate that the conception of an Arab Syria had little
relevance for the Christian middle class of Aleppo. Rather, they took
the idea of a mimicked bourgeoisie to its logical conclusion. Seeking
to create a community on the basis of their conception of their reified
European cognate, they moved to the next step, obliterating the
barriers and distance between themselves and the ideal. Thus, the
Scouts de France did not create Frenchmen but rather young men
and women who believed themselves to be modern, albeit modern
à la Française. In such a construct lies the brilliance—or insidious
nature—of the culture of the mandate and the entire edifice of the
civilizing mission. While presenting itself as the best of all possible
worlds and as an absolute set of values and definitions, this world
and these values—when scrutinized more closely—reappear dif-
fracted through a manifestly French imperial lens. Still, attributing
the force of the movement merely to French imperial machinations
would deny the agency of the middle class shown by the persistence
of the movement in postcolonial Syria. Upon Syria's independence
the Scouts de France in Aleppo re-created themselves as the Catholic
Syrian Scouts and gave themselves an Arabic name and emblem.
That same year the leader of the Arab Scouting movement in Damascus moved to bring all the Scout movements under his direct
control. The Armenian Scout movements compromised with the
authorities in Damascus, agreeing to use Arabic in public, though
in private they continued to use Armenian. The former Scouts de
France in Aleppo were unwilling to make such a deal. Leaders of
the movement in the city who continued to press their case were

46

2. Henri Ayyub (*second row, left*) and his Scout de France patrol, Aleppo, ca. 1936. Reprinted with permission from Keith David Watenpaugh, *Being Modern in the Middle East: Revolution, Nationalism, Colonialism, and the Arab Middle Class* (Princeton NJ: Princeton University Press, 2006).

arrested.[42] To those of the movement still alive in Syria, this event remains a fresh and painful memory.

In contrast to the fond associations of Maggie Homsy with her photograph, while looking at this image of his Scouts de France troop, Henri Ayyub passed his finger across it, mournfully noting as he reached each head who had emigrated and to where. Few of the former Scouts remained in Syria, and most had left for North America, primarily Quebec, or metropolitan France. The same holds for the Franco-Aleppine author and memoirist Marie Seurat, whose ambivalent and romantic vision of interwar Aleppo, as seen through the eyes of her father, also portrays a late-1930s and early-1940s middle-class lifestyle where francophone cultural practice assured cultural mobility and the secure possession of middle-class status that ultimately made ephemeral continued association with Aleppo and permanent the relationship with the metropole.[43]

Notes

The epigraph is from *Salons, coton, révolutions . . . : Promende à Alep* (Paris: Éditions du Seuil, 1995), 80.

1. On the broader historical and political narrative of the French Mandate for Syria see Philip Khoury, *Syria and the French Mandate: The Politics of Arab Nationalism, 1920–1945* (Princeton: Princeton University Press, 1986).

2. On Rabbath see my "Middle-Class Modernity and the Persistence of the Politics of Notables in Interwar Syria," *International Journal of Middle East Studies* 35 (2003): 257–86.

3. Homi Bhabha, "Signs Taken for Wonders: Questions of Ambivalence and Authority under a Tree Outside Delhi, May 1817," in *The Location of Culture* (London: Routledge, 1994), 110.

4. Centre des Archives diplomatiques de Nantes-Ministère des Affaires Etrangères (hereafter CADN-MAE), Fonds Beyrouth Cabinet Politique 575, "Installation de réfugiés arméniens à Alep," Assistant Delegate, Aleppo to Puaux, High Commissioner, Beirut, no. 3754, 8 July 1940. On the Armenian genocide see Vahakn Dadrian, *The History of the Armenian Genocide: Ethnic Conflict from the Balkans to Anatolia to the Caucasus* (Providence RI: Berghahn, 1995); and Richard G. Hovannisian, *The Armenian Genocide in Perspective* (New Brunswick NJ: Transaction, 1986).

5. Ellen Marie Lust-Okar, "Failure of Collaboration: Armenian Refugees in Syria," *Middle Eastern Studies* 32, no. 1 (1996): 53.

6. On pre-genocide relations between Armenians and the Ottoman state in Syria, see Avedis Krikor Sanjian, *The Armenian Communities in Syria under Ottoman Dominion* (Cambridge: Harvard University Press, 1965).

7. Elizabeth Thompson, *Colonial Citizens: Republican Rights, Paternal Privilege, and Gender in French Syria and Lebanon* (New York: Columbia University Press, 2000), 67.

8. On the Nansen Office, see *Convention Relating to the Status of Refugees* (Paris, Nansen Office for Refugees, 1938); and Fridtjof Nansen, "Armenian Refugees," League of Nations C:237 (1924).

9. The film has no visible copyright or bibliographic information. It is no doubt similar to the now-lost docudrama "Ravished Armenia" (Selig, 1919), directed by Oscar Apfel. See Anthony Slide, *Ravished Armenia and the Story of Aurora Mardiganian* (London: Scarecrow, 1997).

10. Public Records Office, Kew, Great Britain, Records of the Foreign Office (hereafter PRO FO) 371/3405, 199352/55708/44, Sykes (Cairo) to Secretary of State (London), 2 December 1918. E. Stanley Kerr had been sent to Aleppo on behalf of Near East Relief. Before arriving in Marash he participated in the rescue of young women from a Bedouin

encampment and narrates the rescue of some fifty children from another tribal chief in his *The Lions of Marash: Personal Experiences with American Near East Relief, 1919–1922* (Albany: State University of New York Press, 1973), 43–48.

11. League of Nations A.29.1927. IV Social, Karen Jeppe, "Report of the Commission for the Protection of Women and Children in the Near East: Aleppo, 1 July 1926–30 June 1927," 2.

12. Kerr, *Lions*, 48

13. Jeppe, "Report," 2.

14. Jeppe, "Report," 4.

15. Jeppe, "Report," 1. For an account of the American efforts on behalf of the Armenian communities of Anatolia, see Peter Balakian, *Burning the Tigris: The Armenian Genocide and America's Response* (New York: Harper Collins, 2003); also Joseph L. Grabell, *Protestant Diplomacy and the Near East: Missionary Influence on American Policy, 1920–1927* (Minneapolis: University of Minnesota Press, 1971); and Frank Ross, C. Luther Fry, and Elbridge Sibley, *The Near East and American Philanthropy: A Survey Conducted under the Guidance of the General Committee of the Near East Survey* (New York: Columbia University Press, 1929).

16. Jeppe, "Report," 4.

17. CADN-MAE Fonds Beyrouth, Cabinet Politique 573, "Note au sujet des Arméniens," 26 October 1929, 2.

18. See, for example, CADN-MAE Fonds Beyrouth, Cabinet Politique 577, Enclosure: "Note de l'Union Générale Arménienne de Bienfaisance à son Excellence Monsieur de Martel, Haut Commissaire en Syrie et au Liban," 12 October 1934.

19. Stephen Hemsley Longrigg, *Syria and Lebanon under French Mandate* (New York: Octagon Books, 1972), 181; PRO FO 371/13074 E 5338/141/8 Monck-Mason (Aleppo) to Lord Cushendon, 30 October 1928; and CADN-MAE Fonds Beyrouth, Cabinet Politique 399, Chief, Sûreté Générale (Aleppo) to Assistant Delegate (Aleppo), no. 110/S.G., 9 January 1932.

20. CADN-MAE Fonds Beyrouth, Cabinet Politique 396, "Summary of the Elections to the Representative Councils of the States of Syria, October 1923"; PRO FO 371/11515 E641/146/89 Hough (Aleppo) to Chamberlain, 15 January 1926; CADN-MAE Fonds Beyrouth, Cabinet Politique 398, "Political Situation in Aleppo" Collet (Damascus) to High Commissioner, 21 March 1928; and CADN-MAE Fonds Beyrouth, Cabinet Politique 398, "1928 Elections," Protche (Aleppo) to Chief, Sûreté Générale, 27 April 1926.

21. PRO FO 371/13074 E 5338/141/8, Monck-Mason (Aleppo) to Lord Cushendon, 30 October 1928.

22. *al-Qabas* (Damascus), 16 March 1931. The article made a connection between Zionist claims to the creation of a state in Palestine and Armenian, Kurdish, and Cherkess

desires to found similar national homes in Syria. It warned that Syria risked transformation into a Tower of Babel.

23. CADN-MAE Fonds Beyrouth, Cabinet Politique 575, "Comité de secours aux refugiés arméniens, Procès-verbal," 24 June 1931.

24. CADN-MAE Fonds Unions Internationales 2ème versement no. 1902, "Rapport de M.B. Nicolsky sur l'œuvre d'établissement de réfugiés arméniens en Syrie," 30 June 1936.

25. CADN-MAE Fonds Unions Internationales, 2ème versement no. 1902.

26. CADN-MAE Fonds Unions Internationales, 2ème versement no. 1902. On the linkage between urban forms and French colonial modernity, see Gwendolyn Wright, "Tradition in the Service of Modernity: Architecture and Urbanism in French Colonial Policy, 1900–1930," in *Tensions of Empire: Colonial Cultures in a Bourgeois World*, ed. Frederick Cooper and Ann Laura Stoler (Berkeley: University of California Press, 1996), 322–45.

27. Andranik Zaroukian's *Men without Childhood*, trans. Elise Bayizian and Marzbed Margossian (New York: Ashod, 1985), provides a touching firsthand account of orphanage life in Aleppo during the interwar period.

28. CADN-MAE Fonds Beyrouth, Dossiers Isolés no. 2387, "Installation des refugiés Arméniens 1930."

29. CADN-MAE Fonds Beyrouth, Cabinet Politique 575, "Arméniens d'Alep." ca. 1924, 3.

30. C. Godard, *Alep, essai de géographie urbaine et d'économie politique et sociale* (Aleppo: Imp. Rotos, 1938), 20.

31. See Michael Rosenthal, *The Character Factory: Baden-Powell and the Origins of the Boy Scout Movement* (New York: Pantheon, 1986). Rosenthal argues that though Baden-Powell, the "Hero of Mafeking," had founded the movement to instill a sense of patriotism and paramilitary preparation among Britain's lower and working classes, the solid middle class embraced and grew to dominate the movement in a way that was surprising even to its founder. Further, he contends that Scouting's success and its rapid spread throughout bourgeois Western Europe and North America was a consequence of the way it eased middle-class anxieties about masculinity in the face of urbanization and passive office work (pages 2–14).

32. Images of British Boy Scouts appeared in the Istanbul press in 1908–9. The first Ottoman scout group was founded by the curiously named Ahmet Robinson, an Anglo-Ottoman teacher at the Imperial Galatasaray High School in Istanbul. Robinson coined the Turkish word for Boy Scout, "Izci" (scouting being "Izcilik"). The first Ottoman translation of Baden-Powell's *Scouting for Boys* appeared shortly thereafter: *Izci Ocagnin Iç Nizamnamesi* (Scouting Hearth's internal organization) (Istanbul: Matbaa-i

hayriye ve Sirketsi, 1930); Gökhan Uzgören, *Izcilik Tarihi* (The history of Scouting) (Istanbul: Istanbul Lisesi Sakarya Izciligi Kitapları, 1984), 59. After the war Scouting was integrated fully into the Kemalist project—see Mustafa Resmi's introduction to his 1925 translation of *Scouting for Boys*, *Izcilik* (Istanbul: Matbaa-i Amiri, 1942). Resmi makes an explicit link between the reform of Turkish society and the kinds of reforms envisioned by Baden-Powell in Britain.

33. On the origins of Arab Scouting, al-Kashafa, scout being "Kashaf," which began at the American University in Beirut in the prewar period, see Shafiq Naqash and ʿAli Khalifa, *Al-Haraka al-Kashfiyya fi al-iqtar al-ʿarabiyya* (The Scouting movement in the Arab regions) (Beirut: Matbʿat al-kashaf Bayrut, 1936); and Anonymous, "Note sur le Scoutisme musulman en Syrie et au Liban," CHEAM 684, Beirut, 4 April 1944. The earliest Arabic translation of *Scouting for Boys* is probably that of the Aleppine high-school teacher Mamduh Haqqi, *al-Kashafa* (Scouting) (Damascus, 1929). See Syrian director general of Public Instruction's 1940 report, "Note sur le scoutisme musulman dans le Mohafazat d'Alep," in CADN-MAE Fonds Beyrouth, 2ème versement Instruction Publique no. 189. Alongside Arab Scouting, which tended to be dominated by Muslims, Jewish groups associated with the Alliance Israélite also formed; Armenian Scouting was linked to organizations like the HoMenEtMen or the more middle-class Armenian General Benevolent Union.

34. On the history of the Scouts de France movement, see Philippe Laneyrie, *Les Scouts de France: L'évolution du mouvement des origines aux années quatre-vingt* (Paris: Les editions du cerf, 1985). Unlike Scouting in the Anglo Saxon world, where unique national Scouting movements emerged, in France and other European countries Scouting tended to follow religious divisions. Hence the Catholic Scouts de France were founded in 1919 by Père Sevin in opposition to the secular Les Éclaireuses et Éclaireurs de France, the Jewish Les Éclaireuses et Éclaireurs Israélites de France, and most recently, *Scouts Musulmans de France*. Unlike the other Scout movements in France, the Scouts de France integrated bellicose Catholic imagery into their repertoire of symbols, including crusaders.

35. CADN-MAE Fonds Beyrouth, 2ème versement Instruction Publique no. 189.

36. Oral history interview with Henri Ayyub, 12 December 1995, conducted by author in Arabic and French. Henri Ayyub was a senior youth leader of a Scouts de France group associated with Aleppo's Marist Brothers high school.

37. Oral history interview with Elie and Lora Hindie, 7 December 1995, conducted by author in Arabic, English, and French.

38. Oral history interview with Pierre Khoury, 10 December 1995, conducted by author in English.

39. Interview with Pierre Khoury.

40. Interview with Henri Ayyub.

41. See, for example, the premier issue of the organization's journal, *Le Scout de France* 1:1 (15 January 1923). The cover shows a crusader, most likely the French king Saint Louis, standing behind a Scout dressed in campaign hat, shorts, and neckerchief. The knight's crown and the boy's hat share the elaborate Jerusalem Cross.

42. Appealing to a provision in the postcolonial Syrian constitution that guaranteed freedom of association, Henri Ayyub filed a formal written complaint against the Ministry of Education in 1952.

43. In addition to *Salons*, see also Marie Seurat, *Les Corbeaux d'Alep* (Paris: Gallimard-lieu Commun, 1988).

3

Race Making and Race Mixing in the Early Twentieth-Century Immigration Debate

ELISA CAMISCIOLI

In *Black Skin, White Masks*, Frantz Fanon responds contemptuously to Octave Mannoni's claim that "France is unquestionably one of the least racialist-minded countries in the world." Fanon writes: "Be glad that you are French, my Negro friends, even if it is a little hard, for your counterparts in America are much worse off than you." He then concludes with conviction that "France is a racist country, for the myth of the bad nigger is part of the collective unconscious."[1]

Rather than isolating the experience of American blacks from those subject to French rule, Fanon juxtaposes the oppression of both groups while refuting the myth of a universalist, color-blind France untroubled by the racial conflict prevalent in the United States. Historians of France, however, have been hesitant to ask whether the American experience of race can teach us anything about France. Such comparisons are dismissed as the product of the American "obsession" with race, an unreflective projection of the great trauma of the United States onto an unwitting France.[2] But the steady rise of the French National Front since the 1980s, with its uncompromising use of racialized language in constructing the "immigrant problem," demonstrates that discourses of racial contamination are not particular to the United States. As historian Tyler Stovall has lucidly explained, "if the Empire provided [France with] one model of race relations, the United States furnished another."[3]

This chapter insists that racial ideologies were elaborated and concretized in a world system rather than confined to the boundaries of one nation. For this reason the American experience of race need not be cordoned off as somehow exceptional, and the use of non-French methodologies in a study of immigration to France is not necessarily ahistorical. Instead I would argue that a more complete understanding of the way racial ideologies passed *between* Europe and the Americas is essential. French observers were keenly aware of the American experience of immigration, its restrictive legislation and quota system, and the trials of a post-emancipation society. Thus, in a 1930 study of immigration in France, Jean Pluyette resoundingly praised American legislation on immigration, which he claimed was "founded on the basis of the fundamental inequality of the human races."[4] In 1923 pronatalist Fernand Boverat, forced to concede that immigration was necessary to rebuild the native population, nevertheless warned against the "mass immigration of men of color [to France], at the risk of witnessing the development of racial conflict on French soil, the disastrous consequences of which we have already seen in the United States."[5]

This transatlantic discourse on race, race science, and racism conformed to the political culture of individual nations yet was also a shared and often syncretic ideology. For example, the eugenics movement was international in scope, linking like-minded thinkers in Europe, Latin America, and the United States.[6] Racial theorist Georges Vacher de Lapouge had the honor of composing the preface to the French edition of Madison Grant's *The Passing of the Great Race* (1916), undoubtedly one of the most influential American accounts of the eugenic view of immigration.[7] To demonstrate the relevance of Grant's essentialist account of race to French society, Lapouge explained in the preface that "a prince, a king, a minister, or parliament can no more make a Frenchmen from a Greek or a Moroccan than bleach the skin of a Negro, widen the eyes of a Chinaman, or turn a man into a woman."[8]

Assimilating into the French national body, then, was more complicated than Republican universalist discourse had promised. Most significantly, it was race that mattered, and the roots of this racialized language are located in the late nineteenth and early twentieth century, when in the particular political economy of mass immigration, colonialism, and Republicanism a discourse of race and race mixing developed that would be transferred to the immigration debate. The predominance of white immigration to France in this period—namely Italians, Belgians, Spaniards, and Poles—has led researchers to assume that race was inconsequential to the rebuilding of the nation.[9] The assimilability of these immigrants, however, was predicated on their membership in what contemporaries defined as "*la race blanche*," allowing mass immigration to play a critical role in the consolidation of a white European identity.

While it has become increasingly difficult to discount race in analyses of contemporary France, some scholars have described a more simple social taxonomy for the pre-1945 period, explaining that immigrant populations were grouped together under general rubrics such as "*travailleurs immigrés*" or "*main-d'œuvre étrangère*."[10] Instead, I will show that racial hierarchies were an integral part of the prewar debate, not only creating profound distinctions between European and colonial labor power but also fragmenting whiteness itself. This essay will therefore trace the emergence of three imbricated racial projects: the "French race," the "white race," and the "Latin race."

Before the Franco-Prussian War of 1870, to cite an approximate date, the concept of race was primarily used to differentiate populations *within* France itself. Since the sixteenth century it functioned as a marker for class, assigning members of the aristocracy to the Germanic-Teutonic-Nordic races and those of the Third Estate to the Gallo-Roman.[11] In the second half of the nineteenth century, however, the doctrines of racism and nationalism fused, and an understanding of race as nation became increasingly prevalent throughout Europe.[12] Individual nation-states fabricated discourses of origin to explain the transmission of national essences across generations, thereby constructing boundaries between European nations while distinguishing the metropole from the colonies. In France the elaboration of the "French race" coincided with the beginnings of mass immigration, preparation for revenge against Germany, and the founding of the colonial empire.[13]

The construction of the French race occurred in tandem with that of the "white race," with each project mutually reinforcing the other. This resulted in the consolidation of a supranational European identity and an image of the French race as fundamentally white. Despite the potency of late-nineteenth and early twentieth-century nationalism, "the colonial castes of the various nationalities . . . *worked together* to forge the idea of 'White' superiority, of civilization as an interest that had to be defended against savages."[14] Mass immigration, like colonialism, generated a variety of discourses distinguishing white Europeans from their colonial subjects. These discourses claimed that European immigration upheld the purity of the white race while assuring the homogeneity of the French national body.

In this period the attempt to create or maintain a white polity through immigration was not a French project alone: similar efforts occurred in the United States, Latin America, and Australia, again attesting to the significance of transatlantic parallels. Restrictive legislation passed in the early 1920s, informed by eugenic nativism, overwhelmingly favored the entry of Anglo-Saxons to the United States.[15] Meanwhile, in Brazil, Argentina, and Cuba, it was argued that European immigrants could "whiten" the nation through successive crossings with indigenous and mestizo people.[16] In Australia the 1901 Immigration Restriction Act was essentially a literacy test which required immigrants to write out a dictation in a specified *European* language.[17]

Despite the ideal of whiteness to which such immigration policies aspired, the white race they invoked was only sometimes viewed as a monolithic grouping of individuals with a common identity distinct from people of color. At other junctures of the immigration debate, the various members of the Latin, Slavic, Nordic, and Germanic races, to use the parlance of the time, were considered relationally, with each group assigned a particular capacity for assimilation.[18] Both Republicans espousing universalist doctrine and their antiparliamentarian critics held that the integration of Italians and Spaniards, fellow members of the "Latin race," occurred by the second generation. Although these "Mediterranean elements," according to early twentieth-century geographer Georges Mauco, were products of a "less evolved civilization," they belonged to the same race as the French and shared with them similar language, culture, and mores.[19]

An intermediate category of "more distant white populations" from "Central and Oriental Europe" consisted of Slavs, Eastern European Jews, "Levantines," and in some cases North African Berbers.[20] Although Dr. Eugène Apert of the French Eugenics Society described these populations as "fundamentally white," he claimed they differed physically, intellectually, and morally from other whites and had less aptitude for productive labor. While their assimilation required several generations, social critics nevertheless claimed that it was possible.[21] This middle group demonstrates what U.S. historian Matthew Frye Jacobson has called the "untidiness of the contest over whiteness," how phenotypical whiteness and European origin cannot always guarantee one a place within it and that the "rules can be rewritten" at any historical moment to allow "borderline Europeans" full membership.[22]

Categories such as the "Latin race," "Nordic race," and "Slavic race," which occur freely in early twentieth-century French writings on immigration, express a notion of cultural *and* biological sameness not necessarily coterminous with the boundaries of the nation-state. In the French context these social constructs did not denote "ethnicity," as it is employed in contemporary America, to signify differences among whites. The language of ethnicity, denoted by words like *ethnicité* and *ethnique*, was rarely employed in early twentieth-century legal, scientific, political, and demographic discourse; moreover, it was not consistently applied to mark purely cultural rather than biological difference. In fact French political scientist Pierre Birnbaum claims that the word "ethnic" does not even exist in the French political vocabulary and is "alien to French political tradition."[23] For this reason critiques of the "ethnicity paradigm" that have been put forth by historians and sociologists of the United States can help us to analyze the French case.[24] For example, why are whites marked by "ethnicity" and nonwhites by "race"? Can the experience of white and nonwhite immigrants be equated with regard to such factors as their perceived incorporation and assimilation? Is it not possible that in early twentieth-century France there existed a system of difference in which one was both white and racially distinct from other whites?

By assigning race to white foreigners, I am not equating their experience in France with that of immigrants of color. A pervasive discourse of hierarchy clearly favored white Europeans while situating Africans and Asians in the least desirable position, thus attesting to the particular salience of a color-based racism in France before the Second World War. Of course European immigrants were also the victims of discrimination, and their assimilation into the national body was an uneven and often turbulent process. This must be underscored because contemporary rhetoric on immigration has cynically juxtaposed the unproblematic assimilation of white foreigners with the recalcitrance of immigrants of color. Yet in fact, many themes invoked by the "New Racism" in France, including the impossibility of assimilation, were previously applied to European immigrants whose racialization has since been effaced.[25]

The racial projects outlined above operated in the interrelated realms of production and reproduction. This was due to the widespread concern for demographic decline shared by social critics from a broad political spectrum who feared the perceived shortage of native-born citizens and laborers was symptomatic of the overall degeneration of the French nation. The question of labor power assumed paramount importance for politicians and industrialists who—confronted with depopulation, continued industrialization, and the upward social mobility of the French working class—were forced to concede that only though recourse to foreign labor could economic growth be sustained. In time the tremendous needs of the wartime economy further heightened the demand for foreign workers from both Europe and the colonies, and after 1919 immigrant labor was to be an integral component of postwar reconstruction. The labor power provided by these various immigrants was evaluated and hierarchized with persistent reference to "racial" origins. According to industrialists, government officials, work scientists, and others, white labor was always preferable to that of Africans and Asians, who were deemed suitable only for unskilled work. However, the same commentators did not assign equal value to the labor performed by diverse European populations in France, thus attesting to the construction of an internal hierarchy within the whiteness itself.

But depopulation was not only construed as a problem of production, it was also seen as a total social phenomenon that had decimated the citizen body as well as the labor force. In order to replenish the nation's population, immigrant workers would have to be assimilable and able to produce children capable of becoming French. For this reason, both the productive and reproductive value assigned to foreigners determined their place in the racial taxonomy. In France depopulation had engendered a "demographic crisis" that forced hybridity upon the nation; race mixture was thus necessary if the citizenry were to be rebuilt. Participants in the immigration debate conceived of the French race as a dynamic construct with the ability to incorporate select elements into its fold. Even in the writings of French eugenicists in the 1920s and 1930s, the dominant racial metaphor was not one of racial purity. In the words of Dr. René Martial, one of the most prolific writers on race and immigration to France, the goal was instead to promote "*le bon métissage.*"[26]

In the realm of production, the first and most important distinction made by politicians and industrialists was between the "white work force" (*main-d'œuvre de l'immigration blanche*, or *main-d'œuvre étrangère*, the latter category not including nonwhites) and the "colonial and Chinese work force" (*main-d'œuvre coloniale et chinoise*). This primary division of whiteness and color can be openly observed for the first time in the factories of the First World War. Between 1914 and 1918, approximately 300,000 workers from Algeria, Indochina, China, Morocco, Tunisia, and Madagascar were brought to France in addition to 330,000 European workers from Spain, Italy, Portugal, and Greece.[27]

Employers, work supervisors, and representatives of the Ministries of War, Labor, and Armaments generally agreed that foreign labor was "more or less useful, depending on its origin."[28] The metaphor of hierarchy was so prevalent in this period that wartime documents are replete with comparative charts, lists, and numerical quantifications of the productivity of different groups. For example, the War Ministry's Colonial Labor Service Organization, which was responsible for bringing colonial workers to France, observed that "three Kabyles furnish approximately the output of two Europeans."[29] A survey conducted by the consortium of coal mine owners (Comité Central des houillères de France) reported that the output of North Africans was inferior to that of French or European workers due to a "less robust constitution" and their need for careful supervision due to the "clumsiness of their movements" and "slowness of their reflexes."[30] In 1916 the same consortium sent a survey to its various associations in order to assess their needs for labor power. Unwilling to envision the work of all foreign men as roughly the same, it requested that each company rank foreigners according to its preference and enumerated the suggested order of Belgians, Italians, and Spaniards at the top, followed by the "not quite white" Slavs and Greeks, and ending with North Africans and Asians at the bottom.[31]

While the hierarchies constructed by industrialists and emissaries of the Labor Ministry were extraordinarily nuanced, they consistently divided white and colonial labor before further hierarchizing the foreign workforce. They claimed white workers were more skilled, more productive, and, by virtue of their membership in the white race, ultimately more assimilable. According to Lt.

61

Col. Lucien Weil and economist Bertrand Nogaro, an attaché of
the Labor Ministry who would later be elected to the Chamber of
Deputies, the recruitment of white and colonial workers were of two
very different "modalities." Upon their arrival, immigrants of color
were forced to live and work apart from their French and European
counterparts.[32] The isolation of the colonial workforce from the
rest of French society was both an effort by French authorities to
circumvent racial conflict and an indication of their predetermined
refusal to assimilate these workers. Thus, a 1914 letter from the
Labor Ministry's Foreign Labor Service (Service de la main-d'œuvre
étrangère) to a chief of staff in the Ministry of Armaments contained
the following observations:

> It seems that we will have to make a choice, or at least establish
> an order of priority with regard to the different categories of
> labor power. It would be best to consider colonials as a reserve
> from which we can draw if needed. . . . It would be preferable to
> direct our efforts toward white labor which, first of all, is of better
> quality, and second, is much more assimilable. Our colonials . . .
> and other colored men will become a source of difficulty both
> here and in the colonies, while on the contrary, white labor can
> help us reconstitute our population.[33]

The Labor Ministry's Office of Economic Studies advised that
after the war it would be "opportune to favor the immigration of
foreigners of the white race," who along with their children were
most likely to assimilate.[34] A similar report from the Ministry of
Armaments claimed that workers who were "members of the white
race, and hence assimilable," should be encouraged to remain in
France, aiding in both the nation's economic recovery and the re-
constitution of the French population.[35] In the end the neutral and
universalist language of political economy was abandoned in favor

of a particularist and racialized idiom. While the demographic crisis and the wartime demand for labor power tempted employers, labor recruiters, and government representatives to view all bodies as potential creators of surplus, they soon distinguished between whites and nonwhites, systematically devaluing the productivity and skill of the latter group. Only those in favor of an untrammeled, radical economic liberalism, they claimed, could hold that any foreigner was capable of performing any task in the French national economy.[36]

Turning now to the question of how race articulates with reproduction, I will show that by linking the "immigrant problem" to the "demographic crisis," social critics strengthened the racialized idiom delimiting national belonging. Mass immigration engendered substantial debate on assimilability and racial compatibility, including detailed considerations of the potential dangers of *métissage*, and the civic and biological fitness of the *métis*. In political, medical, and juridical circles, métissage was explained in terms of two ideological constructions of nationhood. The first, an organicist, blood-based understanding of community, was prevalent among physicians and anthropologists, many of whom were affiliated with the eugenics movement in France. In contrast the assimilationist metaphor was the staple of loyal Republicans with faith in the power of the French language, schools, soil, and women to render immigrants culturally homogenous to the French. In its unadulterated form the Republican position held that all foreigners could assimilate if they were willing to assume the cultural patrimony of the nation.

Organicist metaphors of nationhood have generally been associated with German romantic nationalism, which privileged the *Völk* and its lineage over the universalism of the Enlightenment and the French Revolution. Maxim Silverman and Rogers Brubaker, however, have argued against the overwrought distinction between the "French" and "German" models, for even though the organicist metaphor is inimical to Republican universalism, both views have coexisted throughout modern French history.[37] In the debate on immigration and miscegenation, social critics freely employed both doctrines, sometimes even combining elements of each to explain the stakes of racial mixing. In fact when confronted with the question of assimilating nonwhite foreigners, even Republican universalists resorted to the competing discourse of filiation and biological similarity. Although an organicist understanding of nation abdicates liberal republican principles, this view was far from "marginal" among early twentieth-century participants in the immigration debate.[38] Moreover, the wide currency of biologism in this period does much to explain the transition from the liberal Republic to the Vichy State.

But what Dr. René Martial referred to as "métissage between whites" was another matter. Even the most strident proponents of eugenics stressed that French blood was not "pure," as it had been elaborated since Gallo-Roman times by successive crossings with such populations as the Latins, Celts, and Ligurians.[39] It is likely that French commentators associated "racial purity" with German understandings of race and nation and for this reason strove to differentiate their model from one they viewed as historically inaccurate and ideologically repugnant. The organicist metaphor of nationhood therefore encompassed the belief that the "French race" was in fact of "mixed blood."

Elements of the organicist and assimilationist paradigms were combined to distinguish the possibility of integrating members of the white race from the irreducible difference of immigrants of color. For example, Dr. Victor Storoge argued that the problems caused by the arrival of the "colored races" to the United States should not affect the French, whose immigrants were generally drawn from the "diverse branches of the white race" and hence were more assimilable. Storoge therefore proposed that white immigrants be assimilated by traditionally Republican methods. French authorities, he claimed, should encourage "familial crossings" with French women and focus their efforts on assimilating the second generation, namely through the Republican school system.[40]

Similarly, the work of jurist Jean Bercovici is also situated in a gray zone somewhere between staunch assimilationism and biological determinism. In his discussion of the medical and hygienic repercussions of immigration, he explained that race had both a cultural and a "physiological" dimension. In language redolent of Ernest Renan, Bercovici insisted that a concept of race as a "community of aspirations which constitutes a people" was far more important than an idea of race as a "community of origins," thereby affiliating himself with the contractarian and universalist position. Nevertheless, while he claimed that "individuals belonging to the white race" could mix with and assimilate into the French population, it was only with "much caution" and "in very limited numbers" that France should allow "exotics of the black race, or yellow-skinned people with thick lips and slanty eyes, to settle in France."[41] With the immigrant pool thereby restricted to white immigrants, Bercovici applauded the work of Republican institutions like the Foyer Français, responsible for teaching French language and culture to foreigners.[42]

The confusion of organicist and assimilationist metaphors also characterized a report issued by the French Academy of Medicine which ruled that in spite of the nation's "well-known power of assimilation," the influx of foreigners of different races made immigration a "biological problem" of a "scientific order." Immigration could therefore be studied in terms of current research on acclimation and crossings, notably in the field of "zootechny."[43] In keeping with the medical model, the commission likened immigration to a "cellular transplant" and a "blood transfusion." They wrote: "Results will only occur if the transplanted elements are as close as possible to the autochthonous ones, and thus able to adapt easily to their new humoral milieu."[44]

The report also defined assimilation as a "mutation" that different races were more or less able to perform. While there were few obstacles for members of the "diverse branches of the white race," Africans and Asians were described as impervious to the workings of traditional methods of assimilation. For this reason only foreigners deemed "ancestrally close" to the French, such as northern Italians, Belgians, and Canadians, should be encouraged to immigrate. Men from these nations were to enter "familial crossings" with French women who, due to the casualties of the Great War, could only found a family by marrying a foreigner. The report also held that for white Europeans, assimilation would succeed if they "settled permanently upon French soil, spoke . . . our language, adopted our customs, received our culture, crossed with the autochthonous population, and sent their children to French schools."[45] Whiteness was thus a precondition for access to the mechanisms of the "French melting pot," while Africans and Asians, because they endangered the "physical and intellectual qualities" of the French "patrimony," were excluded outright from the possibility of integration.[46]

We have seen that the proclaimed universality of French citizenship was most easily bypassed through recourse to a particularist language of racial proximity. For the most coveted immigrants—consanguineous whites like the Italians, Spaniards, Belgians—inclusion in the national body was to entail cultural assimilation with homogeneity as its ultimate goal. Assimilation was to occur by the second generation, when the children of immigrants had mastered the French language and by virtue of the homogenizing powers of the

Republican school system absorbed the critical elements of French culture. In the meantime politicians and other commentators hoped that the parents of these children would learn to speak French, request naturalization, accept the norms of capitalist work discipline, and introduce French elements of cooking, clothing, and home decor into the new lives they had established in France. The experience of mass immigration revealed the nuances of French racial belonging, its relationship to Europe and the colonial empire, and the means by which race articulated with national anxieties of depopulation and degeneration. This was to undermine—if not subvert—the liberal and Republican construction of a raceless individual with the capacity to contract into a universalist public sphere.

Notes

1. Frantz Fanon, *Black Skin, White Masks* (New York: Grove, 1967), 92.

2. Sue Peabody and Tyler Stovall, eds., "Introduction: Race, France, Histories," in *The Color of Liberty: Histories of Race in France* (Durham NC: Duke University Press, 2003), 5.

3. Tyler Stovall, "The Color Line behind the Lines: Racial Violence in France during the Great War," *American Historical Review* 103, no. 3 (June 1998): 743–44.

4. Jean Pluyette, *La doctrine des races et la sélection de l'immigration en France* (Paris: Pierre Bossuet, 1930), 5.

5. Fernand Boverat, "Il faut à la France une politique d'immigration," *Revue de l'Alliance Nationale pour l'Accroissement de la Population Française* 129 (1923): 119–20. See also Georges Schreiber, Discussion de la Communication du Docteur Eugène Apert, "Le problème des races et de l'immigration en France," *Eugénique* 3, no. 5 (1924): 162; Victor Storoge, *L'hygiène sociale et les étrangers en France* (Paris: Faculté de Médecine, 1926), 62–63; and Albert Trouillier, "Immigration-Démographie," *L'Economie Nouvelle* (June 1928): 300.

6. Stefan Kuhl, *The Nazi Connection: Eugenics, American Racism, and German National Socialism* (Oxford: Oxford University Press, 1994); Nancy Leys Stepan, *"The Hour of Eugenics": Race, Gender, and Nation in Latin America* (Ithaca NY: Cornell University Press, 1996); and William Schneider, *Quality and Quantity: The Quest for Biological Regeneration in Twentieth-Century France* (Cambridge: Cambridge University Press, 1990).

7. George L. Mosse, *Toward the Final Solution: A History of European Racism* (Madison: University of Wisconsin Press, 1978), 58. On Lapouge, see Schneider, *Quality and Quantity*, 59–63, 236–39; and Pierre-André Taguieff, "Eugénisme ou décadence? L'exception française," *Ethnologie française* 24, no. 1 (1994): 81–103.

8. Georges Vacher de Lapouge, preface to Madison Grant, *Le déclin de la grande race*, trans. E. Assire (Paris: Playot, 1926), 13.

9. Tyler Stovall's work is an important exception.

10. See Max Silverman, *Deconstructing the Nation: Immigration, Racism, and Citizenship in Modern France* (London: Routledge, 1996), 11–12; and Alex Hargreaves, *Immigration, "Race," and Ethnicity in Contemporary France* (London: Routledge, 1995), 10.

11. Benoît Massin, "Lutte des Classes, Luttes des Races," in *Des sciences contre l'homme, volume I: classer, hiérarcher, exclure*, ed. Claude Blanckaert (Paris: Autrement, 1993), 127–32. See also Rogers Brubaker, *Citizenship and Nationhood in France and Germany* (Cambridge: Harvard University Press, 1992), 101.

12. David Theo Goldberg, *Racist Culture: Philosophy and the Politics of Meaning* (London: Blackwell, 1993), 78; and Mosse, *Toward the Final Solution*, 34.

13. Etienne Balibar, "Racism and Nationalism," in *Race, Nation, Class: Ambiguous Identities,* ed. Etienne Balibar and Immanuel Wallerstein (London: Verso, 1991), 53.

14. Balibar, "Racism and Nationalism," 43. See also Charles W. Mills, *The Racial Contract* (Ithaca NY: Cornell University Press, 1997), 29.

15. Matthew Frye Jacobson, *Whiteness of a Different Color: European Immigrants and the Alchemy of Race* (Cambridge: Harvard University Press, 1998).

16. Thomas E. Skidmore, *Black into White: Race and Nationality in Brazilian Thought* (Durham NC: Duke University Press, 1993), especially 136–44; and Aline Helg, "Race in Argentina and Cuba, 1880–1930: Theory, Policies, and Popular Reaction," in *The Idea of Race in Latin America, 1870–1940*, ed. Richard Graham (Austin: University of Texas Press, 1990), 37–69.

17. David Walker, *Anxious Nation: Australia and the Rise of Asia, 1850–1939* (Queensland, Australia: University of Queensland Press, 1999).

18. This racial idiom was also transatlantic: in the United States whiteness was also fragmented and hierarchized, and American and European critics were often informed by a common body of texts. See Jacobson, *Whiteness of a Different Color*.

19. Clearly, Mauco is only referring to "Mediterraneans" from northwestern Europe. See *Les étrangers en France. Leur rôle dans l'activité économique* (Paris: Armand Colin, 1932), 145.

20. On the long-standing tradition in some French discourses of "whitening" the Berbers, see Patricia M. E. Lorcin, *Imperial Identities: Stereotyping, Prejudice, and Race in Colonial Algeria* (London: I. B. Tauris, 1995).

21. Eugène Apert, "Immigration et Métissage. Leur influence sur la santé de la nation," *Presse Medicale* 19 September 1923, 1567. Apert was a member of the French Eugenics Society, but a nearly identical racial hierarchy appears in Republican Fernand Boverat's "Il faut à la France une politique d'immigration," *Revue de l'Alliance Nationale pour l'Accroissement de la Population Française* 129 (1923): 119.

22. Jacobson, *Whiteness of a Different Color*, 5; Mills, *The Racial Contract*, 80; Wallerstein, "The Ideological Tensions of Capitalism: Universalism Versus Racism and Sexism," in Balibar and Wallerstein, *Race, Nation, Class*, 34.

23. Pierre Birnbaum, *Jewish Destinies: Citizenship, State, and Community in Modern France* (New York: Hill and Wang, 1995), viii.

24. See especially Michael Omi and Howard Winant, *Racial Formation in the United States from the 1960s to the Present* (New York: Routledge, 1994), 14–23.

25. Kenan Malik, *The Meaning of Race* (New York: New York University Press, 1996), 35. See also Pierre Milza, "L'intégration des Italiens en France: 'miracle' ou vertus de la longue durée?" *Pouvoirs* 47 (1988): 103–13; and Silverman, *Deconstructing the Nation*, 81.

26. René Martial, "Etrangers et métis," *Mercure de France* 990 (September–October 1939): 517.

27. Bertrand Nogaro and Lucien Weil, *La main-d'œuvre étrangère et coloniale pendant la guerre* (Paris: Presses Universitaires de France, 1933), 25.

28. Archives Nationales (hereafter AN) 94AP 135, Note du SSE de l'Artillerie et des Munitions aux Directeurs des Etablissements du Service des Poudres, 2 October 1916.

29. AN 94AP 130.

30. AN 40AS 48, Enquête de la Comité Général des houillères français concernant l'emploi de la main-d'œuvre nord-africaine dans l'industrie et le commerce de la métropole, 15 November 1937.

31. AN 40AS 40, Projet de circulaire et de questionnaire qui pourraient être envoyés aux principales associations industrielles et agricoles, en vue de déterminer sommairement l'importance des besoins de main-d'œuvre, 1916. No responses to the survey were located in the archives of the Comité Central des houillères de France.

32. Nogaro and Weil, *La main-d'œuvre étrangère et coloniale*, 2, 20–24, 26.

33. AN 94AP 135, SSE, MOE, Note pour M. Simiand, 20 February 1914.

34. AN F22 330, Bureau d'Etudes Economique. Procès-Verbal no. 19, 17 May 1918, Traités du travail et politique de l'immigration. AN F22 330, Bureau d'Etudes Economique. Exposé relatif aux clauses dans les traités au sujet de la main-d'œuvre, reported by Nogaro, 31 May 1918.

35. AN 94AP 120, Ministère de l'Armement et des Fabrications de la Guerre. Direction de la main-d'œuvre. "L'introduction de la main-d'œuvre étrangère pendant la guerre et

la politique de l'immigration." This citation appears virtually unchanged in Bertrand Nogaro, "L'introduction de la main-d'œuvre étrangère pendant la guerre," *Revue de l'économie politique* 6 (October–December 1920): 719.

36. Both sides of the debate are explained by William Oualid in "Le Droit Migratoire," *Revue de l'Immigration* 27 (July 1930): 1–5.

37. Brubaker, *Citizenship and Nationhood in France and Germany*, 2; and Silverman, *Deconstructing the Nation*, 19–27. See also Gérard Noiriel, *The French Melting Pot: Immigration, Citizenship, and National Identity* (Minneapolis: University of Minnesota Press), 10–11.

38. Here I disagree with Noiriel. See *The French Melting Pot*, 17.

39. See, for example, Martial, "Etrangers et Métis," 515.

40. Storoge, *L'hygiène sociale et les étrangers en France*, 62–63.

41. Jean Bercovici, *Contrôle sanitaire des immigrants en France* (Paris: Ernest Sagot, 1926), 2.

42. Bercovivi, *Contrôle sanitaire*, 92.

43. "Rapport de la Commission sur les malades étrangers dans les hôpitaux," *Bulletin de l'Académie de Médecine* 3 (19 January 1926): 68.

44. "Rapport de la Commission sur les malades étrangers," 69.

45. "Rapport de la Commission sur les malades étrangers," 68–69.

46. "Rapport de la Commission sur les malades étrangers," 68.

II

Immigrant Spaces and Identities

4

Shantytown Republics

Algerian Migrants and the Culture of Space in the Bidonvilles

NEIL MACMASTER

S tudies of migration from "Third World" to "Western" societies
have tended to neglect the issue of how migrants have adjusted
to radically different built forms. Since cultural practices in the
society of origin depend on the complex of daily relationships that
are embedded in unique spatial contexts, the fabric of the home,
particular markets, streets, fields, and landscapes, it has proved
almost impossible to reproduce such patterns within the radically
different urban contexts, the brick and concrete geometry of the
European city. Central to sociocultural practices, given the key importance of the family as the site of reproduction, are the internal
domestic spaces of the house, the size and layout of rooms, their
specific functions, furnishings, and sacred meanings.[1] In "traditional" and primarily rural societies peasants generally built their
own houses and this ensured that vernacular architecture was both
an expression of central values as well as the physical carapace, a
defining space that molded cultural practice. But migrants moving
to European cities were dramatically inserted into urban spaces,
both at the macro level (streets, squares, housing estates) and the

micro level (the layout of the individual flat or house), that were already constituted, literally set in concrete, and that they had limited powers to modify or reshape. In most instances it would seem that migrants were radically disempowered in relation to their control of space, but it would be a mistake to underestimate the versatility of migrants in restructuring or adapting "Western" built form.[2]

This process of adaptation is explored here in relation to post-1945 Maghrebian migration to the sprawling shantytowns or *bidonvilles* that mushroomed on the outskirts of North African and metropolitan French cities. Conventionally the bidonvilles have been regarded as inhuman and squalid "Third-World" settlements, and certainly photographs of the giant bidonvilles of Nanterre in the industrial outskirts of Paris give an impression of chaotic disorder, of shacks thrown together from pieces of wood, corrugated iron, and tar paper, an absolute denial of the order implicit in the traditional Maghrebian house. But appearances can be deceptive, and photographs taken externally of the shacks, as panoramic views or at street level, are quite misleading since they do not penetrate into the order of the internal domestic space. Unlike other "Western" forms of housing occupied by Algerian migrants, from worker hostels to cheap lodging houses, the bidonvilles constituted a unique form since autoconstruction enabled migrants to shape their built environment and to reproduce significant components of vernacular architecture and related cultural practices.[3]

The bidonvilles on both sides of the Mediterranean were formed by internal migration and emigration that resulted from the profound colonial dislocation and *déracinement* of rural societies and the devastation of the War of Independence. Between March 1956 and early 1962 the French army forcibly removed 2.5 million peasants from the land, mainly into militarized camps, and the irreversible dislocation of already impoverished peasant economies triggered a vast diaspora as refugees sought refuge on the margins of Algerian and French cities.[4] Already by 1954 there were sixteen major shantytowns in Algiers housing 86,500 people or one-third of the city's Algerian population, while in the Paris suburb of Nanterre by the end of the war there were some 8,000 migrants living in thirteen settlements.[5] At the morphological level, the bidonvilles in Algiers and Paris assumed quite similar forms, and this will be examined first at the macro level in relation to the structure or plan of the total settlement, a minitownship that might contain up to 2,000 people, before looking at the design of the individual house and domestic space.

The Bidonville as "Casbah"

In the early 1950s a young French architect, Roland Simounet, carried out a detailed study of the social conditions of Algiers's most noted bidonville, the Cité Mahieddine, and discovered that the standard form of house construction, the flexible and "organic" relationship of these domestic cellular units to one another and to the landscape, was rooted in the customs and traditions of rural migrants. This was, he claimed, an expression of the "instinctive and profound aspirations of Muslim populations." The layout of the shantytown—the network of open spaces, alleys, blind walls, and closed-in houses—carried a remarkable similarity to the urban fabric of the traditional Algerian medina.[6]

Isabelle Herpin and Serge Santelli in a 1968 study of the bidonville of the Rue des Près in Nanterre came to similar conclusions: aerial photographs and detailed street plans of the bidonville compared with those of a *ksar* in southern Morocco revealed an identical spatial logic.[7] The cafés, shops, and street market were located on the exterior of the settlement, alongside the main entrance, a public space of social intercourse. Anybody gaining entry by this *porte*, a point of transition into the interior of the shantytown, moved first along the major axis and then into increasingly semipublic alleyways and eventually into a maze of private cul-de-sacs, often shared by several households. The Algerian search for family privacy, concealment from the prying eyes of the French and other "strangers," was realized by the totality of the bidonville as a miniature village that was radically segregated from the surrounding society.

Internal to the shantytown, there was a definite ordering of space according to kinship, ethnicity, and village or regional identity. In Nanterre after 1946 the first micro-bidonvilles grew as hut extensions built into the backyards and gardens of café-hotels that were owned and run by North Africans who lodged men from their own village. As families began to arrive, so their location reflected this preexisting pattern of kin and village ties, which was then further consolidated by chain migration.[8] In the normal housing market of cheap rented rooms or public housing, families from the same village or region had little control over access to adjacent lodgings and found it difficult to group themselves in close proximity in contrast to the shantytown where autoconstruction and extensions to shacks enabled kin to form cellular units around shared private courtyards or blind alleys. The contiguity of relatives and fellow villagers facilitated the reproduction of traditional patterns of everyday sociability and mutual support as well as ritual and celebratory moments like the seven-day wedding described by Brahim Benaïcha.[9]

The distinctiveness of the bidonville as a coherent entity can be further recognized through a high degree of economic and political autonomy. Shantytowns possessed an informal economy, particularly in the shape of small commercial enterprises, *halal* butchers, "Arab cafés," coal merchants, hairdressers, unlicensed taxi drivers, bakers and general grocers that provided specialist products (spices, couscous, vegetables, mint), as well as credit facilities that were denied by French shopkeepers outside the settlement. Shantytowns thus showed a considerable degree of economic autarchy, internal circuits of exchange that were independent from the surrounding French society.[10] Oral history and autobiographical accounts by Algerians confirm a powerful sense of the radical segregation of the bidonvilles from the surrounding French society, in the words of Sayad an *"espace de refuge,"* in which inhabitants, in spite of extreme squalor and poverty, felt "at home" in the safety of the hearth and close family, friends, and kin, while the world beyond the boundaries of the settlement was always a perilous zone that had to be negotiated with extreme care—one of powerful authorities, uncharted streets, policemen, and racist French.[11]

The sense of internal cohesion and solidarity, faced with a threatening outside world, became particularly strong during the Algerian War, and the bidonvilles presented an almost ideal terrain for the spread of nationalist movements. The Front de Libération Nationale (FLN) organized a sophisticated support network within the emigrant community, the main function of which was to collect funds to buy arms and to sustain the armed struggle in North Africa. The bidonvilles, an impenetrable warren of lanes, provided a natural redoubt for the FLN, a place in which arms and documents could be concealed, while leading militants could escape police raids through secret back doors or by constantly moving residence between townships.[12] Within the bidonvilles the FLN established an almost absolute control over all aspects of daily life, particularly through local *commissions de justice,* which imposed Islamic law (*sharia*), regulated disputes, marriage and divorce, banned alcohol, and imposed fines, while *Comités d'hygiène et d'aide sociale* organized rubbish disposal and building repairs, and advised on welfare rights.[13]

The Bidonville House: Autoconstruction and Cultural Autonomy

More remarkable in many ways than the extent to which bidonvilles reflected the street layout and beehive plan of the Maghrebian village or urban settlement was the reproduction of the traditional North African house and domestic space. Although vernacular architecture varied by region, there was an underlying unity in the design of the "Algerian house" that related to the absolute respect for family privacy, female seclusion, gender roles, and patriarchal honor. The individual dwelling with high, windowless external walls constituted an *espace coquille* that turned its back on the outside world. The external doorway was concealed by a *skifa* or chicane so that no passer-by could see into the intimate world of the household. Interior rooms had unadorned bare surfaces and were equipped with furnishings low to the ground (tables, cushions, divans), while the use of space was polyvalent, rooms being used for eating, weaving, and sleeping. The courtyard, a well of light open to the sky, was the central hub of domesticity, a space in which women could cook, wash clothing, sit, and weave.[14]

Most accounts of the Paris bidonvilles have emphasized the appalling physical conditions of the settlements, the lack of piped water and sanitation and the damp and rat-infested shacks in which migrant families suffered from disease, overcrowding, and the constant risk of fire from candles, lamps, and stoves.[15] However, conditions varied considerably between one bidonville and another, and in settlements like that of the Rue des Près, when optimum conditions prevailed such as a relative freedom to stake out building plots to a desirable size and access to savings or capital to invest in materials (cement, timber, breeze-blocks, corrugated iron), Algerians built solid structures that replicated the spaces of the traditional home. During the first decade of significant bidonville expansion from 1951 to 1961, migrants moving into large *terrains vagues* and unhampered by police controls had a degree of freedom to construct houses to the size and shape they wished. Many North African immigrants brought with them the skills and techniques learned from building houses and barns in their home villages, and a common practice was for men to cooperate in building work just as they had in Kabylia, following the custom of reciprocal labor, the *tiwizi*. Many Algerians were also skilled workers in the Paris building industry, while some made a living within the townships by undertaking piecework, charging a fixed rate for each line of brick or breeze-block construction. The application of internal plastering and molding was done by women using, as in the Maghreb, their hands rather than a trowel, and walls were painted in brilliant colors, ochre, azure, and green.

During these early years, with space to expand, Algerians typically chose to construct a closed-in cellular habitat in which a key feature was a small, private courtyard complete with a high outer wall and protective door. The yard, although often small in size, was a particularly valued feature, an important extension of the domestic space in which women, while still retaining privacy, would prepare and cook food, wash clothing and hang it to dry, and sit in circles talking with neighbors, while small children could play in safety. Many inhabitants, nostalgic for their peasant roots, would grow flowers and vegetables in minuscule gardens or pots, adding a touch of color and greenery. The house was in most instances a three-room structure, with a hierarchy of space that progressed from the kitchen in which visitors would be received via a more intimate family room containing luxury items of furnishing and where during ceremonial occasions women and children ate apart, through to the most private space, the bedroom of the parents, often decorated with oriental carpets imported from Algeria. The house as a whole, as in Algeria, "belonged" to the women who played a central role in maintaining cultural tradition through child rearing, food preparation (couscous), and the organization of religious festivals.[16]

The French State and Anti-bidonvilles Strategies

During the course of the Algerian War the French state brought all its weight to bear on the autonomy of both Algerian and metropolitan bidonvilles. The refugees who poured into the Cité Mahieddine from the Mitija and Kabylia rapidly formed a revolutionary redoubt that, like the famous Casbah, the security forces found difficult to penetrate or control. Military intelligence officers trained in the theories of psychological warfare were fully aware that the political power base of the FLN within these bastions was integrally linked to the unique built form and the powerful kin and group solidarities of which it was an expression. The anti-bidonvilles, counterinsurgency strategies that were developed under the aegis of the army in Algeria during 1955–60, were rapidly introduced into the metropolis. These consisted of two interlocking approaches, each of which is considered in turn: firstly the physical destruction of the shantytowns as bastions of nationalism and secondly the radical dislocation of Algerian social structures and culture through decanting into Western forms of HLM housing that would lead to the "civilizing" and "assimilation" of migrants.

Urban squatter settlements throughout Algeria, segregated enclaves of revolutionary activity, were bulldozed by the army, and the inhabitants broken up into groups that were rehoused to great fanfare in dreary HLM-type blocks or low-density cabins.[17] In Constantine Maurice Papon orchestrated bulldozing ceremonies before ranks of dignitaries, senior army officers, and journalists. Those rehoused in the new Cité El-Attabia were personally handed a key by the superprefect (IGAME [Inspecteur Général de l'Administration en Mission

Extraordinaire]), who made a long speech on the advances being
made in the battle against "fanaticism."[18] The Plan de Constantine
of 1958 massively accelerated the "pacification" program through
the rapid construction of vast concrete-block estates containing
200,000 housing units.[19] The strategies developed by the military
and technocrats in Algeria to tackle the bidonville "problem" were
introduced into metropolitan France through the creation of a new
funding agency, the Fonds d'Action Sociale (1958) and a housing
corporation, SONACOTRAL (Société nationale de construction de
logements pour les travailleurs algériens [National Company for
the Construction of Housing for Algerian Workers]), which engaged
in constructing worker hostels, *cités de transit,* and HLM flats for
families.

Although senior civil servants like Michel Massenet, Délégué
à l'Action Sociale, were genuinely concerned to improve migrant
housing conditions as a means to win Algerian allegiance to France,
the police and military in Paris engaged in extremely repressive
operations against the bidonvilles. In 1958 Papon flew in officers of
the Sections administratives urbaines (SAU), the special army units
which engaged in anti-FLN operations within the Algerian shantytowns under the guise of social work and established identical units
in Paris, the Service d'assistance technique (SAT). Captain Raymond
Montaner, who led repressive operations in Nanterre assisted by
the *harki* brigades that he founded, brought into Paris his expertise
in "pacifying" the Algiers bidonville of Clos Salembier.[20] In August
1961 the Prefecture of Police banned any new constructions as well
as enlargement, alteration, or improvement of existing huts, and
this decree was enforced by the so-called Z brigades, special police
teams equipped with sledgehammers and crowbars that patrolled
the shantytowns daily. Any alterations, even the repair of leaking
roofs, could lead to the punitive demolition of the entire house.[21]

The savage freeze on extension or repair of shacks severely damaged any Algerian control over the built environment and distorted the "normal" ameliorative processes of self-improvement. As their makeshift shelters were demolished by the Z police, so relatives and friends rehoused them, frequently subdividing existing rooms or building new ones into valuable courtyard space, out of the sight of the brigades. As conditions in the bidonvilles deteriorated, fueled in part by the flood of refugees arriving from rural zones devastated by the army, Algerians found it increasingly difficult to maintain the desired spatial forms of the traditional house. The desperate attempt by Algerians to cling, against the odds, to the central values of domestic privacy is illustrated in letters written in December 1965 seeking official permission to build external walls, "that will protect us from the gaze of passers-by" or, in another instance, enclosing "my courtyard which is open to the lane so that everyone can see into our interior."[22]

The second anti-bidonville strategy, first developed in the colonial context, involved the imposition of modern built forms along with "reeducation" into French domestic norms, an assimilationist project that aimed to radically dislocate Algerian culture. French colonial ideology during the period from 1900 to 1962 was obsessed with the hegemonic project of invading, conquering, and "liberating" the last bastion of Algerian cultural and social resistance, the Muslim woman, as well as the sealed-off domestic space that she inhabited.[23] From 1957 onward the army 5th Bureau concerned with *action psychologique* established teams of female social workers, Equipes Médico-Sociales Itinérantes (EMSI), whose task was to teach Western techniques of hygiene, childcare, and domesticity; to "take control of the female Muslim population"; and to gather intelligence.[24]

Such forms of indoctrination could be best implemented by

decanting Algerians from the bidonvilles into the clean environment of Western-style housing projects. However, planning experts believed that migrants of peasant origin, still bound to archaic ways, would need to be gradually introduced to the complex lifestyle of the modern apartment by passing through a transitional displacement into cheaper, temporary forms of low-density housing, usually prefabricated or breeze-block transit camps or cités, where socioeducative teams would train the Algerians to adapt to modernity. Algerian women in particular would need to learn the skills of domestic economy and hygiene; how to use tapped water, electricity, and modern appliances; and to understand the importance of soap, wcs, and the links between cleanliness and health. After the intermediate phase they could then be transferred into the palatial splendor of the *grands ensembles*, the spotless and functional spaces of the modern apartment, a veritable laboratory for the final transformation into *civilisées*.[25] This paternalist, "progressive" movement was inspired by the objective of both physically destroying the fabric of the shantytowns as centers of cultural, social, and political resistance and simultaneously breaking up the traditional family, "opening" it up to the gaze of the state and weakening the solidarities of the extended family and tribal structures that impeded assimilation.

In metropolitan France the key policy statements and practices relating to the *réabsorption* of the shantytowns, first elaborated in 1958–59, show the unmistakable imprint of the strategies that were developed in the cockpit of war in Algeria and that involved the utilization of built form as a means to fundamentally alter the "Algerian migrant personality." This ideology continued to inform postcolonial state policy, particularly during the decade 1962–72 as the shantytowns were slowly eradicated and Algerians were transferred into cités de transit or HLM estates.

In moving Algerians from the bidonvilles, housing authorities—
as in Algiers—carried out a standard procedure of visiting the immigrants at home and classifying them, usually into two or three
bands, according to the degree of integration into the French way
of life. The small number who were most "evolved" could transfer
immediately to HLM flats (if available); families still attached to the
chaotic way of life of the ghettos would go to the cités de transit for a
two-year phase of reeducation, while the most recalcitrant to change
might be considered fit for repatriation.[26] The Trintignac commission
established in May 1967 to study the liquidation of the bidonvilles
reported on the need for a socioeducative program, implemented by
teams of social workers, with the object of facilitating "the adaptation of the population of the bidonvilles to the conditions of normal
life," their marginality within French society being in part due to
their familial and "tribal" structures.[27] The urban anthropologist
Ralph Grillo, who carried out fieldwork in Lyons in 1975–76, found
fourteen years after the end of the Algerian War an identical social
work practice that measured the degree of "evolution" of Algerian
families according to norms that centered on issues of housekeeping,
cleaning, and "dirt," such as the acquisition and utilization of ac-
ceptable (that is, French) furniture, airing and disinfecting, cooking
skills, making bed covers and curtains, child care, and management
of the household budget. Socioeducative action especially targeted
the role of the woman, who was to be encouraged to "open out"
and to undergo a cultural transformation that would make her into
a model Frenchwoman.[28] A social worker who visited one Algerian
family expressed approval in the following terms: "The lodging
presents a clean and tidy appearance: beds with clean sheets, decorated rooms, green plants, artificial flowers, a TV, kitchen furniture
. . . a bedroom made in plywood that has been embellished. The
household is organized, the children under control."[29]

In the development of this professional discourse the bidonvilles served the function of the lowest denominator, the form of immigrant housing that was most in opposition to the model of society that social workers shared. As in late colonial Algeria, progress would be achieved via the physical destruction of the bidonvilles and the simultaneous radical transformation of migrant culture and identity through the crucial role of the modern built form, the HLM apartment. This socioeducative strategy, which reflected the overall ambiguity of government policy toward Algerian immigrants that showed a mix of control and social welfare reform, was constructed on a Eurocentric concept of domesticity, consumerism, and "normality" that largely failed to recognize the kind of "order" represented by "tradition" and bidonville life. Within the postcolonial order the earlier deep fears of the segregated bidonville as a revolutionary bastion amalgamated with the Jacobin tradition that regarded assimilation as crucial to the construction of the nation as "one and indivisible," a precursor of the negative discourse that was soon to develop in relation to the immigrant "ghettos" of the *grands ensembles*. As the Trintignac Report of 1968 remarked, it was feared that "a population that as a whole has evolved little might assert its rights more than its duties, and that such a way of behaving will rapidly lead the *bidonvilles* or the *cités* [*de transit*] to assert themselves as autonomous sectors, threatening to block rather than facilitate the work undertaken in their favour by the Administration."[30]

Algerian Adaptation to the European House

The previous section has been concerned with the discourse and perceptions of French officialdom. There remains to discuss how Algerians experienced the transition from bidonville to transit camp or HLM flat and to what extent the geometrical spaces of the modern built form disrupted traditional sociocultural practices. Did the trajectory toward "modernity" meet resistance or was it welcomed?

Firstly, within North Africa itself, many commentators have noted how the history of French colonialism was marked by the conqueror's imposition of the straight line, the square grid layout of the European township and of geometric architecture that stood in radical opposition to the curved lines and the private spaces of the Arab Casbah.[31] Bourdieu and Sayad, in their classic study, *Le déracinement*, showed how the dramatic expulsion of over two million peasants from their villages and their relocation in the grid-like resettlement camps so dear to the barrack mentality of the military tradition constituted a profound symbolic violence and an irreversible dislocation of traditional village or domestic space. The suppression of the traditional courtyard in the standardized, box-like housing units of the camps was regarded by some as an attempt to force "occidentalization" and to accelerate the "evolution" of women.[32]

There are signs of resistance to the constraints imposed by relocation into the "western" house. In Algeria those who were rehoused in transit cités or HLM deployed a multitude of "rearrangements" to adapt and reappropriate modern internal spaces to their customary practices, by sealing up external windows or building new walls and partitions.[33] The same pattern can be identified in metropolitan France. The Herpin study of 1968 includes an analysis of how Algerian families tried to adapt to the inappropriate layout and functions of the uniform house of the cité de transit. In the absence of a courtyard and of a large kitchen space that could serve as the semiprivate and multipurpose reception room, Algerians adapted a bedroom into a kitchen or used other bedrooms as inappropriate storage spaces for motor scooters. Families also tried to appropriate external open spaces by putting carpets to sit outside in warm weather or, against official regulations, washing and drying clothes. But attempts by Algerian families to re-create customary spaces, a coherent organization of the household, were largely unsuccessful and led to an impoverished and incoherent deployment of the house that simply confirmed French social worker and official perceptions of the "uncivilized" nature of the migrants.[34] The alienation and deep unhappiness that were often caused by modern housing design were in part reflected in the fact that families, given the opportunity, often moved from cité de transit and HLM flats back into the bidonvilles or went to spend the day there among friends.[35]

While, however, Algerian families showed a strong attachment to the customary social and cultural practices of bidonville life, it would be a mistake to read this—as did French officialdom—as a traditionalist rejection of modernity. Algerians showed an underlying ambivalence in relation to French urban society, a mix of admiration and fascination for some elements of modernity, particularly consumer goods and technologies, along with disquiet or hostility toward built form. Migrants could aspire to mass consumerism and comfort (from washing machines to television sets) while showing a profound attachment to religious practices, traditional gender roles, and family structures. In the "superior" bidonville of the Rue des Près many families embraced modern appliances (washing machines, gas cookers, TVs), while the majority of families in the degraded settlement of la Folie dreamed of the day when they would be able to escape the overcrowded, rat-infested, and squalid bidonville for the cleanliness, water closets, and electricity of the HLM. The latter claimed that if they did not have the modern furnishings and appliances that social workers looked for as a sign of being "evolved" and therefore meeting the criteria for rehousing, this was because cramped space did not allow it and it was pointless to invest in new equipment that might be destroyed by damp or by fire or police depredations. As one immigrant remarked, once rehoused, "we furnished ourselves, a washing-machine, a television and all. The bed from here, the mattresses, and all that, were left behind to be burned in the bidonville; we brought nothing with us from here except our clothes."[36]

The future promotion from the shantytown was imagined as a radical abandonment of dirt for the shining "paradise" of the HLM. North African migrants did aspire to the modern house, to consumerism, and a better life, but contrary to the paternalist perceptions of the French housing authorities and social workers, the "norms" of "civilized" living did not have to be inculcated into a resistant and benighted people. An interesting figure here is "Emma," the mother in Azouz Begag's semiautobiographical novel, *Le gone du Chaâba*, who on moving from the *chaâba* into an apartment is fascinated and delighted by modern tables, chairs, the refrigerator, and Formica surfaces, which she endlessly polishes and "caresses."[37] However, Emma, who shows this love of consumerism and a certain kind of modernity, is simultaneously the least "evolved" of Algerian women, who is tied to tradition, is able to speak barely a word of French, and continues to dress in a *binouar*. In this sense elements of tradition and modernity were not mutually incompatible, as the dominant French official discourse maintained. It seems quite likely that official attempts to mold immigrant families into French forms of behavior had a very limited impact: Algerian women, in particular, had a very strong sense of identity, and social workers suspected that conformity to official regulation and norms was a skilful ploy, an instrumental enactment of "correct" behavior, to gain strictly pragmatic and material goals.[38]

The migrant experience of departure from the bidonville for the cité or HLM flat was a moment of profound ambiguity. Azouz Begag, as a child, drove his father to despair with his insistent chanting, "I want to move!" but once installed in a new apartment he missed the chaâba, while his father, Bouzid, disoriented in the modern city flat, repeatedly abandoned his family to camp out in the old shantytown, "To look after the garden."[39] Bouzid's family knew this gardening was a feeble excuse: the symbolic return to the soil for this illiterate man, who had been an agricultural laborer in Algeria, represented a painful and nostalgic regret for a lost order. Similarly, Brahim Benaïcha, on the day of departure from the Nanterre bidonville, could barely watch the bulldozer flatten the rotting hut in which "we had lived ten years in the best of worlds, one of poverty and a rich inner life."[40] There is a danger in nostalgic recall, a selective memory and amnesia toward the truly appalling hardship and misery of the shantytowns, but if we look to understand what was most valued by the migrants themselves, it undoubtedly lies in the ability to establish a specific kind of urban space, an enclave in which a rich tissue of family, kin, and village relationships could be reconstituted on foreign soil. Begag's mother understood this intimate relationship between cultural practices and space when she remarked, "In which other chaâba can the men pray in the fields or in the garden without appearing ridiculous? In what other place are they going to celebrate *Aïd*? And for the circumcisions, what are they going to do? And to sacrifice their sheep? . . . and the women? Where are they going to hang their washing?"[41]

There are some messages here for how we seek to understand and interpret not only Algerian but many other migration flows from "traditional" to "modern" societies. One central aspect of such processes is the adaptations made to the built environment. For those, like Benaïcha's family arriving directly from a Saharan oasis into the geometric, brick and concrete structures of Paris, the urban landscape, the very shape and scale of private rooms, represented a rigidly fixed and constraining order. "We are ground to pieces in the name of an established order." At the end of ten years in Nanterre Benaïcha contemplated the significance of the bidonville, as it disappeared into a pile of dust and rubble: "It preserved our language, our religion, our identity. It enabled us to remain ourselves despite the tempests of the civilizations that we crossed through. The bidonville forged us a strong personality."[42] By this it is not implied that the bidonvilles enabled migrants to preserve intact their original culture, like some fossil relic; indeed, this would be to overlook the dynamic processes of change and adaptation going on within the settlements.[43] But rather it provided a kind of haven within which impoverished rural migrants were able to exercise a degree of autonomy and demonstrated a remarkable energy, courage, and inventiveness that kept alive some of the unique cultural and social values that they had brought with them across the Mediterranean.

Notes

1. See, for example, Pierre Bourdieu, "The Kabyle House or the World Reversed," in *Algeria 1960* (Cambridge: Cambridge University Press, 1972), 133–53.

2. Alison Shaw, *Kinship and Continuity: Pakistani Families in Britain* (Melbourne, Australia: Harwood, 2000), chap. 3, shows how Muslim peasants arriving in Oxford adapted the gender-related functions of the traditional rural household to the framework of the Victorian terrace house.

3. On the interpretation of "Third World" shantytowns as structured communities see John F. C. Turner, *Housing by People: Towards Autonomy in Building Environments* (London: Marion Boyars, 1976); and Peter Lloyd, *Slums of Hope? Shanty Towns of the Third World* (Harmondsworth, UK: Penguin, 1979).

4. Pierre Bourdieu and Abdelmalek Sayad, *Le déracinement: La crise de l'agriculture traditionnelle en Algérie* (Paris: Minuit, 1964) and Michel Cornaton, *Les Regroupements de la Décolonisation en Algérie* (Paris: Éditions Ouvrières, 1967).

5. Robert Descloitres, J-C. Reverdy, and C. Descloitres, *L'Algérie des Bidonvilles: Le Tiers Monde dans la Cité* (Paris: Mouton, 1961); and Ahmed El Gharbaoui, "Les travailleurs maghrébins immigrés dans la banlieue nord-est de Paris," *Revue de Géographie du Maroc* 19 (1971): 15–17.

6. Zeynup Çelik, *Urban Forms and Colonial Confrontations: Algiers under French*

Rule (Berkeley: University of California Press, 1997), 110–12. Descloitres, *Algérie des Bidonvilles*, 70, shows the similarity in cellular form between the *bidonville* of Mahieddine and the Casbah of Algiers.

7. Isabelle Herpin and Serge Santelli, *Bidonville à Nanterre: Étude Architecturale* (Paris: Ministère des Affaires Culturelles, Institut de l'Environment, 1971), 80–81, 85, 87–95.

8. On this pattern of kin- and village-linked migration and settlement see Neil MacMaster, *Colonial Migrants and Racism: Algerians in France, 1900–62* (London: Macmillan, 1997). On ethnic groupings internal to the *bidonvilles* see Brahim Benaïcha, *Vivre au Paradis: D'une Oasis à un Bidonville* (Paris: Desclée de Brouwer, 1999 edition), 39.

9. Benaïcha, *Vivre au Paradis*, 209; for such an elaborate wedding see also Monique Hervo, *Chroniques du Bidonville: Nanterre en Guerre d'Algérie* (Paris: Seuil, 2001), 257–58.

10. On the "closed and autonomous economy" see Imhof, "Le 'bidonville' du Petit Nanterre," *Cahiers Nord-Africains* 89 (May 1962): 50–51.

11. Abdelmalek Sayad, *Un Nanterre algérien, terre de bidonvilles* (Paris: Éditions Autrement, 1995).

12. Hervo, *Chroniques*, 43, 58, 60, 124.

13. On FLN organization in Paris and the *bidonvilles* see Ali Haroun, *La 7e Wilaya: La Guerre du fln en France, 1954–1962* (Paris: Seuil, 1986); Benjamin Stora, *Ils Venaient d'Algérie: L'immigration algérienne en France, 1912–1992* (Paris: Fayard, 1992), 343–51; *Sou'al* 7 (September 1987): 22–55; and Muriel Cohen, "Les algériens des bidonvilles de Nanterre pendant la guerre d'Algérie: histoire et mémoire," Mémoire de maîtrise, University of Paris 1, 2003.

14. Marc Côte, *L'Algérie ou l'Espace Retourné* (Paris: Flammarion, 1988), chap. 2; and Pierre Robert Baduel, ed., "Habitat traditionnel et polarités structurales dans l'aire arabo-musulmane," in *Habitat, État et Société au Maghreb* (Paris: CNRS, 1988), 231–56.

15. See, for example, the detailed account of two social workers, Monique Hervo and Marie-Ange Charras, *Bidonvilles, l'enlisement* (Paris: Maspero, 1971); and François Lefort, *Du Bidonville à l'Expulsion: itinéraire d'un jeune Algérien de Nanterre* (Paris: Editions CIEMM, 1980).

16. Herpin, *Bidonville à Nanterre*, provides a detailed household survey including ground plans, sixty interior photographs, and interviews with family members. Other photographs of internal yards and rooms can be found in Imhof, "Le 'bidonville' du Petit Nanterre," 53; Hervo, *Chroniques*; Sayad, *Un Nanterre algérien*; and Abdelmalak Sayad, *L'immigration ou les paradoxes de l'altérité* (Brussels: De Boeck-Westmael, 1991), 140.

17. Çeylik, *Urban Forms*, 112, 173–74, 211n57.

18. *La Dépêche de Constantine*, 10 October 1956 and 9–10 June 1957.

19. Çeylik, *Urban Forms*, 97–179.

20. On the SAT and Montaner see Jim House and Neil MacMaster, *Paris 1961: Algerians, State Terror, and Post-Colonial Memories* (Oxford: Oxford University Press, 2006).

21. On the Z brigade see Charras, *Bidonvilles*,370–86; Benaïcha, *Vivre au Paradis*, 49, 196; and Hervo, *Chroniques*, 145–54.

22. Hervo, *Bidonvilles*, 380–81.

23. Frantz Fanon, *Studies in a Dying Colonialism* (London: Earthscan, 1989), 38–39; M. Lazreg, *The Eloquence of Silence: Algerian Women in Question* (London: Routledge, 1994), 134–37; and Neil MacMaster, *Burning the Veil: The Algerian War and the "Emancipation" of Muslim Women (1954–62)* (Manchester: Manchester University Press, 2009).

24. Service historique de l'armée de terre, Vincennes, 1H. 2461/D1, "Action sur les Milieux Féminins en Algérie." Hervo, *Chroniques*, 82, notes that EMSI teams operated in the Nanterre *bidonvilles* in August 1960.

25. Çelik, *Urban Forms*, pp. 97–179.

26. Hervo, *Bidonvilles*, pp. 392–93; and A. and J. Belkhodja, "Les Africains du Nord à Gennevilliers," *Cahiers Nord-Africains* 97 (1963): 126.

27. On the Trintignac Report, see Hervo, *Bidonvilles*, 387–402.

28. Ralph D. Grillo, *Ideologies and Institutions in Urban France: The Representation of Immigrants* (Cambridge: Cambridge University Press, 1985), chap. 6.

29. Ralph D. Grillo, "Social Workers and Immigrants in Lyon, France," in *"Nation" and "State" in Europe: Anthropological Perspectives,* ed. R. D. Grillo (London: Academic Press, 1980), 84.

30. Hervo, *Bidonvilles*, 296–97.

31. See Côte, *L'Algérie,* for an analysis of the colonial "inversion" of space.

32. Cornaton, *Les Regroupements*, 86–87.

33. Côte, *L'Algérie,* 137; Çeylik, *Urban Forms,* 166–79.

34. Herpin, *Bidonville à Nanterre,* 98–104.

35. Imhof, "Le 'bidonville' du Petit Nanterre," 52.

36. Hervo, *Bidonvilles,* 33.

37. Azouz Begag, *Le gone du Chaâba* (Paris: Seuil, 1986), 173.

38. Grillo, *Ideologies and Institutions,* 161.

39. Begag, *Le gone du Chaâba,* 197–200.

40. Benaïcha, *Vivre au Paradis,* 301.

41. Begag, *Le gone du Chaâba*, 147. See also Sayad, *Un Nanterre algérien*, 111–15, "la nostalgie du bidonville."

42. Benaïcha, *Vivre au Paradis*, 62, 301.

43. On the contemporary transformation of Maghrebin domestic space in both state and private housing see Rabia Bekkar, Nadir Boumaza, and Daniel Pinson, *Familles maghrébines en France, l'épreuve de la ville* (Paris: PUF, 1999).

5

Excluding the *Harkis* from Repatriate Status, Excluding Muslim Algerians from French Identity

TODD SHEPARD

It was not until the last years of the Algerian Revolution (1954–62), roughly late 1959 to early 1962, that public discussions in "mainland" (metropolitan) France overwhelmingly presumed the need for Algerian independence. Such arguments took for granted what now may appear obvious: that Algeria and Algerians were so different from France and the French that the French Republic could not encompass the former. The most telling indication that this "fact" was both novel and remained far from obvious was the Constitution of 1958, which had extended political rights equal to other French citizens to all Algerians. On through the war's close, government officials, military officers, as well as pro-French Algeria propaganda continued to affirm that "Muslims" from Algeria were French citizens.[1] This was also evident in the Evian Accords, which established a cease fire between government and National Liberation Front (FLN) forces and set the conditions for Algeria's independence. While affirming that a clear distinction existed between French and Algerian territory, the text continued to link all people from Algeria to other French people. Indeed, when the accords were announced on 19 March 1962, there was no official hesitation concerning what it meant for those people now officially referred to as Muslim French citizens from Algeria (*citoyens français musulmans d'Algérie*, hereafter FMAS). A telegram from the National Defense Headquarters in Paris to army headquarters in Algeria "convey[ed] the Prime Minister's instructions" concerning their future: "Question: Will they have the same possibilities as the French of [European] Origin to settle in the metropole with French citizenship and the benefits of the Law on Assistance to French repatriates? Response: YES." "Question: Will this possibility remain available to French Muslims? Response: Yes, by returning to the metropole at any moment after self-determination they can reclaim French nationality under French law and benefit from the Law [on Repatriate Status]."[2] Radio France broadcast across the metropole the official affirmation that continued French nationality and all measures of the Law of 26 December 1961, which established the legal category of "repatriate," were available to "every inhabitant of Algeria," whether "Muslims or European French." In the metropole supporters of the referendum of 8 April 1962 also specified that "French nationality would be maintained for all in Algeria who currently have it, Europeans or Muslims, and who do not explicitly renounce it."[3]

Thus official documents and official statements continued to define all people from Algeria as French citizens—until the so-called exodus. Between mid-April and September 1962, upward of one million people left Algeria to seek refuge in the metropole. The vast majority of the some one million "Europeans" of Algeria as well as upward of one hundred thousand FMAS, rather than remaining in soon-to-be-independent Algeria, fled to metropolitan France. Most of the FMAS who joined the exodus had been closely associated—either personally or through family connections—with

French control of Algeria; a small number had been administrative elites or had served in the French military; most were so-called *harkis,* members of auxiliary units that had fought alongside French forces during the conflict or *moghazin,* "Muslim Algerians" who had served as guides and scouts for French Armed Forces in Algeria. Despite government expectations and popular impatience that most of these "Algerians" quickly would and should return to Algeria, this did not occur.

In the midst of the exodus the French government abandoned the legally accurate affirmation that all people from Algeria were equally French. Through a series of legal and bureaucratic shifts, officials effectively denied almost all "Arabs," "Berbers," or "Muslims" from Algeria the right to keep their existing French citizenship. In this period of upheaval, the idea that those people whom French law defined as Muslim French citizens from Algeria were part of an ethnoracial group different from that of other French citizens left the sphere of common sense to shape the legal categories that the French government put in place in July 1962. Through extraordinary measures, new laws worked to make the boundaries of the nation resemble what most French people now believed was obvious: Algerians could not be French.[4]

In late April and early May 1962, while publicly denying the existence of anything that could be called an exodus from Algeria (official spokesmen insisted that people were leaving Algeria for "summer vacations"), the government acted to stop only one type of people from coming to the metropole: FMAS. Or as military orders and government decrees increasingly put it, "harkis" or simply "Muslims." Officials charged with assisting Algeria's "Muslim" population received a top secret note of 23 May from de Gaulle's office explaining that they were to "cease all initiatives linked to the repatriation of harkis." To be "welcomed in the metropole, Muslims" were to leave under the control of the Algerian high commissioner, and a list established to this end" named those who were allowed to leave.[5] By late May an officer directed that "Muslims" who were "too old, physically handicapped, or too young" as well as "single women" should not be transported. Such people, he remarked, were "destined effectively either to live off public charity or, with the young women, to turn to prostitution," becoming "deadweights."[6] At the cabinet level the shift in terms was more subtle, and as such easier to interpret. In his April report to the government, the secretary of state for repatriates referred to "Muslims" only as "auxiliaries"— harkis, whom the army would be in charge of dealing with; the May report placed them into one of two distinct categories: "repatriates of European origin (*souche*)" on the one hand and "repatriates of Muslim origin (*origine*)" on the other. With these categories, the government abandoned previous references that tied identity to territory (Algeria) and instead identified people from Algeria on the basis of descent or ethnicity.[7]

Still referred to in May 1962 as "Muslim repatriates," French citizens with Koranic Civil Status would increasingly be named "harkis" or "refugees," a shift that stripped them of the terms "repatriate" and "citizen." This was inextricably linked with another shift in which "Muslim" was no longer an adjective for "French," but an "origin" (*origine*). If the April report to the cabinet noted, regarding "Muslim families whose head served in the French Army in Algeria," that their "lack of preparedness for metropolitan life pose[d] special problems," the May report adopted a new tone and recommended a new approach: "As these Muslims are not prepared for European life, it would be inopportune to give them the aid reserved for repatriates as individuals."[8] De Gaulle pretended on 25 July that "the term repatriates obviously does not apply to the Muslims. In their case, we are dealing only with refugees."

His statement completely disregarded the Evian Accords and the definition of "repatriate," both of which had the force of (French) law.[9] French officials already had affirmed that refugees were not repatriates. In the first weeks of mass departures for the metropole, government officials had embraced a distinction between repatriates and what de Gaulle's chief of staff characterized as "temporary refugees." This euphemism allowed officials to maintain that most French people fleeing to the metropole—"Europeans"—soon would return to Algeria. With the government now recognizing the exodus as a regrettable and durable fact, officials applied the term "refugees" with all its implications almost exclusively to "Muslims."[10] At the beginning of 1963, Prof. Robert de Vernejoul published a *Study of the Problems Posed by the Repatriation of Refugees from Algeria*. The Economic and Social Council, one of the new representative institutions the 1958 constitution had established, submitted it to the Parliament and the government. The official report stated, "[apart from] French repatriates who return to their fatherland, there are Muslim 'refugees.'" The report clearly affirmed a distinction: "these non-French Muslims . . . are not repatriates in the true sense of the term. . . . they are refugees." By ignoring their citizenship and instead pointing to their "choice in the last several years to side with France," De Vernejoul's study explained away the fact that they had "the right to the same benefits, to the same integrative measures" as repatriates. De Vernejoul followed de Gaulle, effacing law and history as well as harki rights.[11]

Shifting Algerian "Muslims" out of the category of repatriates and into the category of refugees of course had material effects. The most dramatic concerned the tens of thousands of actual or suspected harkis who, abandoned by the French, were killed in Algeria during these months. Whether the act of armed groups, units associated with the FLN), or the result of local settlings of accounts, Algerians claiming to punish traitors assassinated, using often inhumane measures, other Algerians accused of collaborating with the French. The French government in response affirmed that the victims were not themselves French. When in September 1962 Prime Minister Pompidou gave instructions to the minister of the armies to "guarantee the transfer to France of former auxiliaries currently in Algeria who have sought protection from French Forces," he made this clear. They were "under threat of reprisal from their compatriots."[12] Pompidou's directive was grounded in humanitarian concern for human beings, not in fraternity or national solidarity for French nationals. A "personal note" in late October from the high commander of French Armed Forces in Algeria to all French generals in Algeria reinforced this point and revealed the limits this placed on humanitarian concern. Despite previous reminders, he observed, "the number of Muslims housed in our camps in Algeria grows steadily." It was thus necessary "to suspend all new admission to our centers." In November 1962 official documents and the newspaper *Le Monde* estimated that over ten thousand Algerians had been killed for being harkis since the cease fire. Although it remains difficult to ascertain verifiable numbers for these killings, evidence suggests that ten thousand is at the low end of the estimates. Many who died, and others who did not, experienced various forms of torture.[13]

Those who made it to the French metropole experienced other effects of being refugees in their own country. Denied their right to government assistance, these French citizens had to confront convoluted restrictions to obtain the more limited aid the French government was willing to give to foreign refugees. By early 1963 the head of the Service for Muslim Affairs (SAM) could insist that "Muslim Algerian refugees in the metropole who have chosen French nationality cannot, *ipso facto*, be considered refugees." According to Circular n. 63–03 AGA.AS of 2 January 1963, these "refugees" could benefit from refugee status only if they could "prove that they left their country of origin because in danger or for political reasons." While those whose "departure [*répli*] was arranged by the army automatically have this status," all others were required to establish a dossier, which would be examined by Technical Assistance Section counselors.[14] Gen. Maurice Faivre (ret.), historian of the Algerian War and of the harkis, highlights how government leaders and officials stymied the efforts of numerous French officers to help harkis escape possible reprisals in Algeria. The most scandalous and most well known was Louis Joxe's 12 May telegram, marked "Top Secret Highest Priority," laying out a new principle: "all auxiliaries landing in the metropole outside of the official repatriation program will be sent back." Although quickly revealed by a number of press sources (*Combat*, *La nation française*, and *Esprit publique*) aghast at Joxe's proposal, the government persisted in its efforts to prevent "Muslim" Algerians from fleeing Algeria. Faivre pays little attention, however, to extensive documentary evidence of high-level military responsibility for these decisions. Military intelligence reports, for example, consistently downplayed the threats harkis confronted in Algeria. The military leadership not only followed government instructions, it also shared basic assumptions about the dubious assimilability of "Muslims."[15]

It was certain officers and officials in the field who continued to take seriously French promises of equality to the "autochtones." This was particularly true of officers involved in "integrationist" programs, services set up after 1955 to bring all Algerians closer to France, or commanders of harki units in Algeria. Military officers repeatedly invoked the question of guarantees for their FSNA (*français de souche nord africaine*—French of North African Origin) subordinates. In January one report even argued that harkis were "more interested in how the new status recognizes that they are French than in the material improvements it promises them."[16] These on-the-ground operatives struggled against the assumptions of their higher-ups in Paris, who denied any reality to earlier French claims that all Algerians were French. Previously in Algeria as elsewhere in the French Overseas Empire, it had usually been Paris-based officials who had held onto republican ideals and rejected abandoning them because of local difficulties, whereas officers in the colonies had shown, at best, lip service to republican and universalist claims (often in the name of defending "indigenous" cultures and practices).[17]

When confronted with the exodus of "Muslims," the government did not treat them as French citizens with rights; instead, it presented and classed the harkis as outsiders whom the French Republic welcomed and assisted only out of charity and only in unavoidable circumstances. Classing them as a group rather than as individuals legitimated this shift. Summarizing the difference between their activities in 1958 and in 1963, SAM officials identified "320,000 legally French citizens" before Algerian independence; afterward, they were dealing with "a group of 480,000 foreigners."[18] The definition of the harkis as a group placed them outside the nation.

In the midst of the exodus, contrary to the Evian Accords, the law, and government directives, only a few people insisted that France offer the harkis the same treatment as other repatriates. Harkis themselves did so with all the very limited means at their disposal. Numerous harkis signed individual copies of one form letter with blanks for addresses and names of the signer, all addressed to M. *le Colonel Commandant* of the Bougie District, to "request my pull-back and that of my family to the metropole." The appeal "to benefit from the advantages of repatriate assistance, in conformity with the applicable texts," was motivated "by the fact that I categorically refuse to stay in an Algerian Algeria . . . I am French and want to remain French with my family."[19] Some state officials made vigorous efforts to assert that "Muslims" should be welcomed in the metropole. All affirmed that the potential repatriates in question were fully French. Military officers sent numerous messages seeking the reinstallation in the Hexagon of FSNA individuals or groups. These letters exhaustively detailed the personal qualities of these "French Muslims" and the services they had rendered to the nation. The officers' letters stressed assimilability to metropolitan life, most putting special emphasis on the applicants' fitness for work.[20] A battalion leader who sought the reinstallation in France of "a number of civilian families who [were] irremediably compromised with the Armed Forces in Algeria" asserted that the women and children spoke "French and [were] physically and morally apt to settle in the Metropole." He stated further: "their employment will cause no serious problems as they will be immediately usable as maids. All [of the women] are highly moral."[21] Some officers tried to prove the true Frenchness of the individuals concerned. Battalion Leader Roger wrote, in reference to "Mlle. Hamzaoui, Ratiba, Social Worker": "through constant contact with Security Forces, she has acquired a life-style similar to a Frenchwoman *de souche* [of French origin]."[22] Neither personal testimony nor "expert" certification guaranteed that either the harkis in Oudali or Ratiba Hamzaoui, despite their French citizenship, would be transported or authorized to go to the metropole. In both instances, as was generally the case, no investigation was made. No evidence in their folders remains that would indicate that they were being manipulated by an army officer. Yet the official presumption was that they were not French.

Charles de Gaulle left no doubt as to his own conception of what should be done, signing on 21 June 1962 a document concerning the "nationality problem." The note deployed terms without juridical value to assert that the people concerned were "Algerians of European Origin" and "Muslim" Algerians. The document is striking because it employed terms rarely used by French officials, terms that explicitly embraced group identities with no reference to territory or legal definitions in assigning national membership. Note how he stripped both the official military term *français de souche européenne* (French of European origin, or FSE) and the legally meaningful term FMA of their "French" anchor. While de Gaulle affirmed that the former should have their French nationality as before, for the latter each individual should be required to file an application.[23] It was left to Christian Fouchet, High Commissioner in Algeria, to remind the government that "the nationality question is strictly the domain of the law." Thus, he explained, "it does not seem possible, however desirable, to have a very general text that would give total liberty of appreciation to the administration."[24]

With the Ordinance of 21 July 1962, de Gaulle's government unilaterally altered one of the primary elements of the Evian Accord: the right of all people from Algeria to keep French citizenship. This right had been central to governmental explanations of the Accords in the 8 April referendum campaign, which had wholly rejected opponents' criticisms of the "double nationality" measures. An 8 June 1962 draft project for what would become the Ordinance of 21 July 1962, affirmed that "French with Common Law Civil Status living in Algeria on the date of the official announcement of the vote for self-determination will keep French nationality even if, at the close of the three-year period posited by the General Declaration of 19 March 1962 (chap. 2, art. 2/2), they acquire Algerian nationality." The opposite was done for French with Local Civil Status, mainly Koranic Law Civil Status ("Muslims"), whose access to French citizenship was heavily restricted and dependent on the government's discretion.[25] They could keep their French nationality only if they submitted "a declaration accepted by the Judge responsible for the area where they live[d] on the territory of the French Republic." Not only did French citizens with Koranic Law Civil status have to claim a nationality they already possessed and do so while living outside of Algeria (and on French territory): (1) they would lose their nationality if this declaration was not accepted by a judge and then registered with the Ministry of Public Health and the Population by 1 January 1963 and (2) the ministry had the right to refuse to register the declaration or, for a period of three years, to reject the declaration for "reasons of unworthiness." What these reasons might be remained vague but ranged from suspected or known nationalist activity to moral or personal character flaws.[26]

The government acted as if it was now clarifying uncertainties about "double nationality" that concerned all people from Algeria. In fact the government moved to exclude Algerian "Muslims" not from the complicated situation of "double nationality" but quite simply from their right to hold onto their French nationality.[27] According to the Juridical Counsel for the newly named French ambassador to Algeria, Article 2 of Ordinance n. 62–825 of 21 July 1962 meant, "Algerians with Local Civil Status . . . lose at the very least the use of this nationality as of the day Algeria became independent."[28]

Of course, the government wanted many "Muslims" who were in the metropole to stay in order to provide needed labor but only as Algerian citizens, not French. If not all could be sent back, the head of SAM urged that, among "Algerian Muslims residing in France wishing to be recognized as French nationals," the government should exclude "the un-deserving and all morally or physically retarded people who, later, will need to be gotten rid of." Immediate attention was to be given, as "the prefects request, to sending back to Algeria any undesirables."[29] The late 1962 report emphasized that the French "man in the street would welcome with relief the return of Algerians to their country and he d[id] not hide his surprise that new immigrants [were] arriving." Government moves to exclude all "Muslims" from their rights as French citizens—moves that allowed thousand to die often horrifying deaths—were made not for legal or bureaucratic reasons, but in the name of common sense.[30]

Shifts in government terminology, which excluded all "Algerian Muslims" from French citizenship, aligned bureaucratic rules with the assumptions about people from Algeria that now dominated popular metropolitan discussions. This happened when the Hexagon finally began to confront the exodus: it saw not one flight from Algeria, but two. The media, to take one crucial vector of nongovernmental opinion, offered "Muslims" a welcome very different from other—European—"families from North Africa." In *Paris-Match*, and this was true throughout the Gaullist and left-wing press, "Muslims" appeared, above all, as exotic additions to the exodus. One report describes "five families of harkis" arriving just as the boat is about to leave, "with haggard eyes, some twenty men, women and children" whom an "ex-officer had gone to find in their village in Kabylie, to get them away from reprisals."[31] Among many on the French left, there was concern that the harkis were the Trojan horse by which the Secret Army Organization (OAS), a pro-French Algeria terrorist movement, threatened the metropole. An editorial, "Return of the *Harkis*," in *France-Observateur* primarily emphasized the role the "Muslim" arrivals might play in "reconstituting the OAS in certain regions." The article detailed what the government could do to restrict and monitor harkis' arrivals and "reported" on numerous clandestine landings of harkis. While another editorial in the same issue, "Exodus to Marseilles,"

SHEPARD

described "those who [were] leaving Algeria" as acting "despite the OAS" and "in fear of the OAS," *France-Observateur*'s discussion of the harkis cautioned, "as normal as it is that France should shelter and protect the lives of the French Army's Muslim soldiers who consider themselves menaced by the FLN, it would be dangerous to allow the return to the metropole of veritable Muslim commandos of the OAS."[32] In late June, the Communist Party, the new left political party the PSU (Parti Socialiste Unifié), and the Communist-aligned labor union the CGT (Confédération Générale du Travail) protested against the reception given to the harkis, comparing the conditions they encountered favorably with what FLN prisoners were forced to endure. The Communists called for public vigilance against all the repatriates from Algeria, who risked becoming "a reservoir of fascism."[33] The government, unlike the press or left-wing politicians, was far more worried about activist infiltration among the FSE than among harkis. But, despite significant concern about how to detect OAS operatives, at no point during the exodus did any official suggest that the government intervene to prevent non-"Muslims" from fleeing to the metropole. Agencies instead agreed on various intelligence-sharing and surveillance measures to stop such potential infiltrators.[34]

If the government was most concerned about the infiltration of the OAS and its potential "European" relays into the metropole, it chose to act aggressively to exclude "Muslim" Algerians, in particular the harkis. Rather than security concerns or any kind of explicit embrace of the terms of left-wing rejection of harkis as "collaborators" and OAS "stormtroopers," de Gaulle's government affirmed a racialized exclusion. While government officials and the mass media struggled to convince the metropolitan public that the *pieds-noirs* were really French and not Algerian or all "fascists," they concurrently denied any right to French identity for Muslim French citizens from Algeria.

If in this context most French people were willing to ignore the citizenship of the harkis and downplay French responsibility to them, significant numbers of French officials—at the local level, in Paris, elected and not—did express concern about the implications of the 21 July decree for what one termed "Algerians having chosen to remain French." These concerns reinforce the reality of the French identity in question, reminding us of the importance of juridical definitions of citizenship; they also help graph the contours of the denial of that identity that the end of French Algeria produced. The government spurned the rare bureaucratic efforts that proposed to deal with arriving harkis as rights-bearing individuals. The Ministry for Repatriates, for example, proposed establishing a workers' hostel in Paris reserved for "Muslim repatriates." The letter spoke of "isolated Muslims arriving in Paris . . . civilians, who have the right to the status of 'repatriate.'" When an Interior Ministry official rejected the idea, he referred to "Muslims who remained loyal to France" and compared them, not to other French people from Algeria, but to other "migrants."[35] As the deadline for filing "declarations of nationality" approached and officials prepared to act to exclude a group of some 8 million people from French citizenship, the Secretary of State for Algerian Affairs wrote to the Minister of the Interior. He expressed his concerns: "we risk taking the right to vote away from citizens who, according to the ordinance, were guaranteed that they could keep the French nationality that they already possessed." Like the numerous prefects and mayors who wrote to Paris, he invoked not just French obligations but the feelings and sensibilities of the harkis.[36] The Secretary of State was more explicit than most in pinpointing the racially charged character of the exclusion. He warned the Ministry of the Interior that "no criteria exist that would allow the authorities in charge of revising electoral lists to distinguish with certainty those Muslims with Local Status who were able to obtain French status from the others." The complication was purely juridical: "*a contrario*, the only valid proof effectively results from the individual in question's incapacity to prove that he is governed by common law." The approach the Secretary of State sought to avoid was less subtle: he urged Interior "not to begin an automatic exclusion [from the electoral lists] that would concern all electors who have a name that sounds Algerian." Instead, he proposed an approach that at once blatantly revealed the racial nature of the procedure and tried to bend it to republican legality: "it would be better, it seems to me, to instruct those in charge of voting stations to deny, when the case arises, access to the booth to electors of Algerian origin [*souche*] who cannot prove that they have French nationality"; that is, in his system those who looked Algerian would only be dubiously—and not necessarily "un"-French.[37]

Concerns about hurting harkis' patriotic feelings or *amour propre* were not, however, the only or the primary element shaping government policy. After the exodus began, no one accepted that having citizenship was sufficient grounds for "Muslims" from Algeria to keep it. Rather, with Algerian "Muslims," excluding the "bad" was, at best, equally important as admitting the "good," and often more so. As Vernejoul's report of January 1963 emphasized, while it was "unthinkable to make things difficult for those who had fought under our colors," this goal was less pressing than excluding "people who took up arms against us or participated in terrorist activities."[38] By 1964 government legal experts affirmed that it was the combination of submitting a declaration and official acceptance of that declaration that determined the French nationality and citizenship of harkis. It was a result of the government's generosity, not the fact that they previously held French nationality and citizenship. This decision broke with earlier interpretations, which presented the accepted declaration as confirmation of the "maintenance of French national-ity."[39] This bureaucratic gesture—the affirmation that the so-called harkis or FMAs had French nationality and thus citizenship only as a result of official acceptance of their declaration—swept away the entire history of French Algeria and the "failed" assimilation of "Muslims."[40] Government policy emerged as a series of experts and jurists interpreted texts and then interpreted their implications. Without any public debate, or even a single sweeping decision, the French citizenship of Algerian "Muslims" came to seem nonsensi-cal. Distinct from the French and "not prepared for European life," they now appeared virtually unassimilable. Just months before, their assimilation still had seemed reasonable, at least to some.[41]

Government officials, in particular those in the (SAM), had at first conceived the "regrouping" of harkis as a temporary measure, destined as one note in the summer of 1962 described "above all to offer them physical and moral comfort while their repatriate dossier is put together and their reclassification studied." Still working from the assumptions of "integration," (SAM) assessments of the harkis foregrounded the need to make the latter "feel like free men." This reflected a significant body of official opinion that maintained as-similationist or integrationist assumptions. A December 1962 report for the Commissariat for the Plan posited, referring to "Repatriated French Muslims," that for the "young" a "near total assimilation is possible."[42] Such reports presented possibilities for assimilation, first and foremost, as based on material conditions—housing and employment—and not "moral" conditions. Describing the harkis as "much more primitive than [Algerians] who normally settle in France," the (SAM) reports still made clear that their "integration into metropolitan life" could be achieved. The (SAM) and the Eco-nomic and Social Council persisted until early 1963 in asserting that, as the latter's official report stated, "The harkis and their sons, when they reestablish a normal life here, can integrate perfectly into the French national community." [43] On the copy stored at the Bibliothèque Nationale in Paris, two vertical lines and a question mark score this passage. The frequency of such written interrogations next to similar assertions suggests more than one unfriendly reader; they indicate that "integration" no longer made sense to include "Muslim" harkis in the nation.

Historians, harkis themselves, and their sons and daughters have only begun to recount the isolation, poverty, and misery to which their fellow citizens would submit this group of French people. The harkis' status as a group—and what would become their long-term exile in the supposedly temporary camps in abandoned corners of the "French desert" where they were placed—came to seem normal, natural, as they were considered no longer citizens but refugees. By insisting during the exodus that all French citizens with Koranic civil status prove their suitability to have French citizenship, the republic institutionalized what had been an uncodified, if widely held suspicion: "Muslims" were so different from the French that only exceptional individuals (and their families) could be assimilated into the nation.[44]

Notes

1. Throughout this chapter I have chosen to place the term *Muslim* in quotations except when I refer to the legally defined status of Muslim French citizens of Algeria or in the context of a citation. I do this because my French sources use the term "Muslim" without presuming that it corresponds to any particular belief in Islam. In French Algeria "Muslim" was often shorthand for a legal status; it increasingly referred to an ethnic identity, as I argue here.

2. DEFNAT PARIS, "télégramme au Bureau moral" (received 15 March 1962), in Service Historique de l'Armée de Terre (Archives of the French Army, Vincennes, France, hereafter SHAT): 1H/2467/6.

3. Radiodiffusion Française, "Texte de l'émission diffusée au Bulletin de France II (13h) le 4 avril 1962: A qui s'appliquent les Accords d'Evian?" (4 April 1962), 2–3, in Archives Nationales (National Archives, Paris, France, hereafter AN): F/1a/5055.

4. At the end of the Algerian War, I am suggesting, political institutions and the law joined with, reinforced, and sometimes redefined other crucial definitions (scientific, medical, bureaucratic, and cultural, for example) of who was French and how France should be governed, definitions in which race and ethnicity were already explicit. For an overview of how cultural historians analyze these other discourses on racial difference in relationship to French colonialism see Daniel J. Sherman, "The Arts and Sciences of Colonialism," *French Historical Studies* 23 (2000): 700–729.

5. J. J. de Bresson, "Extrait du rélève des décisions du Conseil des Affaires algériennes du 23 mai 1962: Rapatriés Musulmans" (28 May 1962), 1, in Ministère des affaires étrangères/Affaires algériennes (Archives of the French Ministry of Foreign Affairs, Series "Algerian Affairs," Paris, France, hereafter, MAE): 39.

6. Bureau du moral, Commandement Supérieur des forces en Algérie, "Recasement des supplétifs et civils FSNA. menaces" (SP 87.000, 26 May 1962), 2, in SHAT: 1H/1260/2.

7. Secrétariat d'Etat aux Rapatriés, "Comité des Affaires Algériennes du 28 Avril 1962: Accueil des rapatriés," 6, in MAE: 39; Secrétariat d'Etat aux Rapatriés, "OBJET: Personnes rentrant d'Algérie," 5–6, in MAE: 39.

8. Secrétariat d'Etat aux Rapatriés, "Comité des Affaires Algériennes du 28 Avril 1962: Accueil des rapatriés," 6, in MAE: 39; and Secrétariat d'Etat aux Rapatriés, "OBJET: Personnes rentrant d'Algérie," 5–6, in MAE: 39.

9. Maurice Faivre, *Les combattants musulmans de la guerre d'Algérie: Des soldats sacrifiés* (Paris: L'Harmattan, 1995), 197.

10. J. J. de Bresson, "Extrait du rélève des décisions . . ." (28 May 1962), 1, in MAE: 39.

11. Prof. Robert de Vernejoul, *Etude des problèmes posés par le rapatriement des réfugiés d'Algérie; Rapport présenté au nom du Conseil economique et social* (Paris: Conseil économique et social, 1963).

12. Prime Minister Georges Pompidou, "Note pour Monsieur le Ministre des Armées. Objet-Transfert en France d'anciens supplétifs menacés" (Paris, 19 September 1962), in SHAT 1H/1397/8.

13. On estimates of numbers of Algerians killed in the months following the cease fire because they were accused of being pro-French, see Guy Pervillé, *Pour une histoire de la guerre d'Algérie* (Paris: Picard, 2002), 243–44. Estimates range from over 10,000 to close to 150,000.

14. G. Lamassoure, chef du Service des Affaires musulmanes, "à M. le Préfet de l'Isère. Objet: Anciens supplétifs et réfugiés musulmans" (26 February 1963), 1, in AN: F/1a/5125.

15. Louis Joxe, "à Haut Commisaire de la Republique en Algérie" (12 May 1962), in SHAT: 1H/1260/2.

16. Lt. Col. Barthelemy, "Bulletin hebdomadaire de renseignement psychologique (semaine 27/12/61–2/1/62)" (Algiers, 4 January 1962), 6, in SHAT: 1H/2549/ 2.

17. On this phenomenon, see, e.g., Alice Conklin, A "Mission to Civilize": The Republican Idea of Empire in France and West Africa, 1895–1930 (Stanford CA: Stanford University Press, 1997).

18. Service des Affaires Musulmanes, "Bilan des réalisations . . ." (28 November 1963), 1, in IAN: F/1a/5055.

19. (Ouadali, 14 May 1962), in SHAT: 1H/1260/3.

20. See documents in SHAT 1H/1260/D3 folder: "Récasement en France des FSNA menacées."

21. Battalion Chief Troyes, "Objet: récasement en France de militaires, de supplétifs, de civils FSNA et de leurs familles» (SP 86.292, 11 May 1962), in SHAT 1H/1260/3.

22. Battalion Chief Roger, "Rapport sur les services rendus par Mlle Hamzaoui Ratiba, assistante sociale" (SP 86.900, 10 May 1962), in SHAT: 1H/1260/3.

23. Signed: Charles de Gaulle, "Séance du jeudi 21 juin 1962. Rélève des décisions" (21 June 1962), 6, in IMAE: 40.

24. Service des Affaires politiques, "Note pour le Ministre a/s Comité des Affaires algériennes du 21 juin" (21 June 1962), 2–3, in MAE: 40. This note summarizes: Christian Fouchet, Haut Commissaire de la République en Algérie, "Traduction du message chiffré n. 7859/51. Objet: Prochain Comité des Affaires algériennes-Questions de nationalité" (19 June 1962), 1–2, in MAE: 117. My italics.

25. For details of how the executive had obtained the right to exercise legislative powers in this period see Shepard, The Invention of Decolonization, chap. 4. For an explanation of how the French had developed the concept of "local civil status," and Koranic Law Civil status in particular, in governing Algeria see chap. 1.

26. LE PRÉSIDENT DE LA RÉPUBLIQUE sur le rapport . . . ORDONNE" (Paris, 8 June 1962), 1–2, in MAE: 117.

27. The government excluded one group of Algerians with Local Civil Status from the restrictions and the rigamarole to which it subjected all the others: civil servants. Like all functionaries from Algeria, the state dealt with "Muslim" civil servants not as repatriates (or refugees) but under a system specific to state employees. Despite this exception, functionary status was not perceived as transforming or fundamentally changing the racially charged identity of the "Muslim Algerian." The government emphasized this by excluding retired functionaries from the exceptional system. See AN F/1cII/517, in particular, Henri Le Corno, "réponse à la lettre du Préfet de Seine-et-Marne" (2 April 1963), 1, in AN F/1cII/517.

28. A. Bacquet, "A/S Acquisition de la nationalité française par un citoyen Algérien de statut civil local» (Rocher Noir, 29 September 1962), in SHAT: 1H/1260/D3.

29. Michel Lamassoure, Chef du Service des Affaires Musulmanes et de l'Action sociale, "OBJET: Réunion des Conseillers techniques pour les Affaires Musulmanes" (20 November 1962), 4, in Archives nationales/Centre d'archives contemporaines (Center for Contemporary Archives of the National Archives, Fontainebleau, France, hereafter CAC/AN): 770346/10.

30. Services des affaires musulmanes (SAM), "Synthèse des rapports trimestriels . . .— 1er trimestre (1/1–31/3/62)," 34–35, in AN F/1a/5014. According to SAM statistics, the months after the announcement of the Evian Accords did witness a new tendency for more "French Muslims" to leave the metropole for Algeria than vice versa. By September this had ended: once again more "Algerians" or Algerian "Muslims" were coming to the metropole than were leaving.

31. Dominique Lapierre and Maurice Jarnoux, "Avec les passagers d'un nouvel exode," *Paris-Match* 2 June 1962, 109.

32. Editeurs, "Points de repère. 'Retour des harkis' and 'Exode vers Marseille,'" *France-Observateur* 24 May 1962, 3.

33. Direction centrale des R. G., "Sommaire Générale" (Paris, 27 June1962), 1, in CAC/AN: 800280, art. 218.

34. Direction de la Réglementation, Ministère de l'Intérieur, "Note pour M. le Ministre. OBJET: Identification des français de souche européenne rapatriés d'Algérie" (4 May 1962), 2, in CAC/AN: 920172/09.

35. M. Peronu, "lettre à M. le Ministre de l'Intérieur" (18 October 1962), 2, in AN F/1a/5013; C. Ernst, "lettre à M. le Ministre délégué . . . chargé des Rapatriés . . ." (29 November 1962), in AN F/1a/5013. For the effects of Ord. 62–825 in the civil service, see: Marceau Long, "FP/1 n. 003768 Objet: Application de l'ordonnance n. 62–611 du 30 mai 1962" (Paris, 23 August 1962), in CAC/AN: 19770007, art. 210 and art. 212.

36. Secrétaire d'Etat auprès du Premier Ministre, Chargé des affaires Algériennes, "Inscription et radiation" (12 January 1963), 1, in AN F/icII/517.

37. Secrétaire d'Etat auprès du Premier Ministre, Chargé des affaires Algériennes, "Inscription et radiation" (12 January 1963), 1, in AN F/icII/517. On later interpretations that insisted that the déclaration of nationality itself made the "Muslim" Algerians French see, for example, CAC/AN: 950236/09.

38. de Vernejoul, *Etude des Problèmes,* 119.

39. See the 28 September 1962 letter from Marceau Long, Secretary of State attached to the Prime Minister in charge of the Civil Service, "FP/1 n. 4330, à M. Messaoud Djeghloul, attaché de Préfecture, Poitiers (Vienne)," in CAC/AN: 19770007, art. 210.

40. Henri Le Corno, "Application de l'ordonnance n. 62–825 du 21 juillet 1962 . . ." (4 February 1963), 2; and, in response, Bernard Lory, Ministère de la Santé Publique, "réponse à . . ." (18 February 1962), 1, both letters in AN: F/1cII/517.

41. Commission de coordination pour la réinstallation des Français d'Outre-Mer. Commissariat général du Plan, "Rapport Général du 5 décembre 1962" (5 December 1962), 14, in CAC/AN: 80 AJ/254 [[930275/94].

42. Commission de coordination pour la réinstallation des Français d'Outre-Mer. Commissariat général du Plan, "Projet d'avis sur le rapport général du 5 décembre 1962" (14 December 1962), 7, in CAC/AN: 80 AJ/254.

43. SAM, "Synthèse des rapports trimestriels établis par les conseillers techniques pour les affaires musulmanes—4e trimestre/1/10–31/12/62," 41, in AN: F/1a/5014.

44. SAM, "Synthèse des rapports trimestriels établis . . .—3è trimestre/1/7–30/9/62," 25 in AN: F/1a/5014. On the metropolitan welcome of the harkis, see Abderahmen Moumen, *Les Français musulmans en Vaucluse: Installation et difficultés d'intégration d'une communauté de rapatriés d'Algérie 1962–1991* (Paris: L'Harmattan, 2003); Mohand Hammoumou, *Et ils sont devenus harkis* (Paris: Fayard, 1993); and Mohand Hammoumou, with the collaboration of Abderahmen Moumen, "L'histoire des harkis et Français musulmans: la fin d'un tabou?" in *La guerre d'Algérie, 1954–2004, la fin de l'amnésie,* ed. Mohammed Harbi and Benjamin Stora (Paris: R. Laffout, 2004), 317–44.

6

The Transformation of French Identity in Mathieu Kassovitz's Films *Métisse* (1993) and *La Haine* (1995)

ALAIN GABON

This essay examines the postcolonial identity politics of two groundbreaking films by French writer-director Mathieu Kassovitz: *Métisse* (*Café au Lait*, 1993) and *La Haine* (*Hate*, 1995). It offers a comparative reading of those two most significant works by relating their intricate representation of multiculturalism and interethnic youth relationships in contemporary France to the emergence of a globalized, hybrid, and transnational youth culture and to the radical transformation of France under the impact of immigration and globalization, which Kassovitz's cinema often celebrates in a free-spirited manner. This chapter emphasizes how as a result of those breathtaking developments French identity in Kassovitz's films has been appropriated, opened up, and dramatically transformed by minority groups. While *La Haine* is a bleak urban drama that offers a dark and ultimately apocalyptic vision of contemporary France, *Métisse* is a warm, half-realistic, half-utopian romantic comedy that can be read most appropriately as the flipside of the 1995 film. Therefore, Kassovitz's films offer two diametrically opposed ways of representing the mutation of French identity. Ultimately his cinema itself constitutes an important matrix for the new France that is slowly and often painfully emerging from those recent global mutations.

Innovative, cinematographically exhilarating, socially significant, enormously controversial, as well as hugely successful critically and commercially, *La Haine* was Mathieu Kassovitz's second feature film, his first being *Métisse*. Although both films are in dialogue with each other to offer a richly textured and ambivalent vision of the multicultural, transnational, and multi-ethnic future of France, it is with *La Haine* that Kassovitz exploded as a new auteur not only on the French cinematographic stage but also on the social and political scene. In retrospect after the latest *révoltes des cités* and *émeutes des banlieues* of November 2005—the violent youth riots that, as had already happened several times in the 1990s, erupted once again and spread like wildfire in nearly three hundred housing projects throughout France—*La Haine* appears to have been a visionary film. In 2005 the entire French nation felt on the brink of a major disaster. It seemed that far from limiting itself to a few circumscribed housing projects as had been the case in the riots of the previous years, the violence was quickly spreading all over the territory. This time the riots were clearly understood and often explained by the media as the mere symptom of a number of grave failures and dramatic "French syndromes" that could sooner or later put the entire nation in danger, if society did not rapidly find remedies. In other words, the riots were felt to be the sign of "a society that is falling," as Hubert, one of the three main characters of *La Haine*, says at the end of the film right before he himself dies a violent death, a death that seems to allegorize the (self-)destruction of an entire society that had been going down for a couple of decades. (That sentiment of doom is very widely shared in France today as is attested by the proliferation of public discourses, debates, books, TV shows about the "French identity crisis," "the decline of France," the "French malaise," "the France that is losing.")[1]

Like the riots that had already occurred throughout the nineties, the sudden explosion of violence of November 2005 was due to a large extent to France's failure to assimilate (or even just integrate) a significant part of its immigrant and nonimmigrant youth; to the deep economic alienation, exclusion, and disenfranchisement of those youths; and to hidden but quasi-systematic forms of racist discrimination toward the French youths of (mostly) African descent, who constitute the majority of the inhabitants of those governmental housing projects.

Ten years after the release of *La Haine*, the November 2005 *révoltes des banlieues* resonate powerfully with what Kassovitz wanted to show. For the French, *La Haine* was indeed a brutal wake-up call. It helped them awaken to the chilling realities of their own *banlieues*—the suburbs, sometimes also called *cités,* a culturally charged term that inevitably evokes the same grim realities as the American "inner-city ghettos": drugs, poverty, and deprivation; urban decay and socioeconomic exclusion; delinquency, crime, and violence; lack of opportunities and hope for its youth; despair and fatalism; and a widely shared sense that there is "no future in the project."

La Haine is the stylish yet raw chronicle of one day in the life of three alienated and marginalized male youths from a depressing but typical working-class housing project on the periphery of Paris. Beginning with television coverage of the violent riots that took place in the project the previous night during which a young *beur*, Abdel, was fatally wounded, the film then follows the mortal yet often comic trajectory of its central trio of friends—Vinz, a white Jew, Hub, a black-African immigrant, and Saïd, a northern African Arab teenager—through the most harrowing day of their lives.[2]

The trio's twenty-four hours of doom and hardship will eventually lead to the violent deaths of two of them in a shocking and chilling climax. The film takes a brutally uncompromising look at the violence, exclusion, and desperation that at the time seemed to plague the lives of so many French youth. (The November 2005 riots themselves were a far more brutal reminder that nothing had changed and that in the last decade things had actually gotten worse for those living in the projects.)

Written and directed by a then mostly unknown twenty-eight-year-old director and featuring no star (Kassovitz used personal friends, newcomers, and close relatives as cast for his film), *La Haine* can be seen as the political and filmic manifesto of a then-emerging French hip-hop and rap counterculture. Ginette Vincendeau notes that "Kassovitz's trigger for *La Haine* was the real-life racist murder of Makomé, a young Zairian, in a Parisian police station."[3] For Vincendeau it also echoes, particularly in its opening scene, the 1990–91 events in the Lyon and Paris suburbs with their violent street riots and open confrontations between youth and police while foreshadowing other similar occurrences in the summers of 1995 and 1997, during which scores of local businesses and stores were looted and destroyed, cars and busses burned, public facilities (schools, gyms, cultural centers) demolished, and in some cases police stations attacked, leaving many wounded on both sides as would also be the case ten years later. Day after day, week after week, summer after summer, all that mayhem was brought through an avalanche of news headlines and broadcasts to the attention of a stunned and shocked French population, which often felt their country was about to be broken up in an orgy of chaos and violence. Yet, if the roots of those actual riots were to be found in the socioeconomic exclusion, racial discrimination, and sense of despair, Kassovitz's initial gesture was to alter and inflect the events' meaning by mixing

film footage of them with shots from the massive 199.
demonstrations, which were directed mostly against th
tive government of Prime Minister Edouard Balladur. Moreover,
because the opening scene recalled so powerfully the riots of the
1960s and their internationalist struggles (the Molotov cocktails
and cobblestones thrown at cops, the violent clashes with the CRS
(Compagnies Républicaines de Sécurité) urban swat teams, which
became (in)famous throughout France in May 68, the use of Third
World music), Kassovitz located his film from the start within a new
musical and filmic youth culture: a restless counterculture that was
clearly rebellious if not prerevolutionary.[4]

La Haine struck audiences and critics as a remarkably fresh and
significant film on at least three accounts. First, it blended its gritty
and realist documentary feel with highly stylized and aesthetically
beautiful black-and-white photography. Although it was a fictional
work, the film was received by its audiences as a quasidocumentary
on alienated youths, urban decay, and police brutality in France.
Kassovitz himself intentionally constructed that particular "reading
mode." By opening with several minutes of archive news footage
showing actual student demonstrations and urban riots from the
preceding years, the long credit sequence effectively conditioned the
audience to receive the film as a "social issue" type of film, as a film
about "French society today." As reported in the French newspaper
Le Monde, it even led newly elected conservative-populist President
Jacques Chirac to urge every police station in France to organize
screenings of *La Haine* in an effort, one assumes, to help improve
the extremely tense relations between the police and the youth of les
banlieues. Yet, the film has as much to do with cinema in general (and
post–World War II international film history in particular) as with
the social realities of late-twentieth-century France. For example, its
stylish black-and-white images, its on-location shooting, its urban

settings, its often poetic representation of urban drifting are clearly a cinema lover's reference to the great 1950s classics of the French New Wave such as François Truffaut's *Les 400 Coups (400 Blows)* and Jean-Luc Godard's *A Bout de Souffle (Breathless)*, as well as a direct homage to Martin Scorsese's film *Raging Bull*. (Scorsese's cinema from *Mean Streets* to *Taxi Driver* and *Raging Bull* is very much the ghost that haunts Kassovitz's entire film.) The space of *La Haine* is as much the space of transnational art-house film history and aesthetics as it is a representation of contemporary France. Critics such as Claude-Marie Trémois and Carrie Tarr point out that the importance of *La Haine* and many other affiliated films of that period (from Mehdi Charef's 1985 *Le Thé au Harem d'Archimède* to Jean-François Richet's 1997 *Ma 6T Va Crack-er*) also lies with the creation of a new French cinematographic genre, a new type of popular film widely referred to as *cinéma beur* or sometimes *cinéma de banlieue*—although the two are not synonymous, and there have been heated debates about the definition, the corpus, the status, and even the existence of those two genres.[5] In any case, *La Haine* may also be described as a vibrant generic mix between various film cultures: a French cinematographic tradition of critical neorealism; an almost excessively (to some) aestheticizing cinematography that is often reminiscent of *"cinéma du look"* French directors such as Jean-Jacques Beineix (lavish and flamboyant cinematography, striking *mise en scène* effects and pictorial compositions, sudden changes in camera angles, asymmetrical compositions within the frames) and of a more recent and highly stylized *néo-noir* trend within American cinema, from Scorsese to Quentin Tarantino, and others.

The second aspect of *La Haine* that captured the imagination of audiences and critics was the representation of France's banlieues, a space that was becoming more and more critical in the understanding that the nation had of itself. For most critics who have written about that new cinematographic subgenre, the French banlieue is most often represented as a bleak and depressing desert that is neither urban nor rural. It is not a city, it is not part of a city, but it is not the countryside either. Just like the characters themselves, who throughout the film are systematically excluded from the places they try to enter (hospital, art gallery), the French banlieue does not belong. (Kassovitz's acute analysis of how that particular non-space lacks integration within and even connection to the rest of the country echoed and to a certain extent anticipated the current debates about the failure of public policies regarding the housing of immigrants, urban architecture and design—problems which are also partly responsible for the recent violence.) In many films, the banlieue is represented as a no man's land that most of the time deprives its inhabitants of a sense of identity, of a sense of genuine public and private space; it is most often (though not always) a hostile, rejecting, alienating, and potentially violent space.

Yet, even a film like *La Haine*, whose predictions for the future of the nation seem bleak and even apocalyptic, can and maybe should also be read against its dominant grain of banlieue blues and pessimism: despite its bleak narrative trajectory, its "descent into hell" structure, its quasi-apocalyptic sense of doom and lack of final redemption for its characters, it also, to some extent, depicts the banlieue as a potentially utopian space. Countercultural creations of an authentic kind can exist (for example, the scene of the break dancing contest); the often rigidly canonical and elitist culture of France opens up to the creations of minority groups; the housing project itself, though depressing, is also a space of ethnic integration, friendship, and genuine solidarity between minority groups; and no racist feelings or prejudice seems to exist within the cité. Thus, for Kassovitz the banlieue often seems to offer resources that could possibly help France redeem some of its most severe problems such as its often rigidly highbrow culture and widespread racial prejudices and racism.

Through various devices (soundtrack, street fashion, cross-cultural filmic, musical, and political references), Kassovitz firmly locates this ambivalent, half-utopian, half-dystopian space in the realm of hip-hop and rap cultures often pervaded by strong anticop feelings and an aggressive, pull-no-punch youth discourse on urban decay, socioeconomic exclusion, injustice, and violence. Indeed, critics were quick to compare Kassovitz's film to Spike Lee's *Do the Right Thing* and other "American ghetto" or "hood films," such as those of John Singleton, Mario Van Peebles, and the Hughes Brothers (*Boyz N the Hood, Menace II Society, New Jack City*). Most striking at the time was the fact that the deprivation of the French banlieue with its excluded Arab and African immigrant populations suddenly resembled the American black ghetto and its riots, just as the images of young Arabs throwing stones in the opening sequence irresistibly evoked the Middle Eastern Intifada here "relocated" in France. Indeed, one of the most interesting aspects of Kassovitz's cinema was that various centrifugal forces at work in his films (the influence of U.S. commercial and independent cinema, an obviously global, transnational, and highly politicized consciousness) operated to transform, displace, and expand traditional notions and representations of "French identity." *La Haine* seemed to proclaim that the often alienated immigrant youth of contemporary France shared a similar destiny and natural solidarity with the socially and economically excluded segments of American youth (for example, the disproportionate number of young African American males currently behind bars) and more generally with all the oppressed people of the world. As previously stated, the opening images of street riots, stone throwers, and CRS recalled so vividly those of May 1968 and its liberation struggles (still a major cultural reference in today's France) that one could not help receiving *La Haine* as a new type of internationalist film manifesto. In the France of the mid-1990s, the film easily found its place in a new media iconography of politicized riots. It might have played a role in the powerful resurgence of a protorevolutionary kind of cultural imagination, which always simmers below the surface of an apparently normalized French society. At the time Kassovitz's film fit very nicely in a new "discursive revolutionary formation" composed of the images of French students' demonstrations, those (that were soon to follow) of the "battle of Seattle" and antiglobalization riots and demonstrations, those of the continuing Intifada, and more. In a French context but also in a more global cinematographic and cultural context, *La Haine* thus signaled the spectacular rebirth of *cinéma engagé*: a socially committed form of filmmaking whose "avowed intention is to lend . . . voice to those who cannot express themselves" or to those who have none.[6] As noticed by Myrto Konstantarakos, films like *La Haine* and directors like Kassovitz gave the French a new and genuine cinema of social intervention, which Serge Toubiana celebrated in the pages of *Cahiers du Cinéma* as an exciting *retour du politique*: a return to political concerns such as police violence, marginality, racism, exclusion, and youth alienation.[7]

Third, the relevance of *La Haine* and the debates it generated in France were indeed a key cultural and political event of the last decade. Since the film was somewhat naively taken by audiences, media, and the government as an accurate portrayal of societal problems in France—almost a documentary—it alerted the French to a number of imminent threats posed to their society. It also helped many awaken to some major cultural mutations they might have underestimated or ignored up to that point. *La Haine* was instrumental in helping the French bring some painful and crucial but repressed issues to the forefront of their public consciousness and push those issues to the top of their national political agenda and public discourse. Again in retrospect it seems that those issues had not until then fully impacted their collective consciousness. What was it about this film that impressed and sometimes shocked the French so much? What was it about *La Haine* that both excited us and made us somewhat nervous?

Most notable was the sense that in this film, France as a society and a historical project with roots in the universalist ideals of the French Revolution and Republic was abjectly failing: the France shown in *La Haine* is in such an advanced state of decomposition that it was barely recognizable to many in the audience. The film represents a society that is crumbling and imploding around its characters as it seemed to fall apart around the French, who were already at the time in the grip of a devastating economic crisis. Coupled to that, *l'identité française*, sometimes referred to as *l'exception française*, seemed in crisis as well. The French seemed to be losing their belief that their nation was established, solid, stable, and resilient enough to resist a number of developments that were often felt to be threatening. That severe identity crisis was due for the most part to a number of dramatic developments that had been happening over the previous few decades: the massive immigration from Northern and sub-Saharan Africa and the difficulty in assimilating or integrating the new immigrants; the rise of Islam on French soil and the challenges it posed to the well-entrenched secularism of the Republic and the definition of France's identity; the anxiety of being swallowed up in larger geopolitical constructs such as the European Union and the global economy; the fear of *l'américanisation*—an old demon that seemed to undergo a powerful and alarming return in the late 1980s and throughout the 1990s; the sense that France was a country in decline, that it was becoming a third-rate nation, that its values and traditions were being attacked or undermined by its cultural "Others"; and more. In addition, when the film was released, the French had already been exposed to a steady flow of ghastly TV images of actual riots, destruction, and mayhem. All those developments, which had started to shatter the confidence they had in their own country—its institutions, its identity, its resilience, its capacity to integrate and assimilate those who came from different cultures—were amplified by Kassovitz's film, which seemed to crystallize and give shape to the many doubts and fears the French had developed about themselves. With its emphasis on socioeconomic exclusion and injustice, banlieue segregation, the radical marginalization and alienation of so many French and foreign youth, and the ensuing criminality and violence, *La Haine* seemed to partake of the then dominant discourse on what was referred to as *la fracture sociale*: the alarming and everincreasing socioeconomic disparities between the haves and the have-nots. That discourse was most prominent in the 1995 presidential campaign of conservative candidate Jacques Chirac, who was then running for a second term. The *fracture sociale* themes of his campaign later migrated in the similar discourse on *la France d'en haut* versus *la France d'en bas* (the France of the rich versus that of the poor), with the everpresent fear the country was turning into a two-tier society like the United States, which the French often perceive as the evil alter ego of their own country. Kassovitz's film fit neatly within that larger and powerful "discursive formation," which tended to dominate public debates and the mediasphere throughout the 1990s. Alongside an unending string of television newscasts on *la violence des banlieues*, prominent and highly influential texts such as Pierre Bourdieu's 1993 *La Misère du Monde* (which detailed the institutional mechanisms of socioeconomic exclusion), his *Raison d'Agir* pamphlets against capitalism and neoliberalism, bestsellers such as Viviane Forrester's 1996 essay *L'Horreur Economique* (a nightmarish vision of the future of our societies within global capitalism), or the editorials of the influential leftist French monthly *Le Monde Diplomatique*, Kassovitz's film contributed powerfully to the catastrophist and even apocalyptic tone that dominated so much of the cultural atmosphere of France throughout the 1990s and that the film crystallized in powerful cinematic form.[8] The image of France that emerged through those articles, pamphlets, books, TV images, political discourses, and more echoed powerfully the representation of *la fracture sociale* in Kassovitz's film. In *La Haine*, all those themes coalesced in art, form, and fiction to produce maximum impact.

In *La Haine* the corruption and decomposition of France's most important and cherished institutions appear to be beyond redemption. Indeed for Vinz, Hub, and a young Saïd, who at the end can only close his eyes in horror, there will be no redemption. In its pessimistic and even apocalyptic predictions, *La Haine* turned the French Republican utopia and its generous ideals of *Liberté, Egalité, Fraternité* into a nightmarish inverted utopia: a "dystopic" future world order dominated by violence, institutionalized brutality, racism (the scene at the police station), and socioeconomic exclusion. In the film and also in the cultural imagination of so many French people, this new world order is more often than not represented by the United States of America and its ultraviolent mass culture, which for the French often seems to prefigure what might happen to their nation if they stop being vigilant or abandon their *exception culturelle*. This sense of imminent apocalypse through the contagion and "invasion" of American mass culture is present in several scenes such as the rooftop scene at the beginning, when a group of teenagers feverishly discuss Mel Gibson's guns in *Lethal Weapon* with an obvious sense of excitement and exhilaration. Vinz, Hubert, and Saïd already inhabit this nihilistic, self-destructive, and ultraviolent new world order. In another scene a dejected Hub plays with the needles that litter the ground, while a graffiti on the wall behind him reads "We are the future." That new world order they inhabit will thus soon be ours. Equally prominent in *La Haine* is the disturbing and painful awareness that although France as a nation had always proudly struggled to create and maintain social cohesion, equality, and solidarity between all its citizens, large segments of its population were rapidly falling through the cracks of the system and were abandoned in utmost indifference and cruelty by their motherland. In that sense the film was the perfect complement to and the filmic mediation and continuation of the shock felt by the nation during the real urban and suburban riots of the early 1990s. Vinz, Hub, Saïd, and virtually all the other young people in this film have no job, no money, no sense of identity and national community (they throw stones at the mayor's delegation that comes to make peace with them after the riot), no prospect in life, nothing to do other than walk endlessly with no purpose or intent. As Myrto Konstantarakos observes, they are "in perpetual motion,"[9] running from the police squads, running after a train, yet they are on a road to nowhere. They are not only ejected from localities (the comic scene at the art exhibition) but prevented from entering and driven away from their familiar places such as the rooftop where they try to have a barbecue party. They cannot even enter the hospital room where their friend Abdel is dying. Excluded from all places, they are as Konstantarakos writes, *"enfermés dehors"* (locked outside).[10] In *La Haine,* the prison is outside, the prison *is* the outside. It is the totality of their social and geographic space that has become jaillike. There is therefore no way out. To that extent the police brutality is symptomatic and symbolic of a much deeper, more generalized, and more extensive type of socioeconomic violence visited upon them by their society. As is the case in the cinema of Martin Scorsese, the frequently hysterical violence of Kassovitz's films is always deployed in a *critical* and ethical manner to allegorize and amplify a much larger and more pervasive societal violence.

La Haine also targeted the canonical and humanist culture historically promoted and disseminated by the most prominent French institutions (most notably the public-school system) in an attempt to forge a coherent "cultural nation." In one scene Hub sells drugs in front of a giant mural representing da Vinci's *Creation of the World*. Kassovitz creates an ironic and critical visual tension between the two images, between foreground and background: the hands of Hub and his partner exchanging drugs and money are shot against the backdrop of the fingers of God and Adam touching each other in the act of the Creation. That powerful visual counterpoint seems to debunk the humanist hope shared by most French that exposure to the arts and the culture of Western humanism could regenerate at once subjectivity, community, and nation, that they could have redeeming powers. The film's chilling ending takes place under the giant murals of the La Noë housing project on which the faces of the greatest French poets—most notably Baudelaire, Victor Hugo, and Arthur Rimbaud—have been painted by well-meaning urban planners, designers, and architects in the hope, one assumes, that exposure to the celebrated literary and cultural heroes of France would inculcate in the alienated multi-ethnic youth of those suburbs a sense of purpose, a sense of national integration and pride. Ginette Vincendeau observes that as Vinz and Hub fall under Baudelaire and Rimbaud's lifeless gaze, *La Haine* "stresses the failure of the [governmental] cultural policies that were supposed to help the *cités*" through state intervention in the form of an avalanche of after-school programs and grants.[11] In a previous scene, a sympathetic cop of Arab origin offers Hub and Saïd a city grant for repairing their gym, which had been burnt to the ground in the riots of the previous nights. That gesture of solidarity irresistibly evokes the generous cultural activism and emphasis on youth culture promoted throughout the 1980s by Socialist president François Mitterrand's Ministre de la Culture Jack Lang. Firm believers like André Malraux in the guiding and heroic role of the central Republican state, Mitterrand and his wonder boy Jack Lang promoted a new French cultural Renaissance by making full use of state patronage through an astonishing policy of lavish public subsidies on a scale literally unseen since Colbert's days. For a while and with his truly mystical and messianic belief in the power of culture to redeem and transform everything, to "guide people into the light," Lang indeed managed to turn France into a state-backed cultural venture of epic proportions. His admirable effort and faith in the redeeming powers of culture often culminated in giant nationwide cultural festivals, such as the Fête de la Musique and Fête du Cinéma, which to this day take place during the summer and in which it seems the entire nation joyfully participates. Many of Lang's programs and systems of public grants were meant precisely to help the youths of the banlieues in an effort to channel their often unused energies into something creative that would also help in their social and national integration, in their sense of belonging. In the film, however, the cop's generous offer is left unanswered. The trio pays no attention at all—they have already passed their point of no return. Most painfully for the French, the shocking climax and violent deaths of Vinz and Hub—at the hands of a colleague of the city-grant police officer, himself present on the scene—seem to stress the tragic failure of all the utopian hopes that the French have always invested in their celebrated and cherished national canonical culture, particularly their revered literary heroes—Victor Hugo being without a doubt the most monumental and canonized of all. In its narrative trajectory, shocking climax, and representations of banlieue as the "nonspace" and blind spot of the French Republic, *La Haine* was thus one among many texts (filmic or other) that expressed, exacerbated, and amplified a very deep sense of national doom—the sense that the French society and the whole nation were now on the brink of an imminent disaster.

The extent to which in *La Haine* French identity appears to have been appropriated by ethnic minorities is also remarkable, and this aspect was not lost on the audience either: in the film, "France" is not only riddled with injustices, violence, racism, and exclusions of all sorts, but the French Republican "melting pot" has been completely replaced by an extreme "global" mix of ethnicities and fragments of foreign cultures. What was striking and still relatively new at the time is that the film featured no "traditional" French characters or actors at all—nothing even remotely close: the Jean Gabin, Jean-Paul Belmondo, Alain Delon, Gérard Depardieu, Daniel Auteuil, Gérard Jugnot, Arletty, Brigitte Bardot, Jeanne Moreau, Catherine Deneuve, Isabelle Adjani (who has since asserted her North African origins), Juliette Binoche, and Emmanuelle Béart, who had until then incarnated and embodied "France" to both the nation itself and the rest of the world were replaced in *La Haine* by a Jew, a North African Arab, and a black African. *Métisse* featured a French créole from Martinique, a black African Muslim, and a working-class French Jew. All the actors were unknown to the public when the films were released. It was as if the space of "traditional France" that so many had become used to, with its traditional Republican melting pot and white Catholic working-class or middle-class majority, had suddenly disappeared altogether. It was as if "France as we know it" (mostly white, whether in film or in reality) had mysteriously dissolved into air to be replaced by a motley crew of ethnic and religious minorities and by a hybrid, multicultural, transnational, and multi-ethnic youth culture of *métissage* with very strong countercultural elements. In *La Haine* France had indeed become barely recognizable.

Historically, as David Blatt explains in his essay on the immigrant politics of the French Republic, France's dominant approach to immigration was assimilation more than integration, namely, to assume that ethnic minority "others" must adapt and conform to as well as assimilate into the dominant culture (white, Catholic, Republican, working class, middle class).[12] The idea was that immigrants had to accept being "reconstructed" and remolded by France's dominant sociocultural institutions. The French language, the public school system, the army, secular Republican values, the study of the official history of the nation as the main symbolic framework for developing that new *identité française* expected of them, the high literary and artistic culture of the French canon, the prestigious historical heroes from Vercingétorix to Charles de Gaulle were all diligently presented as the true incarnation of the essence of the nation. The immigrant "other" was thus expected to embrace and identify with all of those in order to be fully assimilated, since assimilation was supposed to be his ultimate destiny. However, Kassovitz's films showed that *the exact opposite was happening,* that the relationship between center and periphery had been inverted, with the unexpected result that France was now the object of a massive and very creative act of counterappropriation of its national identity by minority groups: French ethnic minorities from the overseas territories of Martinique, Guadeloupe, and La Réunion; sub-Saharan Muslim African immigrants; Arab Muslim or non-Muslim immigrants from Northern Africa; religious minorities such as the French Jews; as well as teenage youths with their own minority cultures, values, street languages, idiolects, and models (often of foreign origins). Kassovitz's first two feature films wanted to help the French realize the extent to which their population, society, culture, and nation were changing under the impact of multicultural and multi-ethnic immigration—a trend that was intensified and radicalized by the emergence of new transnational global youth countercultures, which the films also represented with great accuracy and empathy. Nowhere were those processes of cultural transformation better felt than in two scenes: the one in which Vinz, a French Jew, after imitating Italian American actor Robert de Niro in front of his mirror (the famous "You're talkin' to me?" routine), cuts the hair of his Arab friend Saïd "the American way" in order to make him look like a New York City "homeboy"; and the beautiful scene of the helicopter shot, where the camera itself carries the rap music in a slow-motion spin over the deprived cité, with the "sampled" fragments of an Edith Piaf song (*"non, rien de rien, non, je ne regrette rien"*, that most deliciously old-fashioned and traditional of all French songs) integrated and "morphed" into an Afro-Caribbean and French American global and multi-ethnic musical mix. The use of Edith Piaf is ironic and even "deconstructive" if one remembers that she was also an icon of (and for) the ultraright paratroopers and French Légion Etrangère, whose privileged field of operation was Africa. In a superb and subtle act of cultural reappropriation and with mordant wit, Kassovitz hijacks, perverts, and turns "Piaf" on its head by relocating her song in the cultural and geographical territory—the rap song and the banlieue—of the sons and daughters of those same African populations who so often suffered at the hands of the Légion. The morphing of Piaf in the Arab and African ghettoes of the French capital, with their musical hip-hop/gangster rap countercultures, shows better than any other aspect of those films that Kassovitz's cinema was genuinely involved in postcolonial problematics and politics. Indeed, the France of *La Haine* and *Métisse* seemed to have come a long way.

Both films were carefully constructed to help the French become fully aware of the extent to which their country was being transformed beyond recognition by a process of creative, productive, and highly transformative métissage at work in all areas of life from "ethnic fashion" to world music, from the new *planète internet* to the globalized economy, from language to interracial dating and marriages, which had visibly started to change the makeup of the population itself.[13] It became more obvious to the French that the future of their society, culture, and nation was more than ever multiracial, multicultural, and transnational and that this state of affairs would make it increasingly difficult to maintain a coherent and specific "Franco-French" culture such as the one embodied by Piaf (in its populist version) or Hugo and Baudelaire (in its more elitist version). If *La Haine* suggests that the process will be at best difficult, uncertain, and even agonizing, the profoundly utopian *Métisse* on the contrary suggests that there could be a successful, happy, joyful, and positive new radical métissage of France.

Moreover, while both films portrayed some grim social realities, they fully and joyfully embraced, celebrated, and advocated the radical transformation of France and French culture represented by the populist *franco-française* songs of Edith Piaf, the more highbrow culture of Hugo and Baudelaire present in the final scene of *La Haine,* or the canonical Western humanism symbolized by the da Vinci mural. Kassovitz's films showed that this profound mutation was occurring not only through multiculturalism, ethnic diversity, and interracial relationship but also through the advent of global transnational youth cultures. The films did not simply put on display the reality of those processes at work in every single social space of France today, "at the pool, on the basketball courts, in the gyms, in discos, in bars, in courses at the university",[14] but more than that they *themselves* sought to radicalize those processes through their elaborate constructs and dizzying webs of transnational musical, filmic, and political references, which included but went far beyond "traditional" French culture. By so doing, the films effectively deconstructed and also expanded and opened up dominant, traditional, and stereotypical notions, definitions, and representations of French identity. To give just a few examples, *La Haine* features (as already observed) much of the mannerist, aestheticizing, "neo-baroque" cinematography associated with the *cinéma du look* of directors such as Luc Besson and Jean-Jacques Beineix, but it also features stylish and orgiastic explosions of violence reminiscent of Hong Kong filmmaker John Woo (the final "Mexican stand-off" between Hub and the cop) as well as a néo-noir disturbing kind of violence associated more specifically with Quentin Tarantino, Brian de Palma, and Martin Scorsese (most notably, Scorsese's critical use of graphic violence as a way to emphasize and amplify social violence). Saïd's failed attempt to "switch off" the Eiffel Tower by snapping his fingers is a direct reference to several other French films that feature a similar scene, especially the very "Franco-French" 1989 film by Eric Rochant, *Un Monde sans Pitié (A World without Pity)*. Dina Sherzer and Carrie Tarr also observe that much in both *La Haine* and *Métisse* is a direct homage to Spike Lee's cinema: the Jewish pizza-delivery boy on bicycle played by Kassovitz himself in *Métisse* is an ethnic rewriting of the black character played by Lee in *Do the Right Thing*, while his broken glasses also irresistibly evoke Woody Allen—another famous American Jew and cult figure of French cinema lovers. Sherzer observes that *Métisse* too can be seen as a French postcolonial rendition of Spike Lee's 1996 film *She's Gotta Have It*, where "the African-American Nola, her black male lovers, and the eventual female lover are transformed into the Martinican Lola and her two lovers, a Jewish pizza-delivery boy and a black university student."[15]

A major aspect of Kassovitz's cinema is that he often reads France through the categories and generic conventions and codes of U.S. cinema. In his films the two cultures creatively interact with each other but also displace and transform each other. For example, the character of Félix in *Métisse* displaces "Frenchness" by relocating it somewhere between French Jewishness, American Jewishness (the reference to Woody Allen), and African Americanness (the reference to Spike Lee). On the other hand, Kassovitz's intertextual and transnational constructs transcode and map the situation of a particular ethnic minority in one country (say, African Americans in the United States) onto that of another ethnic minority group in another country (for example, Arabs in France). This profoundly utopian and politicized gesture asserts an inextricable sense of solidarity and collective destiny between marginalized or oppressed groups, even though they might be separated by space, nationality, race, and culture.

As previously observed, the sizzling soundtrack of *La Haine* also displaces the space of traditional French culture by sampling and "morphing" ultimate French cultural icon Edith Piaf within a mix of Franco-American hip-hop and gangsta' rap music (multi-ethnic groups Assassin, Expression Direkt, and Extreme-NTM appear in the film's soundtrack), while the Zairian Belgian female vocalists of Zap Mama are prominently featured in the musical score of *Métisse*. The space of French literature itself, which appears explicitly through the giant effigies of French poets Baudelaire and Hugo at the end, is from the beginning replaced by multiple forms of decentered, eccentric, and alternative writings—most notably the beautiful Arabic hieroglyph of Saïd's name, which he traces in a rebellious gesture on the back of a police van at the very beginning of *La Haine*. By doing so, Saïd asserts not just his will and need for an identity (which in the film will be denied to him) but also a countercultural desire to displace the dominant orthodox culture of France, to replace its language, canonical literature, and symbolic sign systems by cultures from the "periphery" such as

Algeria, where he comes from. In the film the iconic image of Saïd "tagging" his Arabic name on the police van echoes powerfully the final, canonical, and equally iconic image of that supreme French literary hero Charles Baudelaire, thus creating a dialectical tension between the opening and the final scene. The two scenes represent different and (as the film would have it) incompatible forms of writings. The tension between those two images (the image of Saïd tagging his Arabic name on the police van and the image of Saïd's friends dying in front of Baudelaire's mural) constitutes one of the most significant narrative and ideological structures of the film. In Kassovitz's cinema, those other cultures, those cultures of the "other" and *"langues de l'Autre"* always come from geographical zones that historically have been either colonized, exploited, or marginalized: Northern Africa, the Rastafarian protorevolutionary culture of Jamaican music (the Bob Marley "Burnin' and Lootin'" reggae song of the credit sequence), the Martinique dialect of Lola's grandmother in *Métisse*, and so forth. *La Haine* thus forced the French to recognize that the "transculturalization" process by which powerful Western nations historically tried to colonize and assimilate other countries now seemed to have been *inverted*. It suggested that that process was no longer unidirectional. Saïd's tagging—and indeed the whole film—partakes of what Michel Laronde calls *les écritures décentrées* (decentered forms of writing): "celles qui ne sont plus exactement le standard de La Langue [et de la culture], qu'elle soit la française, l'anglaise ou l'espagnole, mais qui y touchent, en dérivent, la frôlent sans vouloir l'épouser complètement ni sans pouvoir s'en détacher non plus."[16] L'écriture décentrée partakes of an ongoing process of cultural hybridity, or *croisement*. Like Saïd's tagging, it creates a new type of *écart*: a gap, a distortion, a hybrid mutation within the dominant culture of contemporary France, within its symbolic "languages" such as its national canonical literature and traditional popular songs. In both *La Haine* and *Métisse,* the cultural codes of dominant nations such as France have lost their preeminence. The former colonial power seems to have become the object of a reverse act of cultural colonization. The historical movement is inverted and the irruption of cultures from "peripheral" regions within the symbolic constructs of dominant nations seems to promise a multicultural, multi-ethnic, and transnational cultural process with greater reciprocity.

Thus, despite its chilling ending, even *La Haine* might also be read against the grain as a utopian film, especially since so much of the film's energy resides in the more exhilarating musical moments (the hip-hop contest, the DJ who plays Piaf in the cité). Much of the cinematic pleasure generated by *La Haine* actually comes from nonnarrative elements such as the dynamic interaction between its multi-ethnic trio of charismatic actors and characters. Despite the doomed narrative trajectory of their characters and the apparent nihilism of the film, the inspired and energizing performances, acting styles, and interaction between the three actors mediate the possibility of interethnic solidarity and friendship in France today. Mark Ingram observed that many banlieue films such as *La Haine* and Karim Dridi's 1996 film *Bye Bye* are "pessimistic about the possibility of reconciling new forms of culture with a French cultural heritage."[17] Indeed. Yet, the last image of *Métisse* opens possibilities that might not be present in *La Haine.* Despite the fact that the three characters continue to fight till the very end about the name of their baby (David, Mohammed, or Clothère) as a way of asserting their own religious identity over the identities of their partners, the fight or competition is a joyful, not a bitter one. It takes place in a final scene of reconciliation that promises hope. The characters seem to be about to finally overcome their racial, socioeconomic, cultural, and religious prejudices in order to establish a bond of genuine friendship, solidarity, and parenthood as suggested by their three hands joined over Lola's womb. Ironically, the character who suggests the very Frankish name of Clothère for the baby is the black Christian Lola herself, whose Creoleness functions throughout the film as the promise of a reconciliation between apparently incompatible ethnicities and religions.

Moreover, this process of cultural transcoding by which the cultures of "weaker" peripheral regions (Algeria, Jamaica, the overseas territories) are introduced within the symbolic productions of the "stronger" nations such as France seems to *de-essentialize* and *de-territorialize national cultures* in ways described by philosophers Gilles Deleuze and Félix Guattari in their groundbreaking and utopian work, *A Thousand Plateaux* (and later on by Guattari's own works such as *The Three Ecologies*). This new type of transcultural/transnational space mapped by Kassovitz's remarkable films is not really a new "multicultural" and multi-ethnic paradigm. It is not a "synthesis" between several national or regional cultures either. Rather, it can best be described as a fluid mosaic and a fluid *drifting* of cultures, nations, and identities. The last scene of *Métisse* is obviously intended to be read as a simple but effective allegory of the new multicultural, multi-ethnic, multireligious, and transnational France. Lola's womb is the matrix of that new France that has not fully revealed itself yet. If the film denies us the image of the face of the new baby born within a family that counts two fathers, three religions (the Christian Lola, the Muslim Jamal, the Jewish Félix), various socioeconomic origins and classes (from privileged to poor), multiple nationalities, and countless geographic and national ancestries from Africa to Central Europe and the overseas territories, it is because the relentless multicultural and transnational activity of the film itself has made it literally *impossible* to define what France is, or even what it is becoming. Kassovitz's films, which belong to those "languages of the Other" described by Laronde, produce a distortion, a profound transformation, a *torsion* in the representation of France. If Dina Sherzer and other critics saw the love triangle and *ménage à trois* of *Métisse* as a French version of Spike Lee's *She's Gotta Have It,* it should also be seen as a witty, ironic, and caustic rewriting of that most "Franco-French" and sacrosanct 1961 François Truffaut film, *Jules et Jim,* which has remained such a quintessential part of the traditional national canon. Yet, one should even go one step further. As previously said, *La Haine* and *Métisse* actually suggest that "France", French culture, French identity—what Roland Barthes would have called "French-ness"—are becoming increasingly de-essentialized and even de-ethnicized postmodern realities akin to those famous "rhizomes" or *ritournelles* Deleuze and Guattari famously wrote about.[18] Kassovitz's films project the vision (accurate or not) that France today is a deterritorialized space in permanent flux and mutation, always reaching out and connecting to other deterritorialized fragments of foreign national and regional cultures that are themselves in exile, from France's canonical literature and classic cinema to U.S. and Asian commercial films, Jamaican music, and more to come.

Those films are, therefore, also about the thorough globalization or *mondialisation* of France—its nation, its culture, its society, its population, its identities. That idea is suggested by the very first images of the credit sequence of *Métisse,* which shows a globe as viewed from a satellite—another obvious allegory of the new transnational global space of *la mondialisation* itself. Since the satellite image of the earth seen from outer space is followed immediately by the scrambled image of France, which suggests that *national* space has now become problematic, those first images announce that the film will be about the tension between nation and globalization, about the ways in which the former is transformed

by the latter: the satellite scanner has problems finding and stabi-
lizing the image and space of *l'Hexagone*, which remains out of
focus and scrambled, just as the existence and even the presence of
"France as we know it" remain uncertain throughout Kassovitz's
film. Yet, interestingly, the disappearance—or at least the radical
mutation—of France as portrayed in the films is never lamented. On
the contrary, *La Haine* and *Métisse* offer a much more positive and
hopeful vision of globalization and multiculturalism than what those
words and realities usually evoke for the French. On the other side
of the Atlantic, mondialisation as well as *multiculturalisme* (now
sometimes called *communautarisme*) are mostly dirty words that
generate powerful anxieties and fears. They evoke threats to the assumed unity and integrity of the nation, loss of national sovereignty,
the impossibility for nations to determine their own destinies and
maintain their differences, especially now that nation-states are
being integrated ("engulfed", "swallowed up", "broken down")
in much larger constructs from the European Union to the global
economy itself. It is telling that French activist farmer José Bové
has now become a veritable folk hero through his dismantling of a
McDonald's fast-food restaurant (for many, the symbol of an evil,
U.S.–led global economy), his highly mediatized campaigns against
genetically engineered food (now widely called "Frankenfood"),
and his staunch opposition to global economic superstructures such
as the World Trade Organization, also frequently represented and
sometimes demonized in the media as threats to the sovereignty of
the French nation. Regarding multiculturalism (a phenomenon that
is different from globalization although it is often equally demonized and feared), one of the most dramatic promises of presidential
candidate Jacques Chirac during his last reelection campaign was
that he would never let France become "a juxtaposition of communities and groups." In a typically conservative French fashion,

Chirac's promise constituted a radical rejection of multiculturalism *à l'américaine,* which is seen by most French politicians and intellectuals as a dangerous threat of fragmentation or *balkanisation,* an unacceptable menace to the integrity of the "indivisible Republic." Besides constituting an expression of France's fear of what it often perceives as its "others" (America, immigrants, multiculturalist politics), Chirac's promise was also a very typical nationalist defense of the assimilationist model of the "unitary and indivisible" French Republic as a fundamental of *l'exception culturelle*: France's "exceptional," unique identity. *Métisse* on the contrary offers a countertext to that widespread fear of multiculturalism and *communautarisme* expressed in Chirac's remark (a fear that is certainly not limited to the electorate of the conservative right). Kassovitz's first film elaborates a warm, multiculturalist, and multi-ethnic utopia of France that dissolves more traditional representations and unitary concepts of French identity and would no doubt make Chirac nervous! The originality of Kassovitz's cinema also lies in the way he reads the processes of globalization (including Americanization, immigration, multiculturalism, transnational global youth countercultures) in a positive and utopian manner, mostly against the grain of the way those are predominantly understood—or misunderstood—and represented on the other side of the Atlantic. For Kassovitz, far from constituting threats to the unity and integrity of the nation, things to be feared and opposed, those trends represent benign and vital cultural processes whose resources, logics, and effects have the potential to *regenerate* the old nation-states with their traditional cultures and identities rather than destroy or degrade them as the French commonly believe. Against the grain of most of the rest of French culture, including media representations, political discourses, and public debates, Kassovitz's films are not afraid, far from it, of métissage. As the French rap song that opens *Métisse* suggests, they are not afraid of globalization either. Not only do those films seem to proclaim that there can be an authentic global youth culture that would escape the "reification" and loss inherent to the penetration of capitalist logics everywhere, but they actually welcome and *embrace* the dissolution of borders; the *de-territorialization* of nations and cultures; and the erosion of traditional national identities, concepts of national purity (ethnic or other), and canonical national cultures.

One of the main originalities of those very postmodern films was that they very powerfully and joyfully celebrate the emergence in France and everywhere of *impure cultures and identities* as an antithesis and antidote to essentialized national identities.[19] *Métisse* in particular, with its joyful, charismatic, and sexy characters who drink Coca-Cola in wine glasses and play basketball with Superman or "Elvis Shot JFK" T-shirts constitute the positive flip side and utopian antidote to the much bleaker *La Haine* and also to the French anxieties of seeing their cherished nation and culture absorbed and erased altogether in the maelstroms of globalization, immigration, and multiculturalism. Although at first glance *Métisse* is merely a charming multi-ethnic comedy, it was actually quite radical at the time of its release (it still is) since it seemed to advocate métissage, racial mixing, transnational and transcultural permutations, and exchanges at all levels of cultural and symbolic production, personal relationships, romance, sexual relationships, and family life. In this cinema métissage offers solutions to many of France's most severe national syndromes, including racism, fear of immigration, fear of the "other," and fear of la mondialisation—all of which still continue to plague France's confidence in itself.

For Kassovitz radical métissage—*without* assimilation or reduction of differences—offers solutions and resources to eliminate racism, prejudices, national anxieties, and the separation of peoples by ethnic, sociocultural, and national boundaries. As such his cinema constitutes a matrix for the new France that has been slowly and often painfully emerging in the last three decades. As noted above it also offers a healthy antidote to French ideal fantasies of national origins, integrity, purity, and essentialized identities—notions that powerfully resurfaced during the recent *émeutes de banlieue*. (Coupled with the one-hundredth-year anniversary of the separation of church and state, those riots, which were often misrepresented as riots by immigrants, gave new strength to *le discours Républicain*: the defense and celebration of the (idealized) French Republic, with its themes of unity, indivisibility, universalism, and integration, if not assimilation of all.) Last but not least, at a moment when the pluralistic models of the U.S. and British multiculturalist states are being even more violently rejected by prominent intellectuals and politicians alike in the name of the integrity of the unitary and indivisible Republic, *La Haine* and *Métisse*, a decade after their release, still successfully challenge those hegemonic, essentialized, and autochtonous conceptions of national integrity through the fetishism of *l'identité Républicaine de la France*. Kassovitz's cinema can be credited for having courageously, creatively, and dramatically expanded the definitions and representations of France and French identity by opening them up to experiences, characters, and so forth that were traditionally not considered typical. Each in its own particular way, using opposite narrative and representational strategies (the urban drama for *La Haine*, the romantic comedy for *Métisse*), both films managed to do so with generosity and vision.

In a nation as uncertain as France today, where it seems most people just want security and certainty out of a sense of vulnerability and fear for their own future and the future of their country, it is hard to tell whether those new original cultures, those postmodern and de-essentialized multicultural and transnational identities and that radical experience of métissage envisioned in the films will ultimately win out. Yet in the vibrant cinema of Mathieu Kassovitz, they already have.

Notes

1. For representative examples of such discourses see Viviane Forrester, *L'horreur économique* (Paris: Fayard, 1996); and Nicolas Baverez, *La France qui tombe* (Paris: Perrin, 2005).

2. The term *beur*, slang for "Arab," was widely used throughout the 1980s and the 1990s to designate the "second generation": the sons and daughters of Northern African immigrants who came to France after World War II, more often than not as cheap labor to help in the reconstruction and modernization of the country during the postwar boom. Many of them emigrated from Morocco, Algeria, and Tunisia under family reunion laws or were born in France—as such, they are French citizens—while those who came from North Africa have often acquired French citizenship through naturalization. Although up until a recent past, the word "beur" was widely used and accepted as a mark of historical, cultural, and ethnic identification, today it is often felt to be disrespectful, derogatory, if not frankly insulting at a time when many just crave integration. Yet, it is still often used self-ironically.

3. Ginette Vincendeau, "Designs on the Banlieue: Mathieu Kassovitz's La Haine (1995)," in *French Film: Texts and Contexts,* ed. Susan Hayward and Ginette Vincendeau (London: Routledge, 2000), 321.

4. Today, however, rap culture has largely become mainstream, as is also the case with Kassovitz's cinema. In France, break dance, hip-hop, and rap cultures have even been thoroughly tamed and institutionalized—some would say coerced and neutralized—through public initiatives such as state-sponsored and often publicly funded rap and hip-hop festivals, and public grants made available to rap and hip-hop artists upon application to the official local and regional administrations, city halls, or *conseils régionaux*, and more.

5. Claude-Marie Trémois, *Les enfants de la liberté: Le jeune cinéma français des années 90* (Paris: Seuil, 1997); Carrie Tarr, "Ethnicity and Identity in the *Cinéma de Banlieue*," in *French Cinema in the 1990s: Continuity and Difference,* ed. Phil Powrie (Oxford: Oxford University Press, 1999), 172–84; and Carrie Tarr, "Questions of Identity in *Beur* Cinema: From *Tea in the Harem* to *Cheb*," *Screen* 34, no. 4 (1993): 321–42.

6. Myrto Konstantarakos, "Which Mapping of the City? *La Haine* (Kassovitz, 1995) and the *Cinéma de Banlieue*," in Powrie, *French Cinema in the 1990s*, 170.

7. Serge Toubiana, "Retour du politique (suite)," *Cahiers du Cinéma* 511 (1997): 28–29.

8. Pierre Bourdieu, *La misère du monde* (Paris: Seuil, 1993); *Contre-feux* (Paris: Raison d'agir, 1998); and Forrester, *L'horreur économique.*

9. Konstantarakos, "Which Mapping of the City?" 168.

10. Konstantarakos, "Which Mapping of the City?" 168.

11. Vincendeau, "Designs on the Banlieue," 324.

12. David Blatt, "Immigrant Politics in a Republican Nation," in *Post-Colonial Cultures in France,* ed. Alec G. Hargreaves and Mark McKinney (London: Routledge, 1997), 41–55.

13. During the 1990s more than 10 percent of marriages in France were between a French citizen and a foreigner. About 50 percent of those marriages involved Africans, especially Africans from the Maghreb (Algeria, Tunisia, and Morocco). Within a very short period of time a whole new generation of "mixed-blood," binational, and often multicultural children was thus created. See Jacques Audinet, *Le temps du métissage* (Paris: L'Atelier, 1999).

14. Dina Sherzer, "Comedy and Interracial Relationships: *Romuald et Juliette* (Serreau, 1997); and *Métisse* (Kassovitz, 1993)," in Powrie, *French Cinema in the 1990,* 154.

15. Sherzer, "Comedy and Interracial Relationships," 153.

16. Michel Laronde, *L'écriture décentrée: La langue de l'autre dans le roman contemporain* (Paris: L'Harmattan, 1996), 7: "those modes of writing which do not obey dominant Language and Culture (French, English, Spanish, etc.), but which approach it, drift from it, brush past it, without trying to either adopt it or break from it altogether." See also his *Autour du roman beur: Immigration et identité* (Paris: L'Harmattan, 1993).

17. Mark Ingram, "Interdisciplinary Perspectives in the French Civilization Class," *The French Review* 74, no. 6 (May 2001): 1160.

18. Deleuze and Guattari described their "rhizomes" as "incorporeal transformations that are not apprehended in themselves," and as "*nomadic essences,* vague yet rigorous, ... continuous variations, which go beyond constants and variables; *becomings,* which have neither culmination nor subject, but draw one another into zones of proximity and undecidability," *A Thousand Plateaus,* trans. Brian Massumi (London: Athlone, 1988), 506–7. That definition captures exactly what happens to the "France" of *Métisse* and to its trio. For example, toward the end of the film, one observes that Félix and Jamal have unconsciously started to exchange characteristics. For example, Jamal puts on Félix's "urban fashion" clothes while Félix, the would-be gangsta' rapper, listens to Jamal's favorite classical Wagner music. This process of subjective identification, which in the film is largely unnoticed by the characters themselves, suggests that the two rival young men—and through them, the ethnic, religious, and geographic identities they have so far represented and promoted (African pride mixed with highbrow Western culture for Jamal vs. French/U.S. rap and street culture for Félix, etc.)—are also being "drawn into zones of proximity and undecidability," as Deleuze and Guattari would have it.

19. Here it would be useful to analyze the representation of fascism, violence, and Jewishness in other films by Kassovitz as both actor and director such as his 2001 thriller *Les Rivières Pourpres (The Crimson Rivers)* or his roles in the Costa Gavras film *Amen*; the recent 2005 Steven Spielberg's thriller *Munich*, where he plays a Jewish Mossad assassin; and the 1996 Jacques Audiard film *Un Héro Très Discret (A Self-Made Hero)*, where he plays a coward who usurps the identity of a real French Resistance hero when the war is over and there is no more danger. A close analysis of all of Kassovitz's cinema as both actor and director would reveal that he is primarily interested in deconstructing essentialized and idealized national identities as dangerous protofascistic constructs based on fantasies of origins, unity, and purity—which is also why his work revolves around and constantly returns to World War II and the Holocaust (the Auschwitz story in the bathroom of *La Haine*, the grandfather of *Métisse*, himself a Holocaust survivor). Interestingly, Kassovitz cast himself as the neo-Nazi skinhead whom Vinz tries to kill in *La Haine*. A systematic study of his cinema would also reveal how he relates those dominant representations and concepts of "Frenchness" and unitary essentialized identities to their "others" (most notably Jewishness) in order to better challenge and deconstruct them.

III

Writing Algerian Identities

7

A Poet's Politics

Jean Sénac's Writings during the Algerian War

ROBERT ALDRICH

O ver forty years after the end of the Algerian War of Independence and thirty-three years after his murder, Jean Sénac remains a relatively little known figure in modern literature and the history of anticolonial politics. Only recently have collections of his poems, prose writings, and art criticism—including many pieces originally published in limited editions or unpublished—made his writings easily accessible. The meticulous work of Hamid Nacer-Khodja, an Algerian *préfet*, poet, and friend of Sénac, in gathering and editing these writings shows the respect in which Sénac is held by many Algerian intellectuals.[1] Renewed interest in francophone literature and the Algerian war has also contributed to a rediscovery of Sénac's life and works.[2] Sénac has become a symbol of the hopes and deceptions of the Algerian revolution, especially in the context of recent Algerian history and its tragedies, and has figured as the subject of a French play and a Franco-Algerian film.[3] The interest testifies to the dramatic nature of Sénac's life and death and to the paradox of a *pied-noir* supporter of Algerian independence who was murdered in independent Algeria.

Born in 1926 in Bénif-Saf, near Oran, to an unknown father and a mother of Spanish ancestry, Sénac was educated in French schools, completed his military service, and was briefly hospitalized in a tuberculosis sanatorium. He made his way into the literary circles of Algiers after the Second World War then to Paris in the early 1950s. In 1954 with the aid of his mentor, Albert Camus, Sénac published his first book, called simply *Poèmes,* which included a preface by René Char. Sénac spent the years of the Algerian war, which began in the same year his book was published and continued for eight years, in France, from the outset committed to Algerian independence. In 1962 he returned to Algiers, his literary accomplishments and political support for the nationalists propelling him to editorial, broadcasting, and administrative positions. Political and social changes, especially after Houari Boumediène's coup d'état in 1965, severely affected Sénac's fortunes, and by the early 1970s he was banished from the government-aligned cultural elite, dismissed from a position presenting a radio program called *Poésie sur tous les fronts,* and reduced to poverty. He was killed in his sordid basement apartment at the age of forty-seven. Opinion differs on whether the murder was a *crime de mœurs* committed by a former lover or whether he was killed by a regime no longer willing to tolerate someone, who though generally regarded as Algeria's foremost French-language poet and with an unblemished record of support for independence, was now an outspoken critic of the regime—a man, furthermore, of French and Christian origin and an open homosexual.[4]

Sénac's death, with its parallels to the fates of Federico García Lorca and Pier Paolo Pasolini, brings together the themes of politics, literature, and sex. Elsewhere I have written about links between Sénac's homosexuality and his anticolonialism. The handsome French and Maghrebi men whom Sénac cruised, and with whom he fell in love, represented the pleasures of a sun-drenched Algiers and the promise of a nation where Europeans and North Africans might each find their place. "Et maintenant nous chanterons l'amour / Car il n'y a pas de Révolution sans Amour" (And now we will sing of love / Because there is no Revolution without Love) read the opening lines of one of his best known poems, "Citoyens de beauté," published soon after Algerian independence.[5] Sénac's poems, speaking straightforwardly and explicitly of his erotic and romantic encounters, figure among the most powerful works of homosexual literature in French in the 1950s and 1960s.[6]

The present chapter focuses on Sénac's political writings, particularly the prose published between 1954 and 1962 (as well as pieces written at the time but not published until 1999). These voiced opposition to French rule, enunciated an analysis of the colonial situation, and set out Sénac's ideals for an independent Algeria. They are valuable as pleas to fellow pieds-noirs to support the nationalists' cause by committing themselves to a free Algeria. They show the way Sénac mobilized poetic language in the service of a political project, skillfully using ideas and words intended to appeal to the Français d'Algérie, and draw on various currents of metropolitan and Algerian culture. The poems present Sénac as an example of the well-intentioned if ill-fated pieds-noirs who tried before and after 1962 to reconcile their identities as French and Algerian.[7]

Sénac's first published works, experimental poems bearing the influence of Char and Paul Eluard, reveal little of the political cast of his later writings. The evocations of Algiers or Oran owe much to Camus and the *algérianiste* school of Robert Randau more than to nascent political consciousness. Sénac's delight in walking the streets of Algiers at dawn or spending the afternoon at the beach of Pointe-Pescade conjures up the environment so celebrated by pieds-noirs. Inalienable attachment to the sights and sounds, savors and sentiments of the country of his birth loomed large in Sénac's subsequent support for Algerian independence. Even at the end of his life, while Sénac was suffering bouts of despair at new political and social conditions and his personal state, these sensual pleasures survived as the heart of his cultural nationalism. He steadfastly refused to renounce the allegiance to Mère Algérie that marked his first works.

By his mid-twenties, Sénac was certainly politically cognizant of the nature of colonialism in Algeria and of the responsibilities incumbent on a man of letters. In a text dated 1950 (published posthumously), Sénac—speaking as he would customarily do, "to all my brothers"—noted, "everyone has become aware of the racist and colonialist situation, but many have simply adapted or resigned themselves. Let at least the artist, along with the political person, leave his house and cry out that this is unjust and inhuman, that this must end—may he take part in the struggle, no matter what this choice cost him." He affirmed: "The artist, because he addresses himself to everyone, takes responsibility for the misery and the hopes of everyone. He is not simply 'the witness to liberty' but a daily combatant [for it]. His place is on the barricades and wherever still blows the wind of revolt and art. "[8] In private Sénac bemoaned the steadily deteriorating situation, by 1952 denouncing the "assassins" acting against nationalists. "To keep quiet is to be a traitor," he wrote in calling men of letters to action. "Algerians, I love France la Douce, the France of Joan of Arc, Saint-Just, Victor Hugo, Rimbaud, Pasteur and Char, my second homeland. Algerians, I solemnly protest to France la Juste against the injustice done to my friends."[9] Sénac then tried to marshal intellectuals to the nationalist cause when he edited a journal of French-language Algerian literature and presented a cultural program on local radio, though he was forced to leave French-controlled state radio because of his political views.

In early 1954 Sénac lived through a short love affair and wrote a moving journal and poem cycle about it. Even in roaming the streets looking for sexual companions, he could not but notice the Algerians' distress, how "near the small mosque, tonight like every night, hundreds of poor people wrapped in burlap packing sacks are trying to sleep rough on the frozen sidewalks."[10] He discussed the worsening situation with friends, writers and painters, pieds-noirs and Arabs but realized the difficulty of remaining in an Algeria where his opinions were little shared by European compatriots. Sénac decided to go to Paris, though he always foresaw the "the need to return, to witness, to struggle." Already his position was clear: "The pride and the blindness of the Europeans here is mad. We can expect nothing from them, nothing. They have to face the *fait accompli* and make a choice: Algeria or departure. I do not believe there is any other solution." What was needed was a "radical revolution," (an "illusion?"), even though he recognized its complex implications:

> I have no illusions about truly Algerian (Arabic) political parties, about their urge for revenge and their own racism, but I believe that it is necessary to fight with them, even in chaos, so that one day Justice and Truth can emerge in this country. We must hope that some sincere and untainted Frenchmen will agree to contribute to this painful and great undertaking. They will play their part so that one day—after the anger and the anarchy—the country will show its true face, a place where all people—of Arabic, Berber, Jewish, French, Spanish, Italian and other origins—will finally be free (because liberty does exist) under the sun. Faith. Hope.[11]

By November of that year, when the war broke out, Sénac was in Paris, immediately concerned by both literary matters and politics.

He learned for instance of a plan to form an "international brigade" to aid the nationalists, a project that he doubted would succeed. By mid-December he was unsure of what specific action to take, writing in his diary: "Immobile here, I am an accomplice and a coward. . . . Do I leave for the Aurès? Write? Die? Kill? Go to Cairo? Bear witness in Algiers? Be an activist in Paris?" He added other possibilities, with a touch of self-mocking chastisement or real ambition: "Earn lots of money, make a name for myself and place my fortune and my glory in the service of my People. Develop, sparkle, gain a reputation so that some day I can carry more weight, count for more, and really be of use?"[12] In any case, the die was already cast.

Sénac made contact with the French federation of the Front de Libération Nationale (FLN), meeting such leaders as Ahmed Taleb-Ibrahimi, Layachi Yaker, and Mostefa Lacheref. According to Nacer-Khodja,

> Sénac was tireless in the federation—organizing networks, writing tracts, printing the *Bulletin de la Fédération de France du FLN*, maintaining contact between the FLN and the MNA [the Mouvement National Algérien of Messali Hadj, the rival to the FLN], etc. The history of his participation, right from the outset, is yet to be revealed, given the shadows and meanderings that it contained due in part to the necessity to work clandestinely and to avoid suspicion, due to the fact that some Algerians today have a tendency to diminish, if not to overlook, his role. The poet himself was discreet and only confided about his work to several friends and correspondents.

From 1957 to 1960 it is known that Sénac collaborated on the nationalist newspaper *El Moudjahid*. It has been reliably suggested that he considered joining the pro-Algerian *maquis*, but that the FLN leadership told him not to do so.[13] Sénac wrote to Camus in

December 1957, "If I am not in the [Algerian] resistance in the mountains, it is because after three tries, they won't take me. But I serve my people in my own way."[14]

Throughout the war, he associated with pro-Algerian figures in Paris, many of them pieds-noirs, such as the journalist (and later editor of *Le Nouvel Observateur*), Jean Daniel.[15] The cafés of Saint-Germain-des-Prés that Sénac frequented provided rallying points for intellectuals, activists, and Algerians in Paris. Sénac also enjoyed evenings spent in the company of Arabs, listening to recordings of the popular singer El-Anka, eating couscous, and reminiscing about Algeria.[16] He called on François Mauriac to discuss the war, hoping to convince him of the legitimacy of nationalist aspirations, and during the first years, he regularly saw Camus. Although Sénac had met Simone de Beauvoir in Algiers, he does not seem to have been close to Sartre's antiwar circle, and there is no record of participation in the major antiwar demonstrations. Sénac become known to opponents of the war largely because of his writings, including works read at functions in support of the Algerian cause; he gave talks to Algerian student groups in Paris and Grenoble.[17]

Sénac's main role lay in what Philip Dine has called the "cultural politics" of the war, which mobilized many iconic figures in French cultural life.[18] Sénac's known wartime activities are primarily literary through a number of genres: poems, essays, manifestos, open letters, private correspondence, and a play. In 1954 and 1955 he composed "La Patrie," one of his first pieces of political writing (though only printed in 1961). In 1956 a "Lettre à un jeune Français d'Algérie" appeared, his first major public pronouncement on the war, and he also wrote a message to a congress of black writers. A piece titled "Un Français d'Algérie prend la parole—Assez de massacres," offered a brief history of Algerian nationalism, outlined the role that Europeans could play in an independent Algeria, and called for the development of a "shared national consciousness" by Muslim Algerians and Français d'Algérie. Meanwhile, the journal *Simoun* published Sénac's lyrical "Oran ou les statues sous la peau," an evocation of his native region. The following year came a manifesto on literature and revolution, "Le Soleil sous les armes"; other essays were "Les Intellectuels algériens et la Révolution" and "Désertions de l'espérance," a parable about an Arab whose identity papers are checked by uncomprehending and aggressive policemen in the Boulevard Saint-Michel. At the end of 1957 he wrote an essay taking issue with Camus's position on the war.

Sénac's writing continued as the war became even bloodier, threatening to tear apart France as well as Algeria. In 1958 in the Tunis-based *Action*, he published "Les Bourreaux d'Alger," which drew parallels between the Second World War Resistance and the nationalist struggle—a heretical comparison for many Frenchmen. Unpublished was "Le Chant des Africains," in which Sénac commented on the report that the new French leader, General de Gaulle, had been irritated on his trip to Algeria to hear the colonialist song, which gave the title for the essay, sung in place of "La Marseillaise." Sénac retorted acidly: "In the name of 'La Marseillaise,' they have massacred, tortured and bombarded." In "Le Peuple algérien face à l'imposture," he charged that "more than ever France is a prisoner of its myths and its prestigious colonial tradition." In the midst of talk about possible partition of Algeria, some status making it an "associated state" of France or another arrangement falling short of decolonization, he proclaimed: "Nothing will keep Algeria from being independent and the Maghreb united." The following year, as a tribute to the nationalists, Sénac's short collection *Poésies* was published with illustrations by Abdallah Benanteur. In 1961, the year before the war ended, Sénac wrote his last political essay on the conflict, the moving "'Pieds-noirs,' mes frères" and published a collection of poems written since the late 1940s, *Matinale de mon peuple.*

Meanwhile, Sénac also completed works that were only published much later.[19] From 1959 to 1962 he had been writing his only novel (an autobiographical work on his early life), *Ebauche du père.* The book mixed descriptions of everyday life in Algeria—the market, religious festivals, carnival, the discovery of a photo of Sarah Bernhardt, making friends with a Foreign Legion soldier who was one of his mother's lovers—with portraits of his mother and grandmother, and his life-long fantasies about his unknown father. Sénac described the anti-Semitism current in Algeria in the 1940s, which he compared with the anti-Arab racism of many Europeans in later years. He briefly chronicled his life in Paris during the war and included a short section on Camus. Writing of himself in the third person, he revealed his self-appointed fate: "I was born, Sénac said, so that a poor little child from Oran could one day raise his voice against his masters, the masters of prejudice and constraint, so that his worn sandals can splash through the tears of his mother."[20] Writing in Paris or the Drôme (where he had a small house) in the most violent years of the war, his thoughts were riveted on Algeria and the "revolution" that he had adopted, haunted by figures from the past: "I write about an avalanche of people, innocents who fall to the sound of gunfire. I dig into my guts, listening to all of them. I write about my war. . . . . Writing about me, I write about this country that is being built up. I contribute my building block, baroque and delirious."[21]

Sénac's literary output was steady during these years, and he had decided that through his writing, rather than by other types of activism and in France rather than in Algeria, he could best support the *indépendantistes.* The poems in *Matinale de mon peuple* are wholeheartedly engaged with the struggle. One of the opening poems, "Au pas lent des caravanes," speaks about colonialist mirages in Algeria. "Honte Honte Honte" lambastes violence committed by police on children and beggars, and in another appear "children [who] die of thirst in the midst of fountains." "Fait divers" is set in the Algiers slums, while "Les belles apparences" reveals death behind the beautiful façade of Alger *la blanche*. The title of "Massacres de juillet" recalls midsummer massacres, and "1er Novembre 1954" commemorates the start of the war. "Pieds et poings liés," one of several poems about torture, is dedicated to the murdered rebels Mohammed Ben M'Hidi and Ali Boumendjel; another has an epigraph from Henri Alleg, an intellectual whose writing brought the torture practiced by the French to international attention. Lines allude to nighttime meetings of revolutionaries, antiwar campaigns and freedom fighters, curfews, military patrols, and barbed-wire fences, a situation in which his, "homeland" was "imprisoned." In "A quelques-uns," Sénac salutes "French comrades / comrades faithful to the true face of France." A set of poems written after he visited Spain in 1959 compares the situation of wars of liberation against colonialists and against fascists: "As they struck Spain, so they are striking Algeria." The collection closes with poems on Angola, Patrice Lumumba (the Congolese revolutionary), and Cuba. Throughout the book, despite his own suffering, Sénac foresees an inevitable and just victory for the *indépendantistes*, painting an optimistic picture of a free and happy Algeria.[22]

Sénac's other extended work during the war years was *Le Soleil sous les armes*, a fifty-six-page pamphlet published in 1957, characterized by Yvonne Llavador as "the first platform of Algerian poets" and "a landmark in the history of Algerian literature."[23] Subtitled "Eléments d'une Poésie de la Résistance," it constitutes Sénac's manifesto about literature and revolution: "Poetry and Resistance appear as the two cutting edges of the same blade, where man untiringly sharpens his dignity." Morality obliges the poet to voice the concerns of his people, explains Sénac (with mixed metaphors): "In the heat of action, madly on the watch, the poet lives on the very breath of his people. He translates their breathing, oppressed or radiant, the smell of the forests and that of the charnel houses." The poet is not a mouthpiece for a party but a free participant who must report good and bad; the situation authorizes him to condone and condemn. "If he stands up, sometimes with an immoderate violence, to shopkeepers and executioners, that is simply because the arrogance of trade and hatred blocks out the light and mutilates the body of Beauty," added Sénac in an affirmation of the coalescence of an aesthetic (and implicitly erotic) and political vision. Sénac argued that the colonial situation—political and cultural—constrained poets in Algeria and forced some to flee: "By encouraging conformity (pseudo-orientalism, a pseudo-School of Paris, a pseudo-School of Algiers, and so on) and a false avant-garde, the public powers have shown once again that any true art is dangerous because in its very essence it is dynamic and revolutionary and because it is tied to the living roots of the country." The poet's task is to reclaim Algeria: "to affirm without equivocation our presence in the reality of this country, which is indisputably a nation." True nationalists must create a poetic revolution as well as take part in the political struggle: "If the Algerian people are at war, this is also because they demand the right to poetry."[24]

Le Soleil sous les armes then turned to the question of national poetry. Sénac defended French as one of the literary languages of Algeria and defined an "Algerian writer" as "any writer who has definitively opted for the Algerian nation" (a vague definition contested after independence). He spoke about the oral tradition in the Maghreb and reviewed the history of written poetry from Mohammed Belkheir (an Oran writer arrested by the French in 1882) through the algérianiste school, the work of Camus, and contemporaries such as Mohammed Dib and Jean Amrouche. References to Frantz Fanon and Michel Leiris, as well as to Hugo and Rimbaud, connected French-language Algerian poetry to literary and political traditions in the metropole. The manifesto concluded (as did most of Sénac's wartime writings) with a hopeful, if idealistic, view of the *fraternité* that could characterize a liberated Algeria in which poets would find a true and noble place.

Sénac's essays count among his least known works, but they fit into an important genre. According to Dine, in the mass of writings about Algeria, "the most broadly influential pieces which appeared between 1954 and 1962 were polemical essays and/or *témoignages,* with the two categories overlapping."[25] This overlapping was a hallmark of Sénac's contributions. What gives the essays particular interest is that, written by a pied-noir, they are addressed to other pieds-noirs whom Sénac tries to bring around to Algerian independence. Presenting the history of colonialism and asserting that eventual independence is inevitable, Sénac's interventions provide insight into the paradoxes (and perhaps contradictions) of pied-noir support of nationalism. The powerfully worded (if sometimes curiously phrased) and carefully cast texts illustrate great hopes, simplistic though they might now seem, for a multicultural and harmonious Algeria. The achievement of that goal for Sénac depended primarily on the choice made by pieds-noirs.

In the short "La Patrie," written in 1954 in Algiers after he had returned from Paris and revised the following year, Sénac declared his personal and political sympathies. He also reflected on the history of European settlers in Algeria, such as his mother's family, Spanish miners who immigrated in the late 1800s. The essay first expressed his joy at being back in Algiers after his sojourn in France, once again "surrounded by these working people" and enjoying his old haunts, "the Moorish courtyard of a friend, [and] the stone pier where poor, famished and joyous youths reign," and he saluted "Mother Algeria, our tireless love." Homecoming in the midst of upheaval could not engender unmixed feelings:

> The coffee is good here. And it is cheap. Our plates are full and the cooking is fine. The spices also flavor our talk. Is that the secret of this language, which rolls stones and nuggets around the gullet? I would like to speak of things that reassure me, but in the heart of my joy there is sorrow, and old remorse festers. My forefathers imposed on these shores the civilization of the masters, yet deprived of its real honor and its true prestige. Were they really so blinded and uncultivated? I feel so little a part of their race! . . . Because of them, we have lived on this land like nostalgic adventurers, sequestered in our exile. We have defined a hypocritical "superiority", but Virtue, grave and searing, has taken refuge behind a trellis, or a veil, or in the domes of the mosques.

Sénac and his pieds-noirs compatriots carried the "stigmata" of colonization, with redemption only in return for support for independence and justice.[26]

These sentiments reached fuller expression in "Lettre à un jeune Français d'Algérie," published in the Parisian Catholic journal *Esprit* in 1956. The open letter is addressed to a real or symbolic Jean-Pierre, a pied-noir who has accused the poet of being bent on evicting the French from Algeria. Sénac's approach, addressing Jean-Pierre in the intimate "*tu*," is heartfelt acknowledgement of the pied-noir's rootedness in Algeria: "You love Algeria, where you were born, where you grew up, fulfilled; here in the land are your parents and your beloved departed, your memories and your hopes." But, he asks, has the young man considered what that land really is and to whom it belongs? Jean-Pierre, he says, despite boasting about love for Algeria, has not noticed the poor, the starving children, the workers, those beaten by the police. He recounts an exemplary incident in the 1940s when the mayor of Chergas put up a sign forbidding Jews, Arabs, and dogs access to the beach: "Prohibited men thus, the Arab workers from whom bread and dignity had already been taken, could not accept that the sun and the sea were taken from them as well, the only wealth that remained to them in this world, and so—nude and proud—they threw themselves into the waves." The offenders were arrested, some to die of asphyxiation in a police lockup.

Sénac says he does not want, however, to dwell on such horrors. Jean-Pierre himself already understands that "the game is over for the masters in Algeria." Opponents of independence may hold out for a few years, but "the Algerian people have won their battle." If Jean-Pierre and other pieds-noirs persist to the very end of a doomed war in opposition to independence and then die or flee, they are being untrue to the Algeria they claim to love. He pleads with Jean-Pierre to cast his lot with an independent Algeria:

> Algeria will be made with us or without us, but if it has to be made without us, I feel that a measure of leavening will be lacking in the dough. . . . I continue to believe, and I hope despite all appearances, that the Orient and the Occident, united in a new undertaking in the coming years, will present a fresh and redemptive face to the world. I believe that the Orient and the Occident need to rejuvenate themselves and to incarnate a new idea of humanity. Algeria should be the crucible of this culture and of this message of peace.

Europeans do not have the moral right to abandon Algeria, Sénac affirmed, but they do have the obligation to recognize that it was and should be, first and foremost, an Arabo-Berber country. They must give up their seignorial rights and privileges, even weather a period of nationalist vengeance, in order to construct a multiethnic society. "The only choice," he proclaimed, is "sincerely to accept the real Algeria, to accept it, whatever the cost in a night of the 4 August to our vanity as French Algerians"—an allusion to the night of the constituent assembly debates in 1789 in which the nobles of France gave up their aristocratic prerogatives. Predicting the future, however, Sénac was not certain that his friend would see reason: "I fear that this may be only a utopia, and that this Algeria, our Mother, will be constructed in the long run—because of your refusal—without you and against you."[27]

The year 1957, when *Le Soleil sous les armes* had more clearly announced Sénac's position, also brought about a rupture with Camus, the most famous pied-noir author, after his famous choice between "mother and justice" and his refusal to promote independence out of loyalty to Algérie française. The break was an awful decision for Sénac, who had hoped in earlier years to convince Camus of the rightness of the nationalist cause. It was also a personal break: Sénac thought of Camus not only as literary mentor but as substitute father, and Camus sometimes wrote to Sénac as *"mi hijo"* ("my son" in Spanish).[28]

Sénac said that he had respected Camus's silence on the Algerian question since his call for a "civil truce" in 1955, though this became increasingly difficult with escalating violence, including the "blind revolutionary terrorism" and the "crimes of pacification." Camus now had condemned the FLN "crimes" but not those of the MNA or the French authorities, which Sénac said were unacceptable: "To protest against the Nazi, Soviet, and Francoist camps and keep saying nothing about the colonialist camps . . . that is something which is an offence to the dignity of a work or [Camus's professed]

silence." From Stockholm, where he had traveled to collect the Nobel Prize for literature, Camus had called for a "just Algeria," but
Sénac countered that Camus's ideal would only be a variation on
colonial Algeria, and his cause was "not only an error or a utopia
but a criminal imposture, because it maintain[ed] an illusion that
cost dearly." Sénac then lambasted Camus's proposal for a "personal federalism" where Europeans and Arabo-Berbers would be
equally represented (despite the great disparity in their numbers)
in an Algerian parliament. Camus's reference in an interview to an
"Algerian province" enriched by European civilization, typified
by a community of writers constructed "by sole virtue of generous
exchange and true solidarity," particularly incurred Sénac's ire:

> As suggested in these texts, it emerges that Algeria is a province
> that owes everything to France and that only Europe can bring
> it enlightenment. Once again, contained there is a troubling no-
> tion of cultural imperialism. This is not a question of contesting
> the contribution of Europe. We know what we owe it. And that
> is not trivial. But what jumps out [of the writing] is that Camus
> sees only European civilization and culture as valid . . . Camus
> is not far removed from [Jacques] Soustelle's crusade against an
> obscurantist Orient mired in darkness. . . . For Camus, it seems,
> alas, that the admirable message of the West must be linked to a
> certain domination by France.

Sénac then ridiculed Camus's option of defending either the pieds-
noirs or Algerian rights, Camus's "mother" or justice: "Apparently,
the enemies of Madame Camus are the terrorists; apparently, the
politico-military and police apparatus of pacification assure the
safety of Madame Camus. But has Albert Camus not realized that his
mother's safety and justice can be defended together?" Security could
come only through peace, which could be obtained solely through
successful negotiations between the French and the FLN.[29]

Sénac's essay on Camus was his most strongly worded and radical commentary on the Algerian situation. He concluded: "Solidarity with our relatives and our friends consists in forcing them out of their blindness and their habits."[30] Sénac returned to this task in his last major piece of political writing before the war's end. In 1961 he made a final appeal—"'Pieds-noirs,' mes frères"[31]—a historical indictment of colonialism and the attitudes it engendered:

> You are called *pieds-noirs*—and that's already a statement. A tearful legend also. You disembarked on this land with your boots and your shiny shoes. What a black shine when nearby there were barefoot children wearing rags! These little "rats" have grown up washing your floors, carrying your packages, tilling your fields and pruning your grapevines. I say "your," but I should say "our." My [Spanish] ancestors arrived wearing espadrilles. But it didn't take long for them to put on boots.

The colonial past in Algeria, Sénac judged, was a history of land despoliation, laws considered blasphemous by Muslims, prisons, and massacres, though there was also a record of French achievements such as public works projects, education, and medicine. The colonial past must now be shucked off, and the heroes of the moment were the Algerians and the French who recognized the changing order. Sénac evoked the activism of Mohammed Ben M'Hidi, the executed nationalist; Maurice Audin, the communist mathematician and supporter of independence who had died at the hands of French police; and other nationalists and sympathizers, whom most pieds-noirs nevertheless treated as terrorists and traitors. The pieds-noirs must cease talking about the "trading away" of Algeria, abandon hope of a white savior, and stop dreaming of an untroubled future in South Africa or some other haven. Algeria was their land, but they must see it as their future:

So my *pied-noir* brothers . . . the Algerian Revolution of today, this
Republic of Algeria that makes you so afraid, the "cut-throats,"
the "terrorists," the "barbarians," well, they are greeting you!
These "fellaga" are saying to you that the house is big enough
for everybody.

The Revolution could create a new equality between Europeans
and Arabs, with a place for pieds-noirs in a rebuilt country:

For that to happen, you too have to take part in this Revolution,
you must approach him [the nationalist revolutionary] just as he
is coming to meet you: fraternally, you will understand that the
only enemy is colonialism because it diminishes both the one who
imposes it and the one who is subject to it. This will not be easy.
For so long have you been the victims of an insolent caricature, a
fraudulent image in which glory and crime gambol along together—
the History of France, the Colonial Empire, the Civilizing Mission,
churches, schools, hospitals! You arrived in a country that you
were told was "savage" and "uncultivated"—but this was false,
as thousands of letters written by the officers [who took part in
the conquest] in 1830 prove. They expropriated and despoiled
the "resistants" and gave you their best land, French governments
accorded you privileges that became more and more seductive,
and naturally, you wanted to increase them and to defend them.
Little by little, you became the agents of imposture, the soldiers
of colonialism, the lackeys of capitalism.

The colonial system, Sénac charged, had worked its ill effects
not only on Arabs and Berbers but also on Europeans, especially
the "poor whites." They lay at the mercy of metropolitan capital
and political power, abandoned by pieds-noirs magnates who had
already secreted riches overseas and made plans for escape when
Algeria gained independence. The ordinary Europeans in Algeria

were left to the manipulation of demagogues ready "once again to drag [them] into vengeance and bloodshed in order to defend their nostalgic little interests and their outdated visions," a madness that could lead only to collective suicide.[32]

The tenor of Sénac's writings during the war was to sound a general call to his countrymen in Algeria and France, more than to articulate an ideology of independence or to comment on specific strategies of the *indépendantistes*. Sénac did refer to contemporary figures, especially to those engaged in support of the struggle whose individual cases he no doubt hoped could evoke empathy from more open-minded Europeans. "'Pieds-noirs,' mes frères" invokes Djamila Bouhired, the Algerian woman tortured and raped by French soldiers. The start of the war in 1954, the killing of M'hidi, the disappearance of Audin and other episodes inspired particular poems, and they enter too into Sénac's essays, but his works do not attempt to chronicle the war. The Battle of Algiers, the Manifeste des 121 (condoning refusal by conscripts to serve in Algeria), the repression of demonstrations in Paris somewhat oddly did not inspire prose or poetry, perhaps because Sénac knew that getting works with such incendiary themes published would be almost impossible.

On the controversial strategies employed by Algerian nationalists, Sénac made few specific observations. He did comment, however, on nationalists' use of violence. Violence was not the intellectual's way he implied in "Les Intellectuels algériens et la Révolution," but they must not dissociate themselves from the peasants and the *moujahiddin* for whom violence might prove necessary to achieve liberation: "Of course, certain excesses and certain errors risk compromising the spiritual values that are our central reason for acting as we do and the cornerstone of the Revolution," he conceded. He could not approve of actions that "diminish the conscience of man, his dignity and his grandeur," but he could "nevertheless refuse to condemn those of our brothers whom the ignominy of colonialism, broken promises and the stubborn and arrogant blindness of privileged people have sometimes pushed to the extremities of despair, anger and, on occasion, hatred."[33] Violence might be committed in the cause of independence, but he saw it as a response to the exactions committed by French authorities—rape, torture, and executions— and to more than a century of colonialist violence. Violence was not for Sénac, as it was for Fanon, a cathartic and purificatory part of decolonization nor a strategy for forging a new nation.[34] Independence was the sole legitimate aim even if regrettable tactics must contribute to its realization. Independence would bring about the liberation of the Algerians and the French. Paradoxically, only independence could ensure the safeguarding in Algeria of the European culture that Sénac valued. To these ends pieds-noirs must not fight against the nationalists but with them.

Sénac's manifestos are powerful documents of resistance to colonialism, written from the inside. They are not systematic expositions of an anticolonialist or revolutionary theory, although echoes of Fanon, Albert Memmi, and Marxist critics of capitalist colonialism can be heard. They are intended to appeal to pieds-noirs in terms that they could understand. As such they display cogency in employing repeated themes and vocabulary (for example, "blindness," "imposture") targeted at the emotions of the Français d'Algérie.

Claude Liauzu has identified several characteristics of pieds-noirs who became FLN sympathizers.[35] First, most came from a modest background, and this fits Sénac. Sénac's mother (to whom he paid a touching tribute in Ebauche du père) was a seamstress and cleaning lady; his father might have been a barber. Sénac was an illegitimate child, and his mother moved from Béni-Saf to Oran to cover her shame at the pregnancy. Sénac grew up in no more exalted circumstances than those portrayed by Camus in Le Premier homme, much of his life spent in financial difficulty. In his autobiographical novel, Sénac wrote movingly about the poverty of his childhood, the financial ruin of his grandfather, the pain of not knowing his father, the hardships of daily life. Sénac later often relied on temporary work or generally on advances from publishers or handouts from friends to make ends meet. Although he owned a tiny shepherd's hut in the Drôme, at times he lived in a state verging on destitution. Liauzu stresses, secondly, the attachment of pro-Algerian pieds-noirs to Algeria itself, an almost religious allegiance to the land and its life. This he traces to the development of *algérianité* in the writings of Randau and the School of Algiers, and to the idea of a pan-Mediterranean civilization, spanning Christian, Muslim, and Jewish cultures, a popular concept that emerged in the 1930s in the work of Gabriel Audisio.[36] Camus's early writings provide a further development of this "Mediterraneanism." Algeria provided a crucible for the molding of a new society in which peoples of different creeds, ethnic backgrounds, and aspirations would live harmoniously and indeed be fused together. The earth itself—the water of the Mediterranean, the heat and light, the products of the soil—would provide raw material for that new "race" engendered by the vagaries of history and shared commitment to the mother country.

These ideas are particularly strong in Sénac's work. He had met Randau, whom he called "my first mentor,"[37] when a young man, he gratefully mentions Audisio, and he was Camus's protégé. An evocation of Algeria is omnipresent in Sénac's poetry and prose, nowhere more lyrically than in "Oran ou les statues sous la peau." Sénac appended a stylized sun to his signature, and references to the physical features of Algiers appear with the seashore, sea urchins, rocks on the beach, the promontory jutting into the harbor (*môle*), the sun, and the young men and women disporting themselves handsomely at Pointe-Pescade. Camus's descriptions in *Noces* (1938) find resonance in Sénac's vocabulary and poetic *mises en scène* and also in the ways in which he frames political writings to appeal to pieds-noirs. Even though Sénac criticized Camus for a Eurocentric perspective on Algerian culture, his own views were not so far removed from those of Camus's vision as he imagined.[38] His sentiments were also close to those of other Algerian writers of his generation, notably his friend Jean Pélégri, author of *Les Oliviers de la justice* (1959).[39]

Prior political experience also played a role, according to Liauzu, in the decision of pieds-noirs about whether to promote or oppose independence. Many FLN sympathizers—and some who were not, such as Camus—had been members of the Communist Party for shorter or longer periods. A large number first experienced a political *prise de conscience* during the Spanish Civil War and were further politicized during the Second World War. The Algerian War of Independence represented the continuation of earlier struggles against a fascism that in North Africa assumed the form of colonialism; this too was a continuation of the struggles of socialists and communists against capitalism and imperialism.

Sénac's ideological positions draw on these traditions. Though too young to know the Spanish Civil War, he must have heard discussions among descendents of immigrants and Republican exiles. Sénac certainly later developed an interest in Spain as seen in his visit in the late 1950s and the "Diwan espagnol" poems in *Matinale de mon peuple* with their specific reference to the Civil War. He was a teenager during the Second World War—an early "Ode à Pétain" marked a brief flirtation with Vichy—and was marked by the Resistance, particularly honored that a Resistance figure such as Char contributed the preface to *Poèmes*. Sénac was never a member of a Socialist or Communist Party (or any other party) and was not extensively schooled in Marxist theory. Marxist ideas were widely disseminated in Algeria and France in the 1950s, and his poems testify to enthusiasm for Ho Chi Minh's Vietnam and Castro's Cuba. Sénac's writings employ a vernacular Marxism with statements about poor whites versus big businessmen, the links between capitalism and colonialism, and the need to construct a socialist society with workers' management committees, agricultural reform, and political and economic restructuring.

Sénac's political writings also draw on a specific French tradition, what he referred to as the "true face" of France. For instance, the "night of 4 August," as mentioned, alludes to the Revolution of 1789, and on several occasions he mentions Saint-Just and the Jacobin constitution for a radical new state. In one essay Sénac referred to Caribbean slave revolts and the independence of Saint-Domingue (Haiti). He quoted Robespierre's famous 1791 statement: "Let the colonies perish, if the colonists, by threats, force us to decree that which accords with their interests"—a response Sénac felt appropriate to diehard promoters of Algérie française.[40] He lamented the "abdication of the revolutionary spirit in France" in finding a solution to the Algerian problem. References to Hugo evoke the writer's opposition to the Second Empire, and Sénac also quoted Léon Bloy on the social role of the author.

Sénac's ideas were imbued before and after 1962 with *tiers-mon-diste* perspectives popular in France. Sénac made explicit reference to the 1955 Bandung Conference of nonaligned countries. Several times he mentioned Gandhi, and one essay quotes from Gamel Abdel Nasser. He wrote a short eulogy of Fanon: "With him, the Third World throws away its European crutches, and advances by itself."[41] Republicanism, socialism, and *tiers-mondisme* merged in Sénac's views, although in a fairly unstructured and untheorized fashion.

Finally, among traits of supporters of independent Algeria, Liauzu writes of their frequentation of Muslims. Those who promoted nationalism and independence had closer, more regular, and more intimate contacts with Muslims than did other pieds-noirs. They included Europeans married to Muslim or Jewish Algerians. *Ebauche du père*, the major document on Sénac's childhood, encompasses comments on anti-Arab racism. He wrote of his family's trips to Arab markets and Jewish shops and recalled that one neighbor disapproved of his mother receiving an Arab woman in her house. The fictionalized memoir, however, does not suggest particularly amicable links between Sénac's family and Arabs, though such a modest family in Oran would have necessarily had more mundane contacts than wealthier pieds-noirs. In the early 1950s in Algiers, Sénac certainly rubbed shoulders with Muslims in the Bab-El-Oued neighborhood where he lived.

As poet, journalist, and broadcaster, Sénac met most of the young writers of his day, including many Arabs. The journal *Soleil,* which he edited, in 1950 published the first writings of the still unknown Mohammed Dib, Kateb Yacine, and Mouloud Féraoun; and Mouloud Mammeri and Aïcha Nekoud figured on the editorial board of *Terrasses,* a short-lived journal with which Sénac was involved. He also became acquainted with artists who illustrated the magazines and whose exhibitions Sénac promoted through reviews.[42] Contacts with nationalists, such as Mustapha Bouhired and Mohammed Larbi Ben M'hidi, developed during the early 1950s as he became more politicized.[43]

Sénac aided up-and-coming Arab writers and painters whose work he published and discussed on radio programs. Sex provided another way of frequenting Arabs. Some commentators elide the question of his homosexuality or accord it little importance. Yet homosexuality was a crucial element in Sénac's relationship with Algerians and in a general sense in his identification with the downtrodden and damned. It took several years after his sexual initiation for Sénac to accept his homosexuality, but he enjoyed a busy sex life in both Algeria and France. Sénac was by no means interested only in Arab men as bedmates, and some of the most significant encounters—such as the affair with Edgard recorded in the 1954 journal—were with Europeans. But Sénac was able to find numerous partners among the young men in Algiers, whom he met in cafés and cinemas or simply lounging around the street or at the beach. Many evenings were spent cruising for partners, his trysts—successful or failed—often inspiring poems. Although the Arabs did not always view sex and love in the same way as did Sénac, he had no difficulty locating partners with whom to share rich erotic pleasures. Some encounters were casual and brief, while others were longer-lasting affairs or bloomed into friendships. A few left Sénac broken-hearted.

Homosexuality thrust Sénac into the margins of polite and re-spectable colonial society, where he discovered others who were denied a place in the colonial order. On late night wanderings in search of sex, he came upon homeless men and women sleeping on the pavements, beggars scrounging for food, Arab children harassed by police. Homosexual liaisons were equivalents of mixed marriages for heterosexuals—they sensitized Sénac to the political conditions of the colonized. The youths who excited his physical desires by their beauty and seductiveness were the ones for whom he wanted to make a political revolution. For Sénac, as for Jean Genet, the connection between homosexual desire and political sympathies was strong and openly avowed.[44] "I dream of bringing together, as in life, erotics and politics," he wrote,[45] and Sénac's work can be interpreted as an effort to reconcile these aspects of his life.

Sénac's published writings of the war years, both poetry and prose, banish eroticism perhaps because he feared talk of homosexuality—still largely regarded in Europe and the Maghreb as a sin, an illness, or a perversion—would compromise the political message. At the same time as his nationalist writings were being published, however, Sénac was composing a private corpus of poetry detailing in increasingly explicit terms sexual desires and pleasures. The erotic ideal thus helped to animate political engagement, and sexual contacts, just as literary and political ones, contributed to development of a nationalist identification with Algerians.

These influences—the poor childhood and lack of social status, allegiance to the Algerian landscape and life, memories of earlier episodes of European political resistance, a leftist political orientation, and the frequentation of Arabs through sexual liaisons and literary collaborations—engendered Sénac's views. His experiences and perspectives, not unsurprisingly, had limitations. The sincerity of Sénac's commitment to Algeria, land and people, cannot be questioned, but he was aware that he remained a special kind of Algerian. Sénac's personal attachment to Algeria was to Algiers and the Europeanized Mediterranean littoral and seldom (either literally or metaphorically) did he move beyond coastal cities and suburbs or go very far into the mountains or the Sahara. It is doubtful that he possessed a profound knowledge of Algerian history and Muslim culture. His work includes a few quotations from classical authors, such as Ibn Khaldun and references to Abd el-Khader, but Sénac's literary orientation was French not Arabic. There is no evidence that he had read the Koran or systematically versed himself in Arabic and Muslim writing. (Some of his personal habits—from drinking alcohol to engaging in homosexual sex—manifestly departed from the religious precepts of traditional Muslims.) He only half-heartedly, and unsuccessfully, attempted to learn Arabic.

From a more critical point, it might even be charged that the vision of a multi-ethnic Algeria and a trans-Mediterranean civilization perpetuated the position of Europeans who had profoundly transformed Algeria through colonization. This idea of Mediterraneanness, attractive though it might be, minimized differences between historically different countries and ethnic groups. For some (as proved increasingly the case in the 1970s and afterward), Islam was not *one* of the religions practiced in Algeria, but *the* religion that should structure life. Sénac, despite nationalist sentiments and support for the revolution, from this perspective represented a vestige of colonial conquest of Algeria, its people, and its culture. Was a man who did not take on Algerian citizenship or learn Arabic really an Algerian?[46] Such views, gaining ground in the 1970s, betrayed Sénac's belief in an inclusive Algeria. The exponents of these positions targeted men like Sénac and, whether or not his death was politically motivated, made his last years highly uncomfortable.

Such harshly critical judgments displace Sénac from the context of the 1950s and early 1960s when most pieds-noirs were espousing openly racist and authoritarian ideas. In the living memory of many Français d'Algérie, the cult of *latinité* held that Algeria was a Roman and Christian country liberated by colonialism in which Arabs and Islam were barely more than interlopers.[47] Sénac by contrast valorized Arabs individually and collectively. His pan-Mediterrneanism gave pride of place to Berbero-Arabic and Islamic culture. He accepted that in an independent country the privileges of a European minority would be severely reduced. He offered wholehearted support for the FLN. At a time of attempted putsches by renegade generals, torture administered by French officers, and the scorched-earth violence of the OAS (Organisation Armée Secrète), these views were extreme departures from standard pied-noir discourse, and Sénac's positions evidenced political and personal courage.

In 1962 Sénac's poem "Aux Héros purs," a celebration of the

revolution, was distributed to the members of newly independent Algeria's national assembly. Sénac returned joyously to Algiers, participated in an exhibition on his *Poésies* at the national library, obtained a government post, and began broadcasting on the same radio station he had left in opposition to French rule eight years earlier. Despite the exodus of pieds-noirs, he retained high hopes for a multicultural society, where some pieds-noirs, including such figures as his close friend Jean de Maisonseul, had decided to remain. The heady years immediately after the war saw a busy Sénac: he edited an anthology, took part in the work of the Algerian writers' union, traveled abroad, broadcast on the radio, and published widely. Some poems written in the enthusiastic aftermath of independence aroused bemused scorn. A line reading "you are as beautiful as a self-management committee" sparked ridicule from such writers as Kateb Yacine (and was later lampooned by Sénac himself). It is difficult not to see some works as agitprop, though Sénac and many of his generation did not find it unwarranted to dedicate literature to the service of political ideals.

Throughout the late 1960s and into the 1970s, Sénac wrote obsessively, although few poems were published. He continued writing art criticism and prefaces but produced relatively little on politics, although he commented in interviews on various developments, including the events of May 1968. Sénac's personal situation, and that of Algeria, had changed. Eroticism appeared in more unbridled form in his works as did overt criticism of the Algerian regime—denunciations of censorship, the corruption of politicians, persistent poverty, and social injustice. Just eight days before his murder, "L'Algérie d'une libération à l'autre" appeared in *Le Monde diplomatique*. Sénac traced the development of French-language Algerian literature in the twentieth century, showing how novels had illuminated political conditions. He acknowledged present-day developments, such as the Arabization of Algerian culture, though with subtle critiques. Yet Sénac remained hopeful for the success of the agrarian revolution, education, the power of literature in a revolutionary society. He added enigmatically: "Creators and producers have the word. Embers have been brought to the bivouac. The ashes pile up. But the wind is picking up from our sands (and the agrarian revolution heralds them), and we will have more than a fire, a great light in which people will throw off their masks and muzzles, and will affirm their deepest identity in images and words."[48]

Sénac's hopes for a new Algeria born of revolution now seem hopelessly idealistic, even misguided. The years since his death have brought extraordinary suffering to the Algerian people. However, the very disappointments of the Algerian revolution perhaps contributed to the lasting, and ironic, significance of Sénac. He exemplifies a cohort of well-intentioned North African and French activists who saw in the Algerian cause not just a war of independence and emancipation from colonialism but promises for a new society. An undoctrinaire socialism would promote social equality in a country marked by extremes of colonialist wealth and local poverty. Representative institutions and national commitment would create a unified and democratic society on the ruins of arbitrary foreign overlordship. International solidarity would advance the cause of the just in Asia, throughout Africa, and elsewhere. Christians, Muslims, and Jews could live together in harmony, their cultures enriching and fertilizing "Mother Algeria." The "right to poetry" would be recognized and celebrated. Dissident sexualities could find free expression. Such high hopes, whether in 1962 or 1968, would fade in coming years.

The dashing of many of these hopes makes Sénac's case an even more poignant example of the failure of the anticolonial idealism of the 1950s and 1960s. Yet his commitment to a dynamic and open

Algeria may also provide, more than three decades after his death, renewed hope for the country whose destiny he embraced. The tolerance, inclusion, and solidarity he espoused provide an alternative to exclusion and domination that have threatened both European and Islamic societies in our own day.

Notes

1. Jean Sénac, *Œuvres poétiques* (Arles: Actes-Sud, 1999), is a comprehensive edition of previously published poetry; Hamid Nacer-Khodja, ed., *Pour une terre possible: Poèmes et autres textes inédits* (Paris: Marsa, 1999), includes poems, prose writings, and some correspondence; and *Visages d'Algérie: Regards sur l'art*, ed. Hamid Nacer-Khodja (Paris: Editions Paris-Méditerranée, 2002), collects Sénac's writings on artists.

2. The most recent, and comprehensive, biography is Emile Temime and Nicole Tuccelli, *Jean Sénac, l'Algérien: Le Poète des deux rives* (Paris: Editions Autrement, 2003). See also the special issue of *Awal, Cahiers d'études berbères* 10 (1993) and Jamel-Eddine Bencheikh and Christiane Chaulet-Achour, *Jean Sénac: Clandestin des deux rives* (Paris: Séguier, 1999). Two essential earlier works are *Poésie au Sud: Jean Sénac et la nouvelle poésie algérienne d'expression française* (Marseille: Archives de la Ville de Marseille, 1983) and *Le Soleil fraternel: Jean Sénac et la nouvelle poésie algérienne d'expression française* (Marseille: Editions du Quai/Jeanne Laffitte, 1985), volumes that came out of an exhibition on the tenth anniversary of Sénac's death. Sénac's work is also discussed in general works on Maghrebin literature, notably in Yvonne Llavador, *La Poésie algérienne de langue française et la guerre d'Algérie* (Lund: CWK Cleerup, 1980); and Jean Déjeux, *Littérature maghrébine de langue française: Introduction générale et auteurs* (Ottawa: Naaman, 1973). See also the sections on Sénac in Assia Djebar, *Le Blanc d'Algérie* (Paris: Albin Michel, 1995), 152–93; Françoise d'Eaubonne, *La Plume et le bâillon. Violette Leduc, Nicolas Genka, Jean Sénac: Trois écrivains victimes de la censure* (Paris: L'Esprit frappeur, 2000); and passing references in Charles Bonn, *La Littérature algérienne de langue française et ses lectures: Imaginaire et Discours d'idées* (Ottawa: Naaman, 1974).

3. Michel Castillo, *Algérie, l'extase et le sang* (Paris: Stock, 2002), includes the play "La Répétition" and the author's "Lettre ouverte sur la censure." The film is *Le Soleil assassiné* (2003), directed by Abdelkrim Bahloul.

4. Nacer-Khodja, *Pour une terre possible*, 323–80, contains a detailed chronology of Sénac's life. Sénac's novel *Ebauche du père* (Paris: Gallimard, 1989) is largely autobiographical and covers his childhood. On the circumstances of Sénac's death, see Jean-Pierre Péroncel-Hugoz, *Assassinat d'un poète* (Paris: Editions du Quai/Jeanne Laffitte, 1983).

5. "Citoyens de beauté," in Sénac, *Œuvres poétiques*, 399.

6. Robert Aldrich, *Colonialism and Homosexuality* (London: Routledge, 2003), 375–91.

7. Sénac has received little attention in historians' accounts of the Algerian war and its background. He is not mentioned in Alastair Horne's *A Savage War of Peace: Algeria, 1954–1962* (London: Macmillan, 1977) or in such works as Jeannine Verdès-Leroux, *Les Français d'Algérie de 1830 à nos jours: Une page d'histoire déchirée* (Paris: Fayard, 2001). Nor is he discussed in Hervé Hamon and Patrick Rotman, *Les Porteurs de valises: La Résistance française à la Guerre d'Algérie* (Paris: Albin Michel, 1979) or Jean-Pierre Rioux and Jean-François Sirinelli, eds., *La Guerre d'Algérie et les intellectuals français* (Brussels: Editions Complexe, 1991). James D. Le Sueur, *Uncivil War: Intellectuals and Identity Politics during the Decolonization of Algeria* (Philadelphia: University of Pennsylvania Press, 2001), provides a four-line biography in a footnote and discusses Sénac's dispute with Camus (113–15). In Jean-Pierre Rioux, ed., *La Guerre d'Algérie et les Français* (Paris: Fayard, 1990), Sénac is mentioned by Alain-Gérard Slama, in "La Guerre d'Algérie en littérature ou la comédie des masques," only parenthetically as an "authentic poet, a homosexual, a touching bastard of Gide and Maurice Sachs, who died by assassination in Algiers and who did not . . . leave a great *œuvre* on Algeria, as if, because of a certain incandescence of the soul, there was no longer any room for the imagination" (601)—a curious judgment, to say the least. Lack of greater attention suggests that Sénac was not a major figure among French supporters of Algerian nationalism and may result from the scattered nature of his writings and their tardy publication. But one wonders whether his "incandescence" and his homosexuality have marginalized Sénac in standard accounts.

8. "Lettre d'un jeune poète algérien," in Nacer-Khodja, *Pour une terre possible*, 241–42.

9. "Les Assassins en Algérie," in Nacer-Khodja, *Pour une terre possible*, 243–44. "*France la Douce*"—"sweet" or "gentle" France—alluded perhaps to the famous song of the Resistance during the Second World War, "Douce France."

10. Jean Sénac, *Journal Alger, janvier-juillet 1954* (n.p.: Editions Novetlé, 1996), 28–29.

11. Sénac, *Journal Alger*, 71–72; compare 78–79.

12. "Carnets Paris (1954–1955)," in Nacer-Khodja, *Pour une terre possible*, 247.

13. Nacer-Khodja, in the chronology in *Pour une terre possible*, 342.

14. Quoted in Le Sueur, *Uncivil War*, 113. Sénac's letter here provides no further details. Did the FLN think that Sénac would be ineffective in the *maquis*, that he could better serve the cause in other capacities, or perhaps that his personal life might not be compatible with such resistance work?

15. Daniel in *Le Soleil fraternel*, 142–43.

16. Sénac, *Ebauche du père*, 105–16.

17. During the war years in Paris, Sénac met Jacques Miel, who became his adopted son and literary executor. I would like to thank Monsieur and Madame Miel for speaking at length with me about Sénac and showing me documents concerning him.

18. Philip Dine, "French Culture and the Algerian War: Mobilizing Icons," *Journal of European Studies* 28 (1998): 51.

19. The dating of Sénac's writings is taken from Nacer-Khodja's chronology in Sénac, *Œuvres poétiques*, 339–54. Nacer-Khodja dates the writing of several later collections to this period: *Les Leçons d'Egard* (1954, published in 1983), *Les Désordres* (1952–56, published 1972), *La Rose et l'Ortie* (1959–61, published 1964), and *Le Torrent de Baïn* (1959–62, published in 1962).

20. Sénac, *Ebauche du père*, 130.

21. Sénac, *Ebauche du père*, 71.

22. *Matinale de mon peuple* is reprinted in Sénac, *Œuvres poétiques*, 250–339.

23. Yvonne Llavador, "Le Manifeste poétique de Jean Sénac: *Le Soleil sous les armes*," *Awal* 10 (1993): 25–29.

24. Jean Sénac, *Le Soleil sous les armes: Eléments d'une poésie de la résistance algérienne* (Rodez: Editions Subervie, 1957).

25. Dine, "French Culture and the Algerian War," 51–68.

26. Reprinted in *Poésie au Sud*, 55–56.

27. "Lettre à un jeune Français d"Algérie," *L'Esprit* 3 (1956), reprinted in *Poésie au Sud*, 60–63. Sénac was in particularly good company in the pages of *Esprit*, which published comprehensively on the Algerian war and was favorable to the nationalist cause. See David L. Schalk, *War and the Ivory Tower: Algeria and Vietnam* (New York: Oxford University Press, 1991), 72–97.

28. The correspondence has been collected with an analysis by Hamid Nacer-Khodja, *Albert Camus, Jean Sénac ou le fils rebelle* (Paris: Edif 2000/Paris Méditerranée, 2004).

29. "Camus au service de Lacoste," reprinted in *Poésie au Sud*, 69, 71–72.

30. *Poésie au Sud*, 72.

31. It is noteworthy that Sénac places *pieds-noirs* in inverted commas: the term still had a derogatory sound for many Français d'Algérie.

32. "'Pieds-noirs,' mes frères," reprinted in *Poésie au Sud*, 74–76.

33. "Les Intellectuels algériens et la Révolution," reprinted in *Poésie au Sud*, 68.

34. Sénac was closer to Emmanuel Levinas and Tahar Ben Jelloun than to Fanon and Sartre, to use an alignment suggested by James D. Le Sueur in "Beyond Decolonization? The Legacy of the Algerian Conflict and the Transformation of Identity in Contemporary

France," *Historical Reflections* 28 (2002): 277–91. Ben Jelloun, incidentally, has written admiringly of Sénac's work in a preface to Péroncel-Hugoz, *Assassinat d'un poète*, 7–9, and "Le Poète, le Corps, la Mort," in *Le Soleil Fraternel*, 81–84.

35. Claude Liauzu, *Passeurs de rives: Changements d'identité dans le Maghreb colonial* (Paris: L'Harmattan, 2000), 108–15. Liauzu has an interesting section on Audisio, Camus, and Sénac (94–106) but does not apply his categories to Sénac. On the motivations for support of the Algerian cause, as remembered by participants in the campaign, see also Martin Evans, *The Memory of Resistance: French Opposition to the Algerian War (1954–1962)* (Oxford: Berg, 1997).

36. See Philip Dine's chapter in this volume.

37. Sénac, *Ebauche du père*, 109.

38. Similarly, as Patricia Lorcin has pointed out, Camus's views were not so removed from those of Louis Bertrand's vision of *latinité* as he thought (Patricia M. E. Lorcin, "Rome and France in Africa: Recovering Colonial Algeria's Latin Past," *French Historical Studies* 25 [2002]: 295–329.)

39. See Pélégri's introduction to Sénac's *Journal Alger*, 9–12, and his tribute to Sénac, "Le Temple de Janus," in *Le Soleil fraternel*, 155–56; and Dominique Le Boucher, ed., *Jean Sénac, Jean Pélégri—Les Deux Jean: Jean Sénac, l'homme soleil, Jean Pélégri, l'homme caillou. Correspondance 1962–1973* (Clapiers: Chèvre feuille étoilée, 2002).

40. From "Le Peuple algérien face à l'imposture," in Nacer-Khodja, *Pour une terre possible*, 264.

41. "Bonjour Fanon!" in *Poésie au Sud*, 76.

42. Sénac, *Visages d'Algérie*.

43. Nacer-Khodja, *Pour une terre possible*, 333–36.

44. The connection between homosexuality and anticolonialism can also be seen in the stances of Pierre Herbart and Daniel Guérin. See Aldrich, *Homosexuality and Colonialism*.

45. Sénac, *Ebauche du père*, 43.

46. The question of citizenship is a thorny one. Sénac, like many *pieds-noirs*, objected to the provision of the Algerian constitution that restricted automatic citizenship to those of Algerian (Muslim) parentage, although making it available to others if they applied. Sénac felt that having been born in Algeria and having supported independence, he ought not be expected to make this request. It is unclear whether he officially requested citizenship. Although in possession of Algerian travel papers, he retained French identity documents.

47. See Patricia Lorcin, "Rome and France in Africa."

48. "L'Algérie d'une libération à l'autre," *Le Monde diplomatique*, 22 August 1973, reprinted in *Poésie au Sud*, 110–14.

8

Counterviolence and the Ethics of Nomadism

Malika Mokeddem's Reconstruction of Algerian Identity

TRUDY AGAR-MENDOUSSE

> Writing should produce a becoming-woman as atoms of woman-
> hood capable of crossing and impregnating an entire social field,
> and of contaminating an entire social field, and of contaminating
> men, and of sweeping them up in that becoming.—Gilles Deleuze
> and Félix Guattari, *A Thousand Plateaus*

Otto Heim asserts that addressing the theme of violence in
literature answers a decisive challenge. Quoting James Ber-
tram, Heim claims that "the power to shock is surely one of the
marks of an adult and living literature."[1] French-language literature
from Algeria has repeatedly taken up the challenge of its own violent
origins, emerging as a literature of confrontation, contestation, and
condemnation. Malika Mokeddem, an Algerian woman living in
exile in France, divides her time between writing and practicing
medicine. She is the daughter of illiterate nomads and the author of
eight novels and narratives. Her experiences during the Algerian War
of Independence are subject matter for her first published work, *Les
Hommes qui marchent*.[2] Although Mokeddem places this novel in

her first phase of writing, calling it "a storyteller's novel," in contrast to her second phase of writing, which she qualifies as a literature of "urgency" in response to the violence of the early 1990s in Algeria,[3] *Les Hommes*, like her later novels, directly addresses problems of violence. It is in this autobiographical novel that Mokeddem presents her most sustained portrayal of the impact of colonial violence on Algerian society and, in particular, on Algerian women. She traces the history of the Ajalli clan, a fictionalized version of her own family, through some of the violent upheavals of the second half of the twentieth century: the Second World War, the Algerian War of Independence, and the Algerian Civil War.[4] The novel's heroine, Leila, just like the author herself, attended school for the first time shortly before the Algerian War of Independence, in the village of Kenadsa, where the French army had established a large barracks. The war was the background of Mokeddem's childhood, just as it is the setting of *Les Hommes*. A reading of *Les Hommes*, with particular attention to Mokeddem's account of violence and native female identity, will reveal how this Franco-Algerian author accommodates violence in her writing and how she appropriates this violence to her own strategic ends.

In *Les Hommes*, Mokeddem (re)writes the history of Algeria, from the beginnings of the War of Independence to the genesis of the independent Algerian state. Through the violence of this text, she seeks to "decolonize" Algerian identity. In the place of the "native" of the colonial period,[5] she asserts an Algerian identity that is distinctly hybrid. To counter the symbolic violence of the colonial system, the process of decolonization must adopt its own strategies of violence, Frantz Fanon argued in *Les damnés de la terre*. Fanon asserts that decolonization, which is a cultural evolution, must always be a violent phenomenon whose instigators struggle primarily for the liberation of the nation.[6] *Les Hommes* may be considered an act of violence since Mokeddem's project asserts itself as a chapter in the ongoing decolonization of Algeria. Through covert strategies of resistance, Mokeddem accommodates, subverts, and even transforms the symbolic violence inherent in the colonial and patriarchal systems to produce a creative space of hybridity.[7]

In *Les Hommes* Mokeddem exposes the functioning of colonial discourse in which the colonized is codified under the sign of alterity in order to articulate and justify the European's authority. The author demonstrates that colonial ideology is dependent on what Abdul JanMohamed has called the Manichean Allegory: the construction of an essentialist metonymy of the native in which s/he is configured as the "other" of the European. The allegory is built upon binary oppositions in which one term of the pair is negatively connoted and valued.[8] Similarly feminist theory has argued that the "masculine" is constructed in relation to the feminine "other" in a hierarchy of opposing qualities where the masculine is dominant and valued.[9] In Mokeddem's text the pairing of terms such as civilized/savage, individual/community, written/oral, and so on exists within a dichotomy dividing colonizer and colonized into two radically opposed camps, recalling Fanon's vision of the colonial world as two opposed and mutually exclusive zones.[10] Mokeddem then superimposes a second opposition onto her dichotomy, that of gender. The colonizer is associated with the positively valued notions of civilization, the written word, reason, individuality, and the masculine. The colonized is associated with the weak, the irrational, the powerless, and the feminine. Mokeddem's double dichotomy reflects the double oppression of the female Algerian by both imperial and patriarchal ideologies, a situation that some feminists have referred to as a "double colonization."[11]

The author-narrator of *Les Hommes* puts on the mask of the colonizer by reiterating violent colonial discourse in an act of subversive mimicry.[12] Mokeddem adopts a master-slave dialectic, which codifies the native as the slave of the colonizer, and depicts colonial relations in terms of a totalizing metaphor, according to which the native is part of a homogenous mass. When Madame Perez, the French settler who employs Leila's father, asks Zohra, Leila's grandmother, if she really believes she is better than the other "dirty Arabs," she tears down individual difference and imposes on Zohra a stereotype imbued with racism and lack of understanding.[13] The dehumanization of the native in colonial discourse is further emphasized by Mokeddem's strategic adoption of a zoological vocabulary that echoes the colonial opposition of human colonizer to animal colonized. As Fanon has remarked, it was easier for the French to sanction the murder and torture of Algerians if colonial discourse succeeded in its attempt to "animalize" the native, which Fanon saw as Manichaeism taken to its logical extreme.[14] For the colonial oppressors in *Les Hommes*, the natives are nothing but "jackals"; they are enclosed in the police compound at Kenadsa like "beasts" before being locked up "like sheep." Female natives too are animalized when a French girl's mother says that giving them an education is like giving jam to pigs.[15]

Moreover, Mokeddem reiterates the colonial male/female opposition by casting the native as feminine. Traditionally conceived "feminine" qualities characterize the native in the text, particularly in terms of the female activity of storytelling. Zohra, the guardian of nomadism and the oral tradition in *Les Hommes*, underlines the supremacy of the spoken word in nomadic culture when she states, "our story doesn't lie between ink and paper. It explores our memories incessantly and inhabits our voices."[16] Orality, the domain of the native female in *Les Hommes*, is in an antagonistic relationship with the written in colonial ideology, as "proof" of the nonhistory of the native. Mokeddem repeats this opposition when she stresses the power of the written word in the colonial educational system to banish native identity and culture. Mokeddem, speaking through her character Leila, denounces the "aberrations" of colonial schooling. She accuses not only "the litany of 'our ancestors the Gauls'"[17] but also texts, dictations, readings, and subjects for drawings of evoking only France. The scene depicting a visit by General de Gaulle underscores the political stakes of such an education. The town's schools organize a welcome for the general; the children are taught *"La Marseillaise"* and are instructed to make French flags and to wave them when de Gaulle arrives in Kenadsa. Leila, the daughter of an FLN militant, is encouraged to wave her flag while shouting "l'Algérie française," the slogan of the anti-independence *pieds-noirs*.[18] Only when her father becomes furious after seeing her with the flag does Leila start to understand the political implications of the schools' involvement in the welcome ceremony:

> "That crowns it all! My own daughter under my roof with a French flag!" In the face of her father's fury, Leila realized that she hadn't simply been part of a collective game. That actions and words had become stakes.[19]

Shared images of prisons and slavery underline the similarity between native and female oppression. The native, codified in the text as the prisoner and slave of the French, resembles the female Algerian who is imprisoned in the home and guarded by male surveillance and oppressive "protection,"[20] which ensures her compliance with relations of domination.

To the colonial oppositions of colonizer/colonized, human/animal, and masculine/feminine, Mokeddem adds a further binary opposition of nomad and citizen (*sédentaire*), where "nomad" is the positively valued term. These cultures are distinguished from each other principally in terms of radically opposed conceptions of time and space. The nomad lives in perpetual movement in an immeasurable natural space. The citizen lives closed in by the walls of his house within a town. The space of the town is viewed with suspicion by the nomad who avoids this urban enclosure for fear of being contaminated by its alleged immorality. The presence of the colonizer amplifies the danger this space represents, a space that could be called "striated," to borrow Deleuze's term. A striated space is a bordered space that is delineated by closed intervals; in such spaces, the trajectory is always already determined by the points of passage.[21] A smooth or nomadic space, in contrast, is one in which the trajectory determines the points of passage. Colonialism attempts to impose European cultural structures on the nomadic space, seeking to "territorialize" the desert. Colonial territorialization is powerfully evoked in Mokeddem's second novel, *Le siècle des sauterelles*, in the image of the monstrous French train. "El-machina," at once animalized and humanized, is a "devilish wood and iron reptile" that violates the domain of the nomads, bringing men and weapons right into the heart of their country.[22] To emphasize the threat that the train represents, Mokeddem links its presence to that of locusts, the trope of the novel's title that codifies violence and destruction in its many forms and whose referents include soldiers, settlers, brigands, and Nazis (and Leila's brothers, in *Les Hommes*[23]). In the following passage, the soldiers exiting the train are compared to locusts: "At each station, it spits, farts, burps, and from all its orifices, defecates the men in yellow who infest the place like locusts. Not only are they the color of locusts, they are also as voracious and have a propensity to move about in clouds that devastate the very dignity of the ᶜarbi. They have peppered the rail line with forts."[24]

Deleuze and Guattari see the nomad as the deterritorialized human "par excellence," a warrior who combats territorialization, colonialism, and civilization. In *Les Hommes*, Mokeddem presents herself as a Deleuzian nomad-warrior[25] who restakes a claim on nomadic space for the native female.

Mokeddem embraces counterviolence as a response to the violence she unveils in her text, but her writing is no Fanonian call to arms. She rejects physical violence as being restrictive. In her third novel, *L'interdite*, female counterviolence is staged in a scene where women respond to male violence with verbal and physical violence, first by insulting and threatening the mayor, then by burning down the town hall.[26] While the novel's heroine, Sultana, feels solidarity with the women, she refuses to join their resistance group because to do so would entail sacrificing her freedom to the village's customs and conventions.

Instead of proposing physical violence as a counterstrategy, Mokeddem chooses to "slough off the native"[27] through symbolic violence. In *Les Hommes* she deconstructs and subverts the traditional oppositions and the existing hierarchy through strategies of equivocation, ambiguity, and imagery. In this way Mokeddem commits an act of what André Brink has called "violative" violence, in other words actions through which a justifying or sanctioning authority (in this case, male and colonial authority) is broken, interrupted, or profaned.[28] However, Mokeddemian counterviolence is not a negative force but rather one that generates creative power. Brink, stressing the interrelatedness of destruction and creation, asserts that violence loses the one-dimensionality of its usual implication of the negative and destructive use of force when it becomes the expression of a search for meaning. In Mokeddem's revolutionary writing, the search for meaning (her creative counterviolence) is an attempt to inscribe a new native female identity that would escape the symbolic violence of male and colonial ideology. The totalizing binary relationships of colonial and patriarchal discourses are violated and subverted to make way for a hybrid space where the native/the woman is no longer defined in terms of what s/he is not.

Fanon has insisted that the colonial world is founded on a primary Manichaeism according to which the colonizer constructs an embodiment of evil out of the colonized.[29] In his analysis, the colonized also adopts this totalizing metaphor with regard to the colonizer, who is the "enemy." For Fanon, the primary Manichaeism remains intact during the period of the struggle for independence: "On voit donc que le manichéisme premier qui régissait la société coloniale est conservé intact dans la période de décolonisation. C'est que le colon ne cesse jamais d'être l'ennemi, l'antagoniste, très précisément l'homme à abattre."[30] Mokeddem, on the other hand, refuses any antagonistic opposition between the colonizer and the colonized that would repeat the totalizing metaphor of good and evil. She underlines for instance the ambiguity of the French military presence in Algeria. The kindness of individual soldiers contrasts with the terrifying rumors Leila hears about Bigeard's men. The girl is confused and cannot reconcile the soldiers' gifts of candy with the bombs that kill children.[31] The author describes the ravages of colonial violence, which in Leila's dreams disfigures even the natural environment of the nomads, driving away the salt caravans to replace them with groaning sounds, whipped up by the wind. The dune so loved by Leila breathes "like an unhealthy lung" and explodes "in an enormous whirlwind."[32] Yet Mokeddem also evokes the benefits of this violence, planting in her text an equivocality that works to interrogate colonial and patriarchal binary oppositions. She affirms that, thanks to the French educational system and French culture, Leila is able to escape the destiny of other Algerian women: the veil, the harem, and incarceration. Similarly Mokeddem sees her own liberty as resulting from the colonial imposition of culture: "The eldest girl in a family of many boys, I realized very early on that my parents (and beyond them, society) had a preference for boys. Secretly I was mortified, consumed by this injustice. I was condemned to the lot of every eldest girl: to become a model of submission. School provided me an escape, one that I hadn't imagined, from the deadlock of this fate."[33] In this way, Mokeddem implicitly counters Fanon's claim that colonial domination effectively "obliterated" indigenous culture, that domination was total.[34]

Mokeddem subverts the colonial codification of the native under the sign of animal as well as the patriarchal codification of the female under this same sign by employing a zoological vocabulary with positive connotations. This allows her to cut down the primitive human/animal opposition with the tool of equivocality. The animalization of Djelloul-Bouhaloufa, Leila's poet ancestor in *Les Hommes*, is positively connoted as an espousal of the imagination when Djelloul invents a story that turns his banishment from the tribe into a legend. The nickname "Bouhaloufa," which means "pig man," is claimed by his sons, who make it "a point of honor" to preserve this name.[35] Mokeddem also enacts the humanization of animals upon the pig's death. Djelloul avenges the animal's condemnation in the Koran by passing it off as a human, burying it in the cemetery and getting it blessed by the mosque. Djelloul's sacrilegious act undermines not only colonial codification but also religious tradition and customary prejudice. To deconstruct further the codification under the sign of the animal, Mokeddem reverses the opposition, codifying the colonizer under this same sign. Zohra, for example, pays homage to General de Gaulle by calling him a "camel," a metaphor that suggests neither derision nor insult.[36]

In binary patriarchal thought, woman is defined as man's Other, implying a radical separation between the feminine and the masculine. Mokeddem deconstructs this gender opposition in order to confound the two sexes, producing a writing of *bisexuality*, a concept proposed by Hélène Cixous as an alternative to destructive masculine hegemony.[37] A writing of bisexuality opens up the possibility of a new relationship between the Self and the Other and allows their coexistence. Bisexuality is the nonexclusion of sexual difference, a scrambling of opposites that Mokeddem enacts in *Les Hommes*. She assigns new gender roles to several of her characters: Leila flees housework to read on the dune, her aunt Saadia becomes the owner of a small business, and Djelloul takes on the role of mother to the pig. Furthermore, the negatively valued female term in the gender opposition is reversed to take on positivity associated with violence, rebellion, creativity, and freedom. Imagination in *Les Hommes* is established as a dynamic, feminine attribute, especially in the form of storytelling, an activity that passes tribal memory and culture from a woman to her descendants. Even men of imagination and sensitivity are feminized in the text. Both Leila's uncle Khellil and Bouhaloufa are scorned by their tribe for their "feminine" temperament. When Khellil's emotional distress leads him to attempt suicide, the attempt is willfully ignored by his family, and the narrator remarks that "men were only permitted displays of machismo and virility . . . any manifestation of suffering from them was denounced as sentimentalism."[38]

As we have seen, Mokeddem's counterviolence is a creative force that calls into question the authority of colonial and patriarchal discourse to name and inscribe the native female. Mokeddem then seizes this very authority in order to assert a positively valued female and native identity. She articulates this new identity in terms of an ethical system that she terms "nomadism" and that she distinguishes from nomadism understood as the lifestyle of the ethnic group that wanders in the Algerian desert. The Mokeddemian nomad, who supersedes the colonial native, comes into existence in the hybrid space opened up by Mokeddem's writing of ambiguity and

equivocality. Hybridity is codified as the nonexclusion of difference, the coexistence of seemingly opposed terms such as male/
female and human/animal. The desert is the space of ethical nomadism and the locus of hybridity whose duality is reflected in the
very temperatures of the desert.[39] Like the space they occupy, the
characters who inhabit Mokeddem's writing are hybrid. Zohra's
"nomadism of words" sends her wandering in an *entre-deux* as
she points out at the beginning of the novel: "Nevertheless, bear
in mind that storytellers are whimsical beings. They play around
with everything. Even their own past. They doctor it, remodel it in
the space between their dreams and reality's perdition. They exist
only in this in-between. A 'between' that's continually displaced.
Constantly reinvented."[40] The French education Leila receives instills
in her a duality, "with its bitter-sweet joys and its oppositions." Leila
exists in an entre-deux between the worlds of the nomads and the
citizens; like the educated Mahmoud in *Le siècle*, she is "between
the sedentary and the nomadic, between orality, the camaraderie
of stories, and the solitary bewitchment of writing, between flight
and revolt, always at the junction of complementarities, always
at the point of contact between contraries."[41] Mokeddem asserts
hybridity as a characteristic of nomadism, whose ethical principles
are tolerance, imagination and independence.

Intolerance, whether it be refusal to accept racial, religious, or
gender differences, is strongly condemned by Mokeddem as a refusal
to "recognize other paths" and is thus a constraint on nomadic
wandering, as Leila's grandfather Ahmed le Sage avows before
he departs for Mecca: "I will also ask him [Allah] to watch over
our children: may they never know that most formidable of evils,
intolerance, the life that amputates itself from its riches and that
recognizes but one path among the many thousands."[42]

In ethnic nomadism, on the other hand, the imagination is viewed with suspicion as a dangerous (female) characteristic. Their intolerance of the imagination leads the Ajalli clan to banish Djelloul after he discovered a passion for pre-Islamic poetry during his life in Tlemcen, a city the text associates not only with the blossoming of Djelloul's imagination but also with the perfume of women and their veiled silhouettes. His banishment sends him into another form of wandering: that of words. Verbal nomadism, like physical nomadism, has the power to protect the storyteller and his or her listener from the "epidemic" of immobility. For Leila the nomadism of written words liberates the mind and the imagination. It is her "only hope" of survival and a "line of flight" from masculine oppression and her colonized condition.[43] Her grandfather sees learning the language and culture of the oppressor as a weapon of defense for the native. Indeed, the French book serves as a shield that Leila is able to hold between herself and the daily tasks that threaten to engulf her: "She had nothing but the paper ramparts of books to shield herself from all the bottles, the soups, the cries, the pee. Nothing but their stories as journeys."[44] *Les Hommes* is in itself scriptural nomadism on the part of the author who wears the mask of her character Leila. Leila answers Zohra's last request that she walk with the nomads by becoming a storyteller, voyaging back into the past of the women in her family to produce the text of *Les Hommes*.

Mokeddem criticizes ethnic nomadism not only for its refusal of the imagination and for its intolerance but also for the way it demands that the individual's interests be sacrificed to those of the group. Ethical nomadism in contrast embraces individual independence, a principle incarnated by Djelloul and codified in the image of the "grain of sand" or "grain of madness." Those who possess the grain of sand refuse limits on their freedom to act and to think just as nomadic space refuses spatial and temporal limits. The grain saves Djelloul from incomprehension and pressure to conform. Leila's aunt Zina assures her that only the "grain of madness" can save a female Algerian, citing Saadia as a woman whose *folie* helped her escape terrible oppression (incarceration in a brothel). For Leila and Saadia the call to freedom is so strong that whenever it comes up against an obstacle to its realization it manifests itself as aggression, which is read as madness by other characters. Martine Delvaux has underlined the prominence and power of madness in francophone women's writing, suggesting that "the topos of madness" can also be read as a creative "third space."[45] In Mokeddem's writing, hybridity, madness, and creativity are indeed closely interrelated. As Leila becomes more and more trapped between her two worlds—the tantalizing freedom offered to her by her schooling and the repressive traditional female role her parents wish to impose on her—she becomes aggressive, pounding her stomach, shouting, starving herself, and threatening to commit suicide. She only calms down at night, when she barricades herself in the guest room of her house to spend the entire night reading. The conflict at the heart of the entre-deux in which Leila lives seems insurmountable until a moment of epiphany reveals a possible solution. At her brother's marriage Leila comes face to face with the three representative groups who constitute her origins—the nomads, native citizens, and humanist Europeans. After the initial confusion she feels upon contemplating these three origins, Leila realizes that the multiple facets of her identity could be reconciled in a new type of nomadism, one that would lead her along the path of Western culture and female emancipation. The embracing of a Western, humanistic notion of female independence does not isolate Leila from her nomadic origins, since she recognizes her reading of European literature as a sign of nomadic tolerance and openness. This revelation of the embracing of hybridity as reconciliation of multiple identitary origins is evoked in quasireligious terms. Leila is finally able to perceive the nomadic light that contains the presence of her ancestors: "She was puzzled for a moment; then it suddenly dawned on her that the appeal of far-off places and of the unknown was the very essence of the nomads' life. The idea made Leila smile. And, as she lifted her eyes skyward, the light seemed to her at that instant to be the quintessence of nomad gazes that watched over the open horizons, as so often evoked by Zohra."[46]

Although characterized by aggression, Mokeddem's indomitable heroines do not, as we have seen, turn to physical violence against others. The ethical nomad chooses instead to turn her back on physical violence, just as she turns her back on the male town. She responds to oppression by following paths of new possibilities— nomadic flight from territorialization. Leila is able to follow lines of flight (reading and dreaming in the desert) to escape the oppression of both the colonial and patriarchal systems. Mokeddemian lines of flight are always associated with creativity—for example, Yasmine's legendary wanderings are accompanied by her songs and Benichou's lute at the end of *Le siècle*, and Nora's navigations in *N'Zid* give her space to draw.[47] Thus, as well as "answering back" colonial and patriarchal ideologies in a violent interrogation of their authority, Mokeddem also *interrupts* their discourse by drawing lines of flight from oppression. This disruption is a highly creative form of counterviolence that breaks apart the relationship of oppressor and victim to open up new paths of possibility.

Les Hommes has a truly revolutionary dimension as a decolonizing force of counterviolence. By unveiling the mechanisms of the epistemic violence of colonial and patriarchal discourse, Mokeddem is able to subvert these mechanisms to create a hybrid space of inclusive differences. She is concerned to violate binary oppositions; yet, in so doing, she establishes one of her own: the nomad and the sédentaire. As Deleuze and Guattari put it, this involves "a problem of writing"—dualisms are "necessary enemies" we invoke in order to challenge other dualisms.[48] Having violated authoritative discourse, Mokeddem then seizes its power to name and inscribe. She rejects the native female configured as alterity in order to inscribe the nomad warrior. Mokeddem codifies the nomad as feminine, reminding us of the Deleuzian association of women with creativity in the formula "becoming-woman." For Deleuze and Guattari, "all becomings begin with and pass through becoming-woman."[49] Mokeddem's feminized nomad adheres to an ethical code that provides the strategies to fight back against oppressive forces: espousal of difference, creativity, and lines of flight. Like Homi Bhabha, she insists on the creative power of hybridity, embracing alterity, femininity, and madness. Mokeddem's narrative of the colonization of Algeria is not the scenario of a pure violence of appropriation and oppression, it implies instead a creative counterviolence. Mokeddem produces a writing of nomadism, whose principles assert a new identity to counter symbolic violence.

Notes

The epigraph is from Gilles Deleuze and Félix Guattari, *A Thousand Plateaus*, trans. Brian Massumi (Minneapolis: University of Minnesota Press, 1987), 276. Published in French as *Capitalisme et schizophrénie. Mille Plateaux* (Paris: Editions de Minuit, 1980).

1. Otto Heim, *Writing along Broken Lines: Violence and Ethnicity in Contemporary Maori Fiction* (Auckland Australia: Auckland University Press, 1998), 11.

2. Malika Mokeddem, *Les Hommes qui marchent* (Paris: Ramsay, 1990).

3. Christiane Chaulet-Achour, "Portrait," in *Malika Mokeddem: Envers et contre tout*, ed. Yolande Aline Helm (Paris: L'Harmattan, 2000), 185–98. Unless otherwise noted, all translations are my own.

4. The autobiographical nature of *Les Hommes* has been confirmed by the author in interviews. In the first draft version of the text, the members of her nomad family had their real names, and the story was told in the first person. See Chaulet-Achour, "Portrait," 24.

5. Fanon has shown that, since "native" is a metaphorical construct of colonial discourse, the native must disappear along with colonialism. According to Fanon, "Le colon et le colonisé sont de vieilles connaissances. Et, de fait, le colon a raison quand il dit 'les' connaître. C'est le colon qui fait et qui continue à faire le colonisé." *Les damnés de la terre* (Paris: Gallimard, 1991), 66.

6. Fanon, *Les damnés de la terre*, 65.

7. Homi Bhabha has underscored the creative potential of hybridity. In an interview with J. Rutherford, Bhabha stressed that the importance of hybridity lies in the "third space," which enables the creation of new positions. Jonathon Rutherford, "The Third Space: Interview with Homi Bhabha," in *Identity, Community, Culture, Difference*, ed. Jonathon Rutherford (London: Lawrence and Wishart, 1990), 207–21.

8. Abdul R. JanMohamed, "The Economy of the Manichean Allegory: The Function of Racial Difference in Colonialist Literature," *Critical Inquiry* 12, no. 1 (1985): 59–87.

9. Following Simone de Beauvoir's famous assertion, made in *Le deuxième sexe* (Paris: Gallimard, 1949), that one is not born a woman but becomes one, feminist critics have considered gender as a cultural construction rather than a "natural" category and theorized the consequences of a nonessentialist understanding of gender and sexuality. Monique Wittig has taken Beauvoir's assertion a step further in arguing for the deconstruction and indeed eradication of "woman" as a category in order to expose the constructed nature of the naturalized dichotomy of gender. See Monique Wittig, "One Is Not Born a Woman," in *The Straight Mind and Other Essays* (Boston: Beacon, 1992).

10. Fanon, *Les damnés de la terre*, 69.

11. See, for example, Anna Rutherford and Kirsten Holst Petersen, eds., *A Double Colonization: Colonial and Post-Colonial Women's Writing* (Aarhus, Denmark: Dangaroo, 1986).

12. For Homi Bhabha, "mimicry" is a trope of partial presence that articulates native "difference" within and against colonial discourse in order to reveal the ambiguities and lacunae of colonial power and knowledge. Bhabha considers that mimicry represents "moments of civil disobedience within the discipline of civility: signs of spectacular resistance." Homi Bhabha, "Signs Taken for Wonders: Questions of Ambivalence and Authority under a Tree Outside Delhi, May 1817," in *"Race," Writing, and Difference*, ed. Henry Louis Gates Jr. (Chicago: University of Chicago Press, 1985), 181.

13. Mokeddem, *Les Hommes*, 35.

14. Fanon, *Les damnés de la terre*, 73.

15. Mokeddem, *Les Hommes*, 95, 110, 176, 154.

16. Mokeddem, *Les Hommes*, 16.

17. Mokeddem, *Les Hommes*, 159.

18. Mokeddem, *Les Hommes*, 118.

19. Mokeddem, *Les Hommes*, 119.

20. Mokeddem, *Les Hommes*, 169.

21. Deleuze and Guattari, *Mille plateaux*, 624–625.

22. Malika Mokeddem, *Century of Locusts*, trans. Laura Rice and Karim Hamdy (Lincoln: University of Nebraska Press, 2006), 217. Published in French as *Le siècle des sauterelles* (Paris: Ramsay, 1992).

23. Mokeddem, *Les Hommes*, 141.

24. Mokeddem, *Century of Locusts*, 217–18.

25. In their *Mille plateaux*, Deleuze and Guattari view the nomad as inevitably linked to violence. The nomad transforms thought into a "war machine," a nomad invention whose objective is to destroy the State and the Town. A "war machine" can be an artistic, ideological, or scientific movement insofar as this movement constitutes a creative line of flight or smooth space of displacement (467–527).

26. Malika Mokeddem, *L'interdite* (Paris: Ramsay, 1993).

27. The metaphor is borrowed from Robert Bernasconi, "Casting the Slough: Fanon's New Humanism for a New Humanity," in *Fanon: A Critical Reader*, ed. L. R. Gordon, R. T. White, and T. D. Sharpley-Whiting (Oxford: Blackwell, 1996).

28. André P. Brink, *An Act of Violence: Thoughts on the Functioning of Literature*. Inaugural Lecture 165, 16 October 1991 (Cape Town: University of Cape Town, 1991), 5–6.

29. Fanon, *Les damnés de la terre*, 71.

30. Fanon, *Les damnés de la terre*, 81.

31. Mokeddem, *Les Hommes*, 104.

32. Mokeddem, *Les Hommes*, 133.

33. Helm, *Envers et contre tout*, 22.

34. Fanon, *Les damnés de la terre*, 283.

35. Mokeddem, *Les Hommes*, 37.

36. Mokeddem, *Les Hommes*, 119.

37. Hélène Cixous, *La jeune née* (Paris: Union Générale d'Editions, 1975).

38. Mokeddem, *Les Hommes*, 170.

39. In *Le Siècle*, Mokeddem underlines the duality of the nomads' territory, the Tell: "The days there burned with the flame of the desert. The winter nights there outdid the north for frost" (48).

40. Mokeddem, *Les Hommes*, 12.

41. Mokeddem, *Les Hommes*, 159; *Le siècle*, 48–49.

42. Mokeddem, *Les Hommes*, 26.

43. Mokeddem, *Les Hommes*, 124–25.

44. Mokeddem, *Les Hommes*, 141.

45. Martine Delvaux, "Le tiers espace de la folie dans *Ourika, Juletane* et *L'Amant*," *Mots pluriels* 7 (1998): 1, *http://www.arts.uwa.edu.au/MotsPluriels/MP798md.html*.

46. Mokeddem, *Les Hommes,* 238.

47. Malika Mokeddem, *N'zid* (Paris: Seuil, 2001).

48. Deleuze and Guattari, *A Thousand Plateaus,* 31.

49. Deleuze and Guattari, *A Thousand Plateaus,* 277.

9

Interpretation, Representation, and Belonging in the Works of Leïla Sebbar

MARY MCCULLOUGH

B orn of a French mother and an Algerian father in Aflou, Algeria, in 1941, Leïla Sebbar moved to France in her late teens and studied at university in France. She started publishing essays on various topics in the early 1970s.[1] The problematic of how to interpret Sebbar's works, what they represent, and where they belong—in short, how and where to categorize Sebbar's works—is essential to their understanding. Her works of fiction written in the 1980s focus on the experience of Algerian women immigrants and their children in *Fatima ou les Algériennes au square* (Fatima or the Algerian Women at the Public Square) and *Parle mon fils parle à ta mère* (Talk My Son, Talk to Your Mother), which has recently been republished.[2] She is best known for her Shérazade trilogy: *Shérazade, 17 ans, brune, frisée, les yeux verts* (*Shérazade, Missing, Aged 17, Dark Curly Hair, Green Eyes*), *Les carnets de Shérazade* (Shérazade's Notebooks), and *Le fou de Shérazade* (Shérazade's Madman).[3] The first two novels recount the adventures of Shérazade, the daughter of Algerian immigrants, and her peregrinations around Paris and the French countryside. The last volume takes Shérazade to Lebanon, where she is kidnapped and held by terrorists. She eventually returns to the *cité* (housing project) where she grew up and is seemingly reintegrated into her family and society.

After 1991 Leïla Sebbar's works broaden their focus from the Beur generation to include other ethnicities; Michel Laronde posits that they belong to "other post-colonial dialectics [than the Beur corpus]."[4] Reverting to the immediate aftermath of independence, *J'étais enfant en Algérie: juin 1962* (I Was a Child in Algeria: June 1962) presents a child's bewilderment when she and her family must leave Algeria for France.[5] *Soldats* (Soldiers) collects seven short stories recounting, as might be guessed from the title, the horror of wars all over the world: in Algeria, Bosnia, Chechnya, Palestine, Afghanistan, Somalia and Cambodia.[6] *La Seine était rouge* (*The Seine Was Red*) weaves together the testimony of a woman who witnessed the massacre of Algerians in Paris on 17 October 1961 and of several young people—Algerian, Beur, and French of other origins who investigate different truths about what happened that fateful day.[7] This short novel was no doubt inspired by the immense publicity that surrounded the Papon trial in the late 1990s; it exposed the injustices of the French government as well as the media's subsequent successes in concealing the facts about the Algerians killed during the massacre.[8]

After the year 2000 Sebbar has reverted to writing on France and Algeria by writing *Marguerite*, the love story of a French woman and an Algerian salesman; an autobiographical *carnet de voyages* (travel notebook) titled *Mes Algéries en France* (My Algerias in France); and editing *Les Algériens au café* (Algerians at the Café), a collection of short stories by Algerian writers.[9] According to the book's back cover, "*Les Algériens au café* rassemble huit nouvelles inédites d'écrivains algériens" (*Les Algériens au café* brings together eight previously unpublished short stories by Algerian writers). In

2005 she published a collection of short stories on Isabelle Eberhardt, titled *Isabelle l'Algérien* (Isabelle the Algerian man) and *Journal de mes Algéries en France* (Journal of my Algerias in France).[10]

In expanding and shifting her focus, Sebbar problematizes the classification of her works. Because the characters of her 1990s works (*Soldats*, for example) are not immigrants, the collection of short stories cannot be included in "literature of immigration" or "Beur literature." Besides, Sebbar claims: "[*Shérazade*] is not a novel about immigration. None of my novels are novels on immigration. The immigrant background is present, of course."[11] Moreover, "My writing does not center on Maghrebian immigration."[12] The question of "belonging"—that is, where to categorize Sebbar's works—seems to be problematic. She claims to be French (and not francophone or Algerian), yet as mentioned earlier, on the back of *Les Algériens au café* she is listed with the other writers as being Algerian.[13] Because of her Algerian name, her works are placed in the section "Littératures du Monde Arabe" (Literature of the Arab world) or "Littératures d'Afrique du Nord et du Moyen-orient" (Literature of North Africa and of the Middle East) in bookstores in France. This question is not only problematic for bookstore classifications but for literary critics as well.

Critics Michel Laronde and Alec Hargreaves differ on whether Sebbar's works should be included in the Beur literary corpus. Laronde characterizes her as a Beur writer: he includes several of her works in his study *Autour du roman beur: immigration et identité* because the novels she wrote in the 1980s are heavily anchored in Beur politics.[14] He therefore applies the term *littérature beur* more broadly than does Hargreaves. For Laronde what counts is "a dialectic defined by the content of the writing and not by the ethnic origin [of the writer]."[15] Hargreaves does not include her in *La littérature beur: un guide bio-bibliographique* because of her parents' backgrounds. His definition of authors writing "littérature beur" is "essentially sons and daughters of illiterate blue-collar workers from the Maghreb. These authors were born in France or settled there before the end of their teenage years. We exclude from our study writers like . . . Leïla Sebbar, who, until the age of seventeen, lived in Algeria, where her Algerian father and French mother were schoolteachers."[16] Hargreaves contests and criticizes Laronde's inclusion of Sebbar in his study of Beur novelists:

> While Laronde's study contains many interesting insights, the criteria by which his corpus is defined are not altogether convincing. According to Laronde "le terme Beur est à prendre dans le sens ethnique (les romans écrits par les Beurs) et à élargir dans le sens d'une dialectique: celle qui parle de la situation du jeune Maghrébin dans la société française contemporaine" (the term Beur should be understood in an ethnic sense (novels written by Beurs) and expanded in a dialectical sense: that which talks about the situation of the young Maghrebian in contemporary French society) (*Autour du roman beur*, 6).[17] Jean-Marie Le Pen talks a great deal about young Maghrebians in France. Are we to infer from this that Le Pen is an example of "l'esprit beur?"[18]

Needless to say, Le Pen and his followers are definitely not in favor of the Beurs, and no one can claim that anyone belonging to the extreme right is interested in the well-being of immigrants and their descendants or in giving them a voice, whether it be in literature, politics, or any other aspects of society. But can Leïla Sebbar's earlier works to which Beur characters are central and that definitely give the Beurs a voice and speak in favor of them be included in the Beur corpus? "Beur" seems to involve displacement, discomfort, victimization, and a militant reaction against that condition. And although Sebbar denies that her (early) novels derive from the experience of immigration, most literary critics claim they do. According to Charles Bonn, the mainstream press associates Sebbar's works with those of other immigrants because (as of 1994, and still in 2005) she was "the woman writer from the Maghreb and living in France, who has written the most novels about the Maghrebian immigration of the second generation in France." Bonn acknowledges the vexed political issue of finding a definition of Beur literature, as for any "literature qualified as emerging," and he characterizes it as literature that gives the reader "emigration/ immigration 'seen from the inside.'"[19]

Sebbar may be the woman writer who has written the most about the Beurs, but some of her works are now out of print (*Fatima ou les Algériennes au square* and the Shérazade trilogy). Sebbar stated that there was more interest in her work in the universities in the United States than in France.[20] Perhaps the French citizens who claim French ancestry are threatened by her works, whereas North Americans can read them without necessarily feeling directly concerned by the social problems she presents. The topics she presents challenge French readers to confront discriminatory political and social realities faced by North African immigrants. The novels she wrote in the 1980s can also be qualified as belonging to the *écriture d'urgence* (writings about urgent issues) rubric because they touch sensitive colonial and postcolonial wounds in the literary arena—wounds that have been opened and reopened constantly since France's decolonization of its former colonies and protectorates. These wounds include (but are not limited to) repatriation of *pieds-noirs*, immigration, integration, cultural insensitivity, and inhospitality on the part of the French toward the immigrants. Her novels hardly paint a glowing portrait of a glorious France; societal ills lie at the heart of her works. As first-generation immigrants and Beurs are the foci of the four out-of-print novels, it could be that since the 1990s, the French public has become less interested in the Beur plight, although other authors who treat the Beurs' situations have remained in print.[21] Other (Beur) authors treat their situation differently. For example, Mehdi Charef focuses on the Beurs' marginality, and Azouz Begag treats them as picturesquely comical (while still exposing the apathy and racism of French people of other origins).[22]

Sebbar's writings of the 1980s carried urgent messages, exploding the traditional notion of "Frenchness" and creating a new kind of literature dealing with immigration "from the inside" (compare Bonn) by a writer in a position of permanent exile. Beurs and other immigrants are central characters, and French people not of Maghrebian origins are peripheral and in direct conflict with the Beurs. By acknowledging the Beurs as valid subjects, the French readers who appreciated Sebbar in the 1980s were finally moving—at least in the realm of literature—toward "respectful understanding" in the ethnocentric continuum ("physical conquest" and "cultural imperialism" being the two preceding reactions according to Steven Mailloux's formulation).[23] In breaking with tradition and presenting the Beurs at the forefront of her novels, Sebbar's texts are political (in taking a stance in favor of immigration) and historical (in countering an orientalist perspective on colonialism), but they present only a partial reality of the Beurs' situation; the texts are not meant to paint a sociologically realistic portrait of minorities. They concentrate on adolescent energy, but they also depict the interface of emerging French popular culture and Beur culture, implying a possible synthesis.

When questioned on her position as a writer, Sebbar denied trying to explain her political position (which is definitely leftist) but conceded that political readings of her work are definitely plausible. "As long as there are women deprived of rights—men or women, that is—we must write about this wrong. But I do not think about my political positions when I write, even if one can have political readings of my work."[24] And in answer to the question "Do you think that the problems of the young Beurs might come today from this absence of dignity?" Sebbar said, "It's first and foremost the absence of a memory. It's history that provides a conscience and intelligence. When I place these young people on the scene, I identify with them."[25]

In attempting to narrow the cultural divide between the Beurs and the society that surrounds them, Sebbar's works give rise to interpretations of rhetorical hermeneutics (how we state our interpretation of the texts we read), both internally among the multiplicity of cultures that exist in France and externally between Beur minorities within the French majority and other countries. How do we, as readers, absorb another culture and cultural references? According to Mailloux,

> To understand and act within a foreign culture, the differences must be found in the margins of our own. A completely other would be unintelligible. But as the marginal comes into focus or even moves toward the center, the boundaries of our horizons can shift and even be expanded by the other within. Another way of putting this: as we interact with other communities, traditions, cultures, we can reweave our webs of belief to take account of the other, and we do this more or less successfully from differing points of view within and outside our own groups.[26]

Mailloux's interpretation of reader responses clearly favors celebrating multicultural differences and attempting to find common threads among cultures even if none seem apparent at first glance. Sebbar's works encourage such an interpretation; even when these works are read nonanalytically by nonacademics, Sebbar's advocacy of a better understanding of "others" comes across clearly to her readers.

Aside from the issue of a nonconformist foregrounding of ethnicity, critics complain when Sebbar's work does not conform to their expectations and scenarios. They attack from two opposite directions at once: Sebbar's realism trivializes and popularizes what should be high art, and her aestheticism robs her work of any possibilities for political relevance. Both reservations may be enunciated by the same critic. Critics who give Sebbar's work glowing reviews emphasize its attempted connection to reality and in fact seem to confuse it with reality: "Through her extensive sociological researches among immigrant communities, . . . Leïla Sebbar has been able to document two levels of ethnic minority in France. Unless young girls begin to put down their own experiences in writing, and perhaps those of their mothers also, Sebbar's works will remain the only authentic record of a group of people the average reader knows very little about."[27] However, this is changing; other Beur writers and film directors (such as Yamina Benguigui) are also adding their creative works to the Beur corpus. Christiane Achour also highlights what she thinks is represented reality: "the social 'real' stakes its claim. . . . [T]he reader learns or finds quantities of information on immigration, on the way of life of those in the margins of society in Paris, on those from an immigrant background."[28] She links Sebbar's work with sociology, stating that the narration of *Shérazade* is "a little like a sociological enquiry."[29] And finally, Charles Bonn claims

> *Shérazade* is a series of accounts, in a sequence of short chapters
> that narrate the marginal everyday of the young second-generation
> immigrants. Truthful accounts, sociological documentaries: one
> hesitates to talk about a novel per se. However, those in the margins
> of society can find a voice here, which attracts attention.[30]

But Sebbar clearly indicated that she does not attempt to depict reality, as the following quote emphasizes:

> What interests me is to play with extreme realism and the marvelous. In *Shérazade*, there are constantly situations similar to fairy tales, where we have the impression that a guardian angel, a watchful benefactor intervenes at the right moment to save the heroine. In *Les Carnets de Shérazade*, there are also wild, unusual, bizarre situations. Shérazade always is unharmed during very tragic situations. I like this game; it's magic realism.[31]

These citations from book reviews and articles raise several questions. Why are critics overly concerned with Sebbar's "realistic" portrayal of immigrants and their children? Why do they overwhelmingly insist on the sociological aspect of her novels and not the political dimension? Why do most of them criticize the "lack" of literary value of her works? Caroline Clifford, who studied the reception of Sebbar's works, asserts that a more open redefinition of the notion of culture is necessary to understand Sebbar's novels: "Sebbar's work is often read quickly and superficially, a process which leads to misreadings, misunderstandings, and prejudgments, and her work is often expected to reflect directly a certain cultural reality, to give a (French) reader a privileged view of the 'authentic' Maghrebian immigrant experience."[32]

It is necessary to dispel the myth that valid writing about the Beurs means portraying their daily realities. Why must Beur literature automatically be linked to the struggle for identity and the quest for a place in society? Why is late-twentieth-century French literature not criticized for describing the "reality" of life in contemporary France? Although Beur literature was still emerging in the '80s, it can contain literary tropes that are disconnected from questions of displacement and discomfort. In broadening the topics they include in their works, Beur writers demonstrate their capacity to master not only urgent social problems but also their ability to master the richness of the French language.

Certainly partial elements of reality are described, but discerning readers must caution themselves against the idea that fiction always represents reality. Whatever happened to the idea of a suspension of disbelief? Why can this concept not be applied to Sebbar's writings? Why do we fail to see in her texts echoes of reality mixed with fantasy? Readers can become aware (or reminded, if they are already familiar with it) of the immigrants' situation in France from a more lyrical approach through literature, not just from the media. Sebbar dignifies her characters by representing their fantasies and aspirations as well as their daily routines and physical needs. She often does so not by ventriloquizing but rather by bathing them in an atmosphere of iridescent implication.

Because critics fail to recognize that the implied author's lyricism complements the portrayal of her characters by suggesting where (imaginatively and intellectually) they might be, while her realistic transcription of their everyday language shows where they are (under the thumb of white society), they deny that Sebbar's works belong to "quality literature" and also attack the slang she uses. Serge Ménager's position on Sebbar's early works is one of the harshest. He states:

> She collected information on the rebellious youth she describes; her characters speak its language, its slang, with a certain awkwardness. . . . [T]heir way of life is somehow rather artificial. This group of marginalized young people squatting together flirts with the world of drugs, prostitution, fashion, and advertising that is used as an appealing background for the young reader but that is a far cry from reality. The action has very little to do with the universe in which immigrants must fight daily.[33]

Sebbar has commented on the *style oral* of her early works, and by extension, on the "hip" language that her characters speak. She defends herself magnificently: "'In your writing, you seem to express, in the literal sense, what is often only oral.' 'That's what I'm looking for. It's not written orality. It's more like Céline's style, albeit in another register, to restore the emotion of what is oral, but one that comes from the inside.'"[34]

Why can Zola, Céline, and Queneau, for example, be included in the "canon" of French literature and be praised for their style (which contains "popular" and "oral" language), while Sebbar is attacked for it? Is it because they are dead white men? Regardless of their ethnic background, Sebbar's critics fail to appreciate the hybrid language of her texts. Instead of concentrating on the richness of her style and on her remarkable ability to master all levels of the French language, her reviewers see only what appears on the surface during a rapid reading, a fashionable veneer of popular youth culture, which causes them to question the quality of her works.[35]

Sebbar's future plans include continuing to write short stories: "I realize that it's the short story that suits me best."[36] She will continue to write about human rights, about the horrors of wars, and to speak out for those who cannot write. As mentioned earlier, she states: "As long as there are women deprived of rights—men or women, that is—we must write about this wrong. It's that simple, obvious position to which I cling, because it seems to be so clear."[37] She will always fight for the underprivileged and the underrepresented peoples. Because of her own internal exile, the ethnicity of her characters will never be monocultural, her "engagement" will always be for those located in the third space of culture, and the art will always be hybrid forms of both high and popular icons. Instead of seeing her works as "inferior" because they do not represent literary critics' agendas, we should see in Sebbar's texts a clever "'deformation of mastery,' a vernacularism, based on the enunciation of the subject [in this case, the Beur nation] as 'never a simple coming into being, but a release from being possessed.'"[38] The language and cultural representations Sebbar places in her texts demonstrate their hybridity: the representation of the Beurs contributes to the realization that France is indeed a multicultural society, and its citizens who claim French ancestry must learn to accept ethnic others instead of imposing a monolithic French culture on them. They must "reweave [their] webs of beliefs to take account of the other,"[39] because the Beurs and other immigrant ethnic groups are there to stay.

Notes

1. For more information, a regularly updated website on Leïla Sebbar's works is available at *http://clicnet.swarthmore.edu/leila_sebbar/*.

2. Leïla Sebbar, *Fatima ou les Algériennes au square* (Paris: Stock, 1981); and *Parle mon fils parle à ta mère* (Paris: Stock, 1984; Paris: Magnier, 2005).

3. Leïla Sebbar, *Shérazade, 17 ans, brune, frisée, les yeux verts* (Paris: Stock, 1982); *Shérazade, Missing, Aged 17, Dark Curly Hair, Green Eyes*, trans. by Dorothy S. Blair. (London: Quartet, 1991); *Les carnets de Shérazade* (Paris: Stock, 1985); and *Le fou de Shérazade* (Paris: Stock, 1991).

4. Michel Laronde, "Les littératures des immigrations en France: questions de nomenclature et directions de recherche." *Le Maghreb littéraire* 1, no. 2 (1997): 41. Unless otherwise noted, all translations are my own. The term "Beur" has been endlessly defined and politicized. Its origin is the eighties *verlan* (backslang of the Parisian youth, most often from a minority background), which comes from *l'envers* (meaning "backward"). The syllables of a word are switched around. *Musique*, for example, becomes *ziquemu*. *Bizarre* becomes *zarbi*. *Arabe* becomes *Beura*; the "a" at the end was subsequently dropped, and the word became *Beur*. This word usually refers to the children of immigrants of Maghrebian origin; however, many of the *Beurs* were born in France, so are themselves not immigrants. Some of the people of Maghrebian origins embrace this nomenclature, whereas others reject it. For history of the word "Beur" and for a more expanded definition, see the article by Sylvie Durmelat, "Petite histoire du mot 'beur,' ou comment prendre la parole quand on vous la prête," *French Cultural Studies* 9 (1998): 191–207.

5. Leïla Sebbar, *J'étais enfant en Algérie: juin 1962* (Paris: Sorbier, 1997).

6. Leïla Sebbar, *Soldats* (Paris: Seuil, 1999).

7. Leïla Sebbar, *La Seine était rouge* (n.p.: Magnier, 1999).

8. For more information on 17 October 1961, see the article by Anne Donadey, "Anamnesis and National Reconciliation: Re-membering October 17, 1961," in *Immigrant Narratives in Contemporary France*, ed. Susan Ireland and Patrice Proulx (Westport CT: Greenwood, 2001), 47–56.

9. Leïla Sebbar, *Marguerite* (n.p.: Eden, 2002); *Mes Algéries en France* (Saint-Pourçain-sur-Sioule: Bleu Autour, 2004); and Leïla Sebbar, ed., *Les Algériens au Café* (n.p.: Al Manar, 2003).

10. Leïla Sebbar, *Isabelle l'Algérien* (n.p.: Al Manar, 2005); and Leïla Sebbar, *Journal de mes Algéries en France* (Saint-Pourçain-sur-Sioule: Bleu Autour, 2005).

11. Barbara Arnhold, "L'Exil et la fiction," *Cahier d'études maghrébines* 8 (1995): 242.

12. Mohamed El Habib Samrakandi, "Leïla Sebbar: un écrivain de croisement," *Horizons Maghrébins* 11 (1987): 37.

13. Interview with the author, 19 June 1998.

14. Michel Laronde, *Autour du roman beur: Immigration et identité* (Paris: L'Harmattan, 1993).

15. Laronde, "Littératures," 29.

16. Alec G. Hargreaves, *La littérature beur: un guide bio-bibliographique* (New Orleans: Celfan, 1992), 7–8.

17. Laronde, *Autour du roman beur*, 6.

18. Alec G. Hargreaves, "Writers of Maghrebian Immigrant Origin in France: French, Francophone, Maghrebien, or Beur?" in *African Francophone Writing: A Critical Introduction*, ed. Laïla Ibnlfassi and Nicki Hitchcott (Oxford: Berg, 1996), 36.

19. Charles Bonn, "Romans féminins de l'immigration d'origine maghrébine en France et en Belgique," *Notre Librairie* 118 (1994): 99.

20. Interview with the author, 19 June 1998.

21. This may change, however, in light of the riots in France in October 2005, which again drew attention to the plight of immigrants and the racism and discrimination they face.

22. I use the term "French people of other origins" rather awkwardly. The more commonly used "Français de souche" is an absurd term, generally used by right-wing politicians to refer to French citizens of "French" ancestry, whose families have been established in France for several generations, and who have a "French" sounding name. However, France has always been a country populated by immigrants, beginning with invasions in early French history: the Romans in 58 BC, the Visigoths and Burgundians

in the fifth century AD, and the Francs (who of course were Germanic, composed of different ethnicities) in 500 AD. More recent immigrations—from the nineteenth century, for example—have been from Eastern Europe (mostly Poland and Russia) and southern Europe (Spain, Portugal, and Italy). Massive immigration from France's former colonies did not start until the twentieth century. For more details about these immigrant patterns see Neil MacMaster's book, *Colonial Migrants and Racism: Algerians in France, 1900–1962* (London: Macmillan, 1997). As the title indicates, the work concentrates on Algerian immigration; however, it gives information on immigrants from other former French colonies.

23. Steven Mailloux, *Reception Histories: Rhetoric, Pragmatism and American Cultural Politics* (Ithaca: Cornell University Press, 1998), 17.

24. "Tant qu'il existera des femmes privées de droits—hommes ou femmes d'ailleurs—on doit s'inscrire en faux contre ça. . . . Mais je ne pense pas à mes positions politiques quand j'écris, même si on peut en faire des lectures politiques." Evelyne Ballenat, "Entretien avec Leïla Sebbar ou l'écriture de l'oral intérieur," *Nouvelle Donne* 13 (1997): 6.

25. "Pensez-vous que les problèmes des jeunes beurs viendraient aujourd'hui de cette absence de dignité?" "C'est d'abord l'absence d'une mémoire. C'est l'histoire qui donne la conscience, l'intelligence. Quand je mets ces jeunes-là en scène, je me sens eux." Ballenat, "Entretien avec Leïla Sebbar," 4.

26. Mailloux, *Reception Histories*, 15–16.

27. Farida Abu Haidar, "Leïla Sebbar: The Voice of Silence and Protest," *Women: A Cultural Review* 2, no. 3 (1991): 263.

28. "[L]e réel social s'impose . . . [L]e lecteur apprend ou retrouve quantité d'informations sur l'émigration . . . sur les modes de vie de marginaux à Paris, . . . des milieux de l'émigration." Christiane Achour, ed., *Diwan d'inquiétude et d'espoir: la littérature féminine algérienne de langue française* (Algiers: ENAG, 1991), 188.

29. Achour, *Diwan d'inquiétude et d'espoir*, 190.

30. "*Shérazade* est tout récits, en une suite de chapitres brefs qui narrent la quotidienneté marginale des jeunes immigrés de la deuxième génération. Récits-vérité, document sociologique: on hésite à parler de roman, au sens littéraire du terme. Pourtant les marginaux . . . trouvent ici une voix, qui éveille une écoute." Charles Bonn, "Itinéraires d'écritures en Méditerranée," *Annuaire de l'Afrique du Nord* 21 (1982): 856.

31. "Ce qui m'intéresse, c'est de jouer sur l'extrême réalisme et le merveilleux. Dans *Shérazade*, il y a sans arrêt des situations de conte, où on a l'impression qu'un ange gardien, un auxiliaire bienveillant intervient juste au bon moment pour sauver l'héroïne. Dans *Les carnets de Shérazade*, il y a aussi des situations à la fois loufoques, insolites, bizarres. Shérazade sort toujours indemne de situations extrêmement tragiques. Moi, j'aime bien ce jeu-là; c'est le merveilleux réaliste." Arnhold, "L'Exil et la fiction," 243.

32. Caroline Clifford, "Writing Others: Itinerary, Poetics, and Reception of Leïla Sebbar's Novels and Short Stories" (PhD diss., University of Virginia, 1999), 10.

33. S[erge] D. Ménager "Leïla Sebbar," in *Postcolonial African Writers: A Bio-Bibliographical Critical Sourcebook*, ed. Pushpa Naidu Parekh and Siga Fatima Jagne (Westport CT: Greenwood, 1998), 421–22.

34. "'Dans votre écriture, vous semblez exprimer, au sens littéral, ce qui n'est souvent que de l'oral.' 'C'est ce que je cherche. Ce n'est pas de l'oral écrit. C'est plutôt, à la manière de Céline, quoique dans un autre registre, restituer l'émotion de l'oral, mais d'un oral intérieur.'" Ballenat, "Entretien avec Leïla Sebbar," 6.

35. Compare to Clifford, "Writing Others," 10.

36. "Je m'aperçois que c'est la nouvelle qui me convient le mieux." Ballenat, "Entretien avec Leïla Sebbar," 7.

37. "Tant qu'il existera des femmes privées de droits—hommes ou femmes d'ailleurs—, on doit s'inscrire en faux contre ça. C'est cette position simple, évidente, que je continue à tenir, qui me paraît si claire à avoir." Ballenat, "Entretien avec Leïla Sebbar," 6.

38. Homi Bhabha, *The Location of Culture* (London: Routledge, 1994), 241.

39. Mailloux, *Reception Histories*, 7.

IV

Jewish Migrations and Identities

10

Jews from Algeria and French Jewish Identity

SARAH SUSSMAN

The one nonnegotiable trait of all Algerian Jews is their Jewish-ness. After that their identities become more complex. The Algerian Jews in France were Jewish *and* Sephardi on the one hand, French *and pied-noir*[1] *and* Maghrebi *and* Algerian, on the other. They had multiple identities, but so do all peoples, and especially all migrants. Jean-Robert Henry notes that French Algerian history has many "border-zone" situations, or frontiers "of a symbolic nature around which notions of Self and Other are formed in a re-ciprocal process of delimitation and identification."[2] The Algerian Jews were living at the frontiers of several societies; their unique-ness stemmed from the multiple borders that they straddled and the many ways that they fell in-between established categories in both Algeria and France. They were Jewish, but in a different way from the metropolitan Jews; they were Sephardi, but the majority had no roots in Spain. They were French, but from Algeria, and they were pied-noir, but not Catholic. They were from Algeria, but not Algerian, and they were Maghrebi, but neither Arab nor Berber. Just as the Jews were intermediaries between the Arab and

European societies in Algeria and between the Algerian and French societies in France, their identities were on the boundaries of the established categories.

Algerian Jewishness interwove strands of Sephardi, Maghrebi, French, and local identities. It was expressed historically and culturally through memories, experiences, comportment, food, language, and religious rituals. Algerian Jewish culture evolved out of a particular historical context. Algeria was a French colony from 1830 to 1962. In 1962 at the end of the long and violent conflict that resulted in Algerian independence, almost one million French citizens of Algeria, "pieds-noirs," crossed the Mediterranean and began new lives in metropolitan France. Included in this migration were approximately 120,000 Jews. Jewish presence in Algeria dated long before the French arrived in 1830. Under the French, however, government policies had slowly eroded the Jews' autonomy and eased their entrance into colonial French society. The granting of the Crémieux Decree in 1870 bestowed full French citizenship on the Jews, but this legal change neither immediately dissolved their ties with their Muslim neighbors nor did it guarantee instant acceptance by the European community of the colony. As French citizens they continued to be marked as Jews, an intermediary population between the Arabs and the Europeans. When Algeria became an independent state in 1962, the Jews left for the metropole as part of the migration of Algeria's French citizens. Only their religion and the colonial society's definition of them as Jews distinguished them from the other repatriates from Algeria, known in French as "*rapatriés.*"

The confrontation of the French Jews of Algeria and the Jews of France in a postcolonial, postmigration context offers new ways of looking at issues of identity and religious-ethnic communities in France. The Jews from Algeria were at once French, Jewish,

Sephardi and Maghrebin. They were rapatriés, many of whom had never set foot on the soil of the metropole. They had lived in an Islamic, Arab society that had been colonized by France. Within this colonial society, they had become French while remaining defined as Jewish. Their migration to the French metropole was based on this Frenchness, but their welcome in France was also strongly colored by their Jewishness. Within the French Jewish milieu, their "otherness" again stood out. As North African Sephardi Jews, their cultural and historical contexts differed from those of the native *Israélites* and Eastern European Ashkenazi Jews whose experiences and religious and cultural practices had dominated, if not defined, French Judaism until their arrival.

The North African Jews' migration in the early 1960s challenged and changed France's Jewish community by enlarging the scope of its origins, religious and cultural practices, and institutions. The presence of Algerian Jewish rapatriés in France forced both the newcomers and the metropolitan Jews to come to terms with issues of difference and pluralism within the Jewish community. Sources such as oral histories, memoirs, contemporary French Jewish periodicals, and the papers of French Jewish social, cultural, and religious institutions document this process. This chapter uses several points of tension—synagogue rituals, perceived differences in public comportment, food, and language—to explore how Algerian and French Jews addressed the changes in France's Jewish community in the 1960s. In particular these issues strengthened opposing conceptions of Sephardi and Ashkenazi Jews while emphasizing the need for French Jews to recognize their common interests in contemporary French society. In a larger context, the presence of Algerian and other North African Jews in the metropole contributed to the ongoing question of what it means to be French.

The Jews from Algeria distinguished themselves from earlier

waves of Jewish immigration into France in several ways. They were French citizens, spoke French, and had attended French schools and fought in the French army. In addition to their "Frenchness," they were Sephardi Jews whose distinct cultures had been formed by years living in an Arab land. Finally, whereas assimilation into French society and culture had been the goal for earlier generations of Jewish immigrants, the postwar native Jewish community feared that the Algerian Jews would assimilate too much and abandon Judaism altogether, following the path taken by postemancipation Jews of metropolitan France who preferred using the less-religious term *Israélite* to describe themselves. As one scholar has noted, "'Too Jewish, not sufficiently *Israélite*,' one may have told the emigrant in 1930. 'We will assure that he remains Jewish,' said the community leaders in 1962."[3]

According to many participants and observers, the repatriation to the metropole was a logical step for the Algerian Jews. Already "gallicized" and "europeanized" during France's occupation of Algeria, for the Jews the repatriation symbolized a further uprooting (*déracinement*), a separation with the land itself and its hybrid culture, a removal from the melting pot of cultures from which a distinct Algerian Jewish identity had emerged. At the same time, as part of the larger migration from France's former colonies in the late 1950s and early 1960s, they took part in the transfer of social, cultural, and political aspects of colonial society to the metropole.

To ensure that the Algerian Jews were integrated into the Jewish community of the metropole and contributed to its postwar revitalization as well as to respond to the demands of the Algerian Jews themselves, French Jewish institutions constructed new institutional spaces for both religious and cultural activities. In the 1960s and 1970s, the consistories, the institutions in charge of French Jewish religious life, and the Fonds Social Juif Unifié, the central agency for

Jewish social welfare and cultural activities, busied themselves with creating new synagogues, oratories, and community centers. These new structures welcomed Jews of different backgrounds and degrees of religious observance for a wide variety of cultural, social, and spiritual programs. Yet within these meeting spaces, on the street, and among the individual members of the French Jewish community, perceptions of differences between Jews from North Africa and the metropolitan Jews flourished, creating both conflicts over power and questions of what it meant to be a French Jew.

Articulating Algerian Jewish Identity

Two types of ideas dominated the discourse about the Algerian Jews' identity: sentiments of loss and displacement and the acknowledgement of having multiple and interlocking identities or senses of group belonging. The contemporary history of Maghrebi Judaism is fundamentally tied to the colonial history of France and thus to the decolonization of the Maghreb and the resulting repatriation of French citizens. This migration entailed not only a geographic dislocation but also a separation from the origins of these communities' traditions and cultures. With these displacements, the sense of loss, the feeling that something physical (a land, a house, a neighborhood, a family) was missing, became part of the definition of an Algerian Jew. This quality had not been a component of Jewish identity in Algeria; it entered only when Algerian Jewry no longer existed, only Jews from Algeria. Jews from Algeria were not the only ones who felt this loss and looked toward the past with sadness and fascination. Nostalgia is a common theme of pied-noir literature, music, and memory. The term "*nostalgérie*" has entered the French language to describe the specific sense of nostalgia common among rapatriés from Algeria.[4]

Some common themes of this nostalgia appear in conversations with both Algerian Jews and pieds-noirs.[5] Algeria appears as a woman, a lover. But Algeria is also capricious—it calls the rapatriés with its image as *"la terre promise"* and *"la terre natale"* and rejects them because it is ungrateful and dangerous. Some memories of Algeria are constructed in relation to France, especially since France played such an important role in constructing both pied-noir and Algerian Jewish identity. Ties to France unified the various Mediterranean immigrants in Algeria; they also formed an important part of Algerian Jewish identity. Yet the French-Algerian War and the repatriation tarnished France's spotless reputation among the Algerian Jews. In the metropole, they often regarded Algeria as a lost paradise, a place of warmth compared to the coldness of the metropole. As one woman wrote, "I was born in the Jewish quarter of Constantine . . . I lived there, until the day when my destiny uprooted me from the warm familial ambiance to transplant me in a place that was so different, completely impregnated with indifference, coldness, even hostility."[6]

The French-Algerian War transformed the Jews' feelings of belonging. In this conflict, Algerian Jews were pushed further into the sphere of the "Europeans" and away from that of the "Algerians."[7] As Hélène Cixous recently observed, "The noun 'Algerian' was born only recently. Previously, 'Algerian' was only an adjective."[8] Decolonization and Algerian independence gave birth to an "Algerian" as a person. Jews, however, whose ancestors had lived in the land of Algeria before the arrival of many of the ancestors of the "Algerians," as well as their religion, Islam, were denied this noun. Instead, the adjective "Algerian" denoted their past and formed only one part of their identity in the metropole.[9]

As Cixous's comment makes clear, sentiments of belonging and loss emerge in many different forums. One finds them in the discourse of Jewish institutions dealing with the rapatriés, in articles in the general press that attempt to explain the Jewish rapatriés to the general French audience, as well as in the cuisine, literary creations, and memories of Jews from Algeria in France. Religious practices, behavior, food, and language all emerged as sites of difference among France's Jews following the decolonization of the Maghreb.

The Rite and Synagogue Comportment

While the prayers themselves are the same, different prayer melodies and customs for Ashkenazi and Sephardi Jews evolved over centuries of living in different lands. Both the Algerian Jews and the metropolitan Jews constantly brought up the issue of *rites*, or rituals, as a differentiating factor between the two groups. Sephardi rapatriés frequently complained that they could not follow services in Consistorial synagogues. Monsieur Senanès, who had settled in Nice, wrote in November 1963: "I grieve for the Algiers Community, here it is Ashkenazi and I don't understand their prayers at all."[10] Writer Jean-Luc Allouche recalls his father's similar reaction to the Yom Kippur services at the neighborhood "Polish" synagogue. "'They are not like us.' That is all that my father found to say, when he occasionally lifted his nose from his prayer book, which additionally was not the same one as these Polish Jews were using. 'No, really, I don't understand. They are not like us.'"[11]

However, Jews from Algeria were not the only ones who complained about the different melodies. In 1961 a journalist for the Consistory's *Journal des Communautés* commented on the actions of North African Jews who attended High Holiday services at a synagogue in Paris: "Why must certain worshippers, still imbued with their traditional melodies of North Africa, believe it necessary to sing these prayers according to this ritual, thus perturbing a service whose character should not be troubled by this freedom of interpretation that harms the homogeneity of the ceremony?"[12]

The Consistorial services, where an organ accompanied prayers and solemnity ruled, were designed to demonstrate the "Frenchness" of the Jews in accordance with the earlier focus on assimilation to French society and culture. The austere, churchlike services in the Consistorial synagogues of the metropole contrasted with the enthusiastic participation to which the Jews from Algeria were accustomed.

One solution to these disagreements over synagogue rites and conduct was the creation of new places of worship for the Jews from North Africa. The arrival of the Algerian Jews changed the built environment of French Judaism. The construction of community centers, with their multivalent goal of "uniting under the same roof, and on equal grounds, the Synagogue, an educational center and a cultural and recreation center," began in the late 1950s in an attempt to create the physical embodiment of France's diverse Jewish community.[13] Nevertheless, a separation of Sephardi and Ashkenazi spaces reigned in the religious sphere. After much debate in 1958 the Paris Consistory transformed the synagogue on the rue des Tournelles in the Marais district of Paris into a synagogue for the North African *rite*. Rabbi Chekroun, formerly of the southern Algerian town of Ghardaïa, was installed as the synagogue's first Algerian spiritual leader.

In this instance the Consistory reassigned an existing synagogue; yet during the 1960s and 1970s, consistories more often built new synagogues for their new or expanded congregations in the Parisian *banlieues* and in the provinces. North African Jews also often created local prayer rooms, called *oratoires*, and small synagogues on their own initiative. Since the congregants of the new spaces were primarily North African Sephardi Jews, both the rabbis assigned to them and the prayers and behavior that took place within their walls hailed from North Africa.

While the Algerian Jews themselves instigated many of the efforts to maintain their particular traditions, the Consistory also encouraged them as a way of ensuring that the newcomers remained in the Jewish community. Integration, not assimilation, became the goal. By 1966 the Consistory could declare, "We are happy to note that our North African brothers have aligned themselves under the flag of the Consistory, thereby witnessing our active efforts to permit them to find the atmosphere of their land of origin at the heart of the larger community."[14] By undertaking the construction of new synagogues for the Jewish rapatriés and assigning Algerian rabbis to congregations primarily composed of North African Jews, the Consistory gradually came to help the Jews from Algeria celebrate their own traditions. For example, it sponsored celebrations for the holiday of Lag Baomer in certain synagogues, knowing that it was one of the times during the year when many Algerian communities traditionally held a festive celebration, known as a Hiloula. In 1963 after celebrating the holiday in their respective synagogues, Jews from the Algerian cities Constantine and Algiers met for a ball accompanied by the music of musicians such as Enrico Macias, the celebrated Algerian Jewish musician who gained a popular following in France. He is known as much for capturing the pied-noir experience in his music and for bringing arabo-andalouse music to the French public as for his Jewish origins.

As this account also demonstrates, in cities where large numbers of Algerian Jews settled, some synagogues became identified with even more specific *rites*, those of a town or a region, further factionalizing France's Jewish population along the lines of origins and identity. The Tournelles synagogue soon became the domain of Jews from the eastern city of Constantine. Madame Azoulay, who was eighteen years old in 1962 when her family arrived in Paris from Philippeville, near Constantine, explains the importance of the

Tournelles synagogue: "We, who were from Constantine. . . . For us, it was . . . the Tournelles synagogue. . . . Even my father, who now lives far away from this synagogue, will only go to Tournelles. Because he finds all of his friends there, he finds all the ambiance that we had before."[15] In the Paris region associations and synagogues grouping Jews from Algiers, Oran, and Tlemcen rapidly emerged. In Marseille, another city with a large Jewish rapatrié population, the Consistory gave space under the city's main synagogue for oratories for Jews from Algiers and Oran, while those from Tlemcen had their own synagogue as well. These synagogues or oratories became meeting spaces where family members and former neighbors could continue their community relationships and cultural traditions in the metropole. Simultaneously, they imposed themselves as part of France's Jewish community while forcing the recognition of differences within this entity by actively identifying themselves with people and practices from a certain place. Algerian Jewish cuisine functions in a similar way.

Food

Cuisine provides fertile grounds for the articulation of Algerian Jewish identity. Algerian Jews contrast their intricately spiced couscous and tafinas with the bland gefilte fish, the *carpe farcie*, an Ashkenazi Jewish dish that they discovered in the metropole. If their cuisine forms an integral part of their Algerian Jewish identity then the joke is on the Ashkenazi Jews—doomed by their identification with carpe farcie. This interchange demonstrates one of the many ways in which Jews in France increasingly have defined themselves by identity and origins since the arrival of the Jews from North Africa in the late 1950s and early 1960s. Moreover, it illustrates in a provocative way how the contact between the North African Sephardis and the Ashkenazi Jews of Eastern European origin ethnicized both groups, forcing all French Jews to regard their culture and history in a new light.[16]

As Joëlle Bahloul has observed, food preserves the differences between the Jews of Algeria and other North African Jews, Ashkenazi Jews, and the surrounding society. Food both depends on and furthers "the continuation of the Algerian Jewish minority as a social group and as a cultural entity."[17] It is a popular point of reference for Sephardi and Ashkenazi identity in France, as the carpe farcie joke demonstrates. Bahloul has remarked, "The Algerian Jew who eats couscous and *boulettes* on the same nights when the Polish Jew welcomes the Sabbath with stewed carp affirms his or her personality within the larger Jewish sphere, as diversified as it is uniform."[18]

This focus on food as a locus of Algerian Jewish identity gained greater importance in the metropole. Not only a means to distinguish themselves from the Eastern European Jews, cooking Algerian Jewish cuisine offered the Algerian Jews an active way of preserving the past for future generations. Even among Jews who had lost most contact with the organized Jewish community and religion, the social and cultural traditions could remain. One woman, who had a Jewish father and a Catholic French mother, emphasized that food was one of the sole ties that remained to her Jewish origins: "Family relations were not at all based on Jewish culture, but rather on close ties. Except at the culinary level. I had an aunt who used to bring us her couscous every Thursday. Or the cakes, or the famous . . . t'fina."[19]

In the metropole food became an expression of nostalgia. In a work that is part cookbook, part culinary history, and part memoir, one woman writes: "I lost the accent, the friends, the family reunions, the rituals. Chkaimba, t'finas, tadjines, remind me that I am a Jewish woman from Algeria, because our cuisine is all that remains of our identity. Wherever we are, in France, Montreal, or elsewhere, as long as we prepare our cuisine, we still exist as a specific people with a long history behind us. Our cuisine represents our culture that we try to pass on to the children."[20] Published almost two decades after decolonization, this statement illustrates how food is an intrinsic component of Algerian Jewish identity in the metropole—it captures both the pain of exile and the importance of keeping one's culture and identity alive. Food is a cultural marker that can survive migration; it is transportable and it changes with its surroundings, just like the Algerian Jews themselves.[21]

Several examples illustrate food's multiple tasks as a conduit of culture, an expression of nostalgia, and a way of distinguishing the Algerian Jews within French society. In the 1960s Paris was an important Jewish space for Algerian Jews living throughout the Ile-de-France because of the high concentration of kosher food shops in certain neighborhoods. While buying kosher food items certainly provided one motive for Algerian Jews in the greater Paris region to descend on the Rue des Rosiers and the Faubourg Montmartre in the early years after the repatriation, they also frequented these neighborhoods because many of the proprietors of these shops and cafés had also come from North Africa and sold the ingredients specific to North African Jewish cuisine. One man remembered worrying that in Paris he would not find the ingredients to prepare couscous or other traditional dishes, and his happiness when he realized that these ingredients could be found.[22] The matrix formed by the Algerian Jews' preservation of community ties and the continuation of their culinary traditions also includes the factory SA Biscuiterie La Messagerie of Hussein-Dey, Algeria. This business, which produces matzot for the Passover holiday, followed its clientele across the Mediterranean to France, where it continues to make matzot using the Algerian recipe; they are denser and available in both plain and orange water flavors.[23] By 1960 these Algerian matzot were sold by a North African Jewish association located in the temple on the rue des Tournelles.

Traditional cuisine also varied by locality. Under the French occupation local culinary traditions were shaped by the composition of the larger urban population and by the cultural geography of the land. In Oran, for example, Spanish-style butter cookies called montecaos were common. Oranais couscous contained cabbage, whereas in Constantine, near Tunisia, beans, artichokes, and cardoons dominated the dish. Women prepared different holiday dishes in different towns, and local specialties remained a point of pride and identification.

As Jews from different towns in the Maghreb came into contact in the metropole, their traditional dishes became another way of defining their identity. One scholar has noticed that in France, "if one spoke of *bourregh*, *bestel*, or *brik*, one knew (and one knows) the person to be from the Constantinois, Oranie, or Tunisia."[24] In the preface to one cookbook, the journalist Roland Bacri, born in Algiers, disagreed with the name for a certain dessert given by the cookbook's authors, from the town of Mostaganem. "In Mostaganem, for example, they say that the cakes made with matzah meal, they are *sfereets*. In Bab-el-Oued, for us, it was *sfériess*. What is the difference, you will tell me, nothing (perhaps!) for the tongue that tastes, but for the tongue that speaks, yes."[25] Both the names of the dishes and the preparations themselves differed. Being able to eat familiar dishes, if only on holidays, both assuaged Algerian Jews' sense of loss of their former lives and strengthened their feelings of attachment to a locality. One man joked that his marriage contract stipulated that his wife cook in the style of Tlemcen, even though she herself was of Tunisian origins:

"But," he continued, "my wife is extraordinary because she chose to follow my culinary customs. And thus I am entitled to t'fina, I am entitled to Tlemcenian couscous, which is just a bit like Moroccan couscous. So, thanks to God, I have kept my culinary habits. . . . Consequently at each holiday there is effectively a dish that is associated with the holiday and is particularly Tlemcenian. For example, the dinner that breaks the fast . . . we make a certain dish with a base of cardoons, which is truly unique, you will only find it in Tlemcen, you won't find it anywhere else."[26]

Food is such a powerful symbolic expression of identity that this man preserved his local Algerian identity in France by eating his traditional cuisine while his wife "cooked" up a different identity for herself.

As the above example illustrates, Algerian Jewish cuisine did not emerge in a cultural vacuum. In France food links the Algerian Jews to their Maghrebin origins. One woman explicitly located the relationship between the Jews and Algeria's Arab society in the kitchen, recalling that "Mother knew Arabic, but . . . a kitchen Arabic."[27] Even when personal, cultural, and geographical ties are ruptured and their everyday cuisine resembles that found in many French kitchens, the cuisine the Algerian Jews serve on holidays, similar to that of their former Muslim neighbors, is a primary signifier of their identity.

Like the Algerian Jews themselves, Algerian Jewish cuisine is more than just an example of the blending of Muslim and Jewish cultures. Their food is a product of Algeria's colonial society and its three cultures. Couscous is not only the archetypical dish of the Jews, but of the Muslims and the European settlers as well, and this remains true in France.[28] But just as the variants of Jewish couscous differ from the recipes of the Algerians and the pieds-noirs, so do other Jewish dishes. Algerian Jewish cuisine shares spices, techniques, and recipes with the other two communities yet retains its own specificities; it remains in-between North Africa and France. One scholar remarks that this mixing is the root of Algerian cuisine's appeal—a successful assimilation occurred in the kitchen, if not outside of it.[29] In less academic terms, Roland Bacri also understands how this interplay forms the cuisine that arrived in the metropole with the pieds-noirs, Jews, and Muslims: "Mouna (an Easter cake), kosher food, and couscous, three things specific to the three religions of Algeria, which made, the rule of three, the "piénoire" gastronomy."[30]

In the home Algerian Jewish cuisine enlarged the breadth of French Jewish cooking with its t'finas, couscous, salads, and sweet "Oriental" desserts. Yet North African Jews, along with Maghrebi immigrants, and the pieds-noirs, also created a new "Algerian" culinary presence in France. In the public sphere they contributed to a shift in French cuisine by helping to bring North African dishes to the mainstream, something that the Eastern European Ashkenazi Jews and earlier migrations of Sephardi Jews had failed to do.

Language

Language is another powerful marker of identity and belonging. As Frantz Fanon noted, language is especially powerful in the colonial context, for "A man who has a language consequently possesses the world expressed and implied by the mastery of that language."[31] If this is true, then the Algerian Jews possessed many worlds, or more accurately, possessed parts of many worlds and used them in different ways. They were caught between many languages and cultures, primarily French and (Judeo-)Arabic, but Hebrew, Spanish, and Berber, as well.

Arabic tied the Algerian Jews to their Maghrebin roots and culture.

While by the 1950s only a few younger Jews in the south still spoke Arabic as their primary language, many Jews had grandparents or parents who grew up speaking Arabic or Judeo-Arabic in their daily lives. If the younger generations learned Arabic at all, they learned the language as a subject in school, just like they learned Latin or German. Some, like Claudie Georges-François and the scholar Hélène Cixous, took Arabic classes to please their fathers.[32] Even after they forgot what they had learned, certain expressions remained. For Cixous, "I like to exchange two or three words, but I remember only a few words, a few expressions, no more. Yet the language is a familiar one." Georges-François sees how her use of specific sayings ties her and her children to their family's history. "Otherwise, Arabic slowly disappeared, even if we kept some expressions. Perhaps we take it up now to find our roots. The thing that is very funny is that even my children, who are born in France and who have a father from Normandy, have kept expressions in Judeo-Arabic or Arabic." Other Algerian Jews had a more profound knowledge of the language. Jean-Claude Lalou, of the southern town of Laghouat, went to Koranic school in the village before he began his French education and later majored in literary and spoken Arabic at high school in Algiers.[33]

In contrast Hebrew was the language of religion and Jewish roots, not of everyday practice. It too was an expression of the Jews' identity insofar as it represented their spiritual and historical attachments to Judaism. Albert Kadouch, who studied both Arabic and Hebrew at university in France, told me, "I would like to return to my Hebraic origins, I feel a little bit Hebrew." The Hebrew language defined one part of his identity, his spirituality. Yet his Arab environment also shaped his sense of self, as he added later, "Me, I lived in the Casbah of Algiers, I was a bit Arab." In fact, Jewish spirituality and Arab culture were interwoven in everyday life; he remembered: "we had to go to the hammam before going to the synagogue."³⁴

Unlike the Jews of Central and Eastern Europe in France, many of whom spoke Yiddish until World War II, the Algerian Jews' use of Judeo-Arabic had declined rapidly under French colonization to consist mainly of certain expressions associated with food, religion, or emotion. Even though all French Jews spoke French in the postwar period, some Ashkenazi Jews still defined themselves as Jews by their ability to speak Yiddish. For them Yiddish was *the* Jewish language. In contrast Algerian Jews were not defined by their Jewish language culture but rather by their French speech. One woman recounted how the Ashkenazi Jews used language to deny her Jewish identity.

> When I rejoined the World Jewish Congress [in Paris], I heard Yiddish spoken, and I understood nothing. But I felt that these were people who had common roots that I did not share. And the French Jews were very surprised, since for them, if one didn't speak Yiddish, one was not a Jew. End of story. My husband went to bridge clubs and he said that he was Jewish. And they said to him "But do you speak Yiddish?" No, what use was Yiddish in Algeria? So they said "So you aren't Jewish?" But yes he was, but in a different way.³⁵

This story showed the Algerian Jews' multiple exclusion in the accepted Jewish language sphere in France. The rapatriés could not understand the Yiddish being spoken in Jewish milieux in France, yet the Yiddish speakers defined their Jewish identity by their use of this tongue. Moreover, the Algerian Jews' "Jewish language" was the same language spoken by the North African Muslims, who were defined as not French, but "the other"—exactly the definition that the French Jews had been trying to avoid.

For Algerian Jews, *French* was a Jewish language. The French language had a major impact on the Algerian Jews during the nineteenth and twentieth centuries; it was one way by which Algerian Jews defined themselves. Speaking French demonstrated that the *indigène* Jews were not Muslims. It was an active way of strengthening their ties with the colonizing country while distancing themselves from Muslim Algeria. One man, when asked to explain his relationship with France, responded, "France, it is my language above all."[36] Knowledge of French was also a major reason that the Jews gave for migrating to France instead of Israel. They knew French, but not Hebrew; thus they were French, not Israeli.

The French spoken by the Algerian Jews, however, revealed their Algerian origins as soon as they opened their mouths to speak. *Pataouète*, or the French spoken in Algeria's urban centers by the pieds-noirs and Jews, is "a French *patois* upon which were grafted vocabulary and syntax forms from Spanish, Italian, Maltese, and Arabic."[37] The journalist Roland Bacri, *nom de plume* Roro de Bab-el-Oued, is known for his flowery use of *pataouète* in both its written and oral forms.[38] To Bacri Algerian French was an expression of the richness of Algeria's Mediterranean society as he explains in the following quotation: "To be bilingual, pataouète and natural French, is my strength, a trump card. Because I am a polyglot, after all. In the Tower of Babylon, you remember? When all of the languages were mixed up? The super can of worms that that made? The Tower of Bab-el-Oued: the opposite! Like an esperanto of all of the ethnic groups combined!"[39]

This hybrid language, the amalgam of the many origins and languages spoken in colonial Algeria, was the perfect tongue for the Algerian Jews. It was on the fringes of French and combined so well with other languages that linked the Algerian Jews to their origins—Arabic and Spanish. For this reason, the writer Albert

Bensoussan, born in Algiers, claimed that the French spoken by Algerian Jews was an ideal conduit for memory, for remembering the past. "My parents narrated to me so much about it, those village tales of long ago in this far away land of Algeria which plunged with them into the abyss. The . . . family chronicles, proverbs, our words, the bastard expressions in Judeo-Arabic, in local French, even in something resembling Spanish."[40]

Speaking their particular vernacular in the metropole continued their ties to Algeria, even if this affiliation was not desired. The Algerian Jews became pieds-noirs, or *français d'Algérie*, when they spoke this Algerian French with its distinct accent. For the French of the metropole, this accent was yet one more way that the pieds-noirs were different, one more problem that the former colony had sent to the metropole. Jean-Luc Allouche remembers being ridiculed by his high-school classmates in Paris, who gave him the nickname "*marchand de tomates*" for "the speech that was heavy and too songlike, this way . . . of mangling the T's and the D's, of wetting them, diluting them, of making the O's weak, as if closing the mouth like a chicken's ass would have represented an unsurmountable effort, unworthy of me, who in contrast formed them in such a languid manner, so weary that all of the spicy odors of the colony invaded the classroom."[41] Jacques Derrida absorbed the metropolitans' disdain for Algerian French, and "would like to hope, . . . would very much prefer, that no publication permit my 'French Algerian' to appear." In his eyes, accents are not the language of expression for French literature. In speaking Derrida aspires to emit a pure French; by his pronunciation he makes a conscious effort to define himself as an intellectual and not as a pied-noir. "I have never ceased learning, especially when teaching, to speak softly, a difficult task for a '*pied-noir*,' and especially from within my family."[42]

Linguistic loudness of another kind surfaced with the subject of naming. Algerian Jews had very distinctive family and given names. Most family names had roots in Spanish, Hebrew, Arabic, or Berber. Some of these were common throughout the Sephardi world, but many were more common in Algeria than elsewhere. Often Algerian Jews sported names of towns or occupations in Spain (Toledano, Tapiero). Sometimes they wore names of Berber tribes (Touati, Timsit), or other Berber descriptive terms (Chouraqui, Cherqui). And often family names begin with "Ben" or "Bel," meaning "son of" in both Arabic and Hebrew (Belaiche, Benichou, Benyahya).[43]

In 1936 Maurice Eisenbeth, the Chief Rabbi of Algeria from World War I until his death in January 1958, published *Les Juifs de l'Afrique du Nord, Démographie et Onomastique*, which details the common Jewish names found in Algeria and notes the cities in which they were most common. Later, in the metropole youths belonging to the Jewish association Tora ve Tsion used these names to compile statistics on Jewish rapatriés and to identify Jews in the banlieues. In 1962 at the request of the main French Jewish social work organization, the Ministry of Rapatriés carried out an investigation of *israélites rapatriés d'Algérie* using family and first names to determine whether a person was Jewish.[44] Researchers can identify Jews in French archives because of their particular names.[45]

Because of their names, however, both in Algeria and in the metropole Algerian Jews could be mistaken for Arabs, Berbers, or Spaniards. One woman with no real ties to Judaism claimed that society labeled her as Jewish because she carried her father's name. She would also be mistaken for an Arab if her given name were not French. As she explained, "it's only the first name that makes the difference. Because when [the Jews] were made French, they took French names for their children. You only have one page of the Paris phone book—look at the Arab and Jewish names. The only difference is that the first name will be French, it's a Jew, an Arab name, that means that it's an Arab. . . . It's as simple as that, systematic."[46]

In the end the hybridity of Algerian Jewish names paralleled the society from which they came. These names primarily served to identify their bearers as being from Algeria. The young narrator of Daniel Saint-Hamont's novel about the adventures of a pied-noir family in Paris has no illusions about one Monsieur Ganancia:

> With such a name, it was a guy from home, you could have no doubt. For a long time in France we all recognized each other, like that, instinctively, we didn't even need to shake hands like freemasons. Maybe it was in the minute details, the nose a little Jewish, the mouth a little Arab, the eyes a little French, the skin tone a little Spanish, we felt that the other came from *là-bas* even before he had begun to speak. Because after that, of course, with the accent it was easy.[47]

This fictional account tells us several things. The former residents of Algeria in the metropole could use certain names to identify past inhabitants of the former colony. Furthermore, the racial and cultural stereotypes affiliated with the pieds-noirs, Arabs, and Jews contained within themselves the intricate ethnic web of Algeria. The exile of all three populations in the metropole forged a certain identity whose traits were shared by all.

Yet some Algerian Jews attempted to escape this labeling and to change their identity by changing their family names. They profited from their move to a new environment as an occasion to abandon their Jewish identity. Emile Touati labeled this phenomenon "bad assimilation" and remarked, "they take advantage of their transplantation and their isolation, of their Frenchness, of their physical appearance which does not correspond to the stereotype of Jews in

Europe, of their accent, southern but not foreign, to totally break with their natural community."[48] The *Journal Officiel's* lists of registered name changes in the early 1960s contain numerous examples of Jews born in Algeria living in France who went to great lengths to legally gallicize their family names. Examples of this appropriation of a new identity include an El Koubbi from Sidi-Bel-Abbès who requested the new name Lecoubet and a Monsieur Amar born in Mascara who became Monsieur Dubreuil. Benhamou became Benard, or Meunier, while Boumendil transformed into Dumesnil. Another reason for these name changes might have been certain Jews' concerns that people would identify their names as Arab names, this misconception thereby branding them as Arabs. Nevertheless, the very Frenchness of new names that these Jews chose demonstrated their interest in passing as native French rather than as French Jews.

A further way that language defined people was the terms that individuals used to name themselves. In Jewish journals that published the rapatriés' demands for work, the detail "français d'Algérie" (French from Algeria) served to distinguish the Jews from Algeria from their coreligionists from Morocco and Tunisia with whom they competed for employment.

> Man, 44 years old, "*français d'Algérie*," seeks job as waiter, worker.
> Woman, 43 years old, "*française d'Algérie,*" seeks position as an office worker, filer, telephone.

Despite proudly wearing their definition in the public space, the qualifications that they advertise are no more "*évolué*" and "French" than those sought by the Tunisian and Moroccan Jews in the same newspaper columns. The civil servants, high-school professors, doctors, and other members of the liberal professions did not need to advertise in this forum, but those who did felt equally French. Notice as well that the job seekers never neglect to mention that they are both "French" and "from Algeria." This is both their legal status as français d'Algérie as well as their identity in contrast to other Jews from North Africa. Interestingly enough, however, the Jewish rapatriés who advertised for jobs in national newspapers such as *L'Aurore* never mentioned their origins and only very rarely mentioned that they were Jewish. No matter, their distinctive names gave them away.

The arrival of the Algerian Jews in the early 1960s magnified the diversity of France's Jewish population. Centuries of living in different societies had given North African and European Jews different cultural and social practices. After the arrival of the French in Algeria, Jews entered into the colony's European society, yet in the home and in the synagogue local North African cuisines and popular religious beliefs continued to permeate Jewish food and behavior. In the metropole they came into abrupt contact with the native French Jews, whose own food and religious customs were the result of different historical trajectories. The encounter of the metropolitan Ashkenazi Jews with the Algerian Sephardi Jews brought these, and many other differences, into the spotlight. Traditions, persons, and institutions all needed to be qualified with the label Sephardi or Ashkenazi; specific cultures and histories emerged as specific where they had once been recognized as just "Jewish."

Historical memory cannot serve as a unifying factor for France's Jews; their origins, experiences, and cultures are too diverse. Instead, French Jews undertake a conscious attempt to build a united community. As the examples of religious ritual and comportment and food demonstrate, the Jews recognized differences within their population. It is important to remember, however, that both the

North African and metropolitan Jews in the 1960s saw themselves
as belonging to the same community, even though what that community signified, how its members acted, and where they came from
differed. The joke about the carpe farcie depends on the recognition
that the person who tells it and the person at whose expense it is
told are both part of the same community.

Notes

1. *Pied-noir* was a term used to describe a French citizen of Algeria.

2. Jean-Robert Henry, "Introduction," in *French and Algerian Identities from Colonial Times to the Present: A Century of Interaction*, ed. Alec G. Hargreaves and Michael J. Hefferman (Lewiston NY: Edwin Mellen, 1993), 12–13.

3. Colette Zytnicki, *Les Juifs à Toulouse entre 1945 et 1970: Une communauté toujours recommencée*, ed. Chantal Bordes-Benayoun, *Collection tempus-diaspora* (Toulouse: Presses Universitaires du Mirail, 1998), 135.

4. See for example Benjamin Stora, *La gangrène et l'oubli. La mémoire de la guerre d'Algérie*, *Essais* (Paris: La Découverte, 1991), especially part 3, chap. 17; Lucienne Martini, *Racines de Papier, Essai sur l'expression littéraire de l'identité Pieds-Noirs* (Paris: Publisud, 1997); and Joëlle Hureau, *La mémoire des pieds-noirs de 1830 à nos jours* (Paris: Olivier Orban, 1987). Jacques Derrida uses the term in *Monolingualism of the Other or the Prosthesis of Origin* (Stanford CA: Stanford University Press, 1998). The term *nostalgérie* also appears in more popular literature and pied-noir memoires.

5. See the testimonies collected in Monique Ayoun and Jean-Pierre Stora, eds., *Mon Algérie: 62 personnalités témoignent* (Paris: Acropole, 1989). For an analysis of nostalgia in pied-noir memory, see Hureau, *La mémoire des pieds-noirs*.

6. C. El Baz, *Sarah, ou moeurs et coutumes juives de Constantine (Algérie)* (Nice: Imprimerie Meyerbeer, 1971), 7.

7. Aron Rodrigue's work argues that the Alliance Israélite Universelle had the same effect around the Mediterranean. The difference in Algeria was that the French government, not an international Jewish organization, carried out the transformation. Aron Rodrigue, *Images of Sephardi and Eastern Jewries in Transition: The Teachers of the Alliance Israélite Universelle, 1860–1939* (Seattle: University of Washington Press, 1993).

8. Hélène Cixous, "My Algeriance, in other words: To Depart not to arrive from Algeria," *TriQuarterly* 100 (Fall 1997): 262.

9. While they were *français d'Algérie* or *juifs algériens*, the land itself was defined as *Algérie française*, with *française* an adjective. The Algerian Jews were always *français* (noun) while they were never *algériens* (noun).

10. Jacques Lazarus, "Correspondence, 1963." Fonds Jacques Lazarus (Archives du Consistoire de Paris—hereafter PC).

11. Jean-Luc Allouche, *Les Jours innocents* (Paris: Lieu Commun, 1983), 30.

12. "Roch-Hachana au Temple Buffault," *Journal des Communautés* 268 (22 September 1961): 10.

13. "Rencontre des Communautés de Banlieue, 20 décembre 1964." Fonds Jacques Lazarus (PC).

14. "Assemblée générale de l'Association Consistoriale Israélite de Paris, dimanche 15 mai 1966," *Journal des Communautés* 372 (27 May 1966): 2–5.

15. Mme M. Azoulay, conversation with the author, Paris, 29 February 2000.

16. Harvey E. Goldberg, ed. *Sephardi and Middle Eastern Jewries* (Bloomington: Indiana University Press, 1996), 47.

17. Joëlle Bahloul, *Le Culte de la table dressée, rites et traditions de la table juive algérienne* (Paris: A.-M. Métailié: Diffusion, Presses universitaires de France, 1983), 23.

18. Bahloul, *Le Culte de la table*, 23.

19. Michèle Guenoun, conversation with author, Paris, 20 March 2000.

20. Leone Jaffin, *150 Recettes et Mille et un souvenirs d'une Juive d'Algérie* (Paris: Encre, 1980), 228–30. Another cookbook, *La Cuisine Pied-noir, Cuisines du Terroir* by Irène and Lucienne Kersenty, 2nd ed. (Paris: Editions Denoël, 1979), mentions a 1930 work by Ferdinand Duchêne, whose title, *Mouna, Cacher, et Couscous*, illustrates the hybridity of Algerian Jewish cuisine.

21. For anthropological and sociological analyses of Algerian Jewish food, in addition to the work of Joëlle Bahloul, also note Joëlle Allouche-Benayoun's chapters in Allouche-Benayoun and Bensimon, *Les Juifs d'Algérie: Mémoires et identités plurielles* (Paris: Editions Stavit, 1998), in particular the chapter "Rituels festifs et pratiques culinaires: symboles de l'identité juive."

22. Jacques Benichou, conversation with author, Argenteuil, 28 February 2000.

23. "Matsot de Pessah," *Menorah* 7 (December–January 1964): 2. The round Algerian matzot is still made by the same company.

24. Allouche-Benayoun and Bensimon, *Les Juifs d'Algérie*, 202.

25. Kersenty, *La Cuisine Pied-noir*. Preface by Roland Bacri: "A Mostaganem, par exemple, ils disent que les gateaux à la galette de Pâque, c'est des sfereets. A Bab-el-Oued, nous, c'étaient des sfériess. Qu'est-ce que ça change, vous me direz, rien (peut-être!) pour la langue gustative, mais pour la langue lingoiste, hein." Bacri, known for his rich use of pied-noir language, juxtaposes the tongue in one's mouth (*la langue*), with the language (also *la langue*).

26. Joseph Aziza, conversation with author, Marseille, 18 July 2000.

27. Claudie Georges-François, conversation with author, Paris, 31 March 2000.

28. For a humorous account of couscous as the apogee of pied-noir culture, see Daniel Saint-Hamont, *Le Coup de Sirocco* (Paris: Fayard, 1978).

29. Pierre Mannoni, *Les Français d'Algérie: vie, moeurs, mentalités* (Paris: L'Harmattan, 1993), 38.

30. Roland Bacri, *Trésors des racines pataouètes* (Paris: Belin, 73, cited in Mannoni, *Les Français d'Algérie*, 38).

31. Frantz Fanon, *Black Skin, White Masks* (New York: Grove, 1967), 18.

32. Conversations with author, Claudie Georges-François, Paris, 31 March 2000, and Hélène Cixous, Paris, 29 June 2000.

33. Jean-Claude Lalou, conversation with author, Paris, 22 March 2000. See also the beautiful film made by his son, producer Serge Lalou, entitled *In the Beginning: Once upon a time . . . There were Arab Jews* (1997).

34. Albert Kadouch, conversation with author, Paris, 28 January 2000.

35. Ellen Djian, conversation with author, Paris, 11 April 2000.

36. Roland Belicha, conversation with author, Paris, 6 April 2000.

37. Emanuel Sivan, "Colonialism and Popular Culture in Algeria," *Journal of Contemporary History* 14 (1979): 21.

38. For examples of *pataouète* and Roland Bacri's voice, see his columns in *Le Canard Enchaîné* and his books: *Trésors des racines pataouètes* (Paris: Belin, 1983); *Le Roro, dictionnaire pataouète de langue pied-noir, étymologique, analogique, didactique, sémantique et tout . . .* (Paris: Denoël, 1969); and *Le beau temps perdu, Bab-el-Oued retrouvé* (Paris: Editions Seghers, 1978).

39. Bacri, *Le beau temps perdu*, 94–95. With original spelling intact: "Être bilangue, pataouète plus français naturel, c'est ma force, un atout. Comme si j'étais polyglotte en somme. À la tour de Babel, vous vous rappelez? Quand toutes les langues étaient confondues? Le sac de noeuds universel que ça a fait? La tour de Bab-el-Oued: le contraire! Comme un espéranto de toutes les ethnies culturelles!"

40. Albert Bensoussan, *L'Echelle séfarade* (Paris: Editions L'Harmattan, 1993), 16.

41. Allouche, *Les Jours innocents*, 21.

42. Derrida, *Monolingualism of the Other*, 45, 47–48.

43. While all of these names appear in Morocco, Tunisia, and Algeria, some appear with greater frequency in one country or another, or even in one region.

44. Archives départementales des Bouches-du-Rhône (AD BDR) 137W464.

45. Working in the departmental archives of the Bouches-du-Rhône, for example, I was able to identify that a significant percentage of all of the people that presented themselves to the Service des Affaires Musulmanes in Marseille in 1961 and 1962 were actually not Muslims at all, but Jews from Algeria. AD BDR 137W463.

46. Michèle Guenoun, conversation with author, Paris, 20 March 2000.

47. Saint-Hamont, *Le Coup de Sirocco*, 218.

48. Emile Touati, "Fidélité et Continuité," *IJ* 140 (October 1963): 1.

11

Anti-Arab and Anti-French Tendencies in Post-1948 Oriental Jewish Literature Written in French

JOHANN SADOCK

My aim in the following pages is to probe the *simultaneous* forms of anti-French and anti-Arab tendencies in post-1948 Oriental Jewish literature written in French.[1] These tendencies seem to me representative of a central aspect of the Jewish condition as it is expressed in this literature: namely, the Oriental Jews' sense of vulnerability, the degree of which varies depending upon the context but which never disappears completely.[2]

One can expect Oriental Jewish literature to record certain historical events that bring their share of anti-Jewish feelings, attitudes, or actions from Arab Muslims or the French. One expects for instance to see pogroms or the role of the Vichy regime during World War II recorded critically either from the Jewish authors' points of view or from the perspective of their group of origin. Any aggression—physical or verbal, actual or perceived, factual and/or fictionalized—toward the authors themselves, their group of origin, or Jewish characters is bound to provoke reactive feelings directed against the aggressors. Predictably any such aggression tends to lead to the more common forms of anti-Arab and anti-French feelings and representations. In this chapter we will also try to identify the less expected forms these tendencies can take, including the less direct ways of representing the Other and thinking negatively about the Other.

In Oriental Jewish literature, Jews experience both the French and the Arabs as the Other but not in the same way.[3] Even though Jews often have French nationality, the French sphere of influence remains the sphere of the Other. In contrast Jews tend to perceive the Oriental milieu as authentically their own even when they distance themselves from it. Although Arabs can be collectively or individually feared or rejected, they can also be experienced as a version of the Same—especially in the presence of the French. That sense of sameness is rooted in an awareness of a common origin or physical appearance or a common cultural heritage. In the words of the narrator who addresses his cousin in Algerian-born Jean Yvane's *Le dieu jaloux*: "[W]hen one talks to you in Arabic, you pretend not to understand. You open your eyes wide open or you look bored. But I am not worried, cousin; deep inside you, if you cry, it's in Arabic, not in French, because whether you like it or not, it is Arabic that you drank with the milk of your mother. Cousin, it stays with you. Even if sour."[4]

Although speaking Arabic as a "mother tongue" would not be typical for all Oriental Jews, a certain Oriental sensitivity is often acknowledged as characterizing even the more assimilated Oriental Jews. Annie Goldmann, an assimilated Jew born in Tunisia, talks for instance about "all the sensual heat of the Orient that made us sometimes lose our minds and that, I think, did leave indelible imprints on my sensibility."[5]

I will be discussing here relationships among and representations of Jews, Arabs, and the French in two contexts:

1. In North Africa and predominantly Arab Muslim countries (such as Egypt, Iraq, Syria, or Lebanon) after colonization and before independence. In this context, differences may be significant between French colonies and colonies of other European countries as well as between colonies and protectorates since these differences affected the legal status of the Jews.[6]

2. In continental France after the independence of Arab countries.

Relationships between a Jew and an Other are affected by the presence of a third Other, Arab or French, primarily in these two contexts. Of course characters, plots, or narratives can move from one context to the other in the same work. This fluidity also affects the perception of oneself and the Other; anti-Arab and anti-French tendencies are consequently dynamic. The following declaration from the mother of the female narrator in Paula Jacques's *La lumière de l'oeil* clearly shows that such variations exist:

> We got along well with the Arabs. Nowadays they have made something of themselves, but in the past, they were like our inferiors. They were nothing at all: servants, doormen, pitiful people so to speak. We were doing them a lot of good by having them work in our homes. They preferred our European houses to those of the rich Muslims who would beat them, insult them. We treated them well. As inferior accomplices, long-time friends, our secret brothers. It was love in paradise, the years in the Garden.[7]

This superiority of "us" (the Jewish mother likes to see her house as European and herself as French) versus "them" (the Arabs) is grounded in a very specific sociohistorical context, one in which Egyptian Jews were probably the wealthiest and among the most westernized of Oriental Jews.[8] Even so later in the novel the characters take measures to prepare for anti-Jewish riots under Nasser's predecessor, indicating their sense of vulnerability. Alliances were therefore in flux, and the enemy of today could be the ally of yesterday or tomorrow, and vice versa. About her Jewish husband, who studied with the Jesuits, she explains to her daughter:

> One day at the College of the Jesuits, the Father Superior became fanatical. He went all around shouting—may the worms eat him—a terrible story of death to the Jews or of Christian children murdered for Passover. It is a mental epidemic. Catholics persecute their old friends and accomplices but the Arabs do not change. They have a charitable heart, love their Jewish brothers, and recognize them for their good character.[9]

In addition to sociohistorical contexts, other factors influence interactions between Jews and Others. These include social status, the gender and the age of the characters interacting, the exact location where the interaction takes place (inside the house or in the street), the presence of other groups, and the number of people interacting. For example, in Algerian-born Hélène Cixous's short story, "Bare Feet," one cannot easily determine what prompts the aggression of the *yaouled* (shoeshine boy) who stains with red wax the white shoes of the young Jewish girl strolling on the street. It could be her social standing, made clear by her clothes and her shoes; her Frenchness; her Jewishness (so present in her own mind at least); or that she is a girl and he a boy: "I saw the face of the phony little shoeshine boy, and I recognized the sparkle in his eyes: it was the lust of hatred, the first shimmer of desire."[10] The first-person narrator is not sure, and she is tempted to exonerate the little boy: "But how could I accuse a six-year-old child of wanting to commit murder?"[11] The answer to this question seems to be given earlier in the story when the narrator attributes the boy's criminal intent to larger historical forces: "[W]ithout wanting to I had read the whole book written in advance on the walls. . . . And I wasn't the only one. The small boy, who played the role of the shoeshine boy in this children's play, and I was not yet five and he was not seven years old, was already rehearsing the role he was to play when they would present the End of the Two Worlds."[12]

Nevertheless, the historical necessity referred to here does not make the factors of gender, age, and social milieu any less significant.

Another consideration to keep in mind when examining these anti-Other tendencies is that the authors can jump from one position to the other, choose one perspective or another. In their representations of the French, Arabs, and Jews, Oriental Jewish authors have in fact a choice among several cultural perspectives: a French perspective, a Jewish perspective, and an Oriental perspective. In some cases, anti-French and anti-Arab tendencies can be expressed from one, several, or all of these perspectives in the same work. It can also be the case that the perspective of the narrator or the author differs from the one of his or her characters (who can themselves be the medium for different perspectives). Other perspectives can thus be intertwined with the main cultural perspectives mentioned above. For example, in *Les rêveries de la femme sauvage: scènes primitives*, Hélène Cixous writes primarily from a child's perspective about being approached as a young girl by an Arab street vendor nicknamed "Yadibonfromage," who seductively offers to get some blood for her by rubbing his finger against her genitals.[13] However, because the aggressor is ethnically marked as Arab and the young girl is Jewish, there is also an ethnic layer to this anecdote.[14]

Although it is possible to analyze anti-Arab and anti-French tendencies from many angles, I would like to focus on three cultural perspectives: Jewish, Oriental, and French. Clearly these perspectives can be intertwined, but I would like to refer to these perspectives separately in order to outline the main manifestations of anti-Arab and anti-French tendencies from each of these perspectives.

Jewish Perspective

By Jewish perspective I mean that anti-French and anti-Arab tendencies are expressed through a narrative voice or a character's point of view identifiable as Jewish or as speaking within the Jewish group. Jewish populations feel somewhat at home in predominantly Islamic lands—either because their ancestors have been there for generations or because they have developed strong ties there.[15] Yet, in predominantly Arab Muslim countries, Jews are at the mercy of either the French or the Arabs, vulnerable even when they are under the theoretical protection of the French colonizer. Blows can come from both sides, and there is sometimes a feeling of betrayal.

Quite a few authors point to the long presence of Jews in these Islamic lands and to the fact that this presence sometimes preceded that of the Arabs.[16] In some works one thus sees resentment on the part of Jews toward their Arab "half brothers" who in times of upheaval may betray the pact of peaceful coexistence that had prevailed for centuries.[17] There is resentment as well toward France, accused of not fulfilling its commitment to protecting Jews against mobs and as in during World War II of being directly responsible for the Jews' predicament. A rather typical feeling is expressed by the narrator of Tunisian-born Georges Memmi's *Qui se souvient du Café Rubens*: "We the wearers of the kipah, we were Jewish, respectful of our Rabbis and moreover 'protected by the French' . . . this could have lasted for a thousand more years."[18] But as the war starts in Europe, this conditional future is cut short: "Alas, even among the French people, most of them applaud the senile One [Pétain]. I quiver when I see them, walking like drunk people and lying about their own past. The Arabs remain our half brothers.

They reason that a nation that was so shamefully defeated will be beaten again. And they are ready to make a deal with the devil as they dream of independence. . . . And us, what will we become?"[19] This is the most simple and direct example of anti-Arab and anti-French tendencies in the corpus.[20] After independence, this resentment toward Arabs and the French and their authorities grows as Jews become victims of administrative hurdles on both sides. In Paula Jacques's *La lumière de l'oeil*, following their exile in metropolitan France, the mother tells her daughter:

> When the Muslims became citizens, I do not criticize, it is an egalitarian right, your father had to search for the tombs of his ancestors in Cairo's cemetery to prove that they had been there for at least one hundred years. It was the only way to obtain citizenship. Alas, the curse has left me without a country. May God burn the French government that removes the soul of those without a homeland. Do you realize that I have to rush endlessly to the ministry of concerns to renew my right to live? At my age?[21]

The Jewish family too provides a context in which one can see anti-Other tendencies. Sometimes the narrator or the author notices and criticizes negative attitudes among other Jews, often members of his or her family. The most common example is a child's awareness of a family member's feelings of superiority toward Arabs.[22] These feelings of superiority can be directed for instance toward a maid. The intimacy of life inside the house can create a bond between members of a Jewish family—often a child—and the maid.[23] The child thus becomes sensitive to the Arab servant's social status and condition and may feel protective toward him or her. In this type of case, the child is critical of the Jewish parent or group seen as prejudiced and racist.

Outside of the house, while children can have antagonistic

encounters with Arab children, they may also feel drawn to them.[24] In Bensoussan's *Frimaldjézar* (as in Cixous's short story "Bare Feet") the narrator has problems with yaouled "who were throwing their polishing brushes at" him.[25] Yet Bensoussan still confesses to his father that he would like to become a yaouled; his father almost slaps him.

It seems to me that not enough attention has been paid to the at-titudinal changes that came as a result of the shift in power and status that took place between Arabs and Jews in the colonial context. As would be expected after the Crémieux decree (1870), which gave French nationality to Algerian Jews, this shift can be noticed more strikingly in the works of Algerian-born Jewish writers. Among other Oriental Jewish writers, this shift is less clear for reasons that have to do with the legal status of Jews in their particular countries; but to the extent that a French education gives a higher status, these writers see themselves as empowered by French culture (both in their Jewish milieu and in the broader environment). These writers are also quick to notice that Jews could turn this weapon against Arabs. Tunisian-born Gisèle Halimi describes this process in *Le lait de l'oranger*: "As in a construction that a Machiavellian architect would have shaped for a political end, the European masters domi-nated Jews and Arabs, both separated from each other by parallel circles. The Jew despised the Arab located in the inferior part."[26] Although Halimi is right to speak of "European masters," I should emphasize that in some colonial societies Jews can see themselves as just that. The irony is of course that Jews can be despised by the real colonizer, French or European.

Oriental Jewish attitudes toward the French are also complex and, in predominantly Arab Muslim countries before independence, typically ambivalent. This attitude toward the colonizer is ana-lyzed by Memmi in *Le Portrait du Colonisé*, with this important nuance: despite the sometimes painful and typical encounters with the anti-Semitic French, Jews were somewhat aware that the colonial situation could elevate them socially—particularly in relation to Arabs—through acculturation, education, naturalization, or citizenship.[27] This ambivalence toward the French and France has both historical and psychological origins—directly as a result of negative experiences of French anti-Semitism and indirectly in the generational conflicts that can result from the acculturation of children and from the self-hatred often redirected against the parents and against the group of origin.

In continental France itself, anti-French and anti-Arab tendencies intersect in more than one way in Bernard-Henri Lévy's *Le diable en tête* as well as in Claude Brami's *La danse d'amour du vieux corbeau*. Algerian-born Bernard-Henri Lévy makes a clear link between the collaboration of the main character's (non-Jewish) father during World War II and his son's involvement in the Algerian War of Independence on the side of the Front de Libération Nationale (FLN) and later in Arab terrorism.[28] In Tunisian-born Claude Brami's *La danse d'amour du vieux corbeau*, while Arab terrorism is also condemned, more direct attacks are made on the French and French civil servants, who are often represented as anti-Semitic and racist. After terrorists bomb the "synagogue Copernic," a French policeman declares: "they can just blow themselves up, the Jews, the Arabs and the like."[29] Here the implicit accusation against Arab terrorism leads to an implicit indictment by the author of the French racist and anti-Semitic policeman (the involvement of policemen in neofascist organizations is directly pointed out by the narrator of the book).[30] It is to be noted that in the two previous examples, although Arab terrorism is condemned, racism against Arabs is also criticized. In *Le diable en tête*, it comes in the form of a French character's condemnation of torture during the Algerian

War and the murder of Arabs on 17 October 1961 in Paris. It is as if these Jewish authors had to counterbalance the representation of Arabs as terrorists by mentioning racism in France.

Oriental Perspective

By Oriental perspective I mean that a narrative voice or character (Jewish or not) expresses anti-Arab and anti-French tendencies from a perspective that is neither strictly Jewish nor strictly Arab and that can be called "Oriental." From this Oriental perspective, anti-Arab tendencies are usually embodied in a character who laments and deplores the evolution of predominantly Arab Muslim countries after their independence. The lament may not be over what is or has been done to Jews by Arabs but over what has become of the country whose identity was previously Oriental. Here, "Oriental" can be synonymous with "cosmopolitan," as this quotation by Georges Memmi illustrates: "But this means that this country will become only Arab, to our misfortune, exactly as it was once Vandal or Turk."[31] In this quotation the Oriental and the Jewish perspectives intersect: it is both from an Oriental and a Jewish perspective that the departure of Jews is unacceptable, as they had lived there for hundreds of years and therefore contributed to the identity of these countries. One understands that the country is not exclusively Arab, and the historic reference to successive invasions emphasizes this point.

There is, therefore, a certain nostalgia for what the country was and usually a more or less explicit criticism of what Arabs have done to the country. This is true for the few Jews who remain in Arab Muslim countries after independence and for the Jews who go back to their country many years later, as in Algerian-born Alain Meridjen's *Un matelas par terre*,[32] Marlène Amar's *Des gens infréquentables*, or Tunisian-born Jean-Pierre Allali's *Lalou*.[33]

Anti-French tendencies from an Oriental perspective can also take the form of criticism of the French as colonizers or of France as a colonial power. Even though Jews benefited from the French presence in some countries, they can look at the French with the irony or bitterness of the colonized: this perspective is neither strictly Jewish nor strictly Arab, but Oriental. Here the focus is on the common Arab and Jewish experience. Both Jews and Arabs are represented as being equally subjected to a French colonial education as in this sarcastic comment in Moroccan-born Amram El Maleh's *Parcours immobile*: "It is this proud and generous heiress of Gaul [namely France]—'our Gaulish ancestors' Mohammed and Isaac were repeating their lessons—that decided to defend the Oriental people against their own madness."[34] In the denunciation of French colonial schools, the Jewish and Arab perspectives meet. In fact quite a few authors insist on the common marginalization of Jews and Arabs in the French colonial educational system.[35]

One of the most elaborate examples of an anti-French tendency in continental France from an Oriental perspective can be found in Annie Cohen's *Le marabout de Blida*.[36] This is one of the few books that deals extensively with a relationship between a *pied-noir*[37] (wearing "*burnous*" and "*babouches*" in Paris) and a Jew in contemporary France. In this book the anti-French tendency from an Oriental perspective takes the form of the reproach of inauthenticity made by the marabout to his Oriental acquaintance, the female Jewish narrator. Throughout the book, the marabout accuses her (or the character feels accused) of not being faithful to what she knows to be their common heritage, their Oriental roots. This unexpected attack against her Oriental self-hatred is made by a marabout whose identity is not precisely defined but who comes from the same town as the Jewish character, Blida. He attacks her for trying to pass as more French than they both know she is. What is noteworthy about Annie Cohen's text is that it plays on the proximity of an Orientalized pied-noir and a Jew who may have known each other in preindependence Algeria: "The *marabout* and I, we are therefore brother and sister of the city of Blida. That is why I have accepted his words, his sayings."[38] The marabout dislodges the Jewish narrator from her comfort by admonishing her to be true to herself—her Oriental self. In France, both share more with each other than each shares with the continental French.

However, it should be noted that France and Paris are not necessarily inhospitable to Orientals and Oriental ways. France and Paris can be broken into different parts, some of which are somewhat welcoming to Orientals and to Oriental ways of being.

French Perspective

In this perspective France and the French are condemned for failing to live up to the ideals France purports to stand for. The French are criticized from the perspective of what *should* be. Anti-Arab and anti-French tendencies can also be intertwined in this perspective in such a way that self-hatred is induced among Oriental Jews out of fear of being identified as Arabs within a French environment.

First and foremost, anti-French tendencies manifest themselves in the form of a denunciation of the French for their treatment of Arabs in colonial times. This is of course especially true at troubled historical times such as during the Algerian War of Independence. In the criticism of France from a Jewish author who sympathizes with Arabs and their plight, several perspectives can be intertwined. Taking part in the Algerian War in the ranks of the French army becomes a personal conflict for Bensoussan's narrator in *Les Bagnoulis* and *Frimaldjézar*. In *Frimaldjézar*, the shame Bensoussan's narrator experiences chasing *fellaghas* (Algerian independence fighters) is at least partly a French perspective, since representing France means being on the side of the oppressor. The narrator's shame at being a representative of the French colonial army, dressed in *"treillis de la honte"* (fatigues of shame), is made more acute by the realization that his family owes his socioeconomic development to his father's participation in a more noble fight against *"les boches"* (Germans) during World War I ("It is the army that saved us from underdevelopment.")[39] In the following quotation from *Les Bagnoulis*, Bensoussan mockingly endorses the narrational *"nous"* of French colonial discourse: "Such a strange thing this uprising of the *Bagnoulis*, with my all new division that came full of dash, pride, and civilization to restore, so we said, good order. We did not know this remote land . . . these tribes were strangers to us and we had come as messengers of a truth for these people who did not speak our language."[40] In Amram El Maleh's *Le retour d'Abou El Haki*, this anti-French tendency can be seen in the worst example of a high-ranking pied-noir civil servant, Antoine Malifaccio, for whom "contempt and hatred of the Arab, of the native, were instinctive, of a visceral nature."[41] Some tenets of Malifaccio's credo are "force, force, the only thing that the Arab understands";[42] or in a more argued vein, "These people, these nationalist leaders, these Amine Al Andalussi and such, they play the serenade of democracy for you, but they try to cheat you . . . they show that they can be civil, open to dialogue, but this is all fake, the Arab is always cunning and a liar."[43] Anti-Arab sentiments can hardly be made more explicit— or less attractive—by the author. In condoning violence (verbal and physical), Malifaccio is implicitly judged by his own words and condemned by the author. As expressed by a character who is a product of the French colonial system, these sentiments also constitute a condemnation of France.[44]

Anti-French tendencies can therefore take the form of a denunciation of racism toward Arabs prevalent in colonial society and in the French judiciary system (Gisèle Halimi speaks for instance of "*le racisme de la justice*").[45] But they can also take the form of more personal and protective stands toward Arabs. Halimi was called the "whore of the Arabs" (*pute à bicots*) for defending innocent Arabs, as she reports in *Le lait de l'oranger*.

Nevertheless, it is rare to see racism against Arabs explored in depth in the texts situated in contemporary France. This may have to do with the insecurity of Oriental Jews in continental France and the confusion they experience both because they are Jewish and because they may look like Arabs. In Guy Sitbon's *Gagou*, when the eponymous character ends up leaving the Arab country where he hoped to remain after independence, he is advised by his brother-in-law not to mention his former work for the independent Arab government and to avoid some districts because of his looks:

> Always this face. Even he ended up not trusting it: with a face like his, it was risky to walk on the boulevards past ten or eleven at night. Because of arrests. With this face, the policemen were likely to take him for an Arab and it is said that in their police vans you take real blows if your face doesn't please them. The best thing to do, recommended his brother-in-law, is to look less Levantine, that's the best thing to do: never go at night in the neighborhood where the Arabs are. If one does not provoke them, the French are nice.[46]

Finally, the judgmental gaze of the French is painfully internalized as self-hatred, which also creates generational rifts inside Oriental Jewish families. In Marco Koskas's *L'homme de paille*, the author describes the decline of his father in a way that indicates that their Arab heritage is embarrassing—especially in the presence of the French:

No toilet paper. He [Koskas's father] was wiping himself the Arab way. In France, he continued to wipe himself the Arab way. During his last days, just before he was hospitalized, he also started to sing in Arabic. That made us feel ashamed. . . . We said to ourselves that he was becoming mad, completely mad even, to sing in Arabic in front of the French. But we didn't know how to make him shut up. People who passed by in the alley raised their eyebrows and continued their walk. I thought that they would hold it against us, that they would point their fingers at us and that I would lose the few friends that I had at La Drionne Square. In Bougival, each of us had started to make it. We had completely lost our accent.[47]

In this last quotation, Koskas seems to be well aware of both his own fear of rejection and the relative indifference of Others toward his father. Moreover, France is not a homogeneous place. Wealthy suburbs are not popular ones. The author's following remarks about his father make that clear:

In Bagnolet [a popular suburb], he could have made as many mistakes in French as in Bougival and no one would have ever thought to correct him. On Sundays, he would have done like his brothers. He would have gambled on horses and walked in the Belleville market. He would have taken a glass of anisette with a few old acquaintances. In Bagnolet, he would have gotten financial support from the communist city hall; and above all, he could have spoken Arabic without me feeling totally ashamed.[48]

This form of self-hatred—the hatred of the Oriental in oneself as much and often more than the hatred of the Jew in oneself—is caused in part by the high regard in which some of these Jews hold France and the French. In an interesting twist, Koskas's fear that his Tunisian Jewish father will speak Arabic to him becomes acute in front of a friend whose family happens to come from Algeria (and who therefore could be assumed to have a pied-noir accent):

> I feared more and more that he would come and talk to me in Arabic. As *pied-noir* as he was, Gavin would not have understood that my father talked to me in Arabic. The Gavin family had always lived in Algeria without ever becoming acquainted with a single Arab. They were *rapatriés* and we were refugees, or immigrants. . . . I started to be scared. I was terrified by the idea that Gavin would take me for an Arab.[49]

The implicit value that the Tunisian Jewish narrator attaches to the status of *rapatrié* (the pied-noir friend's status) versus *immigré* (Koskas is a Tunisian Jew) does not derive only from his status as an immigrant. Unlike Koskas, Algerian Jews were less *réfugiés* and *immigrés* than *rapatriés* since they were themselves French citizens. Yet even among assimilated Jews, this fear of speaking in the wrong way is pervasive. Even though most Algerian Jews did not speak Arabic, we still find an echo of a similar "oral" concern in Derrida's fear of being identified as pied-noir by his voice and tone: "I have never ceased learning, especially when teaching, to speak softly, a difficult task for a pied-noir, and especially within my family. . . . I was the first to be afraid of my own voice, as if it were not mine, and to contest it, even to detest it."[50]

Having given up on ridding his speech of any accent, Derrida comforts himself with the hope that there is not any trace of his accent left in his written French: "One entered French literature only by losing one's accent. I think I have not lost my accent; not everything in my 'French Algerian' is lost. . . . But I would like to hope, I would very much prefer, that no publication permit my 'French Algerian' to appear."[51] Which "French Algerian" is he speaking of? Not a specific Jewish French but the French accent or tone of North Africa, commonly referred to as "*l'accent pied-noir.*" Here, again, the fear is not so much to be exposed as a Jew but as a North African, which once more underscores the complexity of identities and relationships in this literature.

Notes

1. The "post-1948" framework suggests that authors wrote from a perspective that takes into account the creation of the state of Israel. Whether or not authors wrote about events and characters occurring after 1948, the creation of a Jewish state had to have affected their writing of history and permeates this corpus through additional layers of feelings and attitudes. See in particular Lucien Elia, *Les ratés de la diaspora* (Paris: Flammarion, 1969); Claude Kayat, *Mohammed Cohen* (Paris: Le Seuil, 1982) and *Les cyprès de Tibériade* (Paris: La Table ronde, 1987); Georges Memmi, *Une île en Méditerranée* (Paris: Belfond, 1992); Naïm Kattan, *Adieu Babylone* (Paris: Julliard, 1976) and "Les gardiens," *Pardès* 28 (2000): 195–201; Albert Memmi, *Le Pharaon* (Paris: Julliard, 1988); René Sussan, *La route des voleurs* (Paris: Denoël, 1959); and Chochana Boukhobza, *Un été à Jérusalem* (Paris: Balland, 1986).

The choice of the word "Oriental" rather than "Sephardic" underscores the connection the authors have to an Oriental way of being and feeling. "Oriental" encompasses a shared experience with Arabs—the authors usually speak of "Arabs" without distinguishing between Muslim populations—and a sense of belonging to a world that is not strictly Jewish. I am also using "Oriental" as it is used in French by many Jewish authors. At some point in their personal or group trajectory, the authors also fell under the French sphere of influence (language, culture, values)—at least enough for them to write in French.

By "simultaneous" I mean that both tendencies can appear at the same moment or in the same work. I also mean that while only one tendency may be explicit in a work, the other may be in the vision of the author.

2. Albert Memmi has famously defined Jewish literature as a literature that expresses the Jewish condition. For Memmi the Jewish condition is characterized on the negative side by oppression and on the positive side by values, institutions, and hopes (such as those embodied in religious or secular messianic movements). In regard to the positive side of Memmi's definition, I find it problematic to assert that Oriental Jews within the French sphere of influence share common values, institutions, and hopes that would collectively define them throughout space and time—apart perhaps from the vague hope of living in peace. It also seems to me that the condition of Oriental Jews nowadays as well as in some earlier sociohistorical contexts is one of vulnerability more than outright

oppression. See Albert Memmi, "Condition juive et littérature," in *Le Juif et l'autre*, comp. M. Chavardès and F. Kashi (Paris: Christian de Bartillat, 1995).

3. For an introductory evocation of this distinction between the Arab and the colonizer as Others, see Guy Dugas, *La littérature judéo-maghrébine d'expression française: Entre Djéha et Cagayous* (Paris: L'Harmattan, 1990), 73–81. By opposition, it is worth noting that, as Jean Déjeux pointed out, in Muslim Maghrebi literature the Other tends to be reduced to the Western world. See Jean Déjeux,"Unité et diversité dans la littérature du Maghreb en langue française," in *Convergences et divergences dans les littératures francophones: Actes du colloque, Paris, 8–9 février 1991* (Paris: L'Harmattan, 1992), 83–91.

4. Jean Yvane, *Le Dieu jaloux* (Paris: Denoël, 1989), 12. All translations are mine except when the title is given in English.

5. Annie Goldmann, *Les filles de Mardochée* (Paris: Denoël-Gontier, 1979), 123.

6. For an historical account, see Norman A. Stillman, *Jews of Arab Lands in Modern Times* (Philadelphia: Jewish Publication Society, 2003).

7. Paula Jacques, *La lumière de l'œil* (Paris: Mercure de France, 1980), 23.

8. Although Egypt was under British rule, I am here considering the French sphere of influence that these Jews relate to. When the narrator in Paula Jacques's *La lumière de l'œil* wants to attack her mother's condescending behavior more directly, she accuses her of "[faire] la Française"; in general, her superior attitude is equated to posing as French. From the perspective of the child, the mother who is "racist" in a rather typical, colonial fashion is also condemned for ignoring her, not liking her well enough and being distant—which is equivalent in her mind to "[faire] la Française."

9. Jacques, *La lumière de l'œil*, 80.

10. Hélène Cixous, "Bare Feet," in *An Algerian Childhood*, ed. Leïla Sebbar, trans. Marjolijn de Jager (St. Paul MN: Ruminator, 2001), 58.

11. Cixous, "Bare Feet," 59.

12. Cixous, "Bare Feet," 58–59.

13. Hélène Cixous, *Les rêveries de la femme sauvage: scènes primitives* (Paris: Galilée, 2000).

14. For more portrayals of the sexually menacing or inappropriate Arab, see Annie Fitoussi, *La mémoire folle de Mouchi Rabbinou* (Paris: Mazarine, 1985), 140; Gisèle Coscas, *Accords perdus* (Paris: L'Harmattan, 1994), 34–45; or Jean Daniel, "Dwelling on Images," in *An Algerian Childhood*, ed. Leïla Sebbar, trans. Marjolijn de Jager (St. Paul MN: Ruminator Books, 2001), 98. To add a counterpoint, I should mention that some Jewish children such as Paula Jacques's Mara in *Les femmes avec leur amour* (Paris: Mercure de France, 1999) could be the sexual "aggressor" or initiator of a Muslim adolescent, pp. 291–92.

15. After the national independence of Arab countries, the destruction of all forms of a Jewish presence can exacerbate anti-Arab feelings. In *Lalou* for instance, Jean-Pierre Allali resents the transformation of Tunis's old Jewish cemetery into a public garden. Jean-Pierre Allali, *Lalou* (Paris: Editions A. J. Presse, 2001).

16. See in particular Albert Memmi, *Le Scorpion ou la confession imaginaire* (Paris: Gallimard, 1969), *Le désert ou la vie et les aventures de Jubaïr Ouali El-Mammi* (Paris: Gallimard, 1977), and *Le Pharaon* (Paris: Julliard, 1988); Georges Memmi, *Qui se souvient du Café Rubens* (Paris: Jean-Claude Lattès, 1984) and *Une île en Méditerranée* (Paris: Belfond, 1992); André Nahum, "La Ghriba de Djerba," in *Le roi des bricks* (Paris: L'Harmattan, 1992); Annie Goldmann, *Les filles de Mardochée* (Paris: Denoël-Gontier, 1979); Naïm Kattan, *Adieu Babylone* (Paris: Julliard, 1976); Lucien Elia, *Les ratés de la diaspora* (Paris: Flammarion, 1969); Ami Bouganim, *Récits du Mellah* (Paris: Jean-Claude Lattès, 1981); Edmond Amram El Maleh, *Parcours immobile* (Grenoble: La pensée sauvage, 1980); Nine Moati, *Mon enfant, ma mère* (Paris: Stock, 1974) and *Les Belles de Tunis* (Paris: Le Seuil, 1983); Maya Nahum, *La mal-élevée* (Paris: Editions de L'Olivier, 1994) and *Les gestes* (Paris: Le Seuil, 1999); and Marlène Amar, *Des gens infréquentables* (Paris: Gallimard, 1996).

17. I am referring here to the protection inherent in the former status of *dhimmi* granted to "inferior" non-Muslims in Islamic lands. In relation to Arabs before colonization, there is of course some ambivalence toward the status of *dhimmi,* as this status meant that Jews were both protected in Islamic lands but also considered as inferiors and often humiliated as such.

18. Memmi, *Qui se souvient du Café Rubens,* 122.

19. Memmi, *Qui se souvient du Café Rubens,* 125–26.

20. For an account of how Arabs were viewed as traitors to Jews in Tunisia during World War II see also Gisèle Halimi's recording of these events in *Le lait de l'oranger* (Paris: Gallimard, 1988), 66–67. As a counterexample, Arabs in Algeria were beyond reproach in their treatment of the Jews during World War II.

21. Jacques, *La lumière de l'œil,* 79.

22. Although important distinctions should be made based on the different contexts and factors such as the social status of the Jewish families concerned, I would not agree with the general assessment from Guy Dugas in *La littérature judéo-maghrébine d'expression française: entre Djéha et Cagayous* (Paris: L'Harmattan, 1990), 73, according to which the Other in Jewish Maghrebi literature always appears in a domineering status in one way or another.

23. Claude Brami's *Parfum des étés perdus* (Paris: Gallimard, 1990), which takes place in pre-1956 Tunisia, offers a twist on this bond and exemplifies the web of factors at play such as age, race, class, and gender. In this autobiographical novel, the main

character, a young teenager, exchanges sexual favors with the Arab maid who asks him to steal his parents' money as a payback. In this scenario, who harasses whom? Is it the young Jewish boy who is obviously socially empowered vis-à-vis the maid? Or is it the adult maid who takes advantage of the boy's sexual desire to make him steal his parents' money? What matters most: the age or the social status of the characters? Does age matter, or indeed, do any of these factors matter when both of them seem to get what they are after in a consensual way?

24. Friendships between Jews and Arabs are not uncommon in this corpus. See for instance Katya Rubinstein, *Mémoire illétrée d'une fillette d'Afrique du Nord à l'époque coloniale* (Paris: Gallimard, 1979); Guy Sitbon, *Gagou* (Paris: Grasset, 1980), 114–20; Paula Jaques, *L'héritage de Tante Carlotta* (Paris: Mercure de France, 1987); and Nahum, *La mal-élevée* or Albert Bensoussan, "The Lost Child," in *An Algerian Childhood*, ed. Leïla Sebbar, trans. Marjolijn de Jager (St. Paul MN: Ruminator, 2001).

25. Albert Bensoussan, *Frimaldjézar* (Paris: Calmann-Levy, 1976), 34.

26. Halimi, *Le lait de l'oranger*, 62.

27. Albert Memmi, *Portrait du colonisé* (Paris: Gallimard, 1995).

28. Bernard-Henri Lévy, *Le diable en tête* (Paris: Grasset, 1984).

29. Brami, *La danse d'amour du vieux corbeau* (Paris: Denoël, 1983), 19.

30. In another work, Paula Jacques's *Un baiser froid comme la lune* (Paris: Mercure de France, 1983), the female narrator's father is beaten up by a gang of young French people while hanging posters in the streets of Paris for a Zionist organization (page 165).

31. Memmi, *Qui se souvient du Café Rubens*, 126.

32. Alain Meridjen, *Un matelas par terre* (Paris: L'Harmattan, 1995).

33. Jean-Pierre Allali, *Lalou* (Paris: Editions A. J. Presse, 2001).

34. Amram El Maleh, *Parcours immobile*, 209.

35. Numerous texts, such as Gisèle Halimi's *Le lait de l'oranger*, describe a traumatic encounter with a French instructor. It is important here to point out that, more often than not, the negative influence of these experiences can be countered or neutralized by positive experiences, as in Albert Memmi, *La statue de sel* (Paris: Gallimard, 1963), in Kayat, *Mohammed Cohen*, or in Daniel, "Dwelling on Images."

36. Annie Cohen, *Le marabout de Blida* (Paris: Gallimard, 2000).

37. In France today, *pied-noir* refers to the French colonist from Algeria or more broadly to the French from North Africa. It is even sometimes applied to Jews from North Africa.

38. Cohen, *Le marabout de Blida*, 43.

39. Bensoussan, *Frimaldjézar*, 129.

40. Albert Bensoussan, *Les Bagnoulis* (Paris: Mercure de France, 1980), 10.

41. Edmond Amram El Maleh, *Le retour d'Abou El Haki* (Grenoble: La pensée sauvage, 1990), 125.

42. Amram El Maleh, *Le retour d'Abou El Haki*, 126.

43. Amram El Maleh, *Le retour d'Abou El Haki*, 127.

44. What could be construed in a fictional text as a Jewish author speaking against Arabs through a pied-noir's voice does not hold in light of Amram El Maleh's body of work. For instance, in Amram El Maleh's *Mille ans, un jour* (Grenoble: La pensée sauvage, 1986), the narrator is haunted by the suffering of Palestinians. Many Oriental Jewish authors write more directly against the institutional racism of colonial France. Halimi in *Le lait de l'oranger* is among the most explicit in her condemnation, p. 62.

45. I should point out that Halimi's protective stand in *Le lait de l'oranger*, 175, does not derive from communist beliefs as do her uncle Jacques's and some fictional characters such as Gagou's uncle, Simon, in Sitbon's *Gagou*, or Josué Cramp's in Amram El Maleh's *Parcours immobile*.

46. Sitbon, *Gagou*, 234.

47. Marco Koskas, *L'homme de paille* (Paris: Calmann-Levy, 1988), 95.

48. Koskas, *L'homme de paille*, 16.

49. Koskas, *L'homme de paille*, 48–49.

50. Jacques Derrida, *The Monolingualism of the Other or the Prosthesis of Origin*, trans. Patrick Mensah (Stanford CA: Stanford University Press, 1998), 47–48.

51. Derrida, *The Monolingualism of the Other*, 45–46.

12

The Figure of the Jew in North Africa

Memmi, Derrida, Cixous

BRIGITTE WELTMAN-ARON

In 1946 Sartre asked the questions, "Does the Jew exist? And if he exists, what is he?"[1] These were not merely "rhetorical" questions unfortunately, taking instead a profound resonance from their proximity to the recent Shoah. If his investigation was acutely relevant then, how are we to understand the persistent recourse to the same form of questioning? It is as though the "Jew" forever remained an opacity, an enigma. Indeed most interpreters of the Jewish condition, Jews or non-Jews alike, often wonder, as a first seemingly inevitable preamble, "What is the Jew?"

Beginning in 1962 Albert Memmi took up the question of "who he is as a Jew"[2] in a series of essays, particularly *Portrait of a Jew*, followed by *The Liberation of the Jew* and *Jews and Arabs*, where he addresses the Jewish condition as that of a specific oppression. On the other hand he constantly underscores the untenability of oppression, the fact that no arrangement with or adjusting to oppression is feasible in the long run, for oppression is, as he says in *The Liberation of the Jew*, an "impossible condition."[3] This is why in Memmi's corpus every "portrait" of the oppressed gives way to an anticipation of their liberation. If, according to Memmi, Israel names the liberation of the Jew, it is because the Jews have been oppressed as a people and must, therefore, be liberated as a people.[4]

There is, however, another way of reading Memmi's discourse on oppression, one that suspends or problematizes the teleological assurance of the pattern he describes—oppression followed by liberation. Instead, this other reading remains alert to the rhetoricity of his investigation of Jewishness. To his own question, "What is a Jew?" Memmi repeatedly answers: "A figure." In *Portrait of a Jew*, he purports to analyze "the present figure of the Jew."[5] This figure would be biological, economic: the Jew represents a figure of oppression.[6] This answer keeps open the rhetoricity of the question concerning Jews; it still holds in reserve the proper being-Jewish of the Jew and defers its predicate because it unfolds as a trope, a figure. Nothing of the "Jew" is yet figured out. It might be objected that Memmi asserts time and again that the Jew is not merely absence, a lack, but maintains instead some relation to the self or what he terms positivity, even within oppression. Here is precisely where he situates his difference with respect to Sartre. Memmi does not accept that the Jew is only constituted by the other, "pure gaze of the other" and, what is more, constituted only so as to be negated.[7] If Memmi concedes that the oppressed tends to be reduced to a figure, constantly expropriated, including from his own self, or from the proper as such,[8] he does also assert that this is not the whole picture, even within oppression. In fact, however, Memmi's debt to Sartre's essay is evident, from the diagnosis of the anti-Semite's permanent accusation of the Jew to the affirmation of the Jewish right to difference: "Certainly [the Jews] wish to integrate themselves in the nation, but *as Jews*."[9] The main point of Sartre's essay was to emphasize that whether Jews have a positive relation to their own culture or not is to no avail, since it does not "save" them as Jews. It is, therefore, no accident that Sartre's essay gives the impression that there is no element of Jewish culture that is not *in effect* negatively filtered by a hostile view, that of the "anti-Semite." Memmi is actually in agreement with Sartre's analysis of the Jew's "situation": the ethical decision to embrace authenticity has still not solved the collective conditions of oppression of the Jews, which can only be addressed socially and politically by Jews and non-Jews.[10] While drawing that conclusion, Sartre also calls for the responsibility of all non-Jews toward all Jews, perhaps with the sense of "innocent guilt" toward the other that Maurice Blanchot suggests for "responsibility."[11]

To sum up Memmi follows two converging axes of inquiry regarding Jewishness: one endorses the national liberation of an oppressed people; the other examines how the Jew can accede to being and escape figurality. As far as being Jewish is concerned, when Memmi turns to the positivity of Jewish existence, he does not manage to foreclose entirely the figure of the Jew, for even in his authenticity or self-acceptance, the Jew is still maintained at a second remove; he still is a representation, a trope of the oppressor. The question then becomes, Will the national liberation of the Jew bring about at last the experience of being Jewish in its immediacy? Will it bring an end to figurality? If that is the case, what will "being Jewish" consist of?

Nowhere is the difficulty for the Jew to return properly to himself (*retour à soi*), in himself and as himself better exposed than when Memmi discusses his "identity" of Arab Jew.[12] I write "identity" in quotation marks precisely because Memmi shows that being an Arab Jew constitutes anything but an identity, certainly not a self-identity. Being an Arab Jew corresponds to partial identifications that never amount to a totalized unity. In the preface to *The Colonizer and the Colonized*, Memmi writes that he was "a sort of half-breed of colonization, understanding everyone because [he] belonged completely to no one."[13] He was a "colonized," but French colonization had also brought some privileges to the Jews. In colonial hierarchical society, the Jew was "one small notch above the Moslem."[14]

This situation implies a greater complexity in the process of liberation for the Arab Jew than for the Muslim. In *Jews and Arabs*, Memmi shows that on the one hand, "the arrival of the Europeans, which was a catastrophe for the Moslems, was a sort of liberation for the Jews."[15] On the other hand, when the colonized comes to the conclusion that he cannot or will not assimilate and initiates what Memmi calls a return to his own language and culture, though both Jews and Muslims have suffered from colonization, the Jew finds himself in a singular position: "*With the Jew, however, this return to self does not occur.*"[16] The Muslim was more oppressed during colonization but would return to himself more easily in decolonization; to himself, that is, to his language, religion, and culture. For the Jew, however, no such return to self is possible, because there is no self-same position to which to return. The Jew is condemned to live, and so little at that, in "the others' archives,"[17] Memmi says in a striking formulation. The impossible return to self is illustrated by the Jew's chance and predicament at the same time: How can one be liberated from the "sort of liberation" that French colonization made possible? It might be objected that Memmi opposes too neatly the experience of the Jew to that of the Muslim with respect to decolonization and its aftermath. In fact, Memmi does not always minimize the difficulties met by Muslim Arabs in nations where, to name just one issue, politics of Arabization have at times violently addressed the challenge of the plurality of spoken languages.[18] Yet what he tells of the singular situation of the Arab Jew's decolonization compared to that of his

Muslim countrymen and the specific ambivalence of the relation to his former colonizer remains pertinent and is, as we shall see, similarly addressed by Hélène Cixous and Jacques Derrida. The Jew's "identity" (understood as passport, nationality, language, culture) is not only borrowed, always borrowed, but also lived as such, as a loan that can be taken from him "at any moment and without notice," as he writes in *Liberation of the Jew*, and never is the self's possession.[19]

When near the end of *The Liberation of the Jew* Memmi states that the objective is to "restore the Jew to himself,"[20] it is nevertheless clear from what precedes that nothing but a long (re)construction will be necessary to face the task adequately. Memmi does not appear to hesitate when he locates what properly belongs to the Jew in the sense of his property and what he can appropriate as Jewish in itself. However, assigning a place, a location, or locale (Israel) to Jewishness still says little about what the specificity of being Jewish consists of. Clearly Memmi is more inclined to contemplate being Jewish as a future, a potential. His endorsement of a secular Israel leads him to defend the position that Israelis be considered as "a people like others" and Israel "a nation like others"[21] and that both be given a future in order to be criticized and transformed like any other state. On the one hand such a petition tends to reduce the Jews' will to survive, and the fact that Jewish tradition endured in spite of oppression, to utilitarian criteria, to a defense mechanism or "machinery of survival."[22] And at the other end of the process— liberation through the Jewish nation-state—the same flattening out happens regarding the specificity of being Jewish since Memmi advocates an evaluation of Israel like any other nation.

On the contrary Memmi's statement elsewhere that "the Jew is otherwise [*autrement*]"[23] should be taken seriously and addressed with patience. Memmi asserts the Jew's difference but does not

pursue sufficiently his insight regarding this difference, an otherness
that would display in its singularity the authenticity or the being of
being Jewish. Should the difference of the Jews' thought and experience of dispersion affect the very form taken by Israel, not only
as far as the civic safeguarding of Jews in general or of minorities
within Israel is concerned but for the philosophical thought of the
Jewish state itself, in itself, and to its others within and beyond its
borders?[24]

Maurice Blanchot addresses these questions with an attention that
precisely respects the positive significance of Judaism, as Memmi
could have said. Judaic law, Jewish thought (in particular that of
Lévinas) involve "a certain relation of man with man,"[25] which
defines responsibility and justice. Both Lévinas and Blanchot take
responsibility to involve a relation to the other that is not already
given but must still be elucidated. Blanchot says, "Responsibility,
which withdraws me from my order—perhaps from all orders and
from order itself—responsibility, which separates me from myself
(from the 'me' that is mastery and power, from the free, speaking subject) and reveals the other *in place* of me, requires that I
answer for absence, for passivity."[26] This disengagement from the
proper, from subjectivity, and from a preexisting order, is necessary
to constitute a true responsibility to the other. Responsibility, then,
does not already presuppose the *I* before and therefore in place of
the other. Or as Derrida would say, responsibility responds to no
calculable, decidable, and thus already decided program but lets the
event—that is, the other—come in the sense also that the coming of
the other is "the coming of what does not depend on me."[27]

This understanding of responsibility to the other does not leave
unaffected the thought of location or dwelling. Blanchot and Lévinas think here in terms of a "residence" other than Heidegger's
dwelling, to the extent at least that the latter implies an inherence

and a sedentarity or, as Derrida also says, metaphorically associates the proximity of Being with the values of neighboring.[28] For
these thinkers responsibility entails a dislocation. That dislocation
or untenability is precisely not foreign to what Blanchot shows to
be at work in "being-Jewish": "If Judaism is destined to take on
meaning for us, it is indeed by showing that . . . to go out (to step
outside) is the exigency from which one cannot escape if one wants to
maintain the possibility of a just relation. The exigency of uprooting;
the affirmation of nomadic truth."[29] Because "Nomadism answers
to a relation that possession cannot satisfy," nomadic movement
constitutes an "authentic manner of residing . . . a positive relation
with exteriority, whose exigency invites us not to be content with
what is proper to us."[30] In the sense that it posits a relation to the
other and to the self on the basis of dispossession and nomadism,
being Jewish "poses a universal question."[31] Therefore, being Jewish is not simply being like any other, but proposes instead through
thought and experience a possibility of responsibility and justice
that go through the passage of need, dislocation, errancy, and build
a relation to the other, and first of all to the self as other, on that
very passage. The works of Hélène Cixous and Jacques Derrida
reflect on, and testify to, that other responsibility.

Hélène Cixous has always written on being Jewish in Algeria:
"I was born in Algeria. . . . I am (not) Arab. Who am I? I am 'doing' French history. I am a Jewish woman," she wrote in an early
essay.[32] In introducing herself thus, she noticeably distances herself
from Frenchness, which is not even part of her inquiry. This initial
position does not vary in later texts. She calls herself "inseparab,"[33]
but she looks at her French passport with incredulity and does
not understand the verb *to be* connecting her to Frenchness. Yet,
she does not idealize after the fact a privileged relation she would
have once had to Algerians or Algerian "reality." On the contrary,

she indicates time and again that "Algeria" was never hers, that she was the "uninvited," the excluded, a foreigner on her native land, which therefore was not hers.[34] Her implication in crosscurrents of belonging and dispossession, one of the consequences of colonization, leads her to question notions of authentic dwelling and property (or the proper) in a mode that is close to Blanchot's. Colonization fashions the certainty of irreducible, heterogeneous camps such as illegitimate Arabs against legitimate French and leaves the Jews hanging there, nowhere, or worse, "forcibly played in the play, with a false identity."[35] Neither Jews nor Arabs manage to escape collectively that moment of togetherness in hostility that they first enact against each other before turning, differently, against the colonizer. Cixous draws several conclusions from that foul play and false positioning.

"I am on the side of Moses, *the one who does not enter*. Luckily."[36] Without exilic pathos, Cixous endorses nomadism, rootlessness and errancy, lines of escape, the difficulty of thinking the passage. For Cixous there is only departure, but not from the stability of a legitimate anchoring place; there are only beginnings in the plural, never an arrival; it is a question of departing (so as) not to arrive.[37] This is why, unlike Memmi, she does not see in Israel the opening of a future, but a clear end. In other words she does not believe that Israel represents the ongoing movement of an "arriving" but rather an arrival that entails that "the question *What next?* would have been extinguished."[38] Cixous presents commitment to the other in general, the engagement involved in siding with, being on the side of, as an act without return that ensures no necessary reciprocity.[39] This position also sheds light on the specific consideration of belonging as expropriation, which is characteristic of Cixous. It stems first of all from her experience and thinking of crossing borders, where in the most general way, passing a threshold (that

of school, nationality, citizenship, language) does not guarantee
the safety of a protective community of fellow insiders but on the
contrary brings about the strange realization, or the realization
of strangeness itself, that to be inside is also, is still to be outside:
"Entering gave on to exclusion."[40]

In Algiers, Cixous writes, graffiti was written on the wall for
everyone to read but apparently for no one to see. It simply read:
"You shall see."[41] Precisely the French were blind, deliberately or
by dint of habit. Sometimes absence, the fact that there is nothing
to see, is what provokes thought most acutely. With subtlety and
precision, Cixous evokes scenes from her high-school days in Algiers, this jump into *lycée* and by the same token "FrenchAlgeria" in
one word, a system "nottrue [in one word] to infinity" but for that
reason replacing truth as truth itself, usurpation built into a system
that projects a "plan to efface the Algerian being," a deliberate exci-
sion and spectralization of the Algerian body from the Algerian city
and landscape. Not only were Algerians never mentioned within
the school, but Algeria itself was never studied, not even named,
France was the only object of study.[42]

Unlike Memmi, however, Cixous insists time and again on the
chance for thinking that great complexity brought about. And if she
does revolt against the iniquities of colonization or recalls the painful exclusions she owed to prevailing anti-Semitism, in one respect
at least she does not wish to move one step beyond the recognition
she had when growing up in Algeria that "each scene always had
other contradictory sides."[43] This quote names "sides," which are
not synonymous with abundant positivity but require that one
remain alert to difficulty. Cixous always appeals to the chance, the
luck of exteriority, which should remain as such as a needed horizon
even after, and perhaps especially after the end of oppression, to
keep within Memmi's lexis. In fact her memory of being expelled

from school in Oran because of the pro-Vichy measures against the Jews, and her return to school after the change of government in Algeria, are marked by the same word, "chance," both in the sense of chance and luck: "In Oran we were *fortunate* [*nous avions eu la chance*] my brother and I to have entered outside, at the cardboard school, thanks to Vichy. . . . *Luckily* [*par chance*], once this holy outsiderization was interrupted by the American landing, it was not interrupted either in our minds or in our bodies."[44] Liberation is needed not merely as a rupture with oppression but as a conservatory of the lucky chance opened up through—she even dares say *thanks to*—oppression. Another way of stating this position is to say that while Memmi insists that the figure of the Jew should be separated from being-Jewish properly speaking, Cixous exposes the enduring tropological capacities of being a Jew.

Cixous, Memmi, and Derrida intersect at least at the point when each testifies to a dispossession with respect to the French language. But even their agreement on this point is marked by significant divergences. Memmi says that the Jew is "deprived of a language, without a legitimate language."[45] On the one hand, his mother tongue, Judeo-Arabic, was "a crippled language," and this linguistic trouble was aggravated when he learned French, in a frightening exposure, when he was thrown without a net into the French schooling system and thereby into the French language, as he recounted slightly transposed in *The Pillar of Salt*.[46] Like Derrida Memmi is wary of the notion of richness and surfeit, and both see blur or "trouble" where others would point out abundance (Memmi speaks of "linguistic troubles," Derrida of a "trouble of identity"). Memmi says in that respect that bilingualism is "a double inner-kingdom [that] literally imperils the unity, the psychic harmony of the oppressed. His second language, far from complementing his solidly acquired, self-confident mother tongue, dethrones and crushes it."[47] He remained forever the invited "guest of the French language.[48] In *The Pillar of Salt*, the young *lycéen* speaks like nobody; someone tells him that he speaks French like a German (I think of Cixous and of her at least double linguistic heritage): "I tried to speak this language which wasn't mine, which perhaps will never be entirely mine, but without which I would never be able to achieve self-realization."[49]

Derrida may seem close to Memmi when he tells in *The Monolingualism of the Other* of his "passion of a Franco-Maghrebian martyr" growing up in French Algeria.[50] Unlike Abdelkebir Khatibi, Derrida's friend, and the author of *Amour bilingue*, neither Memmi nor Derrida can rely or simply fall back on bilingualism; that is, a mother tongue, which in Khatibi's case is Arabic, and a second language, French—"a single mother tongue *plus* another language."[51] In Memmi's case, as we have seen, this happens because his mother tongue, Judeo-Arabic, is infirm, and his second language, French, will always be felt to be borrowed, never his proper possession. As for Derrida, he shows a range of interdictions at work as far as his access to language(s) was (and still is) concerned. As was the case with Cixous, and Memmi also, these interdicts are particularly manifested in the context of the French school, which becomes emblematic of a more general cultural inscription under colonial conditions, in fact, in the most general way, of the colonial structure of culture. The first interdict concerns the study of Arabic or Berber languages, the language "of the other as the nearest neighbor. *Unheimlich*. For me, it was the neighbor's language."[52] Unlike Memmi, however, and this is why Derrida's relation to the French language is at the same time more simple and more difficult, there was no possible return home to a mother tongue, even to what Memmi describes as an imperfect mother tongue, for "Judeo-Spanish . . . was no longer practiced" by Algerian Jews.[53] The impossible relation to the French language comes from this double order or interdict: "[T]his *I* of whom I speak is someone to whom, as I more or less recall, access to any non-French language of Algeria . . . was *interdicted*. But this same *I* is also someone to whom access to French was *also interdicted*. . . . In a different manner, surely, but likewise interdicted."[54] What Derrida is defining in this passage is the deprivation of an "authorized mother tongue," the French language being the "language of the master."[55] Memmi meets Khatibi in positing French as his second language, even though he clearly shows the ways in which that secondariness inevitably turns into a redoubted and admired primacy. But Derrida says instead, to remain a little longer within the premises of these terms, that French is neither a second language nor does it constitute the safety and comfort of a mother tongue. He still speaks of dispossession, or more precisely, he writes in a famous, difficult statement, "*I only have one language, yet it is not mine.*"[56] The whole essay elaborates the difficult "compossibility" of that declaration.

In a first sense, explored by Memmi, Derrida tells the story of the colonized when he says that monolingualism, that of the French language, is imposed by the other, by the master, while at the same time the colonized may not ever assume the ownership of French: "It is not mine." However—and this is a major difference with Memmi—Derrida also shows that the master possesses nothing either. There is never a relation of belonging, property, and mastery to language; language is "ex-appropriation," and this is the case even for the master or the colonizer.[57] With the notion of ex-appropriation, Derrida is also in proximity to Cixous's "chance," a term that Derrida also applies to his own experience, calling it for instance "a paradoxical opportunity [*chance*]."[58] As Derrida says elsewhere, ex-appropriation not only is a way of going beyond the opposition between appropriation and alienation but also constitutes "the only chance that is possible."[59] As for the presupposed unity of language, the "One of language" begs the question of legitimacy but does not solve it.[60] These pages are revealing of the ways in which politics and ethics are addressed in Derrida's discourse; that is, how they are not only discussed, but apostrophed, asked to arrive, to happen. First, the notion of alienation shows its limitations, for no property, no self is properly speaking "alienated" in relation to language. If no one possesses language, at the same time no prior plenitude was ever achieved or lost, and this entails that there are only appropriations of a language, to some extent and never entirely. Therefore the master is such inasmuch as he "can give substance to and articulate this appropriation . . . in the course of an unnatural process of politico-phantasmatic constructions."[61] It must be emphasized that Derrida does not thereby deny either the cruelty and humiliation of colonial oppression or the uniqueness, each time, of its manifestations. He also writes—and he is here close to Cixous—that all exiles are not equivalent, "all expatriations remain singular"; each singularity is both taken up in conditions of iterability and at the same time remains irreducible in its event.[62] If he insists on "the *determinable* possibility of a subservience and a hegemony," it is because this determination denounces all naturalized appropriations.[63]

It also corresponds in Derrida to a heterology, an opening to the other. For saying that one speaks one language that one does not have also means that language is always the other's: "Coming [*Venue*] from the other, remaining with [*restée à*] the other, and returning [*revenue*] to the other."[64] It is a monolingualism, yes, but of the *other*, a proposition that immediately codetermines an ethics of relation, exchange, gift, and hospitality. The monolingualism *of* the other also makes the other come, is the coming of the other.[65] Another way of expecting the other to come, or to speak of the monolingualism of the other, is to say that one language is always already in translation, that is to say, one and always more than one. Hence, Derrida's "desire to make it arrive *here*, by making something happen to it. . . . forcing the language then to speak itself, in another way, in its language."[66] Or as Hélène Cixous puts it in her reading of Jacques Derrida's *Monolingualism of the Other*, "it is the untranslatable that remains his dwelling place."[67]

In *Portrait of Jacques Derrida*, Cixous focuses, besides *Monolingualism*, on another essay by Derrida, "Circumfession." Cixous examines the point where confession intersects with circumcision in "Circumfession," both as writings or marks on and from the body. She draws attention, among other motifs, to this double writing, where circumcision "puts its stamp" on the body and circumfession is written, not said, unlike a confession.[68] Her focus and graft take up and extend several lines of argument in Derrida. On the one hand, Derrida is interested in confession as that which would no longer have anything to do with truth,[69] but on the contrary with avowal, asked-for pardon, assumed guilt, and the secreting of order.[70] On the other hand, circumcision is an event writing itself on the body, an inscription that always remains, and it is an event without memory that cultivates the circumcised.[71] In Judaism this sign on the body of male Jews also marks the covenant between God and his people. Because assimilation to the French brought about acculturation and a "handicapped memory"[72] to Algerian Jews, who were in effect "strangers to Jewish culture,"[73] Derrida's circumfession is said to inhabit what remains of Judaism for him.[74] At the same time, since "the Jews know nothing of confession," "Circumfession" both reflects acculturation and subverts the "proper" act of confessing.[75]

While Cixous has always been linking language and body in her writings, she notes that the inscription of circumcision is one that is sexually exclusive in Judaism.[76] As a woman, as the uncircum-cised,[77] she can only talk about circumcision "from the sidelines."[78] If circumcision is a cut, a separation, it is so to begin with in that it is reserved to men, to the exclusion of women. This is why the best attempt at defining what a Jewish woman is is to list the reverse characteristics of male Jewishness: "She is not Jewish (*juif*), she has no bar mitzvah and no tallith, in the synagogue among the Jews she is not there, she is off to the side, she is apart, she is parked in the balcony, she is there to look at him—her son her brother her spouse her lover her father, she is the necessary forgotten, the witness excluded for millennia who is nonetheless bizarrely necessary, from far away and very close."[79] However, Cixous shows that though apparently excluded from the inscription of the covenant on their bodies, Jewish women invent transgressive yet faithful covenants of their own, which ritualize circumcision in reverse. If circumcision concerns the male newborn (*le né*), Cixous inverts the rite by saving her Jewish nose (*le nez*), that figure for the penis, from being cut: "I was afraid of fleeing from my signifier my né-Jewish too big too long nose, my tip of an organ my father. In this way I had myself circumcised in reverse by refusing the operation. There are more kinds of circumcision than we imagine."[80]

The very association in *Portrait* of "né" and "nez"—the two words are homonyms—signals another motif of her investigation of Jewishness beyond the question of sexual difference or of being Jewish in the feminine: "It is always about the born (*le né*), isn't it? Or the nose (*le nez*) *in French*" (my emphasis).[81] Homophony gathers words of different meanings *in one language*, and this assemblage brings forth the chance of unperceived links or leaks of sense. Fur-thermore, one may never know what being Jewish entails, Cixous says, but one is Jewish at least to the extent that one says so, "by Jewsay (*par juifdire*)."[82] And this saying so is always performed in a given language. During World War II, her mother would use a code letter to designate a Jew: "He's a J she would say, to say it without saying, it, J the name of the secret,"[83] but she would pronounce that letter not as a German, but as the French "J." Therefore, the word *juif* is not only always in the masculine or usurped by love and faithfulness when used in the feminine, but what is more, "it is a French word."[84] She meets Derrida when she tackles the acculturation or "countertime" of the Jewish community in Algeria, where the knowledge of Hebrew had almost disappeared, and in which, as she says borrowing Derrida's phrase, "the trouble of identity . . . has also to do with this trouble of saying."[85] The very word *juif* in French becomes the entrusted repository of Jewishness, the "survivor" when all has vanished or been forgotten: "Imagine the enormous weight of the word *juif*, the swelling, the erection of the word, sole survivor of an extinct verbal population."[86]

This analysis of the word *juif* as the survivor that carries the burden of signifying what is not even legible any more but remains as a trace may recall Derrida's adoption for himself of the name "Marrano." In the Middle Ages, that name was given to a Jew forced to convert to Christianity, with the implication that he might secretly hold a faith that he could not profess and consequently, as Derrida argues, that he bore a secret that he did not properly own.[87] For Cixous, Derrida is also a "Marrano" in his relation to the French language, passing between the tours and the turns of French.[88] Here, after a long detour, we come back to Memmi's attempt to separate the figure of the Jew from his being-Jewish, properly speaking. Both Derrida and Cixous retreat from the unattainable literality or properness of being-Jewish and consider instead what the figure of the Jew yields as a question in a way that cannot simply oppose the proper to the figural. Cixous quotes Derrida's *Questions au judaïsme*: "The question remains to know what Judaism is as a figure, precisely."[89] And Cixous proposes a trope called "paragram" in order to paraphrase Derrida's stance on his Jewishness: "AM I JEWISH OR DO I FLEE JEWISH? (SUIS-JE JUIF OU FUIS-JE JUIF?)."[90] This example of a rhetorical turn, an example that is fully significant only in the French language, sums up several aspects that have been examined here. First, Cixous's paragram displaces the question of being-Jewish into that of escape or errancy, an undetermined location. It also figures the question asked of Judaism and of the Jew, always "What *is* the Jew?"; that is, it both stands for the question and turns it around. And, finally, the question remains.

Notes

1. Jean-Paul Sartre, *Anti-Semite and Jew*, trans. George J. Becker (New York: Schocken, 1948), 58.

2. Albert Memmi, *Portrait of a Jew*, trans. Elisabeth Abbott (New York: Viking, 1971), 20.

3. Albert Memmi, *The Liberation of the Jew*, trans. Judy Hyun (New York: Orion, 1966), 263.

4. Memmi, *The Liberation of the Jew*, 278.

5. Memmi, *Portrait of a Jew*, 88.

6. Memmi, *Portrait of a Jew*, 88, 320.

7. Memmi, *Portrait of a Jew*, 262.

8. This article contends that the extent to which a figurative meaning can yield access to a proper meaning is problematic, though in different ways for each of the writers under study. In addition, my argument will often rely on Jacques Derrida's analysis of the notion of "the proper" (*le propre*). The translator of Derrida's *Margins of Philosophy*, Alan Bass, explained in a note that "the proper" is a term that economically condenses the senses of "proper, literal," as well as "that which is one's own, that which may be owned, . . . all the links between proper, property, and propriety" (Derrida, *Margins of Philosophy*, trans. Alan Bass [Chicago: The University of Chicago Press, 1982], 4).

9. Sartre, *Anti-Semite and Jew*, 145.

10. Sartre, *Anti-Semite and Jew*, 138.

11. Maurice Blanchot, *The Writing of the Disaster*, trans. Ann Smock (Lincoln: University of Nebraska Press, 1986), 22.

12. In *Remnants of Auschwitz. The Witness and the Archive*, trans. Daniel Heller-

Roazen (New York: Zone, 1999), Giorgio Agamben discusses a jargon term used in concentration camps, and particularly in Auschwitz. This term is "Muselmann" or "Muslim." It designated a man having reached a state of extreme malnutrition, who out of weakness and suffering became emotionally and intellectually indifferent to everything, too tired, neither alive nor dead, yet or for those very reasons, "the sure candidate for the gas chambers" (51). One of Agamben's remarks darkly intersects with Memmi's concern with the figure. The naked corpses taken out of gas chambers were not named as such by the SS: "We know from witnesses that under no circumstances were they to be called 'corpses' or 'cadavers,' but rather simply *Figuren*, figures, dolls" (51). Agamben also writes: "In any case, it is certain that, with a kind of ferocious irony, the Jews knew that they would not die at Auschwitz as Jews" (45), but in other words as "Muslims." But something is left unsaid in Agamben's explanation for the very recourse to the word "Muselmann" (44–45). He considers the use of the term either in its semantics (in Arabic, the word *Muslim* literally means the one who submits unconditionally to the will of God) or in behavioral terms (their attitude looked like that of praying Muslims). I am not suggesting that Agamben endorses these explanations, he only reports them. But is this sort of etymology sufficient in itself when his analysis shows that Auschwitz achieved the utter degradation of the Jew as "Muslim," transformed the Jew "into a *Muselmann*, and the human being into a non-human" (52), or more precisely made the "Muselmann" into "the human that cannot be told apart from the inhuman" (82)? Slang or jargon is rarely entirely arbitrary but rests on some presuppositions. What does the fact that utter degradation could be apparently appropriately named "Muslim" tell us, including as far as the relation Muslim/Jew is concerned?

13. Albert Memmi, *The Colonizer and the Colonized*, trans. Howard Greenfeld (Boston: Beacon, 1991), xvi.

14. Memmi, *The Colonizer and the Colonized*, xiv.

15. Albert Memmi, *Jews and Arabs*, trans. Eleanor Levieux (Chicago: J. Philip O'Hara, 1975), 40.

16. Memmi, *Jews and Arabs*, 41.

17. Memmi, *Portrait of a Jew*, 202.

18. Memmi, *The Liberation of the Jew*, 183–84; Memmi, *Jews and Arabs*, 180–81. Djamila Saadi-Mokrane shows that the number of languages in Algeria must be thought both historically and politically, in relation to the fact that there has been more than one "Algerian war," not only the War of Independence against the French: "The existence of the pre-Islamic Berber language serves as a reminder of historical periods that many would prefer to see forgotten, a reminder that Algeria was not a blank state before Islamization, and that the Arabization of the country was the consequence of an Arab conquest" ("The Algerian Linguicide," *Algeria in Others' Languages*, ed. Anne-Emmanuelle Berger

[Ithaca NY: Cornell University Press, 2002], 44). In the same collection of essays, Hafid Gafaïti complicates the issue of the Berber opposition to Arabization by showing that the Berber community is not monolithic. Instead, some of its groups, like the Chaouis, have benefited from political, economic, and military power and embraced Arabization. In his analysis the Francophone Kabyle elite has been the recipient of benefits during the French colonization, and therefore at stake is a conflict of interests among different political groups, who are not necessarily aligned on clear-cut ethnic communities ("The Monotheism of the Other: Language and De/Construction of National Identity in Postcolonial Algeria," *Algeria in Others' Languages*, see esp. pp. 37–38).

19. Memmi, *Liberation of the Jew*, 185.

20. Memmi, *Liberation of the Jew*, 273.

21. Memmi, *Liberation of the Jew*, 288.

22. Memmi, *Liberation of the Jew*, 155.

23. Memmi, *Portrait of a Jew*, 313.

24. In fairness to Memmi, it must be pointed out that he often asserts as well the legitimacy of the Palestinians' national vocation (*Jews and Arabs*, 110–11). In *Jews and Arabs* he tries to provide answers that are not "apocalyptic" to the Israeli-Arab conflict. For him, that conflict is above all "a problem of peaceful coexistence" (109).

25. Maurice Blanchot, *The Infinite Conversation*, trans. Susan Hanson (Minneapolis: University of Minnesota Press, 1993), 125.

26. Blanchot, *The Writing of the Disaster*, 25.

27. Jacques Derrida, *A Taste for the Secret*, trans. Giacomo Donis (Cambridge: Polity, 2001), 60.

28. Derrida, *Margins of Philosophy*, 130. Heidegger's formulations of inherence and sedentarity in relation to dwelling have to be assessed together with what works *at the same time* in opposition to them, for example "ek-stasis." In "Letter on 'Humanism'," for instance, Heidegger says: "[T]he way that the human being in his proper essence becomes present to being is *ecstatic inherence* in the truth of being" (in *Pathmarks*, trans. Frank A. Capuzzi [Cambridge: Cambridge University Press, 1998], 251, my emphasis); "Language is the house of being in which the human being *ek-sists by dwelling*, in that he belongs to the truth of being, guarding it" (254, my emphasis).

29. Blanchot, *The Infinite Conversation*, 125.

30. Blanchot, *The Infinite Conversation*, 125, 127.

31. Blanchot, *The Infinite Conversation*, 447.

32. Hélène Cixous and Catherine Clément, *The Newly Born Woman*, trans. Betsy Wing (Minneapolis: University of Minnesota Press, 1986), 71.

33. Hélène Cixous, *Reveries of the Wild Woman*, trans. Beverley Bie Brahic (Evanston: Northwestern University Press, 2006), 24.

34. Cixous, *Reveries of the Wild Woman*, 63.

35. Hélène Cixous, "My Algeriance, in other words: to depart not to arrive from Algeria," *Stigmata: Escaping Texts*, trans. Eric Prenowitz (New York: Routledge, 1998), 156.

36. Cixous, "My Algeriance," 170.

37. Cixous, "My Algeriance," 170.

38. Cixous, "My Algeriance," 170. She seems to meet Blanchot when he says: "Jewish messianic thought (according to certain commentators), suggests the relation between the event and its nonoccurrence" (Blanchot, *The Writing of the Disaster*, 141); "Why the necessity of a just finish? Why can we not bear, why do we not desire that which is without end?" (143).

39. See in that respect what Jill Robbins says of Lévinas's "ethical relation," particularly in his *Totality and Infinity*: "The ethical relation . . . is a relation *without* relation. It maintains the distance of infinite separation, 'without this distance destroying this relation and without this relation destroying this distance' [41]. Lévinas insists on its radical asymmetry" ("Circumcising Confession: Derrida, Autobiography, Judaism," *diacritics* 25, no. 4 [Winter 1995]: 20–38, esp. 22).

40. Cixous, "My Algeriance," 159.

41. Cixous, *Reveries*, 69.

42. Cixous, *Reveries*, 80, 84, 70, 84. Likewise, Derrida says of the history and geography classes taught in his Algerian *lycée*: "Not a word about Algeria, not a single one concerning its history and its geography, whereas we could draw the coast of Brittany and the Gironde estuary with our eyes closed" (*Monolingualism of the Other, Or The Prosthesis of Origin*, trans. Patrick Mensah [Stanford: Stanford University Press, 1998], 44). As for the rare Algerian children in high school, he writes: "I have to forgo here the delicate analyses that the social geography of the habitat would call for, as well as the cartography of the primary-school classrooms where there were still little Algerians, Arabs, and Kabyles, who were about to vanish at the door of the lycée" (37).

43. Cixous, "My Algeriance," 160.

44. Cixous, *Reveries*, 71–72, my emphasis.

45. Memmi, *The Liberation of the Jew*, 185.

46. Memmi, *The Liberation of the Jew*, 182, 187.

47. Memmi, *The Liberation of the Jew*, 188.

48. Memmi, *The Liberation of the Jew*, 191.

49. Albert Memmi, *The Pillar of Salt*, trans. Edouard Roditi (New York: Orion, 1962), 105.

50. Derrida, *Monolingualism of the Other*, 27.

51. Derrida, *Monolingualism of the Other*, 36.

52. Derrida, *Monolingualism of the Other*, 37.

53. Derrida, *Monolingualism of the Other*, 84.

54. Derrida, *Monolingualism of the Other*, 30–31.

55. Derrida, *Monolingualism of the Other*, 31, 42.

56. Derrida, *Monolingualism of the Other*, 2.

57. Derrida, *Monolingualism of the Other*, 24.

58. Derrida, *Monolingualism of the Other*, 53.

59. Jacques Derrida, *Le Droit à la philosophie du point de vue cosmopolitique* (Paris: Verdier, 1997), 32.

60. Derrida, *Monolingualism of the Other*, 28.

61. Derrida, *Monolingualism of the Other*, 23.

62. Derrida, *Monolingualism of the Other*, 58.

63. Derrida, *Monolingualism of the Other*, 23.

64. Derrida, *Monolingualism of the Other*, 40.

65. Derrida, *Monolingualism of the Other*, 68.

66. Derrida, *Monolingualism of the Other*, 51.

67. Hélène Cixous, *Portrait of Jacques Derrida as a Young Jewish Saint*, trans. Beverley Bie Brahic (New York: Columbia University Press, 2004), 119.

68. Cixous, *Portrait of Jacques Derrida*, 73, 102.

69. Jacques Derrida, "Circumfession," *Jacques Derrida*, trans. Geoffrey Bennington (Chicago: University of Chicago Press, 1993), 132.

70. Derrida, "Circumfession," 48, 215, 296.

71. Derrida, "Circumfession," 120, 96, 60.

72. Derrida, *Monolingualism of the Other*, 54.

73. Derrida, *Monolingualism of the Other*, 53.

74. Derrida, "Circumfession," 303.

75. Derrida, "Circumfession," 187.

76. Jill Robbins quotes Howard Eilberg-Schwartz, who says that "[circumcision] establishes an opposition between men and women. Women cannot bear the symbol of the covenant. Only the bodies of men can commemorate the promise of God to Abraham" (Robbins, "Circumcising Confession," 35). And Robbins comments that "the discourse of circumcision represses the question of woman entirely. . . .This forgotten question is the unthought, the hidden ground of the discourse of circumcision" (35).

77. Cixous, *Portrait of Jacques Derrida*, 68.

78. Cixous, *Portrait of Jacques Derrida*, 68.

79. Cixous, *Portrait of Jacques Derrida*, 74.

80. Cixous, *Portrait of Jacques Derrida*, 74.

81. Cixous, *Portrait of Jacques Derrida*, 74.

82. Cixous, *Portrait of Jacques Derrida*, 75.

83. Cixous, *Portrait of Jacques Derrida*, 3.

84. Cixous, *Portrait of Jacques Derrida*, 4.

85. Cixous, *Portrait of Jacques Derrida*, 115, 116.

86. Cixous, *Portrait of Jacques Derrida*, 115.

87. Derrida, "Circumfession," 170–71.

88. Cixous, *Portrait of Jacques Derrida*, 114.

89. Cixous, *Portrait of Jacques Derrida*, 77.

90. Cixous, *Portrait of Jacques Derrida*, 78.

V

Francophone Spaces and Multiple Identities

13

Transnational Identities in the Novels of Amin Maalouf

ANTONY JOHAE

Amin Maalouf emigrated to France with his family in 1976 after the outbreak of the civil war in Lebanon and has lived in Paris ever since. During that time, he has published a history—*Les croisades vues par les Arabes (1983) (The Crusades through Arab Eyes*, trans. 1984)—and, following on from this first success, seven novels, one of which—*Le rocher de Tanios* (1993) (*The Rock of Tanios*, 1994)—won the Prix Goncourt in 1993.

In his long essay, *Les identités meurtrières* (1998) (*On Identity*, 2000), the author complains of frequently being asked whether he feels "'*plutôt français' ou 'plutôt libanais'*" ("'more French' or 'more Lebanese'") to which he invariably replies, "*l'un et l'autre!*" ("Both!"). He accounts for this dual allegiance by saying: "What makes me myself rather than anyone else is the very fact that I am poised between two countries, two or three languages and several cultural traditions. It is precisely this that defines my identity. Would I exist more authentically if I cut off a part of myself?"[1]

For Maalouf cultural identity is not reconcilable with the notion of nation (here France and Lebanon), nor can cultural identity be static as, say, political maps appear to be fixed because they have been inscribed. Identity is rather made up of what José Saldivar in his study of the U.S.–Mexico border zone describes as "crossings, intercultural exchanges, circulations, resistances, and negotiations."[2] This is why one can see the traveler in Maalouf's novels as representative of precisely this heterogeneous cultural being who, because he crosses seas, mountains, and deserts, enters widely differing cultural terrain; through commerce, exchanges of courtesies, ideas, gifts and goods, he feels himself to belong simultaneously everywhere and nowhere.

In his first published novel, *Léon l'Africain* (1986) (*Leo the African*, 1988), Maalouf has re-created the life of the sixteenth-century traveler Hasan al-Wazzan, known by historians in the West as Leo Africanus, who in this fictional autobiography identifies himself at first as his father, the weighmaster (al-Wazzan) of Granada; then with his baptismal name, Jean-Léon de Medici; then as a Granadan from Andalusia (Muslim Spain), a Fassi (that is, coming from Fez in Morocco); and as a Zayyati, his tribe of origin. Yet he rejects these appellations because, as he says, "my country is the caravan."[3] At the end of the account of his life of travel, he offers this advice to his son: "In Rome, you were 'the son of the African'; in Africa, you will be 'the son of the Rumi.' When men's minds seem narrow to you, tell yourself that the land of God is broad; broad His hands and broad His heart. Never hesitate to go far away, beyond all seas, all frontiers, all countries, all beliefs."[4]

This agrees with what Maalouf says of the postmodern conjuncture in *On Identity*: "[I]n the age of globalisation and of the ever-accelerating of intermingling of elements in which we are all caught up, a new concept of identity is needed, and needed urgently. We cannot be satisfied with forcing billions of bewildered human beings to choose between excessive assertion of their identity and the loss of their identity altogether, between fundamentalism and disintegration."[5] And he goes on to warn that if our contemporaries are denied their need to accept multiple affiliations and allegiances and are obliged to choose between negation of the self and negation of the other, the result will be the creation of extremists of the most deadly kind. Clearly, it is to avoid such horned syllogisms that Hasan al-Wazzan recommends his son to distance himself from the constraints of Frontiers, Fatherland, and Faith.

There is a similar sense of detachment from worldly stratification in Maalouf's re-creation of the eleventh/twelfth–century Persian poet-philosopher-scientist Omar Khayyam in the novel *Samarcande* (1988)(*Samarkand*, 1992), when he remonstrates with the politically ambitious court poetess who has encouraged him to vie for the post of Grand Vizir: "Are you after my downfall? Can you see me commanding the armies of the empire, decapitating people or quelling a slave revolt? Leave me to my stars!."[6] Khayyam does not mean by this that he will abdicate from social responsibility— live, as it were, a starry-eyed escapist existence or take refuge in an unscientific astrology—but rather, having found emotional truth in writing verse during the day, at night resort to his observatory in order to pursue scientific truth in astronomy; for Omar Khayyam's research would lead to the inauguration of a new calendar in Persia with the months of the year aligned to the signs of the zodiac, result in unprecedented meteorological predictions, and in mathematics come to be seen by European scientists of the nineteenth century as precursive of non-Euclidean geometry.

One might contrast Omar Khayyam's openness to knowledge with the narrow religious fanaticism of his contemporary and friend Hassan Sabbah, founder of the military and religious sect the Order of the Assassins, whose life is also depicted in the novel. While there is a peripatetic aspect to the poet philosopher's experiences caused often by his expulsion for free thinking and alleged heresies, Hassan Sabbah spends a great deal of his existence enclosed behind the walls of the Alamout—the fortress that became the refuge of the Assassins for 166 years—in order to instill by frequent admonitions and repetitions his teachings in the minds of his adherents; it is an austere place of imprisonment where few pleasures are permitted and where fear is paramount.[7] Hassan Sabbah's biographers have noted that for thirty years he hardly set foot outside his house, and this tells us not only about the nature of his enclosed life but of the prison of his own mind.[8] Perhaps this would not have been harmful if he had not also sought to imprison and harm others, for as the Syrian poet Abu al-Ala cynically once said: "My suffering is the fault of my progenitor, let no one else's suffering be my fault."[9]

While Hassan Sabbah's name has become irrevocably attached to the now-defunct mountain fortress of the Assasins, the Alamout (as Osama Bin Ladin's has to the caves of the mountains of Afghanistan and the twin towers of the World Trade Center), the name Omar Khayyam has come to be associated not with a place but with his lasting achievements as poet, mathematician, astronomer, and philosopher, one who has penetrated the walls of dogma and bigotry, crossed over the boundaries of disciplines, and expanded the frontiers of knowledge.

A propensity for knowledge rather than power is also the ethos promulgated by the protagonist of Amin Maalouf's third novel, *Les jardins de lumières* (1991) (*The Gardens of Light*, 1996), except that here the author seeks to deconstruct the commonly held notion that Mani, the founder of the philosophy known as Manichaeism, was propounding a rigid dualism in which opposites could never be reconciled.

Mani was born in Mesopotamia in 216 AD (that is, in the pre-Islamic era) into a community of religious zealots called the

White-clad Brethren, who had prohibitions almost as austere as those of Hassan Sabbah's Order of the Assassins. But it became clear at the early age of twelve that the boy would not succumb to the sect's extremism when he expressed an irrepressible desire to paint. The narrator comments, "A strange desire for one of the White-clad Brethren, an ungodly desire, a guilty desire. In their society, which was unwilling to accept any form of beauty, any colour, any elegance of form, in this community for whom the most humble icon betrayed an idolatrous worship, by what miracle could Mani's talent and life's work blossom?"[10] The answer is that he will reject the puritanical precepts of the White-clad Brethren as vain and perverse and consequently will centuries later come to be seen as the true founder of oriental painting whose legacy can today be discerned in the art of Persia, India, central Asia, Tibet, and China.

It is to be expected that a painter whose sensitivity to the properties of light, and its determination of a vast range of colors, should spurn a monochrome vision of reality and that he should reject the notion of the irreconcilability of light with dark, of black with white, or, on the moral plane, of the good with the bad, for as Mani himself says, "It is nothing but superstition to talk of pure and impure foodstuffs; it is nothing but madness to talk of pure and impure man."[11] Furthermore, the five senses are upheld by Mani as "the distillers of Light,"[12] a notion which would seem to overturn the traditional view that he preached corporeal existence as belonging only to the Darkness of a world ruled by the Devil. Amin Maalouf's retraction of the stark dualism customarily attributed to Mani is designed to show that such divisiveness was fundamentally alien to the philosopher-artist and that his view of difference was not based on incompatible dichotomies but on a subtle understanding of the diversity of a singular world. That is why he was able to venerate Jesus Christ, the Buddha, and Zoroaster equally, why in his view there should be no inequalities caused by divisive notions of race, caste, or gender, and why attempts to associate him with a royal lineage—as Jesus was with King David and the Buddha with the princes of Sakya—was anathema to a self-identity that would allow him to approach those he had come to heal through words, plants, and painting rather than as a powerful politician or warrior, drawing blood with the knife, fire, or the leech.[13]

One might conclude that as the painter is able to mix a wide range of colors in the creation of his original picture, so too Mani would have regarded each individual as made up of a unique mingling of light and shade, for as he says, "in every one of us there is Light and Darkness, side by side."[14] Perhaps what Maalouf has done in his reconstruction of Mani's life and teachings is to fulfill what he regards as one of the essential roles of writing, namely, the development of positive myths: "History draws on the material needed to construct myths of encounter and of reconciliation."[15] The author's optimistic objectives are clearly perceived by Antoine Sassine, who, in a preface to an interview with the novelist, writes, "As one can see, in *Leo the African*, *Samarkand*, and *The Gardens of Light*, these 'biographies romanesques' demonstrate Maalouf's choice to make known the lives of certain humanist philosophers; they illustrate very well his wish to propagate a wisdom anchored in human brotherhood, a respect for religious diversity, and the right of each individual to multiple cultural affiliations."[16]

This is not to say that such a hopeful state will be easily achieved, for as Maalouf makes clear: "I no more believe in simplistic solutions than I do in simplistic identities."[17] The reality is that cultures are formed out of struggle and resistance, and it is only in this way that coherence and consensus may eventually be apprehended.[18] Minorities and the marginalized need to be particularly resistant to what David Lloyd has called "the monologic desire of cultural nationalism,"[19] which seeks to deny or to neutralize cultural heterogeneity, hybridity, and an aesthetics woven from differing cultural strands. If as Saldivar has said of the U.S.–Mexican border-zone phenomenon, culture has become "a site of social struggle,"[20] all such struggles have to begin with an abrogation of the hegemonic cultural ascendancy of metropolitan centers before a deterritorialized counter-discourse of cultural critique can be set in train.

The full implications of the failure, or refusal, of hegemonic cultures to accommodate border cultures in a globalized world are set out in Amin Maalouf's anti-utopian novel, *Le premier siècle après Béatrice* (1992) (*The First Century after Beatrice*, 1993). The reader is taken into an apocalyptic world of the early twenty-first century, which has become split into a rich, free, and hopeful north and a stagnant, violent, and chaotic south. This world has also been impoverished by a severe depletion of its female population by genetic engineering and by a mass emigration of its population from south to north, causing a further imbalance that in its turn has put in jeopardy the stability of the north. Indeed, one could say that the world has become Dark in a Manichaean sense and that ultimately Light has all but disappeared from the face of Earth.

It should be borne in mind that *The First Century after Beatrice* is an anti-utopian novel and is at its base satirical. The object of such fiction is to warn of what might happen in the future if the existing vices of society are not addressed immediately. The message is only prophetic in so far as a bad place, or dystopia, might actually come into existence if the author's warnings are not heeded. I would argue that for Maalouf the vices, which he apprehends might overturn the world, are rooted in the problem of identity. In the opening chapter of *On Identity*, he states that his task is to try to understand why there are so many who commit crimes in the name of their religious, ethnic, national, or any other identity; at the end of the third chapter, he has already arrived at a conclusion:

> [I]f the men of all countries, of all conditions and faiths can so easily be transformed into butchers, if fanatics of all kinds manage so easily to pass themselves off as defenders of identity, it's because the "tribal" concept of identity still prevalent all over the world facilitates such a distortion. It's a concept inherited from the conflicts of the past, and many of us would reject it if we examined it more closely. But we cling to it through habit, from lack of imagination or resignation, thus inadvertently contributing to the tragedies by which, tomorrow, we shall be genuinely shocked.[21]

A representation of that catastrophic tomorrow can be found in Maalouf's fictional projection into the future and, I would argue, has come about precisely because of the failure of a generous, open, and global transnationality to displace the discriminatory and exclusive tendencies (sexism, racism, homophobism, xenophobism) of an entrenched tribalism.

In *On Identity*, Amin Maalouf has used the word "tribal" as a metaphor to denote a narrow exclusiveness of attitude, while in his novel, *The Rock of Tanios* there is a reversion to a literal tribalism of the nineteenth-century Levant, particularly as it applied to the people of the mountain villages of Lebanon. These communities were formed over time according to religious groupings (Maronite, Druze, etc.), and the fact that the villages were often isolated in the mountains made communication between them and movement away from them difficult. It is from such an (en)closed society that the young protagonist, Tanios, seeks to escape. The first door is opened for him by an English Protestant clergyman who has come to start up a school in the area to which, at the age of fourteen and coming from a Christian Maronite and Arabic-speaking community, Tanios is sent by his family. He is taught English and so is able to enter the Occidental world through the books he is encouraged to read. Four years later he finds himself exiled in Cyprus (then under Turkish rule, as was Lebanon) where he meets Thamar, whose forbears had been brought from Georgia as slaves: "Aged eighteen, restricted and frustrated by his village existence . . . he [Tanios] had found in the arms of this stranger . . . more or less what he had found in this strange town [Famagusta], on this island [Cyprus], so close to his homeland and yet so distant: a haven where he could lie and wait. Waiting for love, waiting for his return, waiting for real life to begin."[22]

It is this experience of a foreign woman in a foreign place that causes Tanios to look again westward—"To Genoa, Marseilles, Bristol. And beyond, to America"[23]—while at the same time being drawn back to the Levant by his tribal need to avenge the hanging of his father by the local emir. This irresolution is settled in the novel by Tanios's unaccounted for disappearance, but it is an end without closure because it does not tell the reader whether the protagonist escaped from the primitive ethos of his tribe or whether he was its victim.

In our postmodern condition, Amin Maalouf would reject the necessity for such double-bind dilemmas of allegiance, for when asked if he feels "'more French' or 'more Lebanese,'" his answer, as we have seen, is "Both!"; but it might equally have been "neither" because as the author has said (in an interview with François Bénichou), "I think that my native land is literature";[24] and in another interview (with Gunther Verheyen), he proposes that the notion of belonging be inverted so that a person can claim to possess several languages, be a part of several nations, and derive belief from a number of religious and philosophical systems.[25] What he is proposing here is not only that identities in our globalized world should be taken as transnational but that they be recognized as inherently transcultural. There is, as Saldivar has noted, a certain "betweenness" in this crossing of boundaries between discourses and cultures,[26] "a new transnational 'becoming,'" as he calls it, which has had the effect of problematizing the notion of a single patrimony[27] and has allowed culture to be apprehended, not in terms of an ideal purity, but of its perceived hybridity.[28]

One can see the lived-out reality of what has been called "crossing as both traversing and mixing"[29] in *Les échelles du Levant* (1996) (*Ports of Call*, 1999), set mainly in twentieth-century Lebanon, where the protagonist experiences no personal tension between tribal atavism and a civilized humanism as Tanios does in the earlier novel. On the larger macrocosmic scale of Middle Eastern politics, however, it is precisely such tensions that prove to be his undoing. Initially, coming from an immigrant background, Ossyane is not burdened by a purist tribal ethos, for his paternal grandparents were of mixed Turkish and Persian origin and his mother Armenian, and Ossyane himself marries a French Jew by whom he has a daughter. Not only has he, with his family, negotiated traversals of frontiers—from Ottoman Turkey to mandated Lebanon, from Nazi-occupied France to conflict-ridden Palestine—but has mixed blood through intermarriage, which in a tribal situation would have been regarded as transgressing taboos—an infringement deserving the *shedding* of blood.

In *On Identity*, Amin Maalouf has drawn attention to the special mediatory role of those he calls *"[les] êtres frontaliers"*: those "who live in a sort of frontier zone crisscrossed by ethnic, religious, and other fault lines."[30] He sees in their multiple belongings (*appartenances}* the possibility of reconciling diverse communities and cultures that find themselves at odds with one another; but these "*êtres frontaliers*" can act as mediators only so long as their several affiliations are not stifled by narrow, exclusive, bigoted, simplistic, and by implication essentialist notions of identity. One experiences such mediation at work in *Ports of Call* where at first Ossyane and his wife, Clara, divide their married life between Haifa and Beirut: "We had two ports of call, and a number of houses, though none to call our own."[31] And the couple are at first able to regard their union as symbolic of a larger reconciliation between Arabs and Jews. But there is also a symbolic moment of ominous import when in 1948 the British mandate in Palestine ends, the state of Israel is declared, and the first Arab-Israeli war breaks out; the road between Beirut and Haifa is blocked, the frontier between Lebanon and Israel is sealed, and telegraph and telephone lines are cut.[32] Not only is Ossyane completely severed from his wife but also from his as-yet unborn daughter, Nadia. There is a poignant paradox here when years later Ossyane remarks to his interlocutor about his daughter, "With us [Muslims], religion is transmitted through the father; among the Jews, through the mother. Therefore, according to the Muslims, Nadia was a Muslim; according to the Jews, she was Jewish. She herself might have chosen one or the other, or neither; she chose to be both at once."[33]

One is reminded here, once again, of Maalouf's response to those who ask him if he feels "'more French' or 'more Lebanese,'" and his reply: "Both!" But the answer is not quite as clear-cut as it sounds, because even his Lebanese identity is a complex one of belonging and not belonging, or even of half-belonging. As he explains in *On Identity*, he was born into a marginalized minority Christian community (the Melchites), even though his name can be found in the register of Protestants because of his father's religious affiliation[34]; his mother tongue is Arabic (the holy language of Islam); and he was educated in French by Jesuit fathers. These, taken with the fact that he emigrated to France, has imbibed French culture, and has written all his novels in French, is evidence enough of the complexity and uniqueness of his individual human identity—and by implication the complexity and uniqueness of all human identities.

It is no doubt because of his own experience of migrating with his family from the place of his birth to another country and also of his having traveled a great deal (India, Bangladesh, Vietnam, Ethiopia, Somalia, Kenya, Tanzania, the Maghreb, South America,[35] and other places besides) that so many of the central characters of Maalouf's novels have been travelers: Hasan al-Wazzan, Omar Khayyam, Mani, Tanios (perhaps), Ossyane, and latterly a seventeenth-century traveler, Balthasar Embriaco, the protagonist of *Le périple de Baldassare* (2000) (*Balthasar's Odyssey*, 2002), whose peregrinations take him from the Levant, through Anatolia, across the Mediterranean, to the Atlantic countries of northern Europe. Perhaps there is an expression of reversed empathy on the part of the author when he has Balthasar contemplate settling in Genoa (from where his forbears originated) and not returning to his home in the Levant where he is sometimes made to feel "a foreigner, an infidel."[36] On the other hand, in the Orient he has been able to live in a society where there is a high degree of harmony between the various communities of the region—"Turks, Armenians, Arabs, Greeks, and Jews, the five fingers of the august sultanate hand"[37]— and a tolerance for one another's religions—Islam, Christianity, and Judaism—which certainly did not pertain in seventeenth-century post-Reformation Europe, torn apart as it was by religious strife, the scourge of the Inquisition, and internecine wars between nation-states vying with each other for colonial mastery.

The traveler and the émigré are the "heroes" of Amin Maalouf's novels because it is they who by crossing borders break down the frontiers of political maps, are obliged to negotiate between cultures, have to learn to communicate in different languages, and through experience, come to understand, respect, and even to participate in the traditions and customs of the foreign other—to such an extent that the space between them can no longer be seen as that which separates but as the place of transition. The empathy that some of Maalouf's travelers have with that otherness, the way they are able to reach out to strangeness, makes it possible for them to think of themselves on occasion as simultaneously self *and* other; for as Maalouf has Balthasar remind us: "I can easily understand people who leave their home and their loved ones, and even change their name, to go and start a new life in another country without any boundaries. . . . Didn't my ancestors do the same thing? And not only my ancestors, but everyone's ancestors. All the towns in the world, and all the villages too, were founded and populated by people from elsewhere. The whole world has been filled by migration after migration."[38]

In short, every one of us has our origin in migration, and every one of us belongs to the diaspora of the world.

Notes

1. Amin Maalouf, *On Identity*, trans. Barbara Bray (London: Harvill, 2000), 3.

2. José David Saldivar, *Border Matters: Remapping American Cultural Studies* (Berkeley: University of California Press, 1997), ix.

3. Amin Maalouf, *Leo the African*, trans. Peter Sluglett (London: Quartet, 1988), 1.

4. Maalouf, *Leo the African*, p. 360. See also, Antony Johae, "Patterns of Travel in Amin Maalouf's *Leo the African*," *Annals of Arts and Social Sciences* 21, no. 163 (2001–2002): 8–52.

5. Maalouf, *On Identity*, 30.

6. Amin Maalouf, *Samarkand*, trans. Russell Harris (London: Quartet, 1992), 80.

7. Maalouf, *Samarkand*, 136–37.

8. Maalouf, *Samarkand*, 135.

9. Maalouf, *Samarkand*, 89.

10. Amin Maalouf, *The Gardens of Light*, trans. Dorothy S. Blair (London: Abacas, 1997), 45.

11. Maalouf, *The Gardens of Light*, 68–69.

12. Maalouf, *The Gardens of Light*, 80.

13. Maalouf, *The Gardens of Light*, 114, 82, 203–4, 128, 191–92.

14. Maalouf, *The Gardens of Light*, 69.

15. Antoine Sassine, "Entretien avec Amin Maalouf: L'homme a ses racines dans le ciel," *Etudes Francophones* 14, no. 2 (1999): 26, my translation.

16. Sassine, "Entretien avec Amin Maalouf," 27.

17. Maalouf, *On Identity*, 40.

18. See Saldivar, *Border Matters*, 14.

19. Quoted in Saldivar, *Border Matters*, 5.

20. Saldivar, *Border Matters*, 40.

21. Maalouf, *On Identity*, 25.

22. Amin Maalouf, *The Rock of Tanios*, trans. Dorothy S. Blair (London: Quartet, 1994), 188.

23. Maalouf, *The Rock of Tanios*, 227.

24. François Bénichou, "Amin Maalouf, 'Ma patrie, c'est l'écriture.'" *Magazine littéraire* 359 (1997): 115, my translation.

25. Gunther Verheyen, "'Faire vivre les gens ensemble.' Un entretien avec Amin Maalouf." *Französisch Heute* 1 (1996): 38.

26. Saldivar, *Border Matters*, 55.

27. Saldivar, *Border Matters*, 29.

28. Saldivar, *Border Matters*, 19.

29. Quoted in Saldivar, *Border Matters*, 12.

30. Maalouf, *On Identity*, 6.

31. Amin Maalouf, *Ports of Call*, trans. Alberto Manguel (London: Harvill, 1999), 123.

32. Maalouf, *Ports of Call*, 136.

33. Maalouf, *Ports of Call*, 255.

34. Maalouf, *On Identity*, 14–17.

35. Sassine, "Entretien avec Amin Maalouf," 25.

36. Amin Maalouf, *Balthasar's Odyssey*, trans. Barbara Bray (London: Harvill, 2002), 240.

37. Maalouf, *Ports of Call*, 30.

38. Maalouf, *Balthasar's Odyssey*, 264.

14

Madwoman in the Senegalese Muslim Attic

Reading Myriam Warner-Vieyra's Juletane
and Mariama Bâ's Un chant écarlate

JOSEPH MILITELLO

S hortly after marrying Mamadou, a Senegalese Muslim, Juletane—the Afro-Caribbean protagonist of Guadeloupan author
Myriam Warner-Vieyra's 1982 novel that bears her name—says of
her life in Dakar: "I had the impression of having arrived on another
planet, since I didn't understand anymore anything around me or
anything people were saying . . . I was surprised by the comportment of the people around me . . . I was struggling in an irrational
and foreign world."[1]

The novel takes place in the landmark year 1961, a time of
newfound independence for many African and Caribbean nations
and a time when the idealism of a Pan-Africanist solidarity and
worldwide brotherhood and sisterhood of "negritude" had a broad
influence. Yet this novel, with the benefit of two decades of hindsight,
reveals the cultural disparities that problematize the assimilation of
a francophone Antillean woman into a francophone West African
society, differences so insuperable that the two parties regard each
other with a profound sense of alterity—as alien "other." Juletane's
alienation drives her into madness, and even before her final descent

into homicidal fury and subsequent institutionalization, the Dakar community had already dubbed her *la folle*, the madwoman.[2]

Such a designation easily brings to mind Sandra Gilbert and Susan Gubar's classic 1979 work of feminist scholarship, *The Madwoman in the Attic*, linking the fate of Juletane with that of Mr. Rochester's "Bertha" in Charlotte Brontë's *Jane Eyre*, a character also of Caribbean origins who lapsed into madness and rage upon finding herself in a loveless marriage in an alien environment. For Gilbert and Gubar, "mad Bertha" represents the archetypal image of woman's repressed fury in an oppressive patriarchal society.[3] She is Jane Eyre's "ferocious secret self," her "avatar," her "Frankenstein's monster," her "dark double." She is a "big woman" with the "virile force" to give vent to her "uninhibited, often criminal self," making her Jane's "truest and darkest double."[4]

Such language, emphasizing Bertha's "darkness," recalls Jean Rhys's location of the source of Bertha's inability to assimilate into English society or to live in marital harmony with Rochester in her having been stamped as a "white nigger" by Jamaican society. In the color-conscious West Indies, her impoverished Creole status paints her a darker shade than a metropolitan Englishman like Rochester, who can barely stand the tropical climate. Her bruised head seems to give her the "mark of Cain" associated with the white mythology insinuated in Rhys's novel that links the dark races with the demonic, just as her red dress contrasts with the gray, repressed English social landscape.

The focus on Bertha's virility as an outgrowth of her "darkness" reminds one of Eldridge Cleaver's analysis of the nexus of race, class, and gender in America, in which black women's femininity has been denied them by their relegation to manual labor, creating a stereotypical image of the black woman as an emasculating Amazon.[5] While Rhys's *Wide Sargasso Sea* attempts to deconstruct such mythology, Gilbert and Gubar's use of a quoted passage from her novel as an epigraph for their chapter on *Jane Eyre* focuses solely on Bertha's homicidal impulses, and nowhere else in their book do the authors discuss Rhys's humanization of Antoinette/Bertha, much less the colonial context Rhys reinscribes.

Gayatri Spivak cites this omission in an article in which she claims that "feminist criticism reproduces the axioms of imperialism" by seeking to impose Western norms as the standard for evaluating women's oppression. She points to Rhys's alternative portrait of Bertha as a sane "critic of imperialism" whose fury is purposefully directed and justified to dismiss Gilbert and Gubar's dismissal of the character as merely "Jane's dark double."[6]

Chandra Mohanty further dismisses the identification of Jane's plight with that of Bertha in her critique of feminist assertions of "the sameness of [women's] oppression" which ignores "the historically specific material reality of groups of women." Mohanty claims that "male violence must be theorized and interpreted *within* specific societies."[7]

Sara Suleri equally challenges the abstractions of a hegemonic feminist theoretical discourse by focusing on the specificity of women oppressed by the "Hudood ordinances" that in the 1990s brought "the criminal legal system of Pakistan in conformity with the injunctions of Islam," citing a case in which a fifteen-year-old girl received "100 public lashes" as punishment for "fornication" after having been raped by male relatives.[8]

Warner-Vieyra's Juletane, therefore, should not be reduced to archetypal status as merely another avatar of "the madwoman in the attic," yet the ubiquity of suggestive images in literature of woman's claustrophobic confinement in prisons, cages, and harems—such as Snow White's glass coffin, an image in turn recalling the narrative frame of the *1001 Arabian Nights*, and the Lady of Shallot in her tower—cited in Gilbert and Gubar's book suggests a certain universality to this metaphor of oppression, especially when one reads Juletane not only against *Wide Sargasso Sea* and *Jane Eyre* but also in relation to Mariama Bâ's 1982 novel *Un chant écarlate*. Ironically, both Bâ's heroine Mireille and Warner-Vieyra's Juletane each get (as Bertha had earlier) just such a claustrophobic room of their own, a peaceful isolation from outside distractions that Juletane, following Virginia Woolf, even uses to write a book. Unfortunately for Juletane that room is in a psychiatric hospital—a fate shared by Bâ's Mireille.

While not dismissing the universalizing claims of a feminist paradigm that can connect Warner-Vieyra's work with Bâ's and Rhys's, one can heed Mohanty's command to study these representations of the maddening alienation of housewives oppressed by patriarchal societies with a detailed attention to the sociocultural specificity of each case. Patriarchal oppression can be transposed into the key of cultural hegemony, and woman's marginalization viewed in terms of the oppression of the cultural minority most clearly in works detailing "mixed" marriages.

One may generalize that *Wide Sargasso Sea* and *Un chant écarlate* represent two distinct representations of this process of alienation. Though rooted in cultural differences, the mutual repulsion Antoinette and Rochester begin to feel toward each other seems to play out on a tacit, intuitive psychological level. Bâ's novel, on the other hand, articulates more explicitly the sociological grounds for the failure of mutual cultural assimilation.

Rhys's couple initially bridges the cultural divide by invoking the transnational concept of an aristocratic family heritage and by the artificial custom of a financially motivated arranged marriage. Rochester's initial attraction, as well as Antoinette's, is primarily a physical and sexual one, however. It is no wonder then that their mutual hatred grows out of equally irrational passions. Aside from Antoinette's more rational objections to an arranged marriage, the growing repulsion of both characters is coded in instinctive reactions to resonant unanalyzed sensory impressions. Even Antoinette's disappointment with England's industrial capitalism, which differs from the ways of both the landed aristocracy (even in its decadent phase) and the communal, even tribal societies she was used to, manifests itself only in a fleeting impression of a gold clock at Rochester's estate, which Antoinette quickly denigrates as "the idol they worship."[9] She has equally visceral reactions to the sound of the name "Bertha" imposed on her by Rochester and to the cold and dark English climate with its strange sensations of snowfall and frost on windowpanes, and she longs for "the smell of the vetivert and frangipanni, of cinnamon and dust and lime trees when they are flowering. The smell of the sun and the smell of the rain," and for her red dress, "the colour of flamboyant flowers" in contrast to the gray wrapper Grace Poole shrouds her in.[10]

Rochester's reactions to Caribbean culture are just as visceral as when he is shocked by the Afro-Caribbean household servant Christophine's dragging the hem of her dress along the ground, despite Antoinette's cultural explanation that such a custom signifies a decorous insouciance over the cost of new clothes. He later reacts with shock to Antoinette's uncombed hair and bare feet and is increasingly perturbed by what he calls "a music [he] had never heard before" and ultimately concludes that "whatever [the local Caribbean people] were singing or saying was dangerous."[11] He begins to regard with suspicion even perfectly rational local customs like spraying white powder on the floor to keep away cockroaches, saying, "So much of what you tell me is strange, different from what I was led to expect."[12] Eventually, the very landscape appears radically alien and threatening to him, and he begins to feel "lost and afraid among these enemy trees," longing for "English trees."[13] He dislikes the scent of the local flowers and finds the heat "unbearable,"[14] hates the colors of the local sunsets,[15] and worries about black snakes and fire ants. His environment becomes to him a "green menace" in which there was "nothing [he] knew, nothing to comfort [him]."[16]

He reads of Caribbean traditions of voodoo or Obeah with incomprehension, while Antoinette all too quickly and with hardly more comprehension accuses him of Obeah when he tries to rechristen her "Bertha."[17] The irrationality and cross-cultural misunderstanding that destroys the couple's relationship reaches its shrill apex in Rochester's equation of her Creole status with a kind of dark Third World racial Otherness. The Jamaicans and local Englishwomen had earlier labeled Antoinette and members of her Creole family with epithets like "white cockroach," "white nigger," "black Englishman," and "old white jumby," marking in advance the ambiguity of her sociocultural and racial status in Caribbean society. Rochester seems to share this prejudice in his reflection that the Creoles "are not English or European either," as he remarks on Antoinette's "dark alien eyes" and use of a "debased French *patois*" with the servants, and he eventually comes to regard her as "a stranger who did not think or feel as [he] did" and finds in her voice a "singing and insolent" quality he compares to "a negro's voice." He seems haunted by her half-caste half brother's self-described "yellow" skin, a coloration reminiscent of Mary Shelley's description of Frankenstein's monster and seems to transfer that image subliminally to Antoinette's yellow silk shawl, making a subconscious association between her estranged brother's racial otherness and her own. Antoinette's mother had been tainted with miscegenation by rape. When she compares her marriage to Rochester with this violent act, her husband undoubtedly seizes upon the vaguely suggested notion of miscegenation within their marriage rather than getting her point about her victimization. Finally, he concludes, "She's one of them." She shares a hermetic knowledge of what Rochester inanely calls "the secret" of an Afro-Caribbean culture he finds inscrutable. It is thus in revenge he wantonly imposes upon her the same cultural isolation of her attic abode. Worried about his social standing and public image back in England, he hides her away in a claustrophobic prison.

Christophine, having experienced her own difficulties with men, had informed Antoinette that "all women, all colours, [are] nothing but fools" in allowing themselves to become dependent on men, who inevitably betray them. She thus expresses an assertion of the universality of Antoinette's situation appropriate to Gilbert and Gubar's use of the Bertha character as the archetype of the wronged, disempowered, alienated, dependent housewife.

Despite the recurrence of this character type and situation in Senegalese author Mariama Bâ's posthumously published 1982 novel *Un chant écarlate*, and the common sources of marital strife in conflicts over music, religion, socioeconomic class, perceived racial differences, and cultural disparities in general, the specific trajectory of Mireille's tragic journey into isolation and madness is informed both by the particular cultural assimilation she is attempting, as a white upper-class Frenchwoman marrying into a Senegalese Muslim family, and by her own unique personal idiosyncrasies and those of her husband and his family. While Bâ had previously documented the daily struggle of an African woman in a patriarchal Senegalese society in her widely read 1979 Noma Award–winning epistolary novel *Une si longue lettre*, her second novel, *Un chant écarlate*, establishes a global feminist solidarity by empathizing with the struggles of a white French protagonist attempting assimilation into this very same patriarchal Muslim society by performing what must still be a relatively rare act by a postcolonial "subaltern" author of ventriloquizing the hegemonic "First World" consciousness in giving voice to a white European protagonist.

One finds in Bâ's novel less of a sense of the purely irrational impulses that motivate the behavior of Rhys's characters and more of an overtly sociological than a subconsciously psychological conflict with the marriage between Mireille and Ousmane. Although there are strong suggestions of Oedipality in Ousmane's relationship with his clinging mother, and this mother-son bond is at the core of the conflict between Ousmane and Mireille, and although the novel seems to flirt with ominous suggestions of animist curses or hexes (like the *Xala* of Ousmane Sembene's 1973 novel and 1974 film)[18] and other antirational rituals playing a role in the breakup of the marriage, the author for the most part eschews a purely psychoanalytic explanation, much less a mythological one, for the forces that rend the couple and drive Mireille into madness. Her "madness," like that which Spivak attributes to Rhys's humanized version of Bertha, is in reality a perfectly understandable, though violent, reaction to her mistreatment by her husband and hostility from his community and her racial marginalization and enforced isolation.

While Mireille and Ousmane, unlike Antoinette and Rochester, came together through shared tastes, interests, values, and educational backgrounds, there are suggestions that the marriage rests on shaky foundations from the beginning. Sexual lust seems to play a large factor in the relationship, and there are suggestions of Mireille's attempt to assuage her "white guilt" as a citizen of a former colonizing power. ("Former colonizer clothed in a phony humanism," she calls her father when he rejects Ousmane.[19]) Even more clearly suggested is Mireille's Juliet-like rebellion against her parents' authority and, as a member of the May 1968 generation, against authority in general in pursuing what her society still perceived as a transgressive relationship. (She even brags that during the May riots, "I enjoyed giving a kick in the face to a defender of the order!")[20]

Ousmane's motives for pursuing the relationship seem to be partly political as well. He argues against the strident black nationalism of his fellow students in favor of a more progressive multicultural engagement with the world, a cosmopolitan attitude in part borrowed from his father's pride at having spent time in Paris during the war and his generally progressive outlook exemplified by his decision to remain monogamous in a traditionally polygamous society and to send his son to the French school rather than the Koranic school. Eventually Ousmane will admit to himself that Mireille was for his youthful self a "trophy wife" whose whiteness and Frenchness might have helped his career.

Ousmane's youthful fantasies of seducing a "rab" (that is, a genie) with "immense luminous eyes and long silken hair"[21] also seem to anticipate his choice of Mireille, who enchants him with "her golden and silken hair and the long fluttering lashes of her blue-green eyes."[22] Although Ousmane's family and Ousmane himself come to refer to Mireille as a dangerously seductive genie, whose "blue-green eyes radiated a bewitching, seductive power,"[23] emphasizing her mystical otherness, the main thrust of the novel is away from such irrational depictions of the forces operating to alienate the couple from each another and toward much more lucid and pedestrian explanations of their personal conflict as rooted in a larger sociocultural conflict.

Bâ describes how differing cultural tastes and customs combine with the objections and behavior of family and friends and racial, class, religious, and political divisions to drive a wedge between Ousmane and Mireille.

Such a seemingly trivial cultural difference as diet becomes divisive. Mireille found the "extremely hot, peppery dishes" of Senegal to be "torture," causing a severe physical reaction. When Ousmane becomes ill, his mother attributes it to his diet of "steak, potatoes, yogurt" prepared by Mireille, as opposed to his more customary diet of "foufou" (mashed gumbo) and "oxtail soup." When Ousmane has an extramarital liaison with the native Senegalese Ouleymatou, he very early on in the relationship instructs his lover to prepare him a nice fish couscous with *Oba* and *Yaboye* (sun-dried fish and sardines). When the meal is prepared, he takes an atavistic "childlike pleasure in eating again with his fingers"[24] in contrast to Mireille's European insistence on his using "a proper spoon" and meticulously washing his hands before dinner, cultural imperatives he finds restrictive and oppressive. He politicizes this preference by reflecting on his nostalgia for the flavor of his native dishes and the strong sensations of African life.

For her part Mireille considered such traditional Senegalese behavior as eating with one's hands as a lack of savoir-faire or a crudeness, recalling Rochester's Eurocentric dismay at Caribbean women dragging their hems along the ground. Ousmane's attachment "to the baobab trees of his country"[25] recalls Rochester's longing for "English trees," adding topographical considerations to the cultural divide. Upon landing at the Roissy-Charles de Gaulle airport, Ousmane had found "the climate and the high-tech world that surrounded him"[26] an alien environment. Ousmane's eventual abandonment of European suits for "more comfortable caftans" brings to mind both Rochester's clothing obsession and Antoinette's chafing at her gray shawl and "loss" of her red dress.

As with the Rochesters, language is also a barrier. Mireille is unable to master the difficult Wolof language, isolating her further from her in-laws, and Ousmane comes to despise the assimilationist tendency of African parents christening their children with Western names like "Ralph, Arthur, Melanie," bespeaking a postcolonial consciousness that resonates with Rochester's renaming of Antoinette as Bertha.

Musical preferences come into play when Mireille, a lover of Mozart, had difficulty coping with "the nightly tom-toms! They pounded her temples and exasperated her nerves."[27] Ousmane decries her lack of appreciation for African music and later relishes the *griot* who strums his Khalam at Ouleymatou's residence and the tom-toms and dancing *griotes* at the baptism of his and Ouleymatou's child. Mireille had found the *griot* tradition incomprehensible, as well as the incessant gift-giving traditions, rituals that were very much in evidence at the baptism. "In marrying a man, one marries also his manner of living"[28] is the patriarchal assertion made by Ousmane.

Even if Mireille had been willing to give up her cultural habits and to adopt her husband's, it is not so easy a thing to adjust one's instincts, despite the fact that this couple was a self-conscious postmodern one actively combating prejudices with a youthful idealism neither Antoinette nor Rochester ever possessed. In praising Ouleymatou in preference to Mireille, Ousmane explains: "She knows the legend of Samba Gueladio, she knows our proverbs. We can communicate in a remark, a greeting, a wink, and that's important. . . . We have the same ancient references."[29]

Although Mireille could never hope to achieve such a deep-rooted cultural kinship with Ousmane, ironically her romance with him began with a similarly meaningful exchange of glances in which could be variously conveyed a shared boredom at a university lecture or other kindred emotions. In particular nonverbal communication between Ousmane and Mireille informed a key moment in their early mutual attraction, when they both used subtle facial signals to help one another through *le bac,* the intensive French university entrance exam.

But in addition to differences in ingrained cultural habits, social institutions began to play a role in dividing the pair. Mireille tentatively accepts Islam "without enthusiasm" but never learns to kneel properly in prayer, prefers the cinema to her father-in-law's ceremonial Muslim hymns and Koranic verse translations, and bristles at the very thought of polygamy or arranged marriage.

Institutionalized class differences also come into play when Ousmane views the 1968 riots at his Dakar university as concerned with "serious causes of agitation of socioeconomic justice" in contrast to the struggles of the Parisian bourgeois "frustration motivated only by the desire for revolt" that Godard had satirized in his 1966 film *Masculin-Féminin* as belonging to "the children of Marx and Coca Cola."[30] Mireille exhibits a bourgeois snobbism toward Ouleymatou in her jealous contempt of the latter's seeming primitivism and lack of subtlety and European sophistication.

While a perceived racial Otherness begins to contribute to marital discord, it is less of the vaguely insinuated subconscious feeling depicted in Rhys's novel and a more overt racial polarization. Ousmane's friends' allegations of a universal white racism work on his growing nationalistic consciousness. Ouleymatou became mingled in his mind with Africa, Bâ tells us. He prefers the pure-blooded African child he produced with her to the "Gnouloule Khessoule" (half-caste) Mireille gave him and the sensuous clinking of the metallic bangles—the rattling suggestive in Ousmane's mind of a Negress's buttocks in the hot colors of her African robe—to Mireille's French charms. The betrayed Mireille regresses from her enlightened racial views and is reduced to calling Ousmane a "dirty nigger" and Ouleymatou "your negress" by the end of the novel.[31]

But just as Othello had his Iago to bring out the worst in him, active scheming and opposition to the marriage by various parties ultimately destroy the relationship. Ouleymatou covertly courts the married man, and Ousmane's friends go out of their way to be rude, inviting themselves over for meals and card playing late into the evening. They make rude jokes, ignore Mireille's presence or status as mistress of the house, and speak Wolof unintelligible to her despite their mastery of French. Ousmane attributes Mireille's displeasure with their behavior to a selfish European failure to comprehend communal African life, yet nothing of the sort had disrupted his parents' household.

Both families oppose the marriage. Mireille's father scratches Ousmane's photo and slaps her face when he discovers the relationship and worries that her marriage will tarnish the family name. Her mother faints at news of the marriage. Ousmane's mother schemes against Mireille and encourages Ouleymatou's advances, fearing that a white daughter-in-law would never relieve her of difficult household chores and wait on her in her old age. She intentionally invades Mireille's privacy by entering the inner sanctum of her bedroom at will and always expecting gifts and money. While the meaning of Ousmane's photo was immediately apparent to Mireille's parents, Ousmane's large collection of framed photographs of Mireille sits on his bureau for many months practically unnoticed by his parents, who assume that such a beautiful blue-eyed blonde could only be a cinema star their son was infatuated with from afar. The idea that such a European beauty could be their son's girlfriend was so alien to them that it was totally beyond their provincial frame of reference, despite the family patriarch's claims to progressive cosmopolitanism.

In Warner-Vieyra's novel, Juletane and Mamadou experience many of the same divisive forces. The novel seems an amalgam of the sociological approach of Bâ's work and the psychological approach of Rhys's. The expected cultural differences between the Europeanized Antillean Juletane and the nativist Senegalese Mamadou again surface. Mamadou's friends and relatives speak "the national language mixed together with French."[32] Juletane grows tired of the steady diet of rice and fish eaten without a spoon. Back in France, she could be seen dining out at a Chinese restaurant in Montmartre and had potentially all the culinary variety of Paris at her disposal. As with Mireille's preference for Mozart over tom-toms, Juletane, weaned on symphonic music, uses a recording of Beethoven's Ninth Symphony to drown out the *pachanga* that they were listening to on the radio. Her Senegalese co-wife Ndeye smashes the record and slaps her face for playing "crazy music."

Religion also intrudes on the relationship. Unlike Mireille, Juletane has never abandoned her Catholicism. In moments of crisis, she says "novenas to all the saints" and attributes her marital misfortune to the curse of having been conceived by her parents during Lent, a time of Catholic abstinence.[33] She does not understand Muslim ways. She is astonished when the local Imam ceremonially spits in her hands and amazed by the fatalism of the community's acceptance of her stepchildren's deaths as the will of Allah. She finds animist traditions equally alien. She sneers at Ndeye's *marabouts* and *griots* and dismisses the custom of wrapping a newborn baby in its mother's *pagne* rather than buying baby clothes. She finds polygamy and arranged marriages horrifying and refuses to accept with equanimity her co-wives and stepchildren, all of whom she directly or indirectly kills or maims. She is openly critical of the hypocrisy of declared Muslims who drink whiskey, avoid Ramadan fasting with claims of stomach ulcers, and only seize with enthusiasm upon the hedonistic aspects of the religion such as polygamy and *tabaski*—a sheep-sacrificing feast—while avoiding its ascetic proscriptions. Rational objections to this religious culture give way to irrational nightmares: "I was awoken in the early morning by a veritable howling of a beast that tore me out of the nightmare in which it was struggling: four masked men, with naked and hairy chests, sneering at and mocking me in a language that I didn't understand, pulled me by the arms and the feet. Between each cry, I heard the voice of the muezzin, who called the faithful to the prayer of the 'fajar.'"[34]

Such a profound alienation occurs despite the fact that unlike Mireille, Juletane is of African heritage. In 1961 a time of negritude, she looks forward to a homecoming to "that African land of my ancestors" as an end to the exile of the African diaspora.[35] Later she refers to her Caribbean birthplace as "my homeland" but mostly longs for a return to Paris. Nonetheless, she is shocked and offended at the denial of her racial identity by co-wife Ndeye, who calls her a *toubabesse* (whitey):

> For her, I am crazy and, what is also completely vexing for me, a *toubabesse*: she has thrown me together, no more and no less, with the white women of the colonizers. She has taken away my black identity. My forefathers have paid harshly for my right to be black, fertilizing the American soils with their spilt blood and with their sweat in hopeless revolts so that I was born free and proud to be black. . . . I would have never imagined at this moment—there, in an African land—that someone would confuse me with a White Woman.[36]

Yet the stage had been set for such racial marginalization of the Afro-Caribbean Juletane. Upon their first meeting at a garden party at the Cité Universitaire in Paris, Juletane was stiffly self-conscious and with her bourgeois upbringing and classical tastes in music didn't know how to dance. While Mamadou had "a light-footedness," Juletane, to Mamadou's amusement, couldn't dance the beguine, "a Negress who dances like a broomstick,"[37] her future husband says mockingly. Juletane was a self-declared ingénue with her hair in braids who dreamed of meeting a monogamous Prince Charming. Mamadou on the other hand fears appearing "like a toubab" when his early attentions to Juletane are overly romantic in the Hollywood fashion.

With her irrational racial marginalization, reminiscent of Antoinette/Bertha's, heaped on top of the more pedestrian social difficulties of cultural assimilation, Juletane dissipates into not merely the homicidal revenge-filled rage of Mireille, but into a schizophrenic state of hallucination, paranoia, delusion, and catatonia closer to Bertha's, the archetypal madwoman in the attic, fulfilling Ndeye's prophetic labeling of her as *la folle*, the madwoman.

Her killing of the children, whether an act of commission or a reckless accident, conjures mythic images of Medea, again suggesting the timeless universality of her fate, which depressingly seems to be shared by countless other women, like Oumy and Nabou, victims of bad marriages not unlike her own who end up in the same psychiatric institution.

Warner-Vieyra's *Juletane* and Bâ's *Un chant écarlate* thus universalize the image of the oppressed, marginalized woman driven to madness by a bad marriage and social ostracism, extending that Gilbert and Gubar motif beyond the early Victorian British setting of *Jane Eyre* and even the postmodern recontextualization and displacement of the setting to the Caribbean provided by Jean Rhys. The contemporary, postfeminist revival of the madwoman archetype and its new placement in West African society both affirms Gilbert and Gubar's identification of that victimization as ubiquitous and central to woman's experience and supplements their analysis by introducing postcolonial Third World nonwhite male authorities and societies as the oppressors.

Notes

1. Myriam Warner-Vieyra, *Juletane* (Paris: Présence Africaine, 1982), 48, 52. All translations mine.

2. Warner-Vieyra, *Juletane*, 76.

3. Sandra M. Gilbert and Susan Gubar, *The Madwoman in the Attic* (New Haven: Yale University Press, 2000), 348.

4. Gilbert, *Madwoman in the Attic*, 357–60.

5. Eldridge Cleaver, "The Primeval Mitosis," in *Norton Anthology of African American Literature*, ed. Henry Louis Gates (New York: W.W. Norton, 1997), 1947–55.

6. Gayatri Chakravorty Spivak, "Three Women's Texts and a Critique of Imperialism," in *The Post-Colonial Studies Reader*, ed. Bill Ashcroft (New York: Routledge, 1995), 269–71.

7. Chandra Mohanty, "Under Western Eyes: Feminist Scholarship and Colonial Discourses," in Ashcroft, *Post-Colonial Studies Reader*, 262.

8. Sara Suleri, "Woman Skin Deep: Feminism and the Postcolonial Condition," in Ashcroft, *Post-Colonial Studies Reader*, 278–79.

9. Jean Rhys, *Wide Sargasso Sea* (New York: W.W. Norton, 1966), 188.

10. Rhys, *Wide Sargasso Sea*, 185.

11. Rhys, *Wide Sargasso Sea*, 90, 149.

12. Rhys, *Wide Sargasso Sea*, 135.

13. Rhys, *Wide Sargasso Sea*, 163.

14. Rhys, *Wide Sargasso Sea*, 147.

15. Rhys, *Wide Sargasso Sea*, 172.

16. Rhys, *Wide Sargasso Sea*, 149.

17. Rhys, *Wide Sargasso Sea*, 147.

18. Ousmane Sembene, *Xala* (Paris: Présence africaine, 1973).

19. Mariama Bâ, *Un chant écarlate* (Dakar, Senegal: Les Nouvelles Editions Africaines, 1981), 44.

20. Bâ, *Un chant écarlate*, 67.

21. Bâ, *Un chant écarlate*, 18.

22. Bâ, *Un chant écarlate*, 25.

23. Bâ, *Un chant écarlate*, 186.

24. Bâ, *Un chant écarlate*, 178.

25. Bâ, *Un chant écarlate*, 58.

26. Bâ, *Un chant écarlate*, 155.

27. Bâ, *Un chant écarlate*, 140.

28. Bâ, *Un chant écarlate*, 133.

29. Bâ, *Un chant écarlate*, 208.

30. Bâ, *Un chant écarlate*, 73.

31. Bâ, *Un chant écarlate*, 241, 244.

32. Warner-Vieyra, *Juletane*, 35.

33. Warner-Vieyra, *Juletane*, 70.

34. Warner-Vieyra, *Juletane*, 35.

35. Warner-Vieyra, *Juletane*, 35.

36. Warner-Vieyra, *Juletane*, 79–80.

37. Warner-Vieyra, *Juletane*, 19.

15

Gender, Exile, and Return in Viêt-Kiều Literature

GEORGES VAN DEN ABBEELE

Upon returning to his native Vietnam, Andrew Lam describes the following scene:

> Saigon—The scrawny street vendor studies my eyes, my lips. "Brother," he observes, "yours is not a Vietnamese face. It's a face that has not known suffering." Then, after a long sigh, he concludes: "Had I escaped to America, brother, maybe I too would have such a face—A Viet Kieu's face."[1]

According to recent statistics, about two million Vietnamese live outside Vietnam.[2] This Vietnamese "diaspora" is an extraordinarily complex phenomenon, however, whose history spans multiple decades and features numerous *different* waves of emigration for different reasons and to different locations. While Americans are primarily familiar with the post-1975 exodus of refugees that brought many to the United States, previous generations left at different moments to escape French colonial rule, Japanese military occupation, communist rule in the north, a corrupt and undemocratic government in the south, or more generally, the pervasive presence of war throughout the region for most of the last century. The so-called Viêt-Kiêu or "overseas Vietnamese" community could not be more heterogeneous, encompassing the most disparate religious affiliations, class backgrounds, educational levels, ethnic-regional origins, and political perspectives (from the most extreme left to the most extreme right and every conceivable shade in-between). To boot, their presence in so many different lands has led to a literature written in as many different languages as their nations of residency.[3]

Yet, for all their manifest differences, these Viêt-Kiêu appear as the fortunate ones, those who managed to leave the miseries and tribulations of the homeland behind, those who sought (and some-times found) greater wealth and prestige abroad. Lam's vignette is instructive then for its poignant reversal of the traditional image of the exiled refugee wandering abroad as the one who suffers. Instead, it is they who stayed (or could not leave!) home who suffer. The Viêt-Kiêu "face" is no longer a "Vietnamese" face, it is "a face that has *not* known suffering."

The lived experiences of the Viêt-Kiêu themselves, as borne out by their own narratives and recollections, do not necessarily bear out this conclusion and often tell a different tale, one rife with its own horror, sadness, and multiple tribulations. Place is all im-portant in Vietnamese culture from the burying of the newborn's placenta and umbilical cord in the family ground (to symbolize the intimacy of one's bond to the soil of one's birthplace) to the ritual cleaning and continuing care of ancestral tombs. To be torn from one's native place, for whatever reason, is felt as an insuperable trauma and wrong.

Across the multiplicity of languages and homelands inhabited by Vietnamese people today and the variety of cultural and religious traditions they claim, there is one text that retains a central and quasi-sacred significance for all Vietnamese, namely Nguyễn Du's long poem, colloquially called *Truyên Kiều*, or *The Tale of Kiều* in English but whose original Vietnamese title, *Doan-Truòng Tân Thanh*, means something more like "New Tones of Sorrow" or more literally "Tormented Bowels, New Version."[4] Often considered the closest thing to a Vietnamese national epic, Nguyễn Du's poem is readily comparable to Dante's *Divine Comedy* both for its defining an ideal of the national language and offering a religious, even cosmological image that defines a national spirit.[5] *Kim-Vân-Kiều*, as the text is also commonly called after the names of its three main protagonists, is used variously as an exemplary text to teach Vietnamese schoolchildren how to read and write, as a tool for fortune telling, and generally, as both personal and national allegory. In her autobiographical reflections, Franco-Vietnamese author Kim Lefèvre remembers her mother in a manner that is as illustrative as it is typical:

> And as if to make sense of her own misfortune, she began to identify her destiny with that of the beautiful and unhappy Kiều—the main character in Nguyễn Du's famous poem. She knew hundreds of lines, which she recited from memory and which for her took the place of philosophy and morals. She had a line adapted to each circumstance, be it to justify the trials she had to endure, be it to criticize my faults or to praise my best efforts. My entire childhood and youth were nourished, I'd even say cradled, by the poignant singsong of the tale of the misfortunes of the beautiful Kiều.[6]

Above all, it is a tragic tale about the loss of place and home, one that since its publication in the early nineteenth century has profoundly endeared it to the Vietnamese, many of whom can recite long passages from it, even if they are otherwise illiterate.[7] Reduced to its most schematic outline, the plot involves a beautiful, talented girl sold into prostitution and domestic servitude to ransom her father from an unjust captivity. Cruelly separated from her family and her betrothed (Kim), Kiều suffers countless indignities and sorrows as she moves from one horrendous situation to another, until she finds solace as a nun in a Buddhist shrine, where fifteen years later Kim finally tracks her down. The "happy" ending is ambiguous though, since the joyful reunion can never erase the intervening years of nightmare and trauma that have made these formerly young lovers not only no longer young but inalterably changed persons.

It is commonly understood that, through his writing Kiều, its mandarin author, Nguyễn Du, expressed his own muted sense of suffering and humiliation at the court of the emperor Gia-Long who came to the throne by suppressing the populist Tây-Son revolution and who first urged his country down the slippery slope into colonialism by his bringing in French soldiers, engineers, and advisors to consolidate his own rule. Various characters in the Kiều have come to name various personality types in Vietnamese society, and it is not uncommon to compare one's own misfortunes with those of Kiều's as an inspiration to one's own effort to endure and persist against all manner of hardship. Kiều herself has come to allegorize the long sufferings of Vietnam as a country, especially in the last century, though the story of woeful separation, loss, and exile applies just as well to the predicament of the overseas Viêt-Kiều.

Beyond its syncretic lesson combining the Confucian sense of familial obligation with the Buddhist acceptance of fate, the Tale of Kiều metaphorizes the loss of home as an absolute change, one equivalent to the loss of life itself: "that cruel separation in life that is the equivalent to death's eternal good-bye! Kiều's very life no longer counted for anything."[8] Or, in one of the Kiều's most striking images, the reversal of fortune that is the heroine's fate is nothing less than a literal "sea change": "Throughout so many upheavals—seas become mulberry fields—what sights to strike sorrow in one's heart."[9] The haunting specter of the sea turned into the bramble of endless "mulberry fields" captures the despair—especially in a country so dependent on the sea as Vietnam with its long coastline—of seeing what most exemplifies freedom, the sea (not just representing freedom of movement but also the all important livelihood of fishing) suddenly inalterably transformed into a barrage of impassible thickets. The image itself, concisely rendered in Vietnamese by the two words, *bê-dâu*, literally "sea and mulberry," is drawn from the Chinese *Stories of Gods and Fairies*, which offers the following prognostication: "Every thirty years, the vast sea turns into mulberry fields and mulberry fields turn into the vast sea."[10] Among many other references, this image of radical change inspired Xuân-Phuc's magnificent poem, "Champs de mûriers sur la mer" (Mulberry Fields over the Sea), about the bloody horrors of the French and American wars: "Peace of offshore sandbars where our dead are buried / Mulberry fields over the sea what sights to strike sorrow in one's heart."[11] The poem closes with evident allusions to Shakespeare and Pascal that also reinforce the traditional Vietnamese message of the *Kiêu* about the value of human perseverance: "the tidal wave has passed full of sound and fury, tears and blood / But the heart of man turns to green the tumultuous waves of history."[12] The perilous conditions undergone by the so-called boat-people in their late-seventies exodus are also readily referenced by this image.

In a country with little history of voluntary emigration, life abroad is fatalistically understood as exile, a cultural sensibility exacerbated by what can only be termed the changed *civil* status of the Viêt-Kiêu. Unlike the seamlessness of many contemporary diasporic communities that maintain active lines of communication and travel between countries of origin and various host nations, sharp and overtly institutionalized divides exist between the Vietnamese and their overseas relations. Until recently Viêt-Kiều were banned from owning property in Vietnam, and when they return to visit, they still pay officially higher prices for goods and services than indigenous Vietnamese (though less than non-Vietnamese foreigners). Hybridity, pace Bhabha, as a strategy of cultural appropriation, does not appear to offer any advantages in the Viêt-Kiều context. Rather, it exacerbates their status as a kind of *tiers-exclu* identity. Those of mixed parentage feel this dilemma even more acutely, as exemplified by Kim Lefèvre's bitterly autobiographical *Métisse blanche*, where she describes the countless rejections she endured growing up in a culture that had no place for "impure fruit":

> Since my childhood, I have never ceased to endure scorn, rejection, and sometimes hate from a people I considered to be my own. This is because I recalled, under the duress of my own body, the humiliating colonization and arrogance of the white man. I was the impure fruit of the treason committed by my mother, a Vietnamese woman.
>
> I had spent my life wanting to prove my innocence by conforming to every rule in my society. But it was my essence that was unacceptable.[13]

For others, such as Edith Simon or Linda Lê, a sense of barred patrimony and ancestral history is paramount in their writings.[14] In literal as well as symbolic ways, exile has meant a loss of family ties catastrophic in a Confucian society. Again the *Tale of Kiều* by its own narrative of loss serves to model the construction of alternate identities in the alienating circumstances of expatriate existence. Trinh Minh-ha's film, *A Tale of Love* (U.S., 1995), features a protagonist named Kiều, who is both doing "research" on the story of her namesake and who extensively references the tale in examining her own personal, familial, professional, emotional, and erotic possibilities in an exilic environment. Just as Kiều herself is traditionally both admired and blamed for her conduct, so the Viêt-Kiều would seem to be likewise subject to a contradictory set of judgments: heroic refugees, or pampered exiles? unjustifiably fortunate (the face with no suffering) or successful only by the ordeal of having survived and persisted against incredible odds (a suffering perhaps unseen)?

One cannot help but be struck at the same time by the prominence of women in the Viêt-Kiều diaspora as writers, filmmakers, or public representatives: Trinh Minh-ha, Ly Thu Ho, Linda Lê, Kim Phuc, Thiana Thi, Lan Cao, Kieu Chinh, Le Ly Hayslip, to name only an obvious few. And while Vietnamese history despite centuries of Chinese-imposed Confucianism offers many examples of strong women from the Truong sisters who led a successful revolt against the Chinese in 39 AD to recent claims that as many as 50 to 70 percent of Vietcong guerrillas may have been women,[15] the visibility of women in a Vietnamese diaspora that draws a good deal of its imagery and cultural inspiration from the character of Kiều is striking. The perils of overseas Vietnamese identity would seem to find their strongest expression not in overt images of ethnic, racial, or class-based difference but in the more pervasive yet shifting contestations of gender. The haunting figure of Kiều was after all created by a man, not unlike the Flaubert who declared, "Madame Bovary c'est moi."

And while the trope of exile as a condition of writing is a common one in many cultures, in the Vietnamese case we again find the exemplary female figure of Kiều, who is presented in Nguyễn Du's poem as a "talented" musician, poet, and writer. Indeed, her talent (*trài*) is also understood to be the source of her misfortune (*tai*), the rhyme underscoring the Karmic (and Taoist) law of equivalences and balance: "such is the law: there is no gift which must not be dearly paid."[16] Fortune and misfortune are as inextricable to the exiled Viêt-Kiều writer as betrayal and love. As Trinh Minh-ha eloquently explains:

[Love, loyalty and betrayal and the experience of foreignness] may be very telling of our times, which are those of the migrant self, of mass refugeeism and of forced immigration. . . . It is through the politics of denationalizing the refugee and the émigré that a person-who-leaves becomes normalized, being systematically compelled to undergo the process of giving up their home, their country, their language, their identity, their proper name. In order to be accepted, one has to abandon one's unwanted self. In order to belong anew, one has to take the oath of loyalty, which entails dis-loyalty to one's home nation and identity. Hardly have the newcomers reached the host territory than they're made to experience the mutilation of their name which, if not entirely changed, can only survive in fragments—shortened, misspelled, mispronounced, or replaced by an equivalent. In this denationalization of the foreigner, we can better grasp the complexity of loyalty and betrayal in relation to love, to freedom, to one's own subjectivity. . . .

Even if you stay in the same place all your life and speak the same language, you cannot avoid the processes of change. The importance of a language's growth and renewal has been a well debated issue in translation. Words take on a new life, expand, shift, suspend, become trite, decline and die within a language. But perhaps such a maturing process becomes all the more de-stabilizing when it intermingles with processes of hybridization and of deterritorialisation, as in the case of *migrants, marginals and of women*. To unsettle what tends to be naturalized, to return to emotion without simply reviving the old discourse of passion and love, or to rewrite differently, one needs to fare—whether in one's own language or in the adopted language—as a nomad and as a foreigner.[17]

Women and exiles inhabit a shared space of marginality, one colored by a lingering love for one's home(land) that is also a betrayal of it. The same goes for the writer or filmmaker: "passion [and foreignness] can be a driving force for writing [and film-making]. ... To be a writer and a feminist (among other things) is to assume one's marginality and to become a foreigner to one's own language, community, and identity. Writing, as Kristeva has affirmed, 'is impossible without some kind of exile.' This is why, for me, to make a film on love is no doubt to betray (one's) love."[18] Working in multiple cross-cultural settings, the diasporic writer can only bridge them by the necessarily unfaithful act of translation, or as Trinh Minh-ha further specifies: "The translator, in Barbara Johnson's term, is a faithful bigamist whose loyalties are split between a native and a foreign language. I feel more like a polyandrist, being torn between the use of Vietnamese, French and English, while loving also Spanish and German. ... To be trilingual, for example, means to be triply faithful *and* unfaithful to the languages that define oneself and one's activity. The place of identity [is] a place of radical multiplicity."[19] And the *name* for this paradoxical identity that is also a multiplicity, the name that conjoins the positions of woman, writer, and exile is none other than that of "Kiều," which she conceives "not as a name belonging to an individual, not as a character in a story, but as a *situated multiplicity*, a mirror that reflects other mirrors."[20]

For Linda Lê, this Viêt-Kiều hall of mirrors is as internal as it is external to the exile, an ego-shattering sense of loss that is also the suicide/murder of a self that is one's own indigenous other: "I have the impression I'm carrying a dead body inside me. It's surely Vietnam that I bear like a dead child. . . . I feel like an alien [*métèque*] writing in French. I say alien with a great deal of pride. I am a foreigner to the world, to the real, to life, to the land in which I live, to my own country."[21] The solution to this situation is not a nostalgic re-cuperation of what once was or might have been. In answer to the question "Do you detest Vietnam?" she answers, "I don't know it well enough to detest it: I see Vietnam as a virgin land whose suf-ferings I know and which I hope one day to sing of by betraying it, that is to say, by making use of another language." Exacerbating the treasonous violence that exile and writing both inculcate ("Ecrire, c'est s'éxiler" [To write is to exile oneself]) becomes paradoxically the only way to remain true to the "situated multiplicity" that is one's identity: "I live on the edge, I want to know how always to live in exile. At this moment, I dream of leaving for elsewhere, in order to redouble the exile, no longer to live in the country whose language I speak. . . . I think it is always necessary to know how to lose your bearings, how to distrust your seat."[22]

Her short story, "Les pieds nus" (Bare Feet), offers another set of images with which to think the contradictory situation of exile among the Viêt-Kiêu. Set in the confusion of war (one readily imagines the turmoil of Tet 1968), the story tells of a young girl fleeing for her life: "She runs barefoot between father and mother, her sister holding her hand. They've fled their home. Father says: It's the war. Mother hides all her jewels on her person. For the child, it's all a game. They've dashed out of the house and they are running in the street. People are running behind them, in front of them. Others are stretched out along the side of the road, motionless, shirts stained red."[23] The red spots of blood mark bodies that do not move, which in the environment of war can only mean death. A proper schoolgirl, "usually" (d'habitude) she wears white socks and shoes, suggestive of a well-to-do (no sandals here!), probably Catholic background, one where going barefoot would be intolerable: "Usually, she wears shoes and white ankle socks. Usually, she is not allowed to run barefoot."[24] But this morning, awoken from her sleep by her parents, she leaves the house so quickly she forgets to put on shoes—this is definitely not a "normal" morning—recognizing her mistake only when the sharp rocks and bits of glass on the road begin to cut and bloody her feet: "There are stones on the roadway, bits of shattered glass. Her feet hurt. She thinks: My feet are bleeding. My blood drips, it's leaving traces behind."[25] But far from being an object of horror, these traces of blood are a singular source of solace to the girl, for they are what keep her still connected to the ground of her home. Should she become separated from her family, should her sister "let go of her hand," should her father and mother leave her lost behind, she thinks, "the traces of red are what will lead me back home" (ce sont les traces rouges qui me ramèneront à la maison). The difference is that, though her "father, mother, sister all have shoes on their feet," they also "know the way back," but she does not.[26] Like the little white stones left behind by the character of Le Petit Poucet in Perrault's fairytale, the red stains of blood (caused by her stepping on similar "*cailloux*") draw a sure line back to the safety of home. The feet may bleed, the body may suffer, but the return to the identity of self and home remains assured. Suffering and loss remain recuperable. And if the Viêt-Kiêu face is one that reputedly knows "no suffering," perhaps the same cannot be said for the opposite extremity of the body, the feet, as they necessarily suffer the pain of flight.

But, then, something unexpected happens:

> Suddenly, the sister stops. She's just noticed that the child is running barefoot. For their part, father and mother come to a stop in

the middle of the street. The child lowers her head; she keeps her eyes fixed upon the three pairs of shoes that form a circle around her little bare feet. Father leaves mother, sister, and child by the side of the road; he goes back to the house, then returns with a pair of shoes. He made a mistake, grabbing one shoe belonging to the sister and one shoe belonging to the child. The left shoe fits her but the right one is too large. The child says nothing, she starts to run again. From now on, she must learn to walk with mismatched shoes.[27]

The family stops—in other words, risks death—to find shoes for the little girl, but they turn out to be the wrong shoes or at least only half right, her father having inadvertently in the rush of things grabbed a "pair" of shoes, only one of which belonged to the little girl, the other belonging to her older sister. No time to go back or complain; necessity requires the little girl to start running again and learn to walk with mismatched shoes, for while the blood stains mark the place of home, they also circumscribe the ground of death. To survive, you run, you leave nothing behind, not even your blood, nothing in sum that would ever let you go back home again. Survival is *absolute* departure: lose your life or lose your home.

But to lose your home is also to lose your identity, to lose the self who once was but is no longer, left behind on the blood-stained ground. The shoes, mismatched or not, save you but at what cost? Near the end of Trinh Minh-ha's *Surname Viet, Given Name Nam* (U.S., 1989), we hear the following voice-over describing a scene in a refugee camp, where the power of shoes uncannily intersects with the gendered division of suffering in exile: "In Guam, I recognized a general, she said, he had been one of the richest men in Vietnam. One morning, in the camp, a mob of women came up to him. They took off their wooden shoes and began beating him about the head, screaming, 'because of you, my son, my brother, my husband were left behind.'"[28]

The final paragraph of Linda Lê's story, as if to follow the narrative outline of a traditional fable, tells us the autobiographical moral of the preceding vignette: "I left the house barefoot. If I had kept on walking barefoot, maybe I would have found the way back home, but I put on shoes that didn't belong to me. French has become my only language."[29] The mismatched shoes, which the fleeing child *must* learn to wear, metaphorize the exiled writer's obligation to write in a language that is not hers. But this necessity of survival (walking in shoes that don't belong to you, writing in a language that doesn't belong to you) at the same time obliterates any chance of returning to one's home or native tongue. Citing the German-Jewish writer, Nelly Sachs, herself an exile who fled to Sweden to escape Nazism, Linda Lê recalls the trope of the murdered inner self: "Foreigners carry their native land in their arms like an orphan girl for whom they seek nothing other than a tomb."[30] The child's flight, both metaphor *and* cause of the writer's exile, is not just another "loss of innocence" but her death as a child, becoming an orphan of one's homeland for which the only solution is the endless search for a tomb, a mourning without end. But given the traditional Vietnamese care for the memory of the dead, their elaborate maintenance of the family tombs in the vicinity of the home, where could one ever find a burial place for an orphaned homeland? "Reconciliation is impossible, impossible to return," responds Linda Lê in a remarkable chiasmus.[31] What makes possible the exile's survival and the writer's words is what simultaneously renders impossible her return and, furthermore, the continual severing of all ties to one's homeland and native identity, even in one's faithful remembrance of them. Again, love and betrayal, survival and suffering refuse to be clearly delineated, naming instead in their insuperable nexus the dilemma of exile itself: "In my head, I keep the image of a child fleeing barefoot in the street, but I will always be she who wears mismatched shoes, and these shoes will never lead her back home."[32] As if to mime the impossibility of that return, the narrative is also written in a kind of *style dépareillé*, shifting between first and third person, between present and past, in a *démarche* that both posits and denies a gap whose insuperable suture is also the narrative's origin and guiding principle.

And yet it would be far too simple to conclude on the absolute impossibility of return, for narratives of return do abound and could even be said to comprise a distinct subgenre of Viêt-Kiều literature. Even in Linda Lê, for whom the possibility of return does nonetheless remain inscribed upon the nether shore of the paroxysm of departure that is the rejection of home and past: "I ate the cadaver of my father, devoured the umbilical cord that binds me to the birth land. But still I return to my country. Will I go back there like a dog returns to its vomit, like a vampire regains its tomb or like a man rediscovers the path to a clearing after having long resigned himself to dwell in the obscurity of the forest? . . . I go back to my country asking my mother to teach me again how to live—perhaps she will know how to give truce to my endless ennui."[33] Here the extreme expressions of (self-)violence that denote the exile as paranoid, cannibal, beast, and vampire coincide with their reversal in images of maternal forgiveness, rebirth, and peace of mind: "But still I return to my country. . . ." But the harder question remains unanswered, namely, that of the modality in which return occurs: like a dog swallowing its own vomit, a vampire regaining its tomb, or more positively (and in a throwback to the Western imagery of Dante or Descartes), like a man at long last finding his way out of the dark forest into a clearing.

M. Trinh Nguyên's short film, *Xich-lo* (U.S., 1995), likewise represents the anxiety of return, "like making a 180° turn without stopping" as the narrator exclaims in her voice-over. The entirety of the "plot" shows the protagonist just off the plane in Saigon being wheeled around town in a pedicab (called a *cyclo* or *xich-lo*), delaying her arrival at her relative's home, while she struggles to come to terms with the insuperable gaps, historical as well as personal, between two times and two places that are also one, just as she is two different people but also one and the same.

Kim Lefèvre's *Retour à la saison des pluies* also deploys a narrative of delay in recounting her returning home after decades abroad. Interestingly her return begins with the writing of her previous book, *Métisse blanche*, whose success brings her into renewed contact first with members of the Vietnamese community in France and eventually with her own family whom she left behind decades before. Writing thus becomes also inextricably exile *and* return. A return in time even more than place via an affirmation of what no longer is. The voyage home, at first undertaken through memories, photos, letters, and phone calls before the strange "nonjourney" of plane travel ("In the airplane, time stands still like a slack sea" [Dans l'avion, le temps est immobile comme une mer étale]),[34] is thus at one and the same time an act of return *and* its denial.

Return and reconciliation are thus both impossible and something that does take place, not unlike the ambiguous ending of the *Kiều*, where the heroine is reunited with her lover and family but in such utterly changed circumstances that the marriage promise of long ago can no longer be naively fulfilled. On Kiều's insistence, Kim marries her younger sister, Vân, as his bride in the full sense of the word while also marrying Kiều in a deliberately unconsummated ceremony that leaves her free to live with Kim and Van while practicing the spiritual life of a Buddhist nun.

Similar consolation in the wise words of a Buddhist nun appears in Phuong Tran's reflections on her "first" visit to her homeland. Here again, we see a rejection of the easy tropes of return to roots or reconciliation of fractured identity in favor of a more genuinely *unheimliche* appraisal of the event:

> The purpose of visiting my homeland wasn't as simple as a search for roots, a cathartic trip to reconcile my bicultural identity, nor was it simply the exoticism or natural beauty that drew me. Perhaps it was tangled karmic ties or maybe it was the hollow silence of my family's history. Or it could have been a desire to find respite in the *hauntingly familiar, yet completely foreign* "home" of Vietnam. And I did find all of that.[35]

Readily perceived in her excursions as returning from overseas ("So, you are Viêt-Kiêu?"), she is asked about her exiled parents: "have they come back? . . . Well, my child, tell them to come back. . . . . Tell them there is nothing to fear and the time has come for them to return to their birthplace." Visiting a Buddhist temple in the old imperial capital of Hue, she is approached by the head sister— aptly named "Su Co Nu Minh" or Sister "True Wisdom"—who proposes a meditative exercise:

> [She] took my hand . . . and led us to the courtyard. After a series of stretches, she started pacing around the courtyard in even measured steps. "Have you ever walked and arrived at your destination but forgotten how you got there?" She continued to walk in slow circles. Two steps—she would silently inhale . . . two steps—exhale. "This helps you to be aware of each step, walking in constant mindfulness of the journey." So we walked and meditated until the sun appeared.[36]

The simple exercise of walking and breathing meant to keep one aware of what one can so easily not notice, namely arriving at one's destination without knowing how one got there, becomes a poignant allegory of Vietnamese history itself:

> I pictured Vietnam taking two giant steps, then meditatively inhaling all of history: Chinese and French colonialism, civil unrest, an international cadre of soldiers. "Tell them to come home." Two steps, exhale. . . .
>
> Yet, Vietnam's exhale is not of resignation, of defeat, or of fatalism, but rather of peace.[37]

The comprehensive and visionary telescoping of these great historical leaps within a single, albeit cosmological, breath is itself occasioned by that specific "art of mindfulness [that] is perfected in small steps": "Two steps—inhale; two steps—exhale. The people, the landscape, the journey. For a moment, all of it is suspended in a fragile timeless web of fellow passengers and True Wisdom speakers." Like the awe-inspiring image of oceans turned to mulberry fields and vice versa, contemporary Vietnamese literature—whether in French, English, or Vietnamese—traces the historical conundrum of a "situated multiplicity" where exile and return, love and betrayal become complex *faces* of each other. If Vietnam departs from and returns to itself within the two-step shuffle of breathing and mindfulness, if staying at home becomes its own kind of estrangement and exile while leaving at least gives one the distant dream of another home, if the purest act of fidelity as in the *Kiều* means the betrayal of all desire, then the travails of the journey, whether literal or metaphoric, across the perilous spaces of exile or during tumultuous times at home, remain the same no matter how differently they are lived, whether they leave the marks of suffering on the face, on the feet, or somewhere in-between.

And if, as the *Kiều* seems to say, the most extreme destinies are reserved for those "rosy-cheeked" girls who have it all (beauty *and* talent) then it would come as no surprise that they—not some hyper-masculine sailor, soldier, or adventurer; no Christopher Columbus!—should be the best guides on a journey as unpredictable as a land- (or sea-) scape turned into its other. Sister True Wisdom's walking exercise offers a potent lesson in how to travel "mindfully," and in the destiny of exile as unending return. And just as Kiều's long travails can also be read as preparatory steps to her finding peace as a Buddhist nun, so also does that same figure appear as the very epitome of courageous and enlightened travel in a poem by the famous eighteenth-century courtesan, Hô Xuân Huong:

> But women go forth, leaning on the Bodhisattva's staff,
> Clutching Buddha's rosary, telling the beads,
> Hoping to raise sails to shores of Enlightenment,
> Afraid of huge waves that might shatter halyards.
> Whoever is lucky enough to become a nun
> Must hold on dearly in order to succeed.[38]

In a similar vein, we might consider the final, concluding voice-over from *Surname Viet Given Name Nam*, a film that begins with a scene of Vietnamese women in traditional costumes. As their dance begins to mimic the movement of boat oars, we hear the sound of rushing water followed by the visual presentation of the film's title distorted by what appear to be raindrops falling against it. Near the end, we see the same dancers, then a side view of a woman peaceably contemplating the sunset while the following words are spoken:

> The boat is either a dream, or a nightmare, or rather both. A no place, a place without a place, that exists by itself, is common to itself, and at the same time, is given over to the infinity of the sea. For Western civilization, the boat has not only been the great

instrument of economic development, going from port to port, as far as the colonies, in search of treasures and slaves; but it has also been a reserve of the imagination. It is said that in a civilization without boats, dreams dry up, espionage takes the place of adventure, and the police take the place of pirates. Hope is alive when there is a boat, even a small boat. From shore to shore, small crafts are rejected and sent back to the sea. The policy of castaways has created a special class of refugees, the rich people.

Each government has its own interpretation of *Kiều*, each has its peculiar way of using and appropriating women's images. First appreciated for its denunciation of corrupt and oppressive feudalism, it was later read as an allegory of the tragic fate of Vietnam under colonial rule. More recently, in celebrations marking its two-hundredth anniversary, it was highly praised by the government's main official writers for its revolutionary yearning for freedom and justice in the context of the war against American imperialism. For the Vietnamese exile, it speaks for the exodus or silent popular movement of resistance that continues to raise problems of conscience for the international community.[39]

Notes

1. Andrew Lam, "To Be Viet Kieu Is to Be Santa Claus," in *New to North America*, ed. Abby Bogomolny (New York: Burning Bush, 1997), 73.

2. Statistics from David Lamb, "Viet Kieu: A Bridge between Two Worlds," *Los Angeles Times*, 4 November 1997; rpt. *Migration News* 4, no. 12 (1997), 24.

3. This multilingual literary diaspora is the subject of a dissertation (in progress) by Lise-Hélène Trouilloud at the University of California, Davis. One of her main concerns is the compartmentalization of various contemporary Vietnamese *literatures* by language, so that Francophone works are studied in almost total isolation from Anglophone works and both in isolation from literature written in Vietnamese (or in other languages such as German, Russian, or Chinese). Though the comparative dimensions of this literary corpus are daunting indeed (just from a linguistic standpoint, not to mention others), scholars are obligated to make as much of an effort in that direction as possible, or risk making serious mistakes of interpretation and/or limiting themselves to partial understandings of

a textual production that is both complex and highly self-aware of not only Vietnamese literary traditions, but Chinese and European as well. I realize the risk of introducing a more robust comparative dimension into a primarily francophone discussion, but it is my contention that the study of Vietnamese francophone literature absolutely requires an approach that transcends the mere use of the French language, not because as is all too quickly claimed that the old colonial language is no longer spoken in today's Vietnam but rather because the very rich literature that is indeed—still today—written by Vietnamese writers in French cannot be extricated from the multilingual context I've described. The beginnings of a good bibliography of purely "Francophone" Vietnamese literature established by Pham Dan Binh and "completed" by Elodie Hai-Duong Thanh Phan can be found on-line at *http://www.sfcc.spokane.cc.wa.us/french/indochineo1/biblio1.htm*. On the situation of the French language in contemporary Vietnam, I refer the reader to the excellent special issue of *Etudes Vietnamiennes* 124, no. 2 (1997), especially the articles by Nguyen Khac Vien, Margie Sudre, and Huu Ngoc. Finally, I would like to dedicate this study to the many students who have taught me enough about the literature and culture of Vietnam that I can offer this still highly preliminary study. In particular, I would like most especially to thank Hoa My Tran, Thi Duong, Lise-Hélène Trouilloud, Mai Anh, Le Tran, and Ali Yedes.

4. I refer both to Huynh Sanh Thông's superb bilingual edition of *The Tale of Kiều* (New Haven: Yale University Press, 1983) and the excellent French translation by Xuân Phuc and Xuân Viêt, *Kim-Vân-Kiều* (Paris: Gallimard/Unesco, 1961), which I cite in this essay both for the benefit of this volume's francophone readers and because this translation is often the direct source for references to *Kiều* in francophone Vietnamese texts. Unless otherwise indicated, all translations are my own. On the title of Nguyễn Du's poem as well as useful considerations on the poem's cultural significance in Vietnamese culture, see Tran Van Dinh, "The Tale of Kieu: Joy and Sadness in the Life of Vietnamese in the United States," in *Unwinding the Vietnam War*, ed. Reese Williams (Seattle: Real Comet Press, 1987).

5. The comparability of these two masterworks comes into focus when one considers the career of Professor Nguyen Van Hoan of the Department of Literature, Hanoi University, who translated both *Kiều* into Italian and *The Divine Comedy* into Vietnamese.

6. Kim Lefèvre, *Retour à la saison des pluies* (Paris: Aube, 1995), 84. Compare also pages 89 and 102. Selecting a passage *au hasard* from the *Kiều* is also a common way to tell one's fortune, turning the poem into an oracular text. On this and other popular Vietnamese customs, much information can be found in Nguyen Du and Vu Van Huan, *Mémoire du fleuve rouge* (Lyon: Jacques André, n.d.), 34 and *passim*.

7. See the especially elucidating remarks on this popular impact of the *Kiều* by the great French ethnographer, Georges Condominas, "Le quotidien du people," in

Littérature vietnamienne: la part d'exil, ed. Le Huu Khoa (Aix en Provence: Université de Provence Service des Publications, 1995), 27–31.

8. Xuân Phuc, *Kim-Vân-Kiêu*, 617.

9. "A travers tant de bouleversements—mers devenues champs de mûriers—que de spectacles à frapper douleureusement le coeur." Xuân Phuc, *Kim-Vân-Kiêu*, 3.

10. See Huynh Sanh Thông's annotation in his edition of *Kiêu*, 169.

11. "Paix de cordons littoraux de sable où sont ensevelis nos morts/ Champs de mûriers sur la mer que de spectacles à frapper douloureusement le coeur." Xuân Phuc [Paul Schneider], "Champs de mûriers sur la mer," in *L'Interculturel et l'Eurasien*, ed. Le Huu Khoa (Paris: L'Harmattan, 1993), 161.

12. "Le raz-de-marée a passé plein de bruit et de fureur de larmes et de sang/ Mais le coeur de l'homme fait verdoyer les flots tumultueux de l'Histoire." Such "multicultural" literary allusions are not uncommon at all in Viêt-Kiêu literature, yet they should not be too quickly dismissed as signs of Western assimilation, for the creative syncretism of Vietnamese literature and culture is traditional and key to its "originality." Even *The Tale of Kiêu* is based on a relatively obscure Chinese novel dating from the seventeenth century, which Nguyên Du rewrites into the quintessential Vietnamese text. See Huynh Sanh Thông's comments in his edition of *Kiêu*, xx–xxi.

13. Kim Lefèvre, *Métisse blanche* (Paris: Bernard Barrault, 1989), 409.

14. Edith Simon, "Le repatriement, in *L'Interculturel et l'Eurasien*, 121–32. Among Linda Lê's novels, *Calomnies* (Paris: Christian Bourgois, 1993) is especially poignant in this regard.

15. This claim is cogently presented and explored by filmmakers Di Bretherton and Cristina Pozzan in their documentary, *As the Mirror Burns* (Australia, 1990).

16. Xuân Phuc, *Kim-Vân-Kiêu*, 5.

17. Trinh T. Minh-ha, "Scent, Sound, and Cinema," Interview with Mary Zourmazi in *Cinema Interval* (New York: Routledge, 1999), 260, 264; emphasis added.

18. Minh-ha, "Scent, Sound, and Cinema," 263.

19. Minh-ha, "Scent, Sound, and Cinema," 265–66.

20. Minh-ha, "Scent, Sound, and Cinema," 257.

21. Linda Lê, "Entretien," avec Catherine Argand, *Lire,* April 1999.

22. "Je suis sur le qui-vive, je veux savoir toujours vivre en exil. En ce moment, je rêve de partir ailleurs, pour redoubler l'exil, ne plus vivre dans le pays dont je pratique la langue. . . . Je crois qu'il faut toujours savoir perdre ses repères, se méfier des assises." Lê, "Entretien."

23. "Elle court pieds nus entre le père et la mère, la soeur la tient par la main. Ils se sont enfuis de la maison. Le père dit, C'est la guerre. La mère cache ses bijoux sur elle. Pour l'enfant, c'est un jeu. Ils se sont précipités hors de la maison et ils courent sur

la route. Des gens courent derrière, devant eux. D'autres sont allongés sur le bord du chemin, immobiles, leur chemise est tachée de rouge." Linda Lê, "Les pieds nus," in *Littérature vietnamienne: la part d'exil*, 57–58.

24. "D'habitude, elle porte des socquettes blanches et des chaussures. D'habitude, il lui est interdit d'aller pieds nus." Lê, "Les pieds nus."

25. "Il y a sur la route des cailloux, des éclats de verre. Les pieds lui font mal. Elle pense, J'ai les pieds en sang. Mon sang coule, il laisse des traces." Lê, "Les pieds nus."

26. "Le père, la mère, la soeur ont des chaussures aux pieds. Ils connaissent le chemin du retour. Mais moi, je ne le connais pas." Lê, "Les pieds nus."

27. "Tout à coup, la soeur s'arrête. Elle vient de s'apercevoir que l'enfant court pieds nus. Le père et la mère à leur tour s'immobilisent au milieu de la route. L'enfant baisse la tête, elle garde les yeux fixés sur les trois paires de chaussures qui font cercle autour de ses petits pieds nus. Le père laisse la mère, la soeur et l'enfant au bord de la route, il retourne à la maison, puis revient avec une paire de chaussures. Il s'est trompé, il a pris une chaussure de la soeur et une chaussure de l'enfant. La chaussure gauche est à sa taille mais celle de droite est trop grande pour elle. L'enfant ne dit rien, elle se remet à courir. Il lui faut désormais apprendre à marcher avec des chaussures dépareillées." Lê, "Les pieds nus."

28. *Surname Viet Given Name Nam* (1989), produced and directed by Trinh T. Minh-ha.

29. "J'ai quitté la maison pieds nus. Si j'avais continué à marcher pieds nus, j'aurais peut-être retrouvé le chemin du retour, mais j'ai mis des chaussures qui ne sont pas à moi. Le français est devenu ma seule langue." Lê, "Les pieds nus."

30. "Un étranger porte sa patrie dans les bras comme une orpheline pour laquelle il ne cherche rien d'autre qu'un tombeau." Lê, "Les pieds nus."

31. "La réconciliation est impossible, impossible le retour." Lê, "Les pieds nus."

32. "Je garde en tête l'image d'une enfant fuyant pieds nus sur la route, mais je serai toujours celle qui porte des chaussures dépareillées et ces chaussures ne la remèneront pas à la maison." Lê, "Les pieds nus."

33. "J'ai mangé le cadavre de mon père, dévoré le cordon ombilical qui me relie à la terre natale. Mais je retourne quand même dans mon pays. Y retournerai-je comme un chien retourne à son vomi, comme un vampire réintègre sa tombe ou comme un homme retrouve le chemin de la clairière après s'être longtemps complu à demeurer dans l'obscurité de la forêt? . . . Je rentre dans mon pays demander à ma mere de me réapprendre à vivre—peut-être saura-t-elle donner trêve à mon ennui sans fin." Linda Lê, *Les Evangiles du crime* (Paris: Julliard, 1992), 226–27.

34. Lefèvre, *Retour à la saison*, 135.

35. Phuong Tran, "A Viet Kieu Visits Her Homeland for the First Time," published

9/1/99 on-line at *http://www.thingsasian.com/goto_article/article.876.html*; emphasis added.

36. Phuong Tran, "A Viet Kieu Visits Her Homeland."

37. Phuong Tran, "A Viet Kieu Visits Her Homeland."

38. Hô Xuân Huong, "Buddhist Nun," in *Spring Essence: The Poetry of Hô Xuân Huong*, ed and trans. John Balaban (Port Townsend WA: Copper Canyon, 2000), 82–83.

39. *Surname Viet Given Name Nam* (1989), produced and directed by Trinh T. Minh-ha.

16

Vietnamese Relationships

Confucian or Francophone Model

ALI YÉDES

Critics like Maurice M. Durand and Nguyễn Tran Huan agree that Western influence on Vietnamese intellectuals could be traced as far back as the year 1840 (the Opium War), when China suffered its defeats at the hands of the West.[1] They explain that this violent encounter with the West triggered the Chinese intellectuals' interest in absorbing Western ideologies and that it was through the intermediary of Chinese progressive writers that the Vietnamese got their first glimpse of Western learning and habits of mind. Later, Durand and Nguyễn add, from 1862 to 1945 Vietnam was a French colony, and Western influence, reflected particularly in the Vietnamese francophone literature, became a matter of fact.

Although Western influence on Vietnamese literature cannot be denied, ideals such as racial equality, individual freedom, political organization, democracy, among others, were already familiar concepts illustrated in Vietnamese texts prior to their encounter with the West. For example, Nguyễn Du's narrative poem, *The Tale of Kiều* where all these concepts were celebrated and where Confucian precepts were challenged, was written in the early years of the nineteenth century, long before the French occupation of Vietnam or the Chinese Opium War for that matter.[2] After a brief historical review illustrating how Buddhism was more suited to the region than Confucianism, this chapter examines Nguyễn Du's poem, *The Tale of Kiều*, and compares it with Ly-Thu-Ho's *Printemps inachevé*[3] and Pham Van Ky's *Frères de sang*[4] in order to demonstrate that the rebellious, liberal trend of Vietnamese francophone literature not only is the direct result of Western influence but also finds its roots in a more indigenous literary tradition. The aspiration to freedom from the cold chains of Confucianism for example was expressed in native literary production long before the French set foot in Vietnam.

The Chinese introduced Confucianism to Vietnam during their repeated and long-lasting occupations of the Vietnamese land.[5] Although Chinese colonization started in 111 BC, Confucianism was adopted as an institution only in the eleventh century. As the people of Vietnam achieved independence from China, Confucianism was to the early Vietnamese dynasties a convenient system of political philosophy and ethical conduct that seemed necessary for the development and management of the kingdom. Confucius stresses the social character of human kind, which binds one person to another. This *jen* (or human kindness) is "expressed through the five relations—sovereign and subject, parent and child, elder and younger brother, husband and wife, and friend and friend. Of these the filial relation is usually stressed. The relations are made to function smoothly by an exact adherence to *li*, which denotes a combination of etiquette and ritual. In some of these relations a person may be superior to some and inferior to others."[6] In order to function efficiently, every element of the social order must adopt the golden rule of correct conduct, treating the superior with reverence and the inferior with propriety.

Both the Ly (1010–1225) and the Tran (1225–1400) dynasties built places for the teaching of Chinese characters and Confucianism in order to train young people as leaders of the nation. It was the Ly Dynasty, which, following the Chinese model, in 1075 instituted the triennial public examinations. These highly competitive examinations became the way to acquire position and authority in the kingdom. Students and scholars dedicated their lives to learning Confucianism and related Chinese authors in order to obtain or keep a position or to advance to a higher one in the administration of the kingdom. Those who passed the examinations became mandarins, having royal title and power; those who failed took teaching jobs or practiced medicine for a living.

Compared to the disinterested, spiritual Buddhist education, Confucian education was then practical and highly rewarding. Not everybody, however, could read Chinese characters, and apart from the few who had the means to afford a Confucian teacher, the predominantly peasant population remained extremely disadvantaged. It was all the more so when mandarins and Confucian educated people used some of the Confucian precepts to reinforce their superiority and dominance over the weak and the poor. Confucianism came to be associated with the ruling class, who identified their relation to the peasantry and women with that between sovereign and subject, where obedience and servility are key elements to the perpetuation of its functioning.

Unlike Confucianism, which entered as a result of Chinese colonial aggression, Buddhism was introduced to Vietnam through missionaries arriving by sea from India and overland from China. Buddhist works trace back the presence of foreign monks in northern Vietnam to the second century AD. The north was then called Giao Chau and was used as a rest station for Buddhist missionaries traveling back and forth by sea between India and China.

The A-Ham "Agma" and the Thien "Dhyana" (Dhyana is the Sanskrit word for Thien; it is Ch'an in Chinese and Zen in Japanese) were the two popular sects that developed in Giao Chau in these early days. It was, however, the Thien sect that prevailed and later gave birth to several original sects and subsects. Thien is one of the numerous sects of Mahayana Buddhism, which is broadly practiced throughout China, Japan, Korea, and Vietnam. Compared to Theravada (Hinayana), found in Ceylon, Burma, Thailand, Laos, and Cambodia, which is a more conservative Buddhism practiced by a minority in the southern part of Vietnam, Mahayana Buddhism is known for its liberal and pliable inclination.

The most important tenet of Thien is the search for truth through an attitude of life rather than a set of beliefs. The right way of concentration, meditation, breathing, eating, drinking is not necessarily conditioned by beliefs in "hell, nirvana, or causality." "The person who practices Zen meditation . . . has only to rely on the reality of his body, his psychology, biology, and his own past experiences or the instructions of Zen Masters who have preceded him."[7] This explains the remarkable adaptability of Mahayana Buddhism. Thich Nhat Hanh explains: "Mahayana Buddhism belongs to the progressive school and is ever ready for change or metamorphosis and for adapting to and accepting the cultural and social conditions of every land and every time."[8] He later asserts that because of the flexibility of Mahayana Buddhism and its disposition to synthesis, "It is no exaggeration to say that there are as many Buddhist schools as there are socio-cultural milieus."[9]

This brings us to deduce that although Buddhism is an imported religion, we can safely assert the existence of a native Vietnamese Buddhism adapted to its culture, society, and beliefs and obviously different from any other Buddhism practiced elsewhere. Whereas Confucian temples are extremely rare, almost every village in Vietnam has both a common house *(dinh)* where people worship their titular god, believed to be the protector of the village, and a pagoda *(chua)* where they worship Buddha.

Since the observance of Zen as practiced in the monasteries was not an easy endeavor, a more accessible form of Buddhism emerged among the masses. It was a combination of some rudiments of Zen and the practice of the Pure Land (Amidist) sect, which is also derived from Mahayana Buddhism. The essential tenets of the Pure Land sect is the concentration of the mind through self-absorption and the recitation of the names of Buddha, as well as the accumulation of merits through the performance of good deeds, all of which would eventually increase the chances of accessing Buddha's "Pure Land" after death.

This Buddhist synthetic doctrine is not the only originality that characterized the Vietnamese Buddhist masters who through the richness of their inner life remained very Vietnamese, always close to their native sociocultural tradition, seeking flexible ways of worship that suited the masses. The uniqueness of the Vietnamese Buddhist monks was further demonstrated by the conservative Vietnamese southern Buddhists who in spite of their religious differences joined hands with northern Buddhism in 1963 and reached unification unparalleled anywhere else in the world. Their identification with other Vietnamese Buddhist monks, progressive as they were, was at least as real as their allegiance to their more conservative school.

Although the beliefs of a typical peasant may include elements of Buddhism, Taoism, Confucianism, and of course other old beliefs as in local spirits and superstitions, common people identify themselves more with Buddhism than any other religious denomination. This was also true with monarchs, nobles, and mandarins, among whom, paradoxically, Confucianism was well established. Under the Dinh and Tien Le dynasties (968–1009) Zen masters acted as imperial counselors not only on religious matters but cultural and political ones too. Although the Ly and Tran kings instituted the triennial Confucian examinations, they were deeply Buddhist. Some of them left their kingdoms to their heirs and sought a spiritual, monastic life. The monarchs' need for Confucian political philosophy did not obviously supplant their hunger for Buddhist spiritual life. They had a deep veneration for Buddhist teachings and perceived Buddhist monks as "the custodians of culture."[10] Nguyễn Ngọc Huy explains that Buddhist monks "played a significant role in education. Being open-minded and learned men, the Buddhist monks not only spread their religious beliefs, but also taught Confucianist philosophy to those who were destined to become civil servants for the administration. The first generation of Vietnamese Confucianist scholars formed by Buddhist monks were, of course, devote Buddhists. But soon Confucianism had at its disposal enough learned men to expand without the help of Buddhist teachers."[11] Because of its political character, however, the rise or the fall of Confucianism depended on the establishment or the elimination of the triennial examination. The elimination of these examinations by colonial France (1918) was the final blow for the precolonial ruling class of nobles and mandarins. When they fell, their Confucianism fell with them. In order to obtain administrative positions within the existing colonial government, young people needed Western, not Confucian education.

After the French conquered Vietnam in 1861 and introduced Catholicism in the country, the Vietnamese traditional way of life was targeted by the colonial force. Because of its disinterested teachings and its powerful inner life, Buddhism was not as affected by the colonial occupation. In times of political disadvantage or crisis, Buddhists could always retire to a life of meditation. For Confucians, however, when stripped of their political and social status, life became meaningless, which led them to either despair or revolution.

"In the 1920s, however, Westernized Vietnamese intellectuals began to criticize the traditional way of life."[12] Fueled by the new system of education set up by the French, their movement aimed at changing the Vietnamese people's mentality.[13] At the same period of time both Confucianism and Buddhism started a movement of revival. While Buddhism managed to be reborn, Confucian-study associations persistently maintained their anachronistic tenets and purposes in a society of rapid change, which led to the gradual disappearance of the remnants of the Confucian religious character. Mahayana Buddhists' dispositions to synthesis allowed them to assimilate Confucian ideas that partake of local culture and combine them with their parallels in Buddhism. "Such Confucian ideals as loyalty and filial piety, humaneness, kindness, gratitude, courtesy, wisdom, and honesty have been assimilated by Buddhism and combined with their parallel in the latter's philosophy. Thus the notion of filial piety in Confucianism is fully realized and exemplified in the Buddhist Vulan Ullambana Sutra. . . . The Confucian notion of humaneness has been merged with the Buddhist notion of compassion or loving-kindness. The process of assimilation has gone so far that at the present time Confucianism has lost all of its religious character."[14]

Its lack of deeper spiritual life together with its focus on sociopolitical conduct explains the rigidity of Confucian philosophy and its reticence to adopt any change even at the risk of vanishing. Changing or adapting any elements of its tightly knit doctrine would amount to denying Confucianism itself. Confucianism had to remain unchanged or disappear. Its resistance to change meant also keeping its foreign character. Indeed, unlike the case of Buddhism there had never been a Vietnamese Confucianism but just Confucianism, which had always been Chinese. Furthermore, Buddhism adapted itself to the Vietnamese population, which led to a native synthetic version of Buddhism. With the advent of Confucianism through colonial China, however, it was the Vietnamese who were supposed to adapt to its principles. Confucianism remained Chinese all along, a foreign concept to Vietnamese tradition, and as such any of its constituents that were not identifiable with the native heritage were bound to fade away.

In Nguyễn Du's long poem from the early nineteenth century, *The Tale of Kiều*, the question of the adaptability of Confucianism is posed at the outset. Faced with her moral duty of filial piety (paying her parents for bringing her into this world and raising her), Kiều raises the issue of the right of a person to naturally love and be loved. Filial piety is a social construct dictated by a Confucian moral code of conduct; love, however, is natural feeling that cannot be ignored or denied. Whereas filial piety requires putting one's parents' need before one's own, the right to choose love and experience its nourishing beauty is an expression and a confirmation of the individual self: "As you must weigh and choose between your love and filial duty, which will turn the scale?"[15] notes Kiều. The incompatibility of the two is further stressed in the following statement: "How could both love and duty be fulfilled."[16]

Kiều eventually chooses to observe filial piety, declaring: "A child first pays the debts of birth and care."[17] This decision, however, is not without suffering, bitterness, and a sense of rebellion against the feudal moral conduct that governs her society: "Crushed by her kinsfolk's woe and her own grief, she crossed the sill, tears flowing at each step."[18] The misfortune that strikes her family comes, obviously, as a result of a social structure where the selective and abusive upper class, which either held political positions or became bourgeois mercantile lords, based its way of relating to common people on Confucian ideas, expecting them to accept a life of submission and resignation.

The incompatibility of love and Confucian moral codes is further illustrated through Kim's obligation to rush back home at his father's request in order to conduct his uncle's funeral. He had to reluctantly and painfully leave Kiều when they had just started nurturing and savoring their love for each other. Kim's presence could have certainly saved Kiều from selling herself and thus prevented a fifteen-year misfortune for both of them. He later recognizes that it was a mistake on his part to have left his love for some funeral rituals: "'Because I had to go away,' he cried, 'I let the fern, the flower float downstream.'"[19]

Nguyễn Du continues his poem in the same vein, with numerous episodes that either evoke the question of adaptability of Confucian precepts to Vietnamese culture or totally refute them as affected principles that do not fit the Vietnamese people as a whole. The relationship between Thuc-Sinh and his father is characterized by tenseness more than by harmonious obedience. Their confrontation represents the clashes between a generation that wants to rid itself of rigid Confucian models as well as from mandarins who want to protect their privileges. Thuc yearns for freedom from restrictive paternal authority. The father's trip to the homeland brings him such relief that he becomes almost drunk with joy: "More bewitched than ever."[20] Thuc marries Kiều in his father's absence, knowing very well that his father will vehemently oppose it. When he returns and rages about it, Thuc does not flinch. He stands firm against his father's attempt to separate them, protecting his right to fall in love and be faithful to it: "Even if I had her for just one day, who'd hold a lute and then rip off its strings? If you will not relent and grant me grace, I'd rather lose my life than play her false,"[21] Thuc declares resolvedly. And the poet continues: "Those stubborn words aroused the old man's bile, so at the hall of law he lodged complaint."[22] By having love win over filial piety, the poet seems to enjoy seeing Confucian ideals diminished when confronted with the individual's right to happiness.

Tù-Hai's heroic confrontation with the monarchy and his aspiration to acquire his own territory spring from his love for freedom that common people like him do not enjoy and cannot hope for within a feudal system. During his five-year control of the part of the country he conquered, he gives Kiều the opportunity to reward those who helped her during her misfortune and punish those who caused it. In a sense, Tù and Kiều, coming from the common people, submit a decadent and corrupt society to popular justice: "All soldiers, crowded on the grounds, could watch the scourge divine deal justice in broad day."[23] Although he succumbs to Kiều's argument to surrender to the emperor's forces, Tù is not persuaded that it is the right decision to make. Kiều is again drawn by her sense of loyalty to the sovereign, nurturing the illusion that by fulfilling their duty of fidelity and obedience as subjects, they will be rewarded and certainly become vassals of the king. Tù's initial response is a heavy critique of the king's circle of nobles and mandarins, which he perceives as corrupt and ludicrous. He would not trade his rebel life for that of a submissive courtier:

> If I turn up at court, bound hand and foot,
> what will become of me, surrendered man?
> Why let them swaddle me in robes and skirts?
> Why play a duke so as to cringe and crawl?
> Had I not better rule my march domain?
> For what can they all do against my might?
> At pleasure I stir heaven and shake earth—
> I come and go, I bow my head to none.[24]

All through the poem, mandarins are associated with negative qualities. The authoritarian and despotic character of Thuc-Sinh's

353

father, the prefect of Lâm-chuy, is obvious. Most important is the way he relates to common people. His rage over his son's marrying Kiều is vented against her alone in spite of the son's avowal that it was all his fault: "She suffers because of me!"[25] The father subjects her to corporal punishment and stops only when his heart softens over his son's lamentations. Although he recognizes Kiều's poetic qualities, his pity and reconciliation are directed exclusively toward his son. What saves Kiều from his rage is neither her honesty, truthfulness, nor her frail body, but her ability to improvise a poem on a subject of the prefect's choice, to the latter's great surprise.[26] As if only mandarins and their emulators were worth any compassion or human consideration. The poet seems also to stress the fact that although they are looked down upon, common people in the figure of Kiều have beauty, talent, and a capacity for sound judgment. The governing upper class needs to make an effort to recognize and appreciate them.

Hô Tôn-Hiên is supposed to be an important mandarin and governor of the provinces: "He thought, 'I am a noble of the realm, whom both my betters and the rabble watch.'"[27] The poet depicts him as a detestable character. Compared to the brave Tù-Hai, he is mean and cowardly. Instead of confronting Tù-Hai face to face, he resorts to trickery, using Kiều's naive concept of loyalty to and trust in the sovereign's promises and protective qualities. After his cowardly act, he is insensitive enough to force Kiều to serve wine and sing to his festive crowd in the presence of Tù-Hai's corpse. In his drunken state, he proposes to her then changes his mind the next day when he sobers up and realizes the social gap that separates them. In the end, ignoring her feelings, he forces her to marry an indigenous chief.

The way Nguyễn Du depicts his female characters runs against the Confucian female model. Thu Trang, a Vietnamese critic, explains that perceiving women to be of lower status than men is more Confucian than Vietnamese: "The misogyny of Confucianism is well known. We may assume that the degradation of the condition of women in an earlier Viêtnam must be attributed to its influence. Such degradation was never characteristic of Viêtnamese mentality and customs, as is particularly evident in numerous provisions of the Lê Judicial Code (the so-called Hông-duc Code), which can be considered an accurate reflection of the common law that was far more egalitarian than the Codes and regulations inspired by Chinese law."[28]

In July 1961 a survey conducted in Nguyễn Du's village by researchers from l'Institut des Lettres de Hanoï reported that women among the peasantry were neither inhibited by nor submitted to men: "faced with an unyielding farmland, women set about to plowing like their husbands. In this way their role in society is no less important than that of men; liberal conceptions of love and relationships between husband and wife have long broken out of the customary framework.' . . . By and large, the local people are noteworthy, even in 1961, for 'a love life that is so special, expressed outwardly with much more vigor than elsewhere.'"[29]

In light of the above, Kiều's heroism, strength of character, and disposition to love more than once, following her heart rather than Confucian models of fidelity to the first love (husband), are not just revolutionary but stem also from a Vietnamese tradition. Kiều's moral qualities are more than obvious. She takes the courageous decision to save her father and her family by sacrificing herself. Apart from Tù-Hai, men she encounters during her long ordeal are no match for her. So-Khanh and Ma Giám-sinh are cowards, and although Thuc-Sinh is sincere, he is helpless in the presence of his first wife. In the eyes of Nguyễn Du, Kiều's fearless engagement in a life of misfortune is as heroic as Tù-Hai's rebellious military actions against the king. Tù-Hai addresses Kiều as his equal in bravery: "To spot a hero took a heroine."[30]

Although mentioned by Kiều,[31] the Confucian theory of the three submissions related to women (to father, husband, and son) has never been observed in the poem. When Kiều expresses her willingness to be submissive, Tù-Hai refuses such an attitude and replies in an admonishing tone: "We read each other's hearts, don't we? Yet you act like some vulgar woman—Why?"[32] As for the other couples, Ma-Giám-sinh is afraid of Tú Bà and is ready to get on his knees to ask for her forgiveness: "If my old broad finds out and makes a scene, I'll take it like a man, down on my knees!"[33] Thuc-Sinh is also afraid of and totally dominated by his wife Hoan-Thu. Unable to admit that Kiều was actually his second wife, he could only weep about it: "Lest he'd betray himself, he'd breathe no word but could not stop his tears from spilling out."[34] Although Kiều is the object of Hoan-Thu's cold revenge, she has a lot of admiration for her strong character: "I'll never look upon her like again. That was true self-command, that was pure sham."[35] Later, Hoan-Thu declared that she too has always admired and respected Kiều.[36]

Nguyễn Du chooses to depict his women characters as strong, capable of active engagement in all aspects of social life. Besides beauty and talent, they are endowed with moral qualities coupled with heroic acts (Kiều); they are also capable of defending their rights, to the point of being cruel (Hoan-Thu's cold revenge and Kiều's punishment of her enemies). Thu Trang remarks that Nguyễn Du's work has certainly opened up the way for liberal ideas in Vietnamese literature: "we are delighted that with the *The Tale of Kiều* a trend of liberal thought has surfaced in literature, thus leading the way to the current renewal of Viêtnamese literature."[37]

Most critics, however, argue that the liberal, progressive aspects of contemporary Vietnamese literature are the direct consequence of Vietnam's encounter with the Western world, through French occupation. In his book *The Vietnamese Novel in French* (1987), Jack Yeager maintains, "the evolution in indigenous literature was itself a profound response to Western social patterns that had been brought by the French. What resulted, in effect, was the telescoping of Occidental literary history—from pre-modern '*romans courtois*' (romance) through romanticism to realism and social realism—into a few short decades."[38] Bui Xuan Bao concurs with Yeager, claiming that 1930s Vietnamese "literary flowering and development were the direct result of the discovery, translation and imitation of French literature. Romanticism in this literature appealed to Vietnamese youth and progressive intellectuals and quickly became popular. The victory of the heart over the mind, the liberation of the senses from the cold chains of Confucian reason, liberated the individual as well."[39]

While one cannot deny the French influence on Vietnam as a whole, one cannot ignore the presence of a Vietnamese literary tradition in the form of verse narrative from which contemporary writers would naturally draw their inspiration. The evolution of Vietnamese literary trends is obviously a complex phenomenon that cannot be linked to the impact of the French presence alone. The so-called new, renovating components introduced by French literature happened also to be very present in traditional Vietnamese verse narrative, such as Nguyễn Du's *The Tale of Kiều*. Aren't social realism and romance part and parcel of Nguyễn Du's poem? The *Kiều* is basically a love story; and the protagonist's encounters with characters belonging to various social milieus are a depiction of the nation's social reality. The break of Confucian "cold chains," as it were, so applauded in the Vietnamese French novel as a rescuing Western import, for example, had already taken place in Nguyễn Du's vision of liberation from the oppressive feudal system, aptly illustrated in *Kiều*'s series of adventures. As for the romantic element, what more than the persistence of *Kiều* and her partners in love in listening to and following the voice of their hearts rather than Confucian or, for that matter, Buddhist precepts or concepts of reality: Thuc resisted his father's will and listened to Kiều's suggestion to go back and inform his first wife; Tù followed Kiều's advice to surrender and died as a result of his heart obfuscating his capacity for reasoning.

When Nguyễn Du wrote his verse narrative in the early nineteenth century, Vietnamese society was already trying to shake itself free from the Confucian feudal system. In 1949 the Vietnamese critic Hoài Thanh wrote, "Nguyễn Du's tragedy is the tragedy of Viêtnamese society, which, during the last years of the Lê dynasty and at the beginning of the Nguyêns', tries to cast off its feudal chains, but, for lack of objective conditions permitting a way out, winds up writhing in its melancholy and pain."[40] With Nguyễn Du, a spirit of freedom and progression came to life, and it is only natural that it would bear its fruits for generations to come. The influence of Western ideals of freedom in the Vietnamese French novel are obviously bound to be there since it is written in French; but Nguyễn Du's legacy of the cult of love and the individual's right to happiness is also bound to infiltrate into the later Vietnamese literary work.

In Ly Thu-Ho's *Printemps inachevé*, although Tuoi and her schoolmate Dung go to French secondary school, the Vietnamese language and literature class is the one they relate to and enjoy the most: "But the class that Tuoi and her friend Dung liked best was that on Viêtnamese language, taught by Mrs Chua. It was with her that, during four years, they came to know and appreciate the refined character of Viêtnamese poetry and literature."[41] The link between national literary heritage and Ly Thu-Ho's novel is also illustrated in its easily detectable affinity with *The Tale of Kiều*'s form and content in spite of the visibly present Western state of mind. Both narratives are a depiction of political, social, and religious reality as well as a love story. Like Kiều, Tran, Ly Thu-Ho's protagonist, is reluctantly separated from her love by forces beyond her power and experiences living terror through the violence of political movements on one hand and the colonial powers on the other. Colonial violence culminates in her being raped by a French soldier in her own home. Like Kiều she then embodies the trauma of feeling no longer worthy of her love, Châu. As Kiều did after her first rape, Tran thinks of suicide: "At first, I had thought of disappearing from this world."[42] But both Kiều and Tran are deeply Buddhist and both take refuge in the healing spiritual power of religion, which allows them to project themselves beyond the bitter reality of a violent world. Tran chooses to become a Catholic "*religieuse*" only for the practical side of physically devoting herself to those who suffer like her, even if it is limited to bodily injuries. Both accounts deal with loyalty and the sense of guilt. Tran feels guilty of breaking the covenant of love of an eventual marriage. Like Kim in the *Kiều*, Châu feels guilty of leaving Tran by herself, unprotected, while he is attending to other national duties: "It is also my fault and I ask you to forgive me for leaving you alone without protection."[43] Both stories celebrate the pursuit of love as well as physical and moral beauty in opposition to the Confucian ideal of denunciation and in spite of the Buddhist warning of its negative results: "Whatever love may be, concluded the bonze, it is always a chain that grips us and hurts us."[44] According to the *religieuse* Tam-Hop, love is one of Kiều's main flaws: "She has woven passion's web wherein at pleasure she'll enmesh herself. Thus, when she dwelt in those abodes of peace, she would not stay, for she could not sit still."[45] Similarly, Tran chooses her own love and holds onto it until her death.

While the defiance of Confucian precepts in the *Kiều* is mostly subtle and refined, in *Printemps inachevé*, it is not only direct but confrontational. This is illustrated in the constant tension between mothers and daughters: from the extreme liberalism of the promiscuous Nam, which distresses her mother, to the rather reserved Tuoi and Tran, who are nonetheless firmly committed to their freedom and right to love and happiness in spite of their mother's strong opposition and attachment to the only Confucian model she knows.

The confrontational attitude toward Confucian binding "relics," together with a certain affinity with *The Tale of Kiều*, is also demonstrated in Pham Van Ky's *Frères de Sang*. As in *Printemps inachevé*, the confrontation with and the rejection of Confucianism carry a sense of mockery: "The slow erosion of things seemed to be a direct consequence of Confucian conformism, which, in its ritual immobility, froze object and subject."[46] The European-educated narrator describes the father, a mandarin and a former judge forced into retirement because of his failure to suppress a riot, in an ironic and a critical tone. Looking at his family ethics, rooted in the lingering filial piety in its wider sense, he denounces the father's persistent feudal mentality in spite of the progressive social changes around him: "Although the League for the Independence of Viêt-Nam, for a year, had destroyed this social triangle, changed the name of the country, renounced the king, discredited the mandarin, Father continued to dictate, given his absolute power. Court orders yielded to common law, as a saying goes, custom was his scepter."[47] The friction between the defiant Western-educated young generation and the father's clinging to Confucian precepts is present throughout the novel.

The mandarin, however, is equally criticized and defied by Lê Tâm, whose education is purely traditional. When in the midst of a party where alcohol is served, the mandarin while drinking decides to judge On Chin's eloping wife, Lê Tâm raises his firmly opposing voice, reminding the former judge that justice is above everybody and that it can be served only by a sober person: "It is written in the books, continued Lê Tâm: 'He who has drunk more than three cups will not cross over the hill!' You will not cross over the hill of justice."[48] This daring confrontation is further reinforced by Hô's rebellious intervention: "You are all cowards!"[49] The furious mandarin spares his son and orders a hundred lashes to be administered on Lê Tâm's frail body, a punishment that is reminiscent of the hundred lashes ordered by Thuc's father, the prefect, on Kiều's frail body, her only offense being that she followed the justice of her heart. For the mandarins, common people and women are always at fault.

The narrator provides us with an interesting clarification concerning Lê Tâm's relationship to tradition to which, paradoxically, he is even more attached than the father: "Lê Tâm clung to tradition more than Father. From under his will to perpetuate its best part, however, filtered out a certain nobility and indulgence toward things beyond him. His rigor opened onto limitless perspectives. That was what I had liked about him."[50] If the triennial exam were still in effect, Lê Tâm would be a mandarin, but an enlightened one in the same way as Nguyễn Du. Both reject rigid Confucian precepts that provide a base for feudal mentality with its abuse of power and oppression of the weak. The Confucian elements that can easily be adapted to Vietnamese popular culture and tradition (humaneness, respect) are readily and naturally adopted and "perpetuated." Lê Tâm is versed in Confucianism, quotes Confucius on more than one occasion to prove or illustrate a philosophical point, but considers himself Taoist: "Thus, I had looked for Confucius, and I found Lao Tse."[51] He had indeed followed a Confucian path only to find himself repelled by its unaccommodating precepts, particularly for peasants and women. It is no coincidence that the person Lê Tâm is defending is a woman who is about to receive the lashes that he receives instead. We can rightly assume that the narrator is a fervent defender of women's rights and would not have the admiration he has for Lê Tâm if the latter did not share his concepts of social justice and equality between men and women. The symbolic "blood" brotherhood between them that infuriated the father leads us to believe that Lê Tâm's charisma forms an important part of the narrator's personality: "Lê Tâm is a part of my truth, if not its entirety."[52]

Both the *Kiều* and *Frères de sang* depict strong women characters who reject Confucian concepts of filial piety and the "three submissions" for women: Ong Chin's wife elopes with a seducer, and the flirtatious and promiscuous Tu, her daughter, is certainly not the image of a submissive woman. She takes pleasure in playing with and exposing the notables' corrupt, hypocritical, and lustful minds. The father himself is not spared from her determination to unveil the illicit conduct of authoritarian mandarins and Confucian adepts. When the former judge is getting ready to condemn Ba, her brother, and his partner, the *trùm*'s wife, who is accused of adultery, Tu, pushed by Dinh, stands up defiantly and speaks her mind: "Who will judge the judges?" she asks, adding, "And if the judge, himself married and a family man, had seduced a helpless servant handed over to his own desires, would he also be accused of adultery and brought before the council?"[53] After this act of bravery, Tu has to escape the mandarin's wrath by running away. But she has at least managed to tell him to his face and publicly that as a married man and a responsible mandarin coveting his servant, herself, is even more adulterous than her brother's single act. Tu and Dinh condemned the father's adulterous conduct before he pronounced his judgment on the adulterous couple. They managed, in their own way, to submit mandarins to the watchful eye of popular justice. This is also reminiscent of the popular justice Kiều and Từ-Hai pronounced and administered on members of the ruling class during their temporary "reign" over a part of the country.

Dinh's cold calculating plan and execution of her revenge on both her father as well as the whole Confucian-based tradition of treating women as inferior to men is again reminiscent of Hoan-Thu's cold calculating revenge, particularly on her weak husband Thuc, who, behind her back, takes Kiều as a concubine. Both female characters avenge themselves by thoughtful preparations and trickery. Dinh is convinced that even if she refuses, her father will force her to marry somebody she does not know. Her only solution is to play the game and escape on her wedding day. The note she leaves to her husband is an assertion of freedom from the cold chains of Confucian ideals: "You should strive to earn my love, my dear friend. And not with jewelry. I am worth more than a Confucian precept. The three 'obediences' I shove in my bag. The 'four virtues' I chew . . . without betel, so as not to dirty my white teeth."[54]

The father and his circle are convinced that Dinh's rebellious character is due to her French education. Her father-in-law is furious when he learns that she had a Western education: "until yesterday we were unaware that she had had such a modern education."[55] The father stops her secondary schooling because he cannot find a school for girls only. One is tempted to believe that that was only a pretext because for him what she needs is not education but marriage. He refers to her as "an eccentric girl that married life will certainly calm down."[56] French education inspires apprehension because of the germs of rebellion it might instill in the young generation. Apart from the narrator, the father manages in one way or another to stop all his children from going to French schools, which for mandarins and Confucians in general are regarded as bad influences that pose a threat to their dominant status in the Confucian social structure. Similarly, prior to the advent of the French, the ideas of Nguyễn Du's *The Tale of Kiều* were also feared as a threat to the established Confucian social structure. It was common practice for fathers to forbid their children, particularly girls, to read this narrative poem.

In light of the above study, we can easily conclude that although the introduction of French education in Vietnam played a major role in the rejection of rigid Confucian ideals and the adoption of a progressive path toward modernity, the seeds of modernity had been already planted by Vietnamese literary figures like Nguyễn Du prior to the nation's contact with Western powers. The march toward freedom from the Confucian feudal system had already begun to take its course and the advent of Western ideologies reinforced and accelerated it. An affinity between both France and Vietnam in terms of literary production already existed before any colonial connection took place. Talking about Nguyễn Du's poem, Pham Quynh remarks:

> This poem, a creation of an Annamite mind over which, apart from the Chinese influence, no single other foreign influence could be exerted, has no small part of its originality in the set of qualities which link it to the best products of the French mind. . . . What can be said other than that there is in the world a certain conception of literature and art that happens to be the same for two peoples at the extremes of the West and of Asia, or rather that there are, between the French mind and the Annamite mind, certain affinities that would be worth cultivating.[57]

Notes

1. Maurice Durand and Nguyễn Tran-Huan, *Introduction à la littérature vietnamienne* (Paris: G.-P. Maisonneuve et Larose, 1969), 25.

2. Nguyễn Du (1766–1820), *The Tale of Kiều*, trans by Huyen Sanh Thông (New Haven: Yale University Press, 1983). *The Tale of Kiều* is a narrative poem. During a long absence of her fiancé, Kim, Kiều, daughter of a family of literati, in order to save her father from debtors' prison, accepts a marriage for money with Ma Giam-Sinh, who turns out to be a rogue. He puts her in a brothel run by an old woman, Tu Ba. Kiều tries to commit suicide. When she recovers, she falls again into the hands of an impostor, So Khanh, and is forced to take the life of a prostitute. A regular client of Tu Ba's house, Thuc, falls in love with her and takes her as his second wife but does not have enough courage to let his first wife, Hoan Thu, know about it. Hoan Thu learns the truth through gossip and takes her revenge by arranging to kidnap Kiều and have her as a servant. Thuc has no courage to defend her. Kiều manages to run away to a Buddhist nunnery and falls in the clutches of an old nun, Bac Ba, who is a trickster. Once again, Kiều is put in a brothel. Tù-Hai, a soldier of fortune, takes her out of it, and marries her after a triumphant warring campaign that makes him master of the country. Kiều is not comfortable with the idea that he is in rebellion against the emperor and begs him to submit, which he does. The imperial envoy, however, has him assassinated and forces Kiều to marry a local chief. Kiều throws herself into the Tsien-tang River and is taken for dead. The Buddhist priestess, Giac Duyen, rescues her, and she is finally reunited with her former sweetheart Kim, who is now married to her sister, Van. Kim insists upon having her as his lawful wife, to which she agrees, Van remaining his second wife. The couple lives happily together but agrees to keep their relationship platonic.

3. Ly-Thu-Ho, *Printemps inachevé* (Paris: J. Peyronnet et Cie, 1962). The narrative in *Printemps inachevé* starts with the peaceful life of the Thai family, whose eldest daughter, Tuoi, graduates from college in 1935. Later in the novel, the outbreak of World War II and the dire consequences of the social and political upheaval on the Vietnamese are portrayed. Dung, one of Tuoi's friends, has to evacuate from town to town. When she returns to the capital by 1946, she meets Tuoi, who relates what has befallen her: her mother died one year before; her husband, André, was killed; her brother, Ba, had been in the hospital with tuberculosis; and her younger sister, Tran, is now a nun working in a Saigon hospital. Before taking the veil, Tran was raped by a French soldier. Later she would die in a leper colony. Tran's diary, read by Dung and Tuoi, gives more details about the devastating consequences of the war on the social and the individual level. The fictionalized destruction of the Thai family by the war is presented in a sociohistorical context. From the personal tragedies of its members emerges a human portrayal of the wreckage caused by wars. The novel closes around 1955 with the anticolonial war leading to the Geneva Agreement.

4. Pham Van Ky, *Frères de sang* (Paris: Editions du Seuil, 1947). *Frères de sang* is a semiautobiographical novel depicting the social and political change that took place in

Vietnam at the end of World War II. The narrator, a Vietnamese intellectual, returns to his homeland after several years of study in France. The narrator's father, a mandarin and judge officially deposed because of his failure to suppress a local insurrection, continues nonetheless his despotic rule over the village. He symbolizes the crumbling Confucian tradition to which he his clinging unsuccessfully. Dinh, one of his daughters, rejects an arranged marriage and escapes to seek her own destiny. Ho, his second son, joins the revolutionary movement. Lê-Tham, the narrator's blood brother, retreats from reality, resorting to a Taoist acceptance of fate. The narrator himself is torn between Vietnamese traditions and acquired Western values. He returns to France, but with a faltering conviction.

5. Unless otherwise indicated, the historical background on Buddhism and Confucianism is inspired by Thich Nhat Nanh, *Vietnam: Lotus in a Sea of Fire* (New York: Hill and Wang, 1967).

6. *Columbia Encyclopedia*, 5th ed., s.v. "Confucianism."

7. Thich Nhat Nanh, *Vietnam*, 4–5.

8. Thich Nhat Nanh, *Vietnam*, 5.

9. Thich Nhat Nanh, *Vietnam*, 11.

10. Durand, *Introduction à la littérature vietnamienne*, 9.

11. Walter H. Slote and George A. De Vos, eds., *Confucianism and the Family* (Albany: State University of New York Press, 1988), 93.

12. Slote, *Confucianism*, 100.

13. Slote, *Confucianism*, 100.

14. Thich Nhat Nanh, *Vietnam*, 14.

15. Nguyễn Du, *The Tale of Kiều*, 33.

16. Nguyễn Du, *The Tale of Kiều*, 39.

17. Nguyễn Du, *The Tale of Kiều*, 33.

18. Nguyễn Du, *The Tale of Kiều*, 35

19. Nguyễn Du, *The Tale of Kiều*, 145.

20. Nguyễn Du, *The Tale of Kiều*, 67.

21. Nguyễn Du, *The Tale of Kiều*, 73.

22. Nguyễn Du, *The Tale of Kiều*, 73.

23. Nguyễn Du, *The Tale of Kiều*, 123.

24. Nguyễn Du, *The Tale of Kiều*, 127.

25. Nguyễn Du, *The Tale of Kiều*, 75.

26. Nguyễn Du, *The Tale of Kiều*, 75.

27. Nguyễn Du, *The Tale of Kiều*, 133.

28. Maurice Durand, ed., *Mélanges sur Nguyễn Du* (Paris: Ecole Française d'Extrème Orient, 1966), 269.

29. Durand, *Mélanges sur Nguyễn Du*, 188.

30. Nguyễn Du, *The Tale of Kiều*, 117.

31. Nguyễn Du, *The Tale of Kiều*, 77.

32. Nguyễn Du, *The Tale of Kiều*, 115.

33. Nguyễn Du, *The Tale of Kiều*, 45.

34. Nguyễn Du, *The Tale of Kiều*, 95.

35. Nguyễn Du, *The Tale of Kiều*, 103.

36. Nguyễn Du, *The Tale of Kiều*, 123.

37. Durand, *Mélanges sur Nguyễn Du*, 273.

38. Jack Yeager, *The Vietnamese Novel in French* (Hanover: University Press of New England, 1987), 1.

39. Quoted by Yeager, *The Vietnamese Novel,* 37.

40. Quoted in Durand, *Mélanges sur Nguyễn Du*, 165.

41. Ly-Thu-Ho, *Printemps inachevé* (Paris: J. Peyronnet et Cie, 1962), 38.

42. Ly-Thu-Ho, *Printemps inachevé*, 173.

43. Ly-Thu-Ho, *Printemps inachevé*, 193.

44. Ly-Thu-Ho, *Printemps inachevé*, 64.

45. Nguyễn Du, *The Tale of Kiều*, 137.

46. Pham Van Ky, *Frères de sang* (Paris: Editions du Seuil, 1947), 21.

47. Pham Van Ky, *Frères de sang*, 25. "La 'Ligue de l'Indépendance du Viêt-Nam,' depuis un an, eût-elle brisé ce triangle social, changé le nom du pays, renié le roi, discrédité le mandarin, Père continuait à sévir, doté d'un pouvoir absolu. Les ordonnances de la Cour cédant à la loi communale, selon un dicton, la coutume était son sceptre."

48. Pham Van Ky, *Frères de sang*, 71.

49. Pham Van Ky, *Frères de sang*, 72.

50. Pham Van Ky, *Frères de sang*, 54.

51. Pham Van Ky, *Frères de sang*, 93.

52. Pham Van Ky, *Frères de sang*, 165.

53. Pham Van Ky, *Frères de sang*, 141–42.

54. Pham Van Ky, *Frères de sang*, 175.

55. Pham Van Ky, *Frères de sang*, 184.

56. Pham Van Ky, *Frères de sang*, 26.

57. Durand, *Mélanges sur Nguyễn Du*, 158. "Ce n'est pas la moindre originalité de ce poème, creation d'un cerveau annamite sur lequel aucune influence étrangère hormis la chinoise n'a pu s'exercer, que cet ensemble de qualités qui l'apparentent aux meilleures productions de l'esprit français ... Qu'est-ce à dire, sinon qu'il y a dans le monde une certaine conception de la littérature et de l'art qui se trouve être la même chez deux peuples de l'Extrème Occident et de l'Extrème Asie, ou plutôt qu'il y a entre l'esprit français et l'esprit annamite certaines affinités qu'il serait intéressant de cultiver."

VI

Postmodern Sites and Identities

17

Feminism and Neocolonialism

Discursive Practices

HABIBA DEMING

In *Nature's Government: Science, Imperial Britain and the "Improvement" of the World*, Richard Drayton shows how a scientific subfield as innocuous as botany came to fit into a discourse of imperial foreign intervention and conquest.[1] By weaving notions of ecological "improvement" into the production of knowledge about exotic places and environments, the European imperial discourse successfully represented exploitation of foreign countries not only as a disinterested endeavor but also as a lofty calling to make the world better with or without the "world's" acquiescence.

Muslim femininity has been an integral part of the European imperial discourse from that discourse's incipience. Colonialism provided not so much the conditions for the discovery of "Muslin femininity" as for its construction. In Algeria from the beginning of the colonial enterprise female subjectivity became part of the structuring of colonial rapports in the realm of an actual geography as well as an imaginary one (see Said's discussion of representation as a site of colonial intervention[2]). The voiceless female, which started as mere pictorial curiosities on the cultural map in the early phase of colonization, became figuratively and literally the focal point in its consolidation phase, in effect turning women into a cultural battleground, fusing aesthetics and politics.[3]

In her analysis of Assia Djebar's attempts to weave together an Algerian and French women's common narrative by inserting strands of Western feminism, represented by the Saint-Simonian revolutionary Pauline Rolland, into the colonized women's experience, Winifred Woodhull underscores the problems inherent in such an approach; yet, in the end she deems the attempt worthwhile: "While it is somewhat troubling that Djebar elides the cultural-imperialist ambitions of the Saint-Simonians . . . her efforts to construct a history linking feminist impulses in two warring nations is still a worthy one."[4]

While women's attempts to bridge historical and cultural divides may be admirable, albeit often contrived, the collapsing of an experience as massively and collectively destructive as the colonial experience into a feminist narrative that would transcend it, in my view, may be leading postcolonial women writers into utopian forms of feminism that will obviate (or at least delay) any real understanding of their own particular historical conditions.

In her essay "Feminism and Difference: The Perils of Writing as a Woman on Women in Algeria," Marnia Lazreg surveys female writings about Algerian women from Hubertine Auclert at the turn of the twentieth century to contemporary feminists and sees a continuity of the paradigms used from the colonial era into the feminist postcolonial period: "What was written about Algerian women by women in the first part of this century is reproduced in one form or another in the writings of contemporary French women and U.S feminists about the same subject matter."[5] Thus, despite the end of direct colonial domination and the waning of the intense ethnographic interest in Muslim women that characterized it, one finds little significant change in the themes or paradigms of Western discourse on Muslim women.

The independence era saw the beginning of modest efforts by postcolonial women to start expressing themselves. Predictably, the nascent feminist consciousness in postcolonial Algerian novels was interwoven with national identity and modernization paradigms. Thus we find that in the earlier novels (those from the period extending from approximately the sixties to the eighties), the ancillary protofeminist discourse was emancipatory but in a framework of national identity and ideology (see Hafid Gafaïti's analysis of Aïcha Lemsine's *La Chrysalide*[6]). Emancipation of women was part of nation building and progress toward economic and social development in the socialist postindependence days.

Recently during the tormented decade of the nineties some women writers started to move away from such broadly defined national and socially inclusive thematics to what might be considered more narrowly identifiable feminist concerns. Thus we find a semiconscious effort by some to merge into a global feminist discourse through the use of an exclusively feminist focus and idiom. These writers have become increasingly part of a commodified transnational feminist discourse largely removed from both the reality and the views of the women they write about. As Lazreg states: "Individual women from the Middle East and North Africa appear on the feminist stage as representatives of the millions of women in their own societies. To what extent they do violence to the women they claim authority to write and speak about is a question seldom raised."[7] While Lazreg raises the question of *representability* (who is writing in the name of postcolonial women), it is just as important to raise the corollary question of *representation*, in other words how Muslim women are being written into the Western feminist discourse and what writing strategies are used to produce these texts and ensure their intelligibility within a global feminist discourse.

In the present chapter I would like to focus on one aspect of this emergent feminist discourse, specifically its attempts to signify complex sociocultural norms and behaviors as unadulterated expressions of oppressive Islamic domesticity. To illustrate this, I shall look at how two novels manipulate old colonial stereotypes of seclusion and repressed sexuality and analogies of religion and backwardness to produce *une écriture* that allows them to be grafted into a neocolonial discourse on Muslim women.

In her *Ordalie des voix* (1983), Aïcha Lemsine undertakes a journey across a wide range of Arab countries. In a loosely structured travel narrative, she engages in exchanges with a variety of women and men, soliciting their opinions on the condition of women in their respective societies and expressing her own views while sharing her experience as a Muslim woman and author.[8] Lemsine's interesting albeit modest undertaking produces traditional as well as dissenting views. Of particular interest in her approach is that she is no mere observer describing events; whatever country she visits, she feels and acts as a direct participant in lively debates on women, their rights, and the development of society at large. This attentiveness to actual utterances of women as they represent their own lives and struggles stands in sharp contrast with the emergent feminist discourse in which a liberated elite "gives voice" to women, in other words, speaks about and for them.

This is not to say that Lemsine's message is devoid of ambiguity or that she succeeds in deconstructing the power structure of the societies she visits and about which she writes. Nonetheless, because she seeks to ground her message of emancipation and resistance for women in their own traditions and values (Islamic) within a specific historical space (pan-Arab), her views cannot be grafted in or coopted by a Western transnational feminist establishment. What is of value in her text is not so much its content (conventional feminist advocacy) but its approach (focusing on women's agency), which constitutes a univocal acknowledgment of Arab and Muslim women's capacity to act on their own, unsubordinated to others' ideologies.

Another example of feminist consciousness emerging from the historical experience of its author is Yamina Mechakra's novel *La grotte éclatée* (The Shattered Cave), a poetic short text about a young woman who joins a group of Algerian nationalist fighters in the Aurès Mountains to care for their wounded. Living in caves alone with the men, she shares their hardships and earns their respect. Kateb Yacine wrote in the preface of the novel the oft-quoted sentence: "a woman who writes is worth her weight in gun powder."[9] Despite its theme (the war of liberation), Mechakra's novel is not ideological nor does it omit or bracket women's concerns. The narrative depicts how colonial rule oppresses male and female equally and also demonstrates how the weight of misogynistic traditions can be an added layer of victimization for women. Through its form, dispassionate language, and content (the historically contextualized structures of oppression), the novel achieves an internal coherence and authenticity not seen in most novels about Muslim women.

In a passage striking for its actuality, the narrator "tunes out" outside opinion of the war, musing instead: "What would be, for instance, my sister's opinion, bent over with the weight of her eighth pregnancy . . . her ear attentive to the voices from Algiers, France, Tunis, Cairo, foreign voices speaking of Algeria, screaming their anger, citing figures, telling everything, absolutely everything, except what she saw, herself, what she thought, herself."[10] In this prescient passage, Mechakra anticipates and preempts what has become the mendacious confiscation of Muslim women's experience by others for their own use. Her rejection of such instrumentalization is contained in the double meaning of "my sister" (family ties and the shared sisterhood of common experience and values).

For Abdul JanMohamed, colonialism has "dominant" and "hege-monic" phases, and though the dominant phase represents the period of direct control over a country and its population, it is during the hegemonic phase, which occurs after political independence, that the formerly colonized start to appropriate the values, attitudes, and morality of the colonizers.[11] In the postcolonial Maghrebian francophone novel, and for Algerian writers in this case, denuncia-tion of traditional cultural norms has become a central theme with only slightly mutated colonial motifs of cultural backwardness and oppressiveness. One finds that these texts and their critical recep-tion symbiotically plug into a universalizing cultural economy that commodifies the experience of Muslim women when such experi-ence is "translatable," in other words, explicitly articulated in a recognizable feminist idiom.

As in the colonial period, Muslim femininity has been re-situated as a space open to outside cultural intervention. Muslim women's lives have become a nexus in a swirling political and ideological storm. As in the past, writing about the condition of women fits in a wider discourse about oppressive, undemocratic, premodern, non-Western societies seen this time through an "insider" lens rather than the outsider's gaze. Gayatri Chakravorty Spivak examines how competing meanings of the Hindu custom of *sati* were elaborated and instrumentalized in the context of colonial and postcolonial India and turned women into an "ideological battleground."[12] Such instrumentalization has its longstanding counterparts in the Islamic cultural realm as is the case most notably for customs such as veiling. Shifting categories such as Third World women writing for a First World readership and the embedding of neocolonial meanings in the larger transnational feminist discourse are, however, increasingly contributing to obscuring such instrumentalizations.

In English postcolonial studies, many critics have questioned

First World feminist hegemony and countered its homogenizing discourse about Third World women with new interpretive strategies. In her essay "Under Western Eyes," Chandra Talpade Mohanty extends her critique of the practices of Western feminism to include the work of middle-class, Third World women when they "employ identical analytic strategies."[13] In contrast Francophone Studies have remained dependent to a great extent on traditional Western feminist models in the study of non-Western patriarchal societies. Both Mohanty's and JanMohamed's views are useful to my discussion as they underline the overdetermined nature of postcolonial cultural production, whether fiction or scholarship.

Almost without exception, novels by Algerian women writers, irrespective of literary worth, are being read as enunciative of a feminist consciousness even when they teem with ambiguities and contradictions, offering often a decontextualized critique of communal values, eliding historical ruptures, and unconsciously bracketing the role of colonization in producing what JanMohamed called "pathological societies, ones that exist in a state of perpetual crisis."[14]

The two novels I consider in this essay have achieved a quasifoundational status as "feminist" texts on the condition of women in Algeria. Nina Bouraoui's *La voyeuse interdite*[15] (Forbidden Vision) and Malika Mokeddem's *L'interdite* (The Forbidden Woman) continue to be seen as emblematic of the two dimensions of Algerian women's experience, Islamic oppression, and women's resistance. Read against the political realities of the 1990s, these novels have been treated to a large extent as cultural texts in which the political, the social, the private, and the public converge.

Bouraoui's text is suffused with a self-conscious literariness, manifest in a sustained effort to transmute ethnographic language into poetics. Thus the text begins by warning against a referential reading "to make oneself a story before contemplating Truth. Real, fictional what does it matter."[16] Despite this ambiguity, the text has been interrogated if not as firsthand experience then at least as a realist description of it. Early on, Jean Déjeux warned "it is certain that a large number of Westerners take at face value what Nina Bouraoui is saying."[17] The object of representation is the secluded woman. The narrative proposes itself to the reader at once as an allegory (sexual segregation as psychosis) and as an actual depiction of the restrictions imposed on the lives of Muslim women by men and religion. This textual duplicity fractures the text aesthetically, resulting in a variety of fragments, including political critique, masochist sexual fantasy, sociocultural commentary, and ethnographic explanations. The novel does not fuse these fragments into a seamless narrative; they remain juxtaposed, jarringly exposing the inner workings of the novel like a series of sketchy drafts.

Below the stereotypic theme of women's seclusion and subjection, we find the more ambitious attempt to build a model of a sexual psychopathology based on a religious taxonomy. The novel locates not only the narrator's neurosis in religion, but subsequently in all of society, "this vast psychiatric asylum,"[18] is seen as marked by a religiously mandated sexual repression. Painstakingly, the text constructs a young Muslim woman's neurosis using not only "secular" psychoanalytical terminology but curiously manipulated Christian symbology as well. Thus the text remains fractured and discordant with incongruent utterances like "sex is a cursed flower planted between Satan's horns."[19] Demonological symbology of carnal love, as expressed in the images of a horned Satan and "cursed flower" suggestive of the fall and original sin, are alien concepts to Islamic theology and not part of the cultural stock of images in which repressed sexuality would normally be expressed. It remains unclear whether this peculiarity results from ignorance of the material needed to construct the psychosexual from within or represents a form of cultural mimicry. Examples of this kind of discordance abound in the text, such as the father's rejection of his daughter's femininity with the strange string of words: "Girl, come, woman, fornication, weakness, stain, start with the same letter" (see the original French[20]). While the alliteration has a definite suggestive power in French, it is certainly not the case in Arabic, presumably the language of the characters.

In the novel's context of the representation of a traditional Arab-Muslim family, Christian allusions constitute a culturally incongruent and as such a problematic aspect of the work, yet it is these questionable fragments that have provided the most readily used grid for its reading. Bouraoui anchors her narrative of psychosis and aberrant sexuality in images of "Satan" and "curse," which would not be associated with sex for a Muslim reader, who lacks a concept corresponding to original sin. Bouraoui's text, on the other hand, provides the Western reader with readily recognizable categories. Her facile manipulation of Western religious and sexual phantasmagoria dressed up in Islamic garb is thus easily recognized and consumed by a dilettante feminism.

It is particularly in its depiction of Muslim femininity that the narrative unravels and further loses its internal coherence. The narrator begins by claiming her solidarity with the cloistered young women: "I am one with the girls from the neighboring houses."[21] She wants to help them: "Kneeling before my window, I mixed with my song prayers addressed directly to God; I did not implore his grace just for me, I mostly wanted that he deliver these poor little girls from hell."[22] However, these attempts to identify with the young women are subverted throughout the text. Thus, the narrator's claims of feminist sisterhood are recused by the text itself. More objects of scorn than of study, women in the text are uniformly described as repulsive and grotesque.

The gaze of the *voyeuse* is an outsider's gaze. The *voyeuse* creates the object of her *voyeurisme*, then in an ultimate gesture of domination and exploitation, objectifies these women under her pen: the women are "bags of flesh"[23] and "rolls of grease."[24] She writes: "all those breasts bobbing disgracefully like monsters make me sick."[25] In the novel women are often described as an undifferentiated mass that then becomes the abstract category of "Muslim women" in the mind of the reader. This silent and in effect absent mass is only given form and existence by the narrator who speaks about them and for them. The narrator's strange repulsion toward women and the fleshiness of female bodies she describes must not be read simply as a symptom of the narrator's obsessions with her body; rather, it encodes the author's own alien aesthetic canons and ideals of feminine beauty. For Bouraoui Muslim femininity is essentially a diseased femininity; so an attractive young woman's face already bears the mark of its future disfigurement: "she could have been charming, that pleasingly plump Moorish girl, were it not for the beginning of a goiter that made her look like an ox in heat!"[26]

The narrator signifies the Muslim woman not only by brandishing the phallic symbol of the paintbrush: "Dominating the Moorish women, I hold the perspective, I own the horizon and nothing escapes my brown brushes."[27] She also objectivizes them under her gaze through her projection inside their world. However, she does so in a system of signs they do not understand. Thus, these uneducated and muted (because non-French–speaking) women are sequestered not just by walls but also by the graphemes of the French language, becoming victims of the ultimate textual violence. The text, which seeks to construct female seclusion from the inside, succeeds only in expressing the author's own terror and repulsion of a fantasmatic seclusion, dramatically underscoring her own status as an outsider (see *Garçon manqué*, Bouraoui's autobiographical novel about her own sense of foreignness and alienation from Algerian culture and Muslim values).

Feminists in France and the United States have embraced the novel while for the most part ignoring its contemptuous treatment of women. However, this disturbing aspect of the text remains to be addressed. Ironic readings unpersuasively attempt to circuitously salvage the text's feminist status by presenting it as a subversion of traditional European Orientalist clichés of Muslim women (a clever nightmarish reversal of an Oriental fantasy) and as resistance to the patriarchal structure of Muslim society.[28]

For Winifred Woodhull, Algerian women's writing has been generally considered mostly for its ideological content rather than for its literariness: "their writing is considered to be trite and to serve, at best, to demonstrate pregiven ideologies, especially anti-colonial, democratic, and feminist ideologies."[29] This description fits perfectly Malika Mokeddem's heavily ethnographic and at times plainly documentary novel *L'interdite*, which relies throughout on facile and superficial imagery of the life of the liberated "emigrant" and narrator to carry a straightforward message of feminism. With its ideologically saturated prose and scant concern for the manipulation of symbols or the transmuting of events into discourse, Mokeddem's novel was embraced not for its literariness but mainly for its message.

In the novel the narrator, who returns to her village after a long absence, immediately sets out to face off with Algeria's traditional society. By accentuating the character's rejectionism of her society's mores and saturating the text with images of Sultana's assertiveness, the author seeks to construct an exemplar of a modern liberated female, a feminist heroine: "Sultana's story shows a woman facing her destiny while, symbolically, she fights for the collective destiny of Algerian women trapped in a macho world."[30] However, Sultana's gratuitous challenge to societal norms and her contemptuous discounting of religious traditions are also signs of a pretentious and self-absorbed ego because they are not connected to a sustained effort at reflection about underlying meanings and the complexities of intersecting historical, cultural, and environmental factors to account for women's lives. Her impatient outbursts and trite comments about Algerian society betray at once the cultural void and intellectual narcissism of the character under a superficial feminism.

In the novel, alcohol, sex, and cigarettes are used as tropes of a naive modernity. These tropes do not require elucidation: they are a recognizable cultural currency of the emancipated woman, and their literal and liberal use imparts to the novel the superficial quality of a popular novel. Mokeddem also eschews linearity and weaves a metadiscourse on the oppression of women with the events. Sultana's feminist and secular message is clear in its Manichean simplicity. It is axiomatic that religious men are bad, like the mayor, who is a nasty bearded smuggler, and Dalila's brothers, who are misogynistic. Religious men are not only uniformly mean, they are physically ugly too. The "good" characters are atheists, or at least secular, and are intelligent, liberal, and handsome like Yacine, the deceased lover, who was even blond. The tendency of the author to assign slots for "good" and "bad" characters gives the novel the predictability of a morality play, and there is little nuance or ambiguity to give the characters depth.

The character of Vincent, a Frenchman visiting Algeria, quite simply becomes the narrator's other voice in the text to carry the feminist message. He does not just bemoan or deplore traditional macho male attitudes; in fact, he totally identifies with Sultana to the point of experiencing the violence of the male "look" women are supposed to experience. Thus he states, "I would not want to be a woman here. I would not want to bear constantly the weight of these looks, their many forms of violence, fueled by frustration."[31]

On close examination, *L'interdite* is more about a woman's social exclusion and concomitant pain at being an outcast as a young girl than about questions of gender inequality. The exclusion suffered in her youth was the defining moment in her alienation from society more so than her later conscious rejection of its norms and traditions. While the questions of class and gender discrimination often overlap, it is important to distinguish between the two. In this case, the social and cultural exclusionary mechanisms operating have been generally overlooked. Situated in its socioeconomic context, Mokeddem's novel depicts the experience of a young misfit who metaphorically reinvents herself as a feminist. Sultana's rebellion underneath its feminist veneer is about the raw emotions of "settling scores" and "getting back" at the tormentors from her past. Mokeddem's characterizations have a narrow range; her female characters tend to be unidimensional. The "feminist" is often a vociferous misfit who models a "liberated" lifestyle for greatest impact in rural "backward" areas, provoking some and enlightening others. Sultana and Nour (the heroine of *La nuit de la lézarde*) end up being mirror images, just like the sidekick characters Dalila and Dounia.[32]

Thus, in spite of its thick feminist message, the novel is as much about the structures of social exclusion as it is about gender discrimination. In fact it is the haunting past of Sultana as a social outcast that permeates the novel and leads the narrator to articulate harsh and superficial assessments of women's experience in her society. One could say that "feminism" here is used as a means of retroactively transcending social exclusion. Just as society excluded her when she was young and vulnerable (in her mind, there is an amalgamation between class and gender exclusion so the whole society is tainted with the sin of misogyny), the excluded now takes on the role of the excluder, showing off her modernity and rejecting those who shunned her. The newly arrived former outcast (a physician and immigrant in France) can stand and face what she considers a backward lot.

As we can see, Sultana's behavior cannot be fully accounted for by looking at it solely through a feminist lens. The focus on the male/female paradigm magnifies and thus distorts the picture in order to turn her into a feminist heroine. The obsessiveness and pathological narcissism at the core of the character make her more singular psychologically and less typical sociologically. When her friend Salah contrasts her gratuitously provocative behavior with that of the majority of Algerian women who work quietly and diligently to achieve greater equality in the society, Sultana does not disagree. In fact, there is a faint awareness in the character of her own singularity as opposed to her exemplarity for Algerian women. Thus she states: "And then, 'true Algerian women' do not have problems with their being. . . . They are whole."[33] As she concedes this, Sultana comes to the realization that her problem is situated elsewhere, not just in the society she blames but mostly in herself. Despite the character's insight into her situation, however, she does not achieve the self-knowledge necessary to move from a self-centered confrontational attitude to a genuine exchange with others. She instead falls back into the trap of transgression for transgression's sake.

The merging of the two strands of modernism and feminism in Sultana's criticisms of her society brings Mokeddem's practice closer to the colonial and neocolonial paradigms of "disassociating"[34] herself from the entire culture, not just men's culture, in order to become modern and feminist. This fact is illustrated by Sultana's reactions to her patients as an ignorant, superstitious group of people. One does not get the sense that their problems in her thinking are in large part a result of poverty and disenfranchisement but rather derive from their beliefs. It is their cultural and religious beliefs that are keeping them poor and backward. The assumption is that if they rejected their beliefs and culture as Sultana did (after all she was one of them at one time) they too would become emancipated and modern.

Like the previous novel, *L'interdite* encodes its own "reading instructions." Fragments of ethnographic explanation, various political and social analyses, and commentaries are inserted throughout the text to provide directions to the reader. Thus in addition to the "translatability" of its feminist idiom, each of the novels considered here provides its audience with interpretive strands that guide the reader back to the text. By tapping into a deeply embedded symbology and well-entrenched paradigms about Muslim women, both novels are readily consumed as "feminist" novels, in other words as works that promote and advance the cause of women despite their reductive and their sometimes contemptuous views of Muslim women.

The question as to why the main critical impulse has been and continues to be that these texts are an univocal expression of a genuine feminist consciousness is a vexed issue that has as much to do with the constitution of feminism as a field of study and its dependence on Western cultural assumptions, including assumptions about Islam, as with any formal characteristics of the works in question. At the base of what Lazreg refers to as "gynocentrism" we find the same sets of cultural beliefs regarding Western superiority in relation to Islam as in the colonial discourse. In this perspective Western feminism operates from the belief that while patriarchy is bad, its cultural forms and expressions are worse in some unique way in Islam.

On the whole, we can say that whether these texts are to be considered as expressions of individual rebellion with more denunciation
than reflection or as failed attempts to signify the muted women of
the tradition, they end up merely recirculating old colonial stereotypes about an Islam designated as misogynistic and opposed to
women's freedom (implicitly a Western value) and thus reinscrib-
ing neocolonialism as feminism. Despite their "native status" the
authors' chosen interlocutionary positions put them in polarity
with the women they write about. The texts were constructed for
and destined to ultimately fit in a sanctioned feminist discourse,
and thus their intelligibility and relevance to Muslim women were
never really an overriding concern.

Notes

1. Richard Drayton, *Nature's Government: Science, Imperial Britain, and the "Improvement" of the World* (New Haven: Yale University Press, 2000).

2. Edward W Said, *Culture and Imperialism* (New York: Vintage, 1994).

3. Malek Alloua, *The Colonial Harem*, trans. Myrna Godzich and Wlad Godzich
(Minneapolis: University of Minnesota Press, 1986).

4. Winifred Woodhull, *Transfigurations of the Maghreb: Feminism, Decolonization,
and Literature* (Minneapolis: University of Minnesota Press, 1993), 82.

5. Marnia Lazreg, "Feminism and Difference: The Perils of Writing as a Woman on
Women in Algeria," *Feminist Studies* 1 (1988): 83.

6. Hafid Gafaïti, *Les femmes dans le roman algérien* (Paris: L'Harmattan, 1996).

7. Lazreg, "Feminism and Difference," 89.

8. Aïcha Lemsine, *Ordalie des voix: Les femmes arabes parlent* (Paris: Nouvelle
Société des Editions Encre, 1983).

9. Yamina Mechakra, *La Grotte éclatée* (Alger: Entreprise du livre, 1986), 8.

10. Mechakra, *La Grotte éclatée*, 35.

11. Abdul R JanMohamed, "The Economy of Manichean Allegory: The Function
of Racial Difference in Colonialist Literature," in *"Race," Writing, and Difference*, ed.
Henry Louis Gates Jr. (Chicago: University of Chicago Press, 1985), 80.

12. Gayatri Chakravorty Spivak, "Can the Subaltern Speak? Speculations on Widow-
Sacrifice," *Wedge* 7, no. 8 (1982): 124.

13. Chandra Talpade Mohanty, "Under Western Eyes: Feminist Scholarship and

Colonial Discourses," in *Third World Women and the Politics of Feminism*, ed. Chandra Talpade Mohanty, Ann Russo, and Lourdes Torres (Bloomington: Indiana University Press, 1991), 52.

14. JanMohamed, "The Economy of Manichean Allegory," 80.

15. Nina Bouraoui, *La Voyeuse interdite* (Paris: Gallimard, 1991).

16. Bouraoui, *La Voyeuse interdite*, 11.

17. Jean Déjeux, *La littérature féminine de langue française au Maghreb* (Paris: Editions Karthala, 1994), 94.

18. Bouraoui, *La voyeuse interdite*, 21.

19. Bouraoui, *La voyeuse interdite*, 25.

20. "Fille, foutre, femme, fornication, faiblesse, flétrissure commencent par la même lettre"; Bouraoui, *La voyeuse interdite*, 33.

21. Bouraoui, *La voyeuse interdite*, 11.

22. Bouraoui, *La voyeuse interdite*, 118.

23. Bouraoui, *La voyeuse interdite*, 34.

24. Bouraoui, *La voyeuse interdite*, 49.

25. Bouraoui, *La voyeuse interdite*, 87.

26. Bouraoui, *La voyeuse interdite*, 79.

27. Bouraoui, *La voyeuse interdite*, 99.

28. Nicole Buffard-O'Shea, "Ecrivaines de l'im/émigration, écrivaines algériennes: Écritures politiques," in *Algérie: Nouvelles Écritures*, ed. Charles Bonn, Najib Redouane, and Yvette Bénayoun-Szmidt (Paris: L'Harmattan, 2001).

29. Woodhull, *Transfigurations of the Maghreb*, 78.

30. Valérie Orlando, *Nomadic Voices of Exile: Feminine Identity in Francophone Literature of the Maghreb* (Athens: Ohio University Press, 1999), 107. See also Valérie Orlando, "Ecriture d'un autre lieu: La déterritorialisation des nouveaux rôles féminins dans *L'interdite*," in *Malika Moukeddem: Envers et contre tous*, ed. Yolande Aline Helm (Paris: L'Harmattan, 2000), 105–15.

31. Malika Mokeddem, *L'interdite* (Paris: Editions Grasset et Fasquelle, 1993), 93.

32. Malika Mokeddem, *La nuit de la lézarde* (Paris: Editions Grasset et Fasquelle, 1998).

33. Mokeddem, *L'interdite*, 191.

34. Lazreg, "Feminism and Difference," 88.

18

The Self as Other

Yasmina Bouziane

DAVID PROCHASKA

MOUKHTAR KOCACHE: Your work refers to historic ethnographic practices and the role that documentary and Orientalist photography plays in the construction of "image" and its justification of certain ideological discourses. What brought you to this?

YASMINA BOUZIANE: Initially, when I first started out, I did documentary photography; more specifically, I studied Moroccan women in the work-force. My work shifted when I began to understand photography as a construction, with the power to alter truths and fabricate imagery. . . . At the same time, I had to take a closer look at myself as a woman photographer shuffling between at least three cultures. . . . The result is, in part, this series of self-portraits.—Moukhtar Kocache, "Conversation with Yasmina Bouziane"

Yasmina Bouziane is one of several contemporary visual artists based in the "West," especially New York, revisioning the "East," especially the Middle East and North Africa. A striking number of these artists are women; gender figures prominently as well in the work of Ghada Amer, Jananne al-Ani, Mona Hatoum, Shirin Neshat, Mikal Rovner, and Shahzia Sikander. Bouziane is a filmmaker and photographer; her father is Moroccan, her mother is French, and she lives in the United States. In her films and photographs she ranges from Morocco and Palestine to New York and Georgetown. She collaborated with her screenwriter sister Anissa on her films: *Imaginary Homelands* (1993) and *Yellow Nylon Rope* (1994).[1] In her photographic series, Untitled Self-Portraits, Bouziane interrogates earlier Orientalist studio photography practices. As a postcolonial critique and reworking of colonial practices, Bouziane looks back and responds from her contemporary vantage point on the colonial past, although from her postcolonial location in New York she addresses more a "Western" audience than an "Eastern" one. Foregrounding her own body, her project has everything to do with gender: how the colonial photography studio was gendered, the gendered gaze of colonial postcards, and what it means to be a woman photographer and filmmaker of French and Moroccan background living in America and in a postcolonial world today. To be sure there is always the risk in such work of lapsing into narcissism, a narrow focus on the self. Taken as a whole, Bouziane's work simultaneously probes issues of identity and gender, hybridity and postcoloniality. Here I focus on selected photographs from the Untitled Self-Portraits series, using them as a springboard for a series of reflections on Orientalist photography and beyond.

> DAVID PROCHASKA: What is your personal experience of Orientalist or colonial postcards and photographs? Did you know people who had postcard collections or family albums?
>
> YASMINA BOUZIANE: My background as both French and Moroccan and as a photographer was very instrumental in my study of colonial postcards. . . . The interesting thing about how I started this series [of

3. Yasmina Bouziane, *Untitled, Self Portrait*. By permission of the artist.

self-portraits] was that I came across a photograph of my father's uncle and a friend of his in a studio set-up (one with this strange flowered background and some kind of Orientalist art) all the while they were dressed in traditional Moroccan garb. It so happens that apparently they had had their portrait taken at this photo studio and later on down the road had found it being sold on the streets as a postcard. This was done, of course, without their knowledge or consent. I own that postcard now and it is part of an installation.[2] As a personal experience it got me thinking some more about the nature of photography and the appropriation of someone else's image and the distortion of "truth" with the use of photography.[3]

"Untitled, Self Portrait" (figure 3) is Yasmina Bouziane's signature photo. It turns the tables. Instead of the Western male photographing Arab women in Orientalist studio settings, the Arab woman turns the camera on the implied Western male viewer. The voyeuristic male gaze of Orientalist painting and photography is reversed as the viewer becomes the viewed. The passive female object becomes here the active female subject, reinforced by Bouziane's serious mien, her direct gaze. The way the photograph is composed contributes to this effect. Everything here consists of lines and angles; nothing is softened by curves: the trapezoids are formed by the floodlights, and the triangles outlined by the tripod. Very much a constructed, posed photo, it is by no means naturalistic. Bouziane's right hand is on the (cocked) camera shutter (ready to shoot), but she is not looking at us through the viewfinder; she is looking at us slightly above and to the side of the camera. It is not "natural" for her left arm to rest on her hip, thrust out, but it makes her pose more active, in your face. Key to the construction of this constructed photograph is the way it calls attention to its own making. The picture frame includes the top of the canvas backdrop and shows how it is attached to the wall behind it. The floodlights are starkly visible.

"Untitled, Self Portrait" presents both past and present, "tradition" and "modernity," color and black and white. The Turkish rugs, the spathiphyllum and red plastic flowers in a basketry container, and Bouziane's tooled leather cowboy boots (a nice touch) are rich in color. In contrast, everything else is black or white.

A photograph such as this one risks being considered trite; once the viewer gets the point, repeated viewings are not necessary, its meaning is exhausted. But behind the end product is the process, the process of working through and beyond the accumulated weight of Orientalist photography and of colonial representation in general. Here Bouziane takes back the photograph of her great-uncle and his friend that was taken from them.

Bouziane evokes the space of the photographer's studio but undermines the illusion of verisimilitude by calling our attention through her composition to how the space is used to create photographic effects. Generally we may identify three kinds of postcard space. First is the space of the photographer's studio. Second is the space of the "view" photograph, the physical world outside. A third, or optical space, is the way in which the negative is manipulated after exposure and before printing by the publisher to achieve certain spatial effects.[4] Now the archetypal space of the Orientalist postcard is a photographer's studio, a "scenic space" arranged to create an "Oriental" illusion. Besides indoor studios, Orientalist photographs were shot in interior courtyards and other spaces where natural light could be used in controlled environments. All these settings were outfitted in an Orientalist fashion with props and artifacts purchased for the purpose.

Orientalist photographic environments are related to other Western fabrications of "Oriental" spaces, including "Oriental" architecture in the west. Most famous perhaps is the Royal Pavilion, Brighton, by architect John Nash built early in the nineteenth century.[5] Even more numerous were "Oriental" rooms in the homes of the wealthy, especially in the nineteenth century. Best known in England is the Arab Hall designed for painter Frederic Lord Leighton's London house, 1877–79.[6] For those only slightly less affluent, Orientalist "cozy corners," a corner or portion of a room, were an option.[7] American decorators recommended to middle-class women cozy, or "cosey," corners as low-cost Orientalist niches that they could create for their own enjoyment. Common accoutrements included a divan upholstered in Oriental fabric, scattered pillows in Oriental fabric, a Turkish coffee table, and an Oriental rug; but they might also include Japanese fans, Chinese lanterns, draped oriental fabric on the walls, east Asian parasols, potted tropical plants, Japanese tea sets, Turkish coffee sets, and other imported brass and ceramic objects.[8] Other rooms contained Oriental accents. Sigmund Freud's consulting room at Berggasse 19 in Vienna was thoroughly Orientalist with a Qual-qi rug spread on the patient's couch and a night scene of Abu Simbel on the Nile painted in 1906 hanging on the wall.[9]

Key to Orientalist (and other exoticist) studio photographs is the effect of the real they strive to achieve.[10] These are photographs that employ realist strategies of representation to convince the viewer of their "other," in this case Oriental, reality. Chief among these representational strategies is that they bear no mark of their making. Sometimes backdrops, often painted, are visible in Orientalist postcards, yet rarely if ever are the edges of the backdrops as visible as they consistently are in Bouziane's "Untitled, Self Portraits" series. Photographs by Félix-Antoine Moulin (circa 1800–after 1868) may be the exception that proves the rule. The first photographer to produce an important body of work on colonial Algeria, where he traveled in 1856–57, Moulin frequently rigged up canvas backdrops against which he posed his subjects, and in several photographs the backdrops are clearly visible.[11] Although Moulin left no record that

4. Yasmina Bouziane, *Untitled, Self Portrait 8*. By permission of the artist.

tells us why he did this, it may well have been simply haste since he traveled more or less continuously. Similarly it is rare to find postcards that depict a photographer or photographic apparatus; those that do so are often novelty cards with a humorous intent.

> Bible metaphors and parables take on the vividness of their own sunny clime when viewed among the hills of Palestine; and Bible history appears as if acted anew when read upon its old stage.[12]

"Untitled, Self Portrait 8" (figure 4) resembles a stock Orientalist "Biblical" scene. Bouziane, dressed in "Biblical" clothes evocative of Palestine, looks down as if contemplating the infant Jesus in the manger. It recalls all those Bible scenes of the Holy Land from the nineteenth and early twentieth centuries of shepherds herding their flocks and women by the manger. "Both the growth of tourism and pilgrimage to the Holy Places of Palestine . . . produced a deluge of books, slides, postcards and other memorabilia of 'biblical' Palestine and its inhabitants."[13] These stock stereotypes coded Palestine as "Biblical." To produce Biblical tableaux, photographers "simply took pictures of daily life in Palestine and attached a caption with a biblical reference or quotation," for example, "The 23rd Psalm, portrayed in the land of its inception."[14] Similar to Bouziane's image in expression is a photograph taken before 1914 titled "A Judean home, suggestive of 'The Wise Men Seeking the Christ Child.'"[15]

What makes the "Biblical" Biblical in this photographic genre is the way contemporary Palestinians were transformed into figures of the past, how nineteenth- and twentieth-century Arab Palestinians were made to stand in for Jews and Christians of two thousand years ago. It also makes them Orientalist. In the 1890s in Nazareth an American traveler does not name names because she does not need to: "A lad stands just within the threshold of a carpenter's shop.

His tunic was blue serge with a red sash at the waist. At the sight of the levelled kodak, he laughs and his hands chafe one another nervously."[16] This would have particular resonance for Bouziane, whose father is originally from Nazareth. As the narrator puts it in her film *Imaginary Homelands,* "When I walk down the streets of the *medina,* rue des Consuls, the men speak to me in English. They think I'm a 'Nasrania,' the one from Nazareth. They think I'm from 'El Kharij,' from the outside. . . . But what am I supposed to do? I'm the daughter of a 'Nasrania,' who lives in 'El Kharij' and speaks Arabic."[17]

Photographers were fully aware of the "timeless Orient" they were creating. Adrien Bonfils, the son of Félix Bonfils, who founded the leading studio in Beirut in the 1870s, wrote the following about his photographic practice: "Twenty centuries have passed without changing the décor or physiognomy of this land [Palestine] unique among all; but let us hasten if we wish to enjoy the sight. . . . before progress has completely done its destructive job, before this present which is still the past has forever disappeared we have tried to fix and immobilize it in a series of views."[18] Once the image was fixed it was available for circulation; it could be inserted in a visual economy of images largely bereft of their original referents.[19] Thus, stereotypical "Biblical" photographs were made not only in Palestine. They could be set in Egypt, where Lucie Duff Gordon described a Bedouin woman who was "walking away toward the desert in the setting sun like Hagar. All is so Scriptural in the country here."[20] They could be set in Algeria, as Théophile Gautier noted in writing about the 1861 Paris Salon: "The voyage to Algiers is becoming as indispensable for painters as the pilgrimage to Italy; they go there to learn of the sun, to study light, to seek out unseen types, and manners and postures that are primitive and biblical."[21] Or they could be set in India among the Todas, an ethnic group in

5. Yasmina Bouziane, *Untitled, Self Portrait 4*. By permission of the artist.

the Nilgiri mountains of southern India that inspired a voluminous written literature from Richard Burton to Madame Blavatsky to W. H. R. Rivers as well as a stream of photographic representations in which the Todas are made to look "Biblical."[22]

"Untitled, Self Portrait 4" (figure 5) and "Untitled, Self Portrait 12" (figure 6) constitute a diptych. In "Untitled, Self Portrait 4" Bouziane cross-dresses as a turn-of-the-century male Western photographer. Wearing a watch fob, the photographer poses for "his" picture with an early flash camera in hand. The first thing to note is, again, the self-referentiality: photographer Bouziane photographs herself as a photographer in a photographer's studio. Yet she has turned the tables once more, for she assumes here the role of a Western photographer, who at the time would have been much more likely to take Bouziane's photo as an Arab woman than vice versa. Posing as a western male with a camera, just whose picture is she going to take?

This photograph functions, therefore, as a contemporary Derridean *supplément* to past Orientalist photographs. For what remains primarily of Orientalist photography is the product, the actual images produced. What is absent almost entirely is textual and visual evidence of both the production process and audience reception of the photographs. Name a photographer of the time, and chances are no photograph of the photographer is readily available or even exists: James Robertson, Félix Bonfils, Felix Beato, Abdullah brothers, the brothers C. and G. Zangaki, Roger Fenton, Auguste Salzmann, Gustave Le Gray, J. Pascal Sebah, Edouard Baldus, Félix Teynard, John Greene, Louis de Clercq, Francis Frith, Yessayi Garabedian, Félix J.-A. Moulin, Jean Geiser.[23]

The studio props in "Untitled, Self Portrait 4" again mix and match past and present. The same Turkish rugs are present. A

6. Yasmina Bouziane, *Untitled, Self Portrait 12*. By permission of the artist.

largely hidden classical pedestal reminds us of props that sitters leaned against during the long exposure times. Bouziane is decked out here in a *fin-de-siècle* three-piece suit, a shirt with a high white collar, black shoes, and watch chain. But this is (anti)colonial mimicry right out of Homi Bhabha, a copy that is "almost the same, but not quite."[24] Her pants are way too short. Her tie is tied in a rakish knot. Her phony mustache is clearly pasted on. Yet present jostles past. Our eye falls on a small electric fan at lower left, a plastic container of Dawn cleanser, and a brown briefcase with snazzy gold clasp. More flowers have blossomed; in addition to the spathiphyllum, there are now garish plastic yellow sunflowers, giant pink begonias, and what appear to be maple leaves. What we have here is, therefore, a present reworking of past photographic practices underscored by the use of new and old props.

Bouziane's pose with camera in hand also evokes an earlier period of visual culture.[25] The photographer posing for his portrait holding his trademark tool of the trade, a camera, is reminiscent of an earlier form of portraiture, *petits métiers*, in which occupational types were identified by the tools they hold. Connected to these you-are-what-work-you-do representations dating from the sixteenth century are the *Cris de Paris*, and in the nineteenth century the nine-volume *Les Français peints par eux-mêmes*, a compendium of pictorial representations by artists in a variety of media aimed at artists. A related publication illustrated with one hundred engravings, La Bédollière's *Les industriels, métiers et professions en France* constituted a volume in the enormously popular *physiologies* series dating from the 1840s.

Earlier *petits métiers* representations gave way by the end of the nineteenth century to the "scenes and types" genre of picture postcards. In such places as late nineteenth- and early twentieth-century colonial Algeria, "scenes and types" stereotypical images produced and reproduced "typical" Algerians in standardized contexts. Such pictorial typing clearly links up with a typological streak in Western social thought, the impulse to categorize, classify. In France the names Buffon and Cuvier, Quêtelet and Bertillon come to mind. The *physiologie* craze of the 1840s, for example, is tied directly to Lavater's physiognomy, the notion that outward appearance corresponds to inner character, how-you-look-is-who-you-are. Where physiognomy scrutinized the body, Gall's phrenology examined the head to determine mental capacity, literally in the craniometry practiced by Broca. Photography's method was similar.

"Untitled, Self Portrait 12" is almost exactly the same as "Untitled, Self Portrait 4." The same garish plastic flowers, the same *fin-de-siècle* clothes, shot from the same angle, surely it was photographed at the same time. Bouziane again cross-dresses *à l'occidentale*. Coat slung over her left shoulder, holding a big red plastic flower on a stalk, she appears deep in reverie. With her head tilted sideways and back, contemplating the flower, is there not a hint, and more, of Narcissus here? Moukhtar Kocache remarks, "Yasmina Bouziane's project faces two dangers. . . . Her practice of self-examination might run the risk of 'othering the self' rather than 'selving the other.' He [Hal Foster] notes the danger that 'self othering can flip into self-absorption, in which the project of an ethnographic self-fashioning' becomes the practice of a philosophical narcissism."[26]

Dressing up. Cross-dressing. Passing. One intriguing aspect of the Western fascination with the "Orient," especially in the nineteenth century, was the frequency with which Westerners dressed up as Easterners. Such dressing up was rife with the aura of disguise, a masquerade. Often necessary for travel, it was also linked to derring-do. Jean Louis Burckhardt assumed the name Shaikh Ibrahim ibn Abdullah to enter the Kaaba at Mecca early in the nineteenth century.[27] As late as the 1930s in central Asia Robert Byron disguised himself as a lower-middle-class Persian to sneak into the mosque of Gohar Shad in Meshed.[28] In his 1879 novel, *Aziyadé*, Pierre Loti went native in Istanbul. When he decides to return home, he simply ceases his Turkish masquerade. "And that is the end of Arif [his Turkish name]. That personage has now ceased to exist. The Eastern dream is ended."[29] At base, it is a question of passing, of becoming who you are not. Richard Burton shuffled identities like so many changes of clothes.[30]

The precipitate, the trace of this Orientalist fascination—or is it obsession?—is the number of photographs that unselfconsciously preserve the moment of masking: E. M. Forster, Francis Frith, Roger Fenton, Pierre Loti, Warren Thompson. And it is not just individuals whose names we know: in colonial Algeria tourists dressed as Arabs posed against painted studio backdrops, and at Mardi Gras, a world-turned-upside-down time, little European girls dressed like Algerians.

While Westerners may have dressed as Easterners more often for fun or the thrill of it, Easterners dressed as Westerners more often as a sign of their *évolué* status, to use the French term for especially those Algerians who had literally "evolved" toward France. This is the point where Bouziane fits in, the Easterner dressed as Westerner. But Bouziane ups the sexual ante, cross-dressing as male. Singer Umm Kulthoum describes her father's anxiety at her performing in public: "So he began to dress me in boys' clothes. . . . I realize now that my father wanted to deceive himself, to postpone in his mind what he was doing, letting his daughter sing in public. And he also wanted to deceive the audience."[31]

Fewer were the Westerners who cross-dressed, but there were—and are—some. Perhaps the most famous, or infamous, was Isabelle Eberhardt, who switched religion, her racial and ethnic identity, and gender roles.[32] Today the political ante has gone up. In Afghanistan once American bombing began in October 2001 no one much wanted journalists around to report on the fighting, so a few intrepid Western reporters both male and female disguised themselves as Afghani women. "Getting there [to the Pashtun tribal lands around Peshawar] was going to require a little subterfuge," Isabel Hilton explained. "I bought a woman's version of the *shalwar kameez* and wound the wide scarf that comes with it around my head and shoulders, hiding my hair and the lower part of my face. The effect was to render me as anonymous as the women I passed on the street."[33] Bouziane's cross-dressing Western male aesthete is different. Redolent of nineteenth-century Symbolism, of fin-de-siècle decadence, "Untitled, Self Portrait 12" is degeneration of the nineteenth-century variety: Odilon Redon, Huysmans, Octave Moreau.[34]

In Algeria in the late 1970s and early '80s you saw Algerian women who in their chic Parisian styles, expensive coiffures, and fluent French could well pass as French. My temporary Iraqi roommate, who brought his makings for tea from Baghdad, was typical of many from the Mashreq who looked down on Algerians for being "uncultured" because they lacked Arab culture. Meanwhile, militant Algerians vehemently criticized the French for having *déraciné*, deculturated them. For the French the Algerians were *complexé*, they had a psychological problem.

In the affected, exaggerated pose of "Untitled, Self Portrait 11" (figure 7), Bouziane looks like someone aping a *Vogue*-ish pose. Her head in profile, tilted up, she is posing, primping for the camera. Her outstretched fingers jabbing the air are a dead giveaway that she is poking fun at the attitudes of such wealthy women. The clothes she wears suit her body language well. Her red coat and heels, blue skirt, black tights are all solid, primary colors. A fur piece drapes around

7. Yasmina Bouziane, *Untitled, Self Portrait 11*. By permission of the artist.

her neck, an outlandishly large animal tail attaches to her expensive leather bag. Oriental carpets and a wood Mouton-Cadet box type this woman as French and Arab. This is not a new phenomenon. "By the early twentieth century, the upper classes in these cities [of Turkey, Egypt, Syria, and Palestine] were looking to Paris for their fashions. . . . The wealthy paid visits to Europe where they bought clothes, and in large cities such as Cairo, Alexandria and Istanbul, department stores and dress shops opened."[35] Bouziane's pose together with her sartorial get-up parodies the well-off, contemporary, Westernized Arab woman; it signs her as snobby and snotty, a person for whom Paris and things French are the epitome of sophistication, elegance, refinement, and culture.

Bouziane deals little in her self-portrait series with either politics or class. What about her own class position? We learn little from either her photographs or her films, except that there is considerable geographical mobility in this triangular Moroccan-French-American milieu. Her mother's family is French and her father's is Arab, but otherwise we are left to guess. "Untitled, Self Portrait 11" comes closest to an explicit comment on class in this satire of the wealthy Arab woman, by someone presumably coming from a somewhat lower class position. The photography studio here might just as well be a changing room from which this lady could emerge to continue shopping until she drops on north Michigan Avenue or Fifth Avenue, Rodeo Drive, or the Champs Elysées.

In "Untitled, Self Portrait 6" (figure 8) we have the young professional with her signifiers, a laptop PC and red plastic whistle. As in "Untitled, Self Portrait 11," Bouziane's wardrobe runs to primary colors, but here more black: black tights; medium black heels instead of red ones, professionally, modestly short; black sequined vest over black blouse; red above-the-knees puff skirt. Staring directly at the

8. Yasmina Bouziane, *Untitled, Self Portrait 6*. By permission of the artist.

viewer, she again gives us that look with eyebrows lifted, forehead furrowed: "Yes? You wanted something? You said something?" All of Bouziane's self portraits play with juxtaposition, mixture, hybridity, East and West, new and old. Few of the studio props here, the Oriental carpets for one, sign this Western-looking woman as Arab. Past and present: the personal computer occupies exactly the same picture plane as the classical pedestal.

This photo is the young professional woman about town wearing the "Don't fuck with me" look. Nothing here codes her as Arab. Once she emerges from this interior Oriental space into the outside world she will pass as Western. She will have erased her Arab identity. She will be an other, another Western woman, but who exactly has she become? The juxtaposition—Western woman, Eastern setting—suggests the question: Who is she? "We never thought of entering ourselves in Moroccan society. I was a bystander to my own culture and people, allowed only to peek through the keyhole of the door we had locked ourselves. . . . How may I choose one side over the other? How may I give up one part of my puzzle? Pull out any piece, and it all comes crashing down."[36]

Perhaps in other, less expensive clothes an Arab woman cannot pass in Paris or Washington as French or American. But disguised as she is in this interior studio space, is her masquerade not complete? "As an Arab woman you're suspect." Outside the Métro in Paris the subway police asked a friend for her papers. "She didn't want to prove that she was what she was not. She was Arab but she was also French and her papers were French. What do they do, these keepers of law and order with those elements that straddle both?"[37] Or, again: "Two suspicious-looking females were reported to the Washington, D.C. police . . . possibly of Hispanic origin. . . . Why is it that we have to go through so much to prove that we are legitimate? You see, I pay rent for the building on the edge of the sidewalk in Georgetown. . . . Does the color of my skin determine where I can sit?"[38]

The woman in this photograph can perhaps pass as Western, but she is still a woman negotiating heavily male spaces. The red whistle she dangles has about it an aura of potential danger. She carries it just in case she may need it. And it is because of her sex. In Paris and in Georgetown it is her race, her ethnicity that is reacted to. In the *medina*—which *medina* Bouziane does not specify—it is her gender that is responded to. Sexual comments, sexual taunting, sometimes sexual danger? In *Le Regard* (1993) a young Moroccan male street seller staring at her camera holds up a pair of white panties, turns them inside out, stretches them, shows the crotch panel in a long sequence while Bouziane films him playing with them.[39]

> I thought I would write a story and a book called "Where Are You From?" It would be about this kid who would go from one place to another asking people if they could help him find out where he was from not because he didn't know, but because there was too long an answer because there was a different answer depending sometimes on whom you were talking to.[40]

Documentary. Photography. Truth. Appropriation. Power. Identity. Identity drives Bouziane's photographic project, her aesthetic. Stealing identity: her great-uncle's photo for sale on the streets. Fashioning an identity: no single photograph sums up, constitutes Bouziane. Instead her photos employ disguise as a conceit; in every one she dresses up, masquerades.[41] Yet as facets, faces of identity, her approach to identity emerges. Postmodernism as pastiche, indeterminacy, body parts intersect in Bouziane's work with postcoloniality as diasporic, multicultural identity. But Bouziane's postcolonialism is not so much beyond colonialism as what comes after it.[42] Bouziane's *oeuvre* presents us with neither history, in the form of documentary, nor class, nor politics, let alone "straight" autobiography. Rather, Bouziane self-consciously uses autobiographical materials to essay an identity, one based on body parts and multiple personae that is liminal and contingent. As the narrator in *Yellow Nylon Rope* expresses it, "who I am has been defined by my struggle to fill that chasm between east and west. That struggle to complete a circle around two points that shall never meet."[43]

Yet however shattered, fragmented into shards, however many metaphors of chasms, circles that do not meet are employed, Bouziane's identity lies behind the different identities she stages. Her identity as fragmented, in shards, is not given raw; it is mediated, processed, constructed, performed, all of which assumes an identity, an authorial presence, an author in charge—in short, a Bouziane identity who stages these facets of her identity. Moreover, this identity is sufficiently strong and ego-centered to perform its own identity as autobiography, even at the risk of narcissistic self-regard. "Caught between two worlds of not belonging to one or the other side neither Muslim nor Christian. It is a hurt . . . not many would willingly impose on anyone else. Yet it is an identity, my identity."[44]

Notes

The epigraph is from Moukhtar Kocache, "Conversation with Yasmina Bouziane," *aljadid*, no. 21 (Fall 1997): 11.

1. Yasmina Bouziane, *Imaginary Homelands*, video, 20 minutes, trilingual (English-French-Arabic) (1993), script by Anissa Bouziane; Yasmina Bouziane, *Yellow Nylon Rope*, video, 18 minutes, trilingual (English-French-Arabic), English subtitles (1994), script by Anissa Bouziane.

2. Yasmina Bouziane, *Inhabited by Imaginings We Did Not Choose*, installation, New York: La Maison Française, Columbia University (1997).

3. Email communication, 8 February 1999.

4. Aline Ripert and Claude Frère, *La carte postale. Son histoire, sa fonction sociale* (Paris: Editions du CNRS, 1983).

5. Patrick Connor, *Oriental Architecture in the West* (London: Thames and Hudson, 1979), 131–53; and John Sweetman, *The Oriental Obsession: Islamic Inspiration in*

British and American Art and Architecture, 1500–1920 (New York: Cambridge University Press, 1988), 103–8.

6. John MacKenzie, *Orientalism: History, Theory, and the Arts* (Manchester: Manchester University Press, 1995), 44, 53, 81–82; and Sweetman, *The Oriental Obsession*, 189–92.

7. William Seale, *The Tasteful Interlude: American Interiors through the Camera's Eye, 1860–1917*, 2nd ed. (Nashville TN: American Association for State and Local History, 1981).

8. Details supplied by Prof. Kristin Hoganson. See her more general discussion, "Cosmopolitan Domesticity: Importing the American Dream, 1865–1920," *American Historical Review*, 107 (2002): 55–83, especially 70–74.

9. *Sigmund Freud: Conflict and Culture*, an exhibition at the Library of Congress, Washington DC, 15 October 1998–16 January 1999; and Lynn Gamwell and Richard Wells, ed. *Sigmund Freud and Art: His Personal Collection of Antiquities* (New York: Abrams, 1989).

10. Roland Barthes, *The Rustle of Language*, trans. Richard Howard (New York: Farrar, Straus, and Giroux, 1986), 141–48.

11. André Rouillé and Bernard Marbot, *Le Corps et son image* (Paris: Contrejour, 1986), 66; and David Prochaska, "All in the Family," unpub. ms.

12. J. L. Porter quoted in Nissan N. Perez, *Focus East: Early Photography in the Near East (1839–1885)* (New York: Abrams, 1988), 95.

13. Sarah Graham-Brown, *Images of Women: The Portrayal of Women in Photography of the Middle East, 1860–1950* (London: Quartet, 1988), 45.

14. Graham-Brown, *Images of Women*, 46.

15. Graham-Brown, *Images of Women*, 105.

16. Yeshayahu Nir, *The Bible and the Image: The History of Photography in the Holy Land, 1839–1899* (Philadelphia: University of Pennsylvania Press, 1985), 147.

17. Yasmina Bouziane, *Imaginary Homelands*, script by Anissa Bouziane.

18. Quoted in Graham-Brown, *Images of Women*, 45.

19. Deborah Poole, *Vision, Race, and Modernity: A Visual Economy of the Andean Image World* (Princeton: Princeton University Press, 1997).

20. Lucie Duff Gordon, *Letters from Egypt* (London: Virago, 1983), 21.

21. Théophile Gautier, *Abédécaire du Salon de 1861* (Paris: Dentu, 1861), 253.

22. Dane Kennedy, "Guardians of Edenic Sanctuaries: Paharis, Lepchas, and Todas in the British Mind," *South Asia: Journal of South Asian Studies* 14 (1991): 57–77.

23. For a useful compendium, see Perez, *Focus East*, "A to Z of Photographers Working in the Near East," 123–233.

24. Homi Bhabha, "Of Mimicry and Man: The Ambivalence of Colonial Discourse,"

in *October: The First Decade, 1976–1986,* ed. Annette Michelson, Rosalind Krauss, Douglas Crimp, and Joan Copjec (Cambridge: MIT Press, 1987), 318–19.

25. See David Prochaska, "The Archive of *Algérie imaginaire,*" *History and Anthropology* 4 (1990): 373–420.

26. Kocache, "Yamina Bouziane's 'Inhabited by Imaginings We Did Not Choose': Photography, Identity and Choice," *aljadid* no. 21 (Fall 1997): 11.

27. Zahra Freeth and Victor Winstone, *Explorers of Arabia from the Renaissance to the Victorian Era* (New York: Holmes and Meier, 1978), 93.

28. Robert Byron, *The Road to Oxiana* (1937; repr., New York: Oxford University Press, 1982), 211–13.

29. Pierre Loti, *Aziyadé* (Paris: Calmann-Lévy, 1877), 156, quoted in Tzvetan Todorov, *On Human Diversity* (Cambridge: Harvard University Press, 1993), 313.

30. Richard F. Burton, *Personal Narrative of a Pilgrimage to Al-Medinah and Meccah,* 2 vols. (1893; repr., New York: Dover, 1964), 1:19.

31. Quoted in Graham-Brown, *Images of Women,* 190.

32. See, among others, Julia Clancy-Smith, "The 'Passionate Nomad' Reconsidered: A European Woman in *L'Algérie française* (Isabelle Eberhardt, 1877–1904)," *Western Women and Imperialism,* ed. Nupur Chaudhuri and Margaret Strobel, 61–78 (Bloomington: Indiana University Press, 1992); and David Prochaska, "Writing Colonial Algeria," in *The Sphinx in the Tuileries and Other Essays in Modern French History,* ed. Robert Aldrich and Martyn Lyons, 235–245 (Sydney: University of Sydney, 1999).

33. Isabel Hilton, "The Pashtun Code," *New Yorker,* 3 December 2001, 60.

34. Richard Gringeri, "Exquisite Corpses: The Decadent Imagination of French Anthropology," unpub. ms.; and *Gustave Moreau: Between Epic and Dream,* exhibition catalog (Chicago and Paris: n.p., 1999).

35. Graham-Brown, *Images of Women,* 125.

36. Bouziane, *Yellow Nylon Rope.*

37. Bouziane, *Imaginary Homelands.*

38. Bouziane, *Imaginary Homelands.*

39. Bouziane, *Le Regard,* video, 12 minutes, trilingual (English-French-Arabic) (1993).

40. Bouziane, *Yellow Nylon Rope.*

41. Compare Cindy Sherman, *Cindy Sherman: Retrospective* (New York: Thames and Hudson, 2000).

42. Kwame Anthony Appiah, "The Postcolonial and the Postmodern," in *In My Father's House: Africa in the Philosophy of Culture,* 137–57 (New York: Oxford University Press, 1992).

43. Bouziane, *Yellow Nylon Rope.*

44. Bouziane, *Yellow Nylon Rope.*

19

Displaying World Culture in Provincial France

Francophonie in Limoges

DAVID G. TROYANSKY

In the fall of 1984 the Mouvement socialiste autonomiste occitan "Volen vivre au païs" (délégation limousine) called for a boycott of the first Festival de la Francophonie occurring in Limoges and the surrounding area. In a bilingual communiqué (Occitan-French), it claimed: "The occitan language is dying. The associations that defend it receive pitiful support or run up against haughty refusals. It's the culture of the Limousin people that elected officials and administration erase from the map."[1] The call to boycott characterized the festival as Parisian and saw it as "parachuting" into the Haute-Vienne and gobbling up official aid and subventions.

The organizers responded quickly, trying to fold regionalism into their own agenda. They began with the national and international nature of the festival and argued that there were two criteria for inclusion: quality of performance and possibility of cultural dialogue. A south-north dialogue devoid of cultural imperialism was a stated goal. It was rooted in the Limousin because of the local theater and the connections between the university and African and francophone entities. Then they addressed the argument of the boycotters:

The Limousin is a region where the French language is in relation with a regional language. In all the countries represented in the Festival, the French language is in contact with other languages of identity, mother tongues or languages of culture. The Festival invites troupes that use the French language for its international vocation; they make use of it to promote their own culture which doesn't always express itself principally in French. The cultural patrimony of the Limousin language and of Occitania ought to benefit from this encounter around a common vehicular language to make itself heard on the global map. The university colloquium, first event of the Festival, opened symbolically in the Occitan language. The National Dramatic Center is preparing projects with Occitan poets, storytellers and people of the theater. We will see the results beginning in 1985. In our mind, the comparison of situations is rich in meaning, in new ideas and exchanges of experiences.

Lo Limosin es uros de recebre lo Festenau de la Franco-fonia.[2]

When I discovered the festival for myself while teaching in Limoges in 1992–93, the Limousin variant of Occitan had some presence on the cultural landscape, a presence that had been strengthened somewhat in the 1970s and 1980s and was kept alive by a small group of activists such as Jan Dau Melhau, who published a series of books on the subject.[3] I heard him perform songs and recount local history in the dialect on two occasions. Others in the audience, both in Limoges and in a village north of the city, admitted that the language was dying out and that only the oldest members of their families really understood it. Nonetheless, the idea of preserving the language appealed to people keen on maintaining a regional identity, and the reaction of Occitan activists in 1984 serves as a useful point of departure for an examination of how a different politics of language, focusing on the use of French throughout the world, would move to the center of debate in Limoges and the Limousin. One form of language politics was giving way to another.

The topic appealed to me as a way of doing something scholarly and contemporary with my own experience in the region, but it also fit conveniently into the context of one strand of my historical research. I have been writing a series of articles on French provincial culture since the eighteenth century—they ranged from a study of a Norman poetry contest in the eighteenth century and the politics of language in Revolutionary Alsace to monuments and their commemoration in Picardy in the Third Republic, all of which concerned the juxtaposition of local history and national history, the province and the capital, and questions of multiple identities—and Limoges offered itself as a setting for the examination of the provincial role in the development of francophone culture in France.[4] Provinciality has principally to do with distance from Paris, but in a more decentered world a provincial city now serves as a major site of international cultural exchange and collaboration. It's not that the regional past has been forgotten, but the regional present has come to involve a complicated global network.

Limoges and the Limousin have long suffered from a reputation as cultural backwaters. Certainly memories of the Hundred Years War, the development of enamel art in the Middle Ages, the Wars of Religion, a regional Enlightenment touched by Turgot, faithful revolutionary Jacobinism, the development of the porcelain industry and French socialism in the nineteenth and early twentieth centuries, and the resistance during the Second World War brought the place some notoriety, but locals looking for something to cheer about in more recent decades have had little to point to other than the perennially successful *équipe de basket*, Limoges CSP.[5] Still, beginning in the 1980s, the city and region managed to address a national problem—how was France to deal with its own relative decline as a world power, even as a world cultural power? At the national level, the government, cultural figures, and academics recognized that France might maintain a global presence by asserting itself as the center of a culture that defined itself as francophone rather than strictly French. Within that context, the cultural leaders of Limoges carved out a major space in an international culture organized around the use of the French language.[6] One page of a very glitzy publication by the city traces that development: one paragraph for medieval enamel, one paragraph for nineteenth-century porcelain, and one paragraph for *la francophonie*.[7]

The city and region's efforts took at least three forms: the annual festival of francophone theatre that began in 1984, the inauguration and development of a new municipal library that placed world literature in French at the heart of its mission, and related curricular developments at the Université de Limoges. The literary curriculum took on a definite francophone slant—still rare in the French university system—and a research group including Michel Beniamino and Claude Filteau became active in organizing conferences and publishing scholarship.[8] Right from the start of the festival, the university played a role, and in 2002 it organized a Semaine de la coopération internationale et de la francophonie to coincide with the festival and bring together representatives of universities from at least seventeen foreign countries.

The Municipal Library of Limoges has been a partner in the promotion of francophonie for several years. Following upon an agreement signed in 1994, the library receives for deposit all manuscripts, typescripts, publications, and other products of the festival. In 1996 the city of Limoges entered into an arrangement with the Bibliothèque Nationale de France to create a francophone "pole." In 1998 a new library building, the Bibliothèque Francophone

Multimédia de Limoges, was inaugurated. The library not only has established itself as an important cultural presence in the region but now presents itself on the World Wide Web as "the only Internet server in the world to offer freely the international loan of works of francophone writers." The old municipal library was a particularly unpleasant place to work and was very much a provincial institution. The new building has extended its reach around the world (www.francophonie-limoges.com). The Pôle Francophone is where I did the bulk of my research into the festival's annual reports and clippings from the regional, national, and international press. Typescripts and tapes are available in the open stacks in that basement section of the library where a director and a couple of other librarians work. In the fall of 2001 an intern there inventoried course offerings in francophone literature at universities around the world, and the librarians, with the cooperation of the Bibliothèque Publique d'Information of the Centre Pompidou and the city of Limoges, organized an international conference on access to francophone resources.[9]

In one corner of the main floor of the library is a book and journal collection in francophone studies that seems to enjoy greater patronage than the Pôle Francophone from the general public. The library as a whole bustles with activity—a regional history section, the multimedia area, and the main collection appear to get a lot of use. In a sense, I'm interested in how the francophone section figuratively infiltrates the regional section. The library has a lecture hall that was often used during the festival, and during festival time, the lobby displays exhibits of related interest. In 2001 it was a photography exhibit of portraits of interracial couples; in 2002 the life and work of Léopold Sédar Senghor. The library has a significant presence in the city and region, and it forces people to think beyond the Limousin to a wider world.

The most notable event on the cultural calendar of the Limousin is the Festival de la Francophonie, which almost accidentally became the Festival International des Francophonies en Limousin and more recently the Festival International des Théâtres Francophones en Limousin.[10] The festival was the brainchild of Pierre Debauche, named in 1983 director of the Centre dramatique national du Limousin by the Ministry of Culture. The CDNL was part of an effort to encourage a decentralized dramatic culture in France. After a period of uncertainty, the center found a home in the Ciné Union, the movie theater that had begun as a cooperative at the turn of the nineteenth to twentieth century and is still one of the larger venues for the festival. Limougeauds still refer to it as "L'Union" and associate its location in the rue des coopérateurs with the cooperative and socialist past. Debauche stayed only a short time but gave a certain impetus to theater in Limoges and to the festival. He claimed to have come up with the idea of a festival ten years earlier while conversing in a train with Jean-Marie Serreau, who was associated as much with Third World writers as with the Parisian avant-garde of midcentury. "*On cherchait une pédagogie Nord-Sud qui se fasse à égalité, enfin.*"[11] The festival was directed by Monique Blin, who had been Debauche's collaborator at the Théâtre des Amandiers de Nanterre and who remained director for sixteen years and continued thereafter to play a role (see below). All along the idea was to create such a festival in provincial France, not in Paris. Debauche spoke of inventing "*des fraternités nouvelles.*" Most of the financial support came from government ministries but much came from regional and local politicians, particularly Jean-Claude Peyronnet, the socialist Président du Conseil Général de la Haute-Vienne and by training an eighteenth-century historian; Président du Conseil Régional du Limousin Robert Savy; and the mayors of Limoges, Louis Longequeue and Alain Rodet. Indeed, the department was

at first more active than the city in supporting the festival. Some
newspaper articles suggest that some city notables didn't appreciate
the national presence, but what's more striking is the cooperation
of the different levels, all, throughout most of the history of the
festival, in the hands of the socialists. Eventually the departmental
contribution was lowered while the regional share increased, but
national support has been remarkably strong. Cuts came in 1994,
when press coverage also suggested a slippage in quality.

The national press, particularly *Le Monde* and *Libération* in the
mid-1990s, suggested there was an institutional francophonie, a
wooden language, something less creative than at the beginning.
But the very idea of francophonie has been accompanied by an
institutional odor, its meaning elaborated in a series of international meetings.[12] Still the festival continued to thrive, the result
no doubt of the hard work of the local organizers. I've seen them
court visitors from Paris, especially from the Haut Conseil de la
Francophonie. Here my own attendance yields some insights that
I might not have gained just by reading the press. It's one thing to
read of visits by the president of the Republic or the Minister of
Culture. It's another to see the interactions between the local staff,
the performers, and the Haut Conseil officials, who represent the
authority of Paris over the provinces.

Among the features of the festival was that it would serve as a
place for interaction by different troupes. They would attend one
another's performances and participate in educational encounters
with teachers, schoolchildren, actors, and conservatory students.
In an effort to decentralize the decentralization policy that brought
the festival to the Limousin, towns other than Limoges would host
events. In 1984 they included Saint-Junien, Eymoutiers, and Saint-
Yrieix; in 1985 Aixe-sur-Vienne, Eymoutiers, Bessines-sur-Gartempe,
Magnac-Laval, Saint-Junien, and Saint-Yrieix. In 1997 and again

in 1998 thirty-two communes from all three departments of the Limousin hosted events, and while the number fell to twenty in 1999, it was estimated that one hundred people attended the average performance in towns of two to four thousand inhabitants. Works by living authors would have priority over the dead. French and foreign (especially African) artists would work together. Some productions would travel nationally and internationally. Coordination with the university would be encouraged.

At first the emphasis was African. Participating troupes came from Cameroon, the Ivory Coast, Martinique, and Réunion as well as Québec, Switzerland, and France and in 1985 from Burkina Faso, Congo, Ivory Coast, Tunisia, Mali, Mauritius, and Sénégal as well as Guadeloupe, Haïti, Belgium, Canada, Vietnam, and France. Newspaper stories feature the encounter between the African artists and residents of the surrounding towns where the actors were housed. Accounts of enthusiastic audiences, schoolchildren who welcomed the visitors to their schools, and communal meals fill the local newspapers. In the early years, many performers were housed in *Centres de vacances* outside Limoges. Some articles emphasize the cultural distance between the African artists and the somewhat taciturn residents of Eymoutiers or St-Yrieix.[13] The Limoges journalists may have been distinguishing their city from the surrounding towns. The national press featured the literary qualities of the plays and the political nature of such a festival. The African press laid claim to the festival as one of African theater, but the French national press and conversations with long-term attendees reveal a sense that it's hard for the Africans to keep up, a sensitive point for the organizers. They have wanted to avoid condescension or a focus on the merely exotic. The music remains impressive, and some theatrical performances have been extraordinary. One Congolese writer, Sony Labou Tansi, was seen as a real star whose short career benefited enormously from his passage in Limoges; and the 2000 production of *Rwanda 1994*, which involved Belgian direction and Rwandan performers, remained the talk of the festival thereafter. Apart from those highlights, perhaps a bit less is expected of the African troupes than for example the Belgian and Canadian ones. Typical of this way of thinking is the 15 October 1988 article in *Le Monde* that speaks of *"inégalités fraternelles."* But it is clear that Limoges has served an important role as *lieu de rencontre* of writers from all over the African continent. Linked to the festival but extending into the rest of the year is the Maison des Auteurs, a program of writers in residence founded in 1988. Over the last decade about one hundred writers have spent three-month periods in Limoges.

Comparisons between national cultures get at the heart of the problem of francophonie. What does a Romanian play modeled after Pirandello's *Six Characters* have in common with a monologue by an Algerian washerwoman? People of the theater translated language questions into their own concerns, seeing a pendulum movement between theater as performance and gesture on the one hand and text on the other. But pedagogy and politics were rarely ignored. Some journalists and participants have spoken of a kind of neocolonialism. Others rejected the term in describing cultural relations with the *pays du sud*. What seems clear is that the accusation of neocolonialism came primarily from French commentators, not Africans, and it seemed to become a tired debate by the early 1990s. But right from the start, African participants and those from the African diaspora valued the use of French both as a vehicle for communicating with France and for finding common ground with others from their part of the world. As the student actor playing Gueido, a West African Oedipus, remarked, "We perform in French because there is no major language among the two hundred or so spoken in Cameroon."[14]

Although sub-Saharan African participants seemed to confirm the centrality of French in an emerging global culture, an important language controversy emerged with a general opening of the festival to the Maghreb in the early 1990s. Not writing in Arabic had been seen as a betrayal of new national cultures. Theater itself, and a theater that called into question the wearing of the veil by Muslim women, was extremely political. Sliman Benaïssa presented *Au-delà du voile* or *Tu es mon frère . . . Mais moi, qui suis-je?* in 1991 both in French and in Arabic and had to deal with the criticism of Rachid Boudjedra, who argued that in Algeria the theater should be in Arabic or Berber, not French. Yet, writers wanted to be read and to be published. French and Belgian publication has meant a great deal. The festival director, Patrick Le Mauff, began publishing a series, Passages Francophones, with Editions Théâtrales of Paris, and Belgian publisher Emile Lansman has long been an active participant in the festival and publisher of African writers. I heard him ask a black writer born in Cameroon, raised in France, and living in Paris whether he considered himself Camerounais, African, French, francophone, or what? The response was a very Gallic gesture that essentially dismissed the premise.

Festival organizers sometimes reached beyond the sphere of francophonie. Flemish was an invited language in 2001, and while I heard suggestions that English might be invited the next year, the invited language for 2002 turned out to be Tunisian Arabic. For director Patrick Le Mauff, it was a way of emphasizing theater as much as language, and the theater of people living beside those who speak French, but he did face some opposition. In the 2001 program he recounts how at the end of the previous festival he was asked by a woman, wineglass in hand, "Pourquoi les avez-vous invités, ces salauds?" She was referring to the Flemish-speaking Belgians. In his 2001 text Le Mauff explained the need to recognize zones of friction between languages and between cultures and to appreciate similarities and differences:

> To say, in the same sentence, we are all the same and we are all different. That is in itself admirable but in concrete terms more difficult to realize. Similarity of language does not add up to the same story if one is a young Malgache [from Madagascar] who has learned verses of Hugo by force, a Québécois who was defending his language as he protects his soul, an exile who will make it a point of honor to employ a borrowed language with the most elegant syntax, or, like my father, a Breton peasant who alertly mixed patois and the French of the cities.[15]

It would be hard to imagine a festivalgoer speaking of the Tunisians in the same way that woman spoke of the Belgians. We certainly wouldn't hear of it from the director. But it would be easy to imagine such a reaction if English had been chosen, for there is another partly stated theme that runs through discussions of francophonie in Limoges and elsewhere, and that is resistance to English. In a 2001 text festival president Robert Abirached doesn't mention English per se, but he compares *la langue unique* to *la pensée unique*, he sees the universality of French and Spanish as antidotes to *mondialisation*, and he sees francophonie as a guarantee of diversity and liberty and opposition to the omnipotence of money.[16]

Even within the context of francophone theater, regional differences have been striking. Theaters from French-speaking Canada represented an opening to America. Despite the strand of *québécois* thought that presents the province as living under colonization, here we have an example of the francophonie of the First World, a North American culture. Production values were extremely high, and local theater-goers who weren't particularly interested in the pays du sud may have found what they were looking for. Asia has been less well represented. In 2001 the festival included the work of Gao Xingjian, 2000 Nobel Prize winner from China, who became a French citizen in 1998, but Vietnamese and Cambodian works have been presented from time to time. Press clippings suggest an emphasis on the exotic and also an opening to the local population of Asian immigrants in the working-class neighborhood of Beaubreuil in the northern *banlieue* of Limoges.

I've already suggested that attending the festival, as I did in 2001 and 2002, provided me with some insights that I would not have gained solely from archival and library research. I spent weekdays working through the press clippings at the Bibliothèque Francophone Multimédia and evenings and weekends attending plays and readings, lectures, panel discussions, and musical performances. Panel discussions ranged from the aesthetic to the political with much attention devoted to questions of immigration. Readings took place in small theatrical spaces and cafés. Concerts by African and Caribbean performers were given every night in a former industrial building transformed into a performance space. Lunches and dinners were served at the festival headquarters, and one of the local bookstores set up a very large display of francophone literature.

For a historian trying to understand the festival, it's natural to think of the legacy of colonialism, decolonization, and immigration. Some readings and performances were explicitly political. A reading of Aimé Césaire's "*Discours sur le colonialisme*" in 2001 may have taken on a new significance in the wake of September 11, or it may have been an opportunity to revisit a historical document from the 1950s.

Over the years the organizers of the festival have tempered the politics and ideology to emphasize cultural exchange. One of Monique Blin's last initiatives, before giving up direction to Patrick Le Mauff, was to organize a *résidence nomade*, sending about ten writers from different francophone countries for a six-week residence in a francophone country that was foreign to them. In 2000 the first group spent six weeks in Lebanon, reflecting on the theme of "*frontières.*" At the 2001 festival they read some of their resulting work. In 2002 a Montréal-based playwright of Lebanese descent, Wajdi Mouawad, introduced a film of his Canadian troupe's passage in Beirut, and he directed and acted in a lively production of Chekhov's *Three Sisters*.

For me the real interest lay in how a city and region of *la France profonde* integrated themselves within the Francophone world. Performers and writers use Limoges as a *point de rencontre*. The people of the Limousin have used the festival to connect with an extraordinary variety of cultures. As might be expected, the audiences were often dominated by *universitaires*, teachers, and students, more bourgeois than popular. But a broader public has been developing, and a territory that had had little experience with theater now identifies with an evolving global culture.[17] More youthful, working-class, and immigrant audiences cheered performances of hip-hop artists from Madagascar in 2001 and singers and dancers from Namibia and Réunion in a multicultural production of Jean Cocteau's *Les mariés de la Tour Eiffel* in 2002, both productions taking place in Limoges's Grand Théâtre, normally used for opera. A father in the 2001 audience was heard telling his son that the production didn't exactly match his memory of Africa. The point is that this version of African culture was influenced by European and African American artists, a far cry from any simple francophonie.

The organizers still have to avoid the wooden, politically correct language that may trap them. What should we make of the words of Michèle Gendreau-Massaloux, Rectrice de l'Agence Universitaire de la Francophonie, at the inauguration of the Hôtel de l'Université on 4 October 2002: "*Les français de Limoges sont aussi des francophones?"* Of course they are. But what does that mean? To what extent have locals, especially the young, incorporated the francophonies of the pays du sud into their identity? Perhaps to a significant extent. I spoke with secondary school teachers whose students' introduction to theater and live music comes from the festival. And some of those students will encounter an altered curriculum at the university. But we should recognize that francophonie at the university level goes beyond the literary and aesthetic. The university's francophone week involved people in the sciences, medicine, and engineering, not just arts and letters. And for them francophonie means political and economic relations between France and the wider world. Money and development are key, and so is the problem of the *fuite des cerveaux* [brain drain].

The Limousin experience of francophonie involves institution building across the university curriculum as well as dramatic arts in search of new and traditional audiences. Academics and artists along with politicians and administrators have a stake in the city and region's calling as francophone center. A provincial city has become a crossroads for global encounters, a transnational space in which a multicultural population works out the most current questions of identity.

Notes

1. "La langue occitane crève. Les associations qui la défendent reçoivent des aides dérisoires ou se heurtent à des refus hautains. C'est la culture du peuple limousin qu'élus et administration rayent de la carte." Text published in local press; extrait, Revue de Presse, Festival International des Francophonies, Pôle Francophone, Bibliothèque Francophone Multimédia de Limoges.

2. "Le Limousin est une région où la langue française est en relation avec une langue régionale. Dans tous les pays représentés au Festival, la langue française est au contact d'autres langue d'identité, langues maternelles ou de culture. Le Festival invite des troupes qui utilisent la langue française pour sa vocation internationale; elles s'en servent pour promouvoir leur propre culture qui ne s'exprime pas toujours principalement en langue française. Le patrimoine culturel de la langue limousine et de l'Occitanie doit profiter

de cette rencontre autour d'une langue véhiculaire commune pour se faire entendre au plan mondial. Le Colloque universitaire, première manifestation du Festival s'est ouvert symboliquement en langue occitane. Le Centre Dramatique National prépare des projets avec des poètes, des conteurs et des hommes de théâtre occitans. On le verra dès 1985. Dans notre esprit, la comparaison des situations est riche de signification, de connaissances nouvelles et d'échanges d'expériences. Lo Limosin es uros de recebre lo Festenau de la Francofonia." *L'Echo du Centre*, 17 October 1984.

3. See, for example, Jan Dau Melhau, *Proverbes limousins* (Limoges: Lucien Souny, 1992).

4. "La 'vierge révolutionnaire': Marie dans les poèmes du Palinod de Caen à l'époque révolutionnaire," in Michel Vovelle, *L'Image de la révolution française: Communications présentées lors du Congrès Mondial pour le Bicentenaire de la Révolution—Sorbonne, Pais, 6–12 Juillet 1989* (Paris: Pergamon, 1989), 2005–13; David G. Troyansky, "Alsatian Knowledge and European Culture: Jérémie-Jacques Oberlin, Language, and the Protestant *Gymnase* in Revolutionary Strasbourg," in *Francia* 27, no. 2 (2000): 202–10; David G. Troyansky, "Monumental Politics: National History and Local Memory in French *Monuments aux Morts* in the Department of the Aisne Since 1870," in *French Historical Studies* 15, no. 1 (1987): 121–41; and David G. Troyansky, "Memorializing Saint-Quentin: Monuments, Inaugurations and History in the Third Republic," in *French History* 13, no. 1 (1999): 48–76.

5. A rich historical literature in French and English includes works by Michel Cassan, Michel Kiener and Jean-Claude Peyronnet, Paul d'Hollander, Alain Corbin, John Merriman, and Sarah Farmer, but the regional self-image may be better understood through a literature of *haute vulgarisation*, such works as Georges Cerbelaud Salagnac, *Histoire du Limousin* (Paris: France-Empire, 1996); and Georges Chatain, ed., *Le Limousin: Terre sensible et rebelle* (Paris: Autrement, 1995). Alas, the basketball team has fallen on hard times.

6. Remarkably this was a phenomenon completely missed in a Mémoire de DEA: Serge Proust, "La transformation du champ culturel local: Animation socio-culturelle et légitimité culturelle à Limoges" (Bordeaux: Institut d'Etudes Politiques, 1993).

7. "Limoges XXIe" (Limoges: Mairie de Limoges, n.d.), 18.

8. Beniamino is the author of a major theoretical work on francophone literature, *La francophonie littéraire: essai pour une théorie* (Paris: L'Harmattan, 1999), and directeur du centre "Textes et langages des francophonies"; Filteau edits a series of books in francophone studies with the Presses Universitaires de Limoges.

9. "L'accès aux ressources francophones. Actes du colloque international, Limoges, 22–23 novembre 2001" (Ville de Limoges, 2002).

10. Béatrice Castaner, "Le Festival International des Francophonies: Aboutissement

de la Politique Sociale et Culturelle de la Ville de Limoges au XXème siècle?" (Mémoire de Maitrise de l'Institut d'Etudes Théâtrales, Université de Paris III Sorbonne Nouvelle, 1991). Castaner has become the Secrétaire Générale of the Festival. I thank her for providing me with a copy of her mémoire, agreeing to an interview in 2001, and responding to questions on subsequent occasions.

11. *Le Monde*, 27 October 1984.

12. For a good summary of that institutional history, see Xavier Denau, *La francophonie*, 5th ed. (Paris: PUF, 2001).

13. See, for example, Jean-Pierre Fremont's account of a visit of Réunionnais artists to a lycée d'enseignement professionnel agricol, *Le Populaire du Centre*, 19 October 1984, 3.

14. "Nous jouons en français parce qu'il n'y a pas de langue majeure parmi les quelque deux cents pratiquées au Cameroun," *Libération*, 26 October 1984, 32.

15. "Dire, dans la même phrase, on est tous pareils et on est tous différents. Ce qui est en soi admirable mais qui dans le concret se vit plus difficilement. Le semblable de la langue n'a pas la même histoire selon que l'on est un jeune malgache qui a appris les vers de Hugo sous la contrainte, un québécois qui défendait la sienne comme on protège son âme, un homme en exil qui mettra un point d'honneur à manier une langue d'emprunt avec la syntaxe la plus élégante, ou, comme mon père, un paysan breton qui mélangeait allègrement le patois et le *français des villes*."

16. Abirached's text is on p. 1, Le Mauff's on pp. 2–4 of the Programme 2001.

17. For a reminder of an earlier era of theatre in Limoges, see Marc Précicaud, *Le théâtre lyrique à Limoges, 1800–1914* (Limoges: Presses Universitaires de Limoges, 2001); Castaner, "Le Festival International des Francophonies," presents the subsequent period as a theatrical wasteland.

Contributors

TRUDY AGAR-MENDOUSSE lectures in French language and literature at the University of Auckland (New Zealand). She has published a study on violence in the writing of Djebar, Mokeddem, and Bouraoui, *Violence et créativité de l'écriture algérienne au féminin* (2006). Her current research centers on crossings and cross-dressing in Algerian literature.

ROBERT ALDRICH is professor of European history at the University of Sydney. He is the author of a number of works on colonial history. Recent publications include *Colonialism and Homosexuality* (2003) and *Vestiges of the Colonial Empire in France: Monuments, Museums and Colonial Memories* (2005). He has also edited *Gay Life and Culture: A World History* (2006) and *The Age of Empires* (2007).

ELISA CAMISCIOLI is assistant professor of history and women's studies at Binghamton University, State University of New York, where she teaches a wide range of courses on French history, colonial culture, and gender history and theory. Her book, *Embodying the French Race: Immigration, Reproduction, and National Identity in the Early Twentieth Century*, is forthcoming from Duke University Press.

HABIBA DEMING has written on postcolonial women writers and taught French and international studies for twenty years. She is currently writing a book, *Francophone Algerian Intellectuals (1962–2000)*.

PHILIP DINE is senior lecturer in French, Department of French, National University of Ireland, Galway. He is the author of *Images of the Algerian War: French Fiction and Film, 1954–1992* (1994). He has published widely on representations of the French colonial empire, including particularly decolonization, in fields ranging from children's literature to professional sport. Other published research includes *French Rugby Football: A Cultural History* (2001) as part of a broader reflection on leisure and popular culture in France.

ALAIN GABON is assistant professor of French in the Department of Foreign Languages and Literatures at Virginia Wesleyan College, Virginia Beach, Virginia. He previously held several other positions in France, England, and the United States. He has published and lectured throughout the United States on French cultural and artistic production. His current research focus is on contemporary French cinema and postmodern fiction and on French popular amateur theater as alternative historiography. He serves actively on the boards of several nonprofit organizations, especially the Hampton Roads Alliance Française and the World Affairs Council.

HAFID GAFAÏTI is Horn Professor of Romance Studies and Qualia Professor of French and Francophone Studies at Texas Tech University. He is also Andrew Mellon Distinguished Professor. His books and edited books include *Les femmes dans le roman algérien* (1996); *Cultures transnationales de France* (2001); *La Diasporisation de la littérature postcoloniale* (2005); and *Migrances, Diasporas et identités immigrées en France et dans le monde francophone* (with Patricia M. Lorcin and David G. Troyansky, 2005). He authored three bilingual collections of poetry: *la gorge tranchée du soleil / the slit throat of the sun* (2006), translated into Italian under the title *la golia tagliata del sole* (2007); *le retour des damnés / the return of the damned* (2007); and *la tentation du désert / the temptation of the desert* (2008). He is director of the book series Etudes Transnationales, Francophones et Comparées (L'Harmattan Press).

ANTONY JOHAE is associate professor at Kuwait University. He has taught in the United Kingdom, Ghana, and Tunisia. His areas of specialization are English and comparative literature, including postcolonial literature. He is preparing a book on the novels of Amin Maalouf. His publications include articles in *Comparative Literature* (on Wole Soyinka), *Research in African Literatures* (on Soyinka), *Michigan Germanic Studies* (on Kafka), *Journal of the Kafka Society of America*, *Dostoevsky Studies*, and *Germano-Slavica* (Dostoevsky and Kafka), as well as articles in collected volumes. He is currently editing a collection on cross-cultural literary interaction with a focus on Europe and the Arab world.

PATRICIA M. E. LORCIN is associate professor at the University of Minnesota–Twin Cities and editor of *French Historical Studies*. She is the author of *Imperial Identities* (1995, French translation 2004) and numerous articles on French imperialism. She edited *Algeria and France 1800–2000: Identity Memory and Nostalgia* (2006) and coedited a special issue of *French Historical Studies* on France and Islam (30:3). She is also the coeditor of *Migrances, Diasporas et identités immigrées en France et dans le monde francophone* (with Hafid Gafaïti and David G. Troyansky, 2005). She is currently coediting a volume titled *War and Its Spaces: France and the Francophone World* and completing a comparative project on women and gender in colonial Algeria and Kenya.

NEIL MACMASTER, of the University of East Anglia (UK), is author of *Colonial Migrants and Racism: Algerians in France, 1900–62* (1997) and *Racism in Europe, 1870–2000* (2001), and coauthor, with Jim House, of *Paris 1961: Algerians, State Terror and Memory* (2006). His research interests relate to the history of decolonization, international labor migration, racism, and Franco-Algerian relations, and he is currently completing a book, *Burning the Veil*, on the impact of the French counterinsurgency campaign to "emancipate" women during the Algerian War of Independence.

MARY MCCULLOUGH is associate professor of French at Samford University in Birmingham, Alabama. She is interested in literature and cinema of the Maghreb and the Maghrebian diaspora. She has published articles on the works of Leïla Sebbar, Azouz Begag, Fatima Mernissi, and Assia Djebar. During the 2007–2008 school year she was a Fulbright Scholar in Tunisia, teaching at the University of Tunis (Institut Supérieur des Sciences Humaines) and working on a project about stereotypes on reverse migrants.

JOSEPH MILITELLO is currently an assistant professor at Emporia State University, teaching world literature. His interests include relations between Modernist aesthetics and politics and relations between Western and non-Western literatures and cultures. He has previously published articles on Joseph Conrad, Chinua Achebe, Ngugi wa Thiong'o, and T. S. Eliot.

DAVID PROCHASKA teaches history and visual culture at the University of Illinois, Urbana-Champaign. He is the author of *Making Algeria French: Colonialism in Bône, 1870–1920* (1990, 2004); coauthor, with David O'Brien, of *Beyond East and West: Seven Transnational Artists* (2004); and coeditor, with Edmund Burke III, of *Genealogies of Orientalism: History, Theory, Politics* (2008).

JOHANN SADOCK teaches in Foreign Languages and Literatures at Massachusetts Institute of Technology. His publications include articles on the cinema of Kassovitz (*Contemporary French and Francophone Studies/ Sites*), Israel Zangwill (*Paragraphes*), and Francophone Jewish writers in Quebec (*Paragraphes*); and the collective memory of Jews from Algeria in relation to French national history (*French Contemporary Civilization*). He was also guest coeditor of a recent issue of *Contemporary French and Francophone Studies: Séfarade-Francophone/Sephardic-Francophone* and has been published in *L'infini* (Gallimard). His Web project, *Au-delà du regard: rencontres multiethniques*, and his documentary, *Black, Blanc, Beur: parlons-en!*, are based on interviews with young people and deal with ethnic diversity in France. These projects were made possible by the support of MIT and the Consortium for Language Teaching and Learning.

TODD SHEPARD is associate professor of modern history of France and the French empire at Johns Hopkins University. His publications include *The Invention of Decolonization: The Algerian War and the Remaking of France* and articles in *Ab Imperio* and *Contretemps*. He currently is studying how the French government pursued social citizenship and antiracist policies in an effort to counter the Algerian Revolution.

SARAH SUSSMAN's research focuses on the migration of North African Jews to France and on immigrants in France more generally. She received her PhD in history from Stanford University and is currently curator of the French and Italian Collections of the Stanford University Libraries. She is also on the editorial board of *French Historical Studies*.

DAVID G. TROYANSKY is professor of history at Brooklyn College and the Graduate Center of the City University of New York. He taught for twenty-one years at Texas Tech University, where he collaborated with Hafid Gafaïti and Patricia Lorcin in the organization of the conference that gave rise to the present volume as well as *Migrances, diasporas et transculturalités francophones: Littératures et cultures d'Afrique, des Caraïbes, d'Europe et du Québec* (2005). He has taught at the Université de Limoges and held a Fulbright senior research fellowship at the Ecole des Hautes Etudes en Sciences Sociales (Paris). Author of *Old Age in the Old Regime: Image and Experience in Eighteenth-Century France* (1989) and coeditor, with Norwood Andrews Jr. and Alfred Cismaru, of *The French Revolution in Culture and Society* (1991), he is completing a book manuscript whose working title is "Entitlement and Complaint: Ending Careers and Reviewing Lives in the French Magistracy, 1814–1853."

GEORGES VAN DEN ABBEELE is professor of French literature and philosophy and dean of the Humanities Division, University of California at Santa Cruz. He is the author of *Travel as Metaphor: From Montaigne to Rousseau* (1992) and currently has two new books in progress: "The Retreat of the French Intellectual" and "The Children of Belgium: Myths of Failed National Identity." Van Den Abbeele is also coeditor of 2003's *A*

World of Fables, a collection of traditional fables spanning the globe and, with Tyler Stovall, *French Civilization and Its Discontents: Nationalism, Colonialism, Race* (2003).

KEITH DAVID WATENPAUGH is associate professor of modern Islamic studies at the University of California, Davis. He is author of *Being Modern in the Middle East: Revolution, Nationalism, and Colonialism in the Arab Middle East* (2006). His current research focuses on the way the large-scale abuse of human rights in the Middle East contributed to the formation of the modern humanitarian régime.

BRIGITTE WELTMAN-ARON is associate professor of French at the University of Florida. She is the author of several articles and of *On Other Grounds* (2001) and is currently working on a book about Hélène Cixous and Assia Djebar.

ALI YÉDES is associate professor of French and francophone studies at Oberlin College. His area of interest is critical theory, North African literature in French and Arabic, Beur literature, francophone literature, and culture related to sub-Saharan Africa, the Caribbean, and Vietnam. He is the author of *Camus l'Algérien* (2003) as well as of several articles related to his field.

Index

bidonville layout: as echo of traditional Algerian medina, 75–76; kinship and ethnicity and, 76, 80; privacy and isolation, emphasis on, 76, 77, 82

bidonville residents: adaptation to European-style houses, xv, 73–74, 85–90; ambivalence toward French culture, 87–90; French reeducation of, 80–85; return to bidonville following relocation, 87, 88–89

bidonvilles: domestic spaces, importance of, 73; French bans on new construction, 81–82; French classification of residents, 84; French dismantling of, 80–85; as haven for Algerian nationalists, 77, 80; house construction and decoration, 78–79; living conditions and sanitation, 78; origins of, 74–75; political structure, 77; studies on, 75–76; women's ownership role in, 79–80

Birnbaum, Pierre, 58

bisexuality, writing of, in Mokeddem, 190–91

Black Skin, White Masks (Fanon), 53

Blanchot, Maurice, 266, 269–70

Blatt, David, 131

Blavatsky, Helena, 398

Blin, Monique, 417, 423

Bloy, Léon, 171

Boissier, Gaston, 12

Boissière, Gustave, 12

Bonfils, Adrien, 396

Bonfils, Félix, 396

Bonn, Charles, 204, 207

Bouhired, Djamila, 167

Bouhired, Mustapha, 172

Boumediène, Houari, 150

Boumendjel, Ali, 158

Bouraoui, Nina, xxi, 377–81

Bourdieu, Pierre, xv, 86, 125

"Les Bourreaux d'Alger" (Sénac), 156

Bouziane, Anissa, 389

Bouziane, Yasmina: biography, 388–89; on photography as construction, 388
—works: *Imaginary Homelands*, 389, 396; *Le Regard*, 408; *Yellow Nylon Rope*, 389. *See also* Untitled Self-Portraits series

Bové, José, 140

Boverat, Fernand, 54

Brami, Claude, 251, 261–62n23

Brazil, immigration policy, 57

Brink, André, 188

Brontë, Charlotte, 304–5, 306

Brubaker, Rogers, 63–64

Buddhism: introduction to Vietnam, 346–47; sects, 347

Buddhism, Vietnamese: assimilation of Confucian ideas, 350; basic tenets of, 347; flexibility of, 348, 350; origins of, 350–51; popular forms of, 348; role in Vietnamese culture, 347–50

Buffon, Georges-Louis Leclerc, Comte de, 401

Bui Xuan Bao, 357

Burckhardt, Jean Louis, 401–2

Burton, Richard, 398, 402

Bye Bye (Dridi), 137

Byron, Robert, 402

Cahiers du Cinéma, 123

Camiscioli, Elisa, xiv, 53

Camus, Albert: challenges to colonial establishment, 14; misrepresentation of colonial realities, 14; and myth of pan-Mediterranean civilization, xiii–xiv, 9, 15–19, 20, 169; Nobel Prize, 16; Sénac and, 150, 154–55, 156, 157, 160, 163–65, 170; on soccer, 9; vision of Algerian future, 164, 169
—works: *Actuelles III*, 16; *Alger Républicain* articles, 14; *L'Express* article, 16; *Noces*, 170; *Le Premier Homme*, xiii, 9, 15–19, 20, 168

Les carnets de Shérazade (Sebbar), 200, 208

EMSI. *See* Equipes Médico-Sociales
Itinérantes
English language, Festival International
des Théâtres Francophones en Limousin opposition to, 420
Englund, Steven, x
Equipes Médico-Sociales Itinérantes
(EMSI), 82
Esprit (periodical), 161, 180n27
ethnicity, absence of concept in French
debate, 58
eugenics movement: and French immigration policy, 63–64; international
scope of, 54–55
European immigrants, and assimilation,
59
L'Evénement du Jeudi (periodical), 6
Evian Accord (1962): and Algerian right
to French citizenship, 94–95, 103;
and Muslim immigration, 112n27;
thirtieth anniversary, 6
exile: gendered division of suffering in,
332–33; writing as, 327–30, 335
L'Express (periodical), 16

"Fait divers" (Sénac), 158
Faivre, Maurice, 100
Fanon, Frantz: on colonialism, 189,
197n5; on language in colonial context, 231; Sénac and, 160, 171
—works: *Black Skin, White Masks*, 53;
Les damnés de la terre, 183
Fatima ou les Algériennes au square
(Sebbar), 200, 204
Fauque, Jean, 17
Félix (Kassovitz character), 135, 138,
145n18
feminine as "other": in colonizers' discourse, 184, 185–86; feminist theory
on, 184; Mokeddem's deconstruction
of, 188–89, 190–91
"Feminism and Difference" (Lazreg),
372
feminist paradigm, Western: Algerian

women writers' efforts to merge
into, 373, 377–86, 384–85; Algerian
women writers who avoid, 374–75;
assumptions about Muslim women,
385–86; efforts to escape hegemony
of, 376–77; imposition on Muslim
women, 372–73, 376–77; reiteration
of colonial paradigms in, 372, 376,
384–86
feminist theory: construction of Muslim
femininity, 372–73; on feminine as
"other," 184
feminist writers: authentic voices among,
374–75; representability of, 373
Fenton, Roger, 402
Féraoun, Mouloud, 172
Festival de la Francophonie, 417. *See
also* Festival International des
Théâtres Francophones en Limousin
Festival International des Francophonies
en Limousin, 417. *See also* Festival
International des Théâtres Francophones en Limousin
Festival International des Théâtres
Francophones en Limousin: activities
during, 423; African troupes in,
419–20; decentralization of, 418–19;
emphasis on cultural exchange,
423–24; goals of, 418; history of,
417–18; invited languages, 421–22;
Maison des Auteurs, 420; national
support for, 417–18; opposition to
English, 420; political and ideological aspects of, 423; and political correctness, 424–25; press coverage of,
418, 419, 420, 423; protests against,
412–13; *résidence nomade* program,
423–24
Fête de la Musique, 129
Fête du Cinéma, 129
5th Bureau, and reeducation of Algerian
women, 82
figurative *vs.* proper meaning, 280n8

278–80; concentration camps and, 280–81n12; Derrida on, 279–80; Memmi on, 264–66, 268–69; nomadism and, 270, 271; Sartre on, 264. *See also* Algerian Jewish identity

Jewish literature, Oriental: Arabs as Other in, 244, 248–49, 250, 251–52, 254–59, 255, 261n20; Arabs as Same in, 244, 246, 249–50, 253–54; fluidity of perceptions of Other in, 245–46, 247; French as Other in, 244, 248–49, 250–51, 251–52, 253–54, 254–56; French perspective on French and Arabs, 254–59; Israel and, 259n1; Jewish perspective on French and Arabs, 248–52; Jews as Other in, 249; Oriental perspective on French and Arabs, 252–54; perception of Oriental milieu, 244; self-hatred in, 256–59; sense of vulnerability in, 246, 248, 259n2; socioeconomic factors in perception of Other, 246–47; sources of anti-Arab tendencies, 243–44; sources of anti-French tendencies, 243–44

Jewish thought, responsibility and justice in, 269

Jews: as figure of oppression, 265, 266; impact of decolonization on, 267–68; return to self of, 266–68; status *vs.* Arabs under colonial rule, 250, 267

Jews, Algerian. *See entries under* Algerian Jewish

Jews and Arabs (Memmi), 264, 267

Jews and language: Derrida on, 274–77; Memmi on, 273–74

Johae, Antony, xix, 289

Journal de mes Algéries en France (Sebbar), 202

Journal des Communautés (periodical), 223

Joxe, Louis, 100

Judaism, women's role in, 278

Les Juifs de l'Afrique du Nord, Démographie et Onomastique (Eisenbeth), 236

Jules et Jim (Truffaut), 139

Juletane (Warner-Vieyra), xx, 303–4, 315–18

Juletane (Warner-Vieyra character), 303–4, 306, 315–18

Kadouch, Albert, 232

al-Kashafa, 51n33

Kassovitz, Mathieu: challenges to French identity, 115, 122, 124–25, 130–33, 135–37, 143; embrace of changes in French identity, 133–34, 139–44; embrace of globalization, 139–44; embrace of multiculturalism, 141–44; embrace of transnational youth counterculture, 133–34, 142; interest in deconstructing national identities, 146n19; inversion of cultural colonization, 136–37; vision of new transcultural, transnational space, 137–39, 139–44
—works. See *La Haine*; *Métisse*

Kerr, E. Stanley, 31, 39

Khatibi, Abdelkebir, 274

Khellil, Uncle (Mokeddem character), 191

Khoury, Pierre, 45

Kiều (Nguyễn Du character), 323–25, 327–28, 335, 351–56, 358, 359, 363, 365n2

Kiều (Thinh Minh-ha character), 326–27

Kieu Chinh, 327

Kim (Nguyễn Du character), 324, 335, 352, 365n2

Kim-Vân Kiều. See *The Tale of Kiều* (Nguyễn Du)

Kocache, Moukhtar, 401

Konstantarakos, Myrto, 123, 127

Koranic Law Civil Status, and citizenship, 103–4, 110

Koskas, Marco, 256–58

Kristeva, Julia, 329
Kulthoum, Umm, 402

La Bédollière, Émile Gigault de, 400
Labor Ministry, and race-based ranking of labor, 61–62
Lacheref, Mostefa, 154
Le lait de l'oranger (Halimi), 250, 256, 261n20, 262n35, 263n45
Lalou (Allali), 252
Lalou, Jean-Claude, 232
Lam, Andrew, 321, 322
Lan Cao, 327
Lang, Jack, 129
language: and Algerian Jewish identity, 231–35, 257–59; as barrier, in Bâ's *Un chant écarlate*, 312–13; Jews' relationship to, 273–74, 274–77. *See also* English language; French language; Occitan language
"La Patrie" (Sénac), 155
Laronde, Michel, 138–39, 201, 202–3
Lartéguy, Jean, 13
"Latin race," assimilation of, 57
Lavater, Johann Kaspar, 401
Lazreg, Marnia, 372, 373, 385
Lê, Linda, 326, 327, 329–34
League of Nations, Armenians in Syria and, 29, 33–34, 36–38, 39
Le deuxième sexe (Beauvoir), 197n9
Lee, Spike, 122, 134, 135, 139
Lefèvre, Kim, 323, 326, 335
Leighton, Frederic Lord, 393
Leila (Mokeddem character), 183, 185, 186, 189, 190, 191, 192, 193, 194–95
Leiris, Michel, 160
Lê Judicial Code (Hông-duc Code), 355
Le Mauff, Patrick, 421–24
Lemsine, Aïcha, 374
Leo Africanus (Maalouf character), 290
Léon l'Africain. See *Leo the African* (Maalouf)
Leo the African (Maalouf), 290, 294

Le Pen, Jean-Marie, 203
"Le Peuple algérien face à l'imposture" (Sénac), 156
"Les belles apparences" (Sénac), 158
Le Sueur, James, xii
Lê Tâm (Pham Van Ky character), 360–62
Lethal Weapon (film), 126
"Lettre à un jeune Français d'Algérie" (Sénac), 155, 161–63
Lévinas, Emmanuel, 180n34, 269–70, 283n39
Lévy, Bernard-Henri, 251–52
L'Horreur Economique (Forrester), 125–26
Liauzu, Claude, 168, 169, 170, 172, 181n35
Libération (periodical), 418
The Liberation of the Jew (Memmi), 264, 268
Les lieux de memoire (Nora), x
Limoges, and development of francophone culture, 414–15, 420, 424, 425; Municipal Library of Limoges (Bibliothèque Francophone Multi-média de Limoges), 415–16, 423; Université de Limoges francophone curriculum, 415, 425. *See also* Festival International des Théâtres Francophones en Limousin
Limousin: efforts to preserve culture, 412, 413. *See also* Limoges, and development of francophone culture
La littérature beur (Hargreaves), 202–3
La Littérature judéo-maghrébine d'expression française (Dugas), 261n22
Llavador, Yvonne, 158
Lloyd, David, 294–95
Local Civil Status, and citizenship, 103–4, 112n27
Lola (Kassovitz character), 138
Longequeue, Louis, 417

Papon, Maurice, 80, 81

Parcours immobile (El Maleh), 253

Parfum des étés perdus (Brami), 261n23

Paris: bidonvilles, 78; kosher food shops, 228

Paris-Match (periodical), 105

Parle mon fils parle à ta mère (Sebbar), 200

Parti Socialiste Unifié (PSU), 106

The Passing of the Great Race (Grant), 54–55

Pataouète, and Algerian Jewish identity, 234–35

patriarchal system, Mokeddem on escape from, 195

"La Patrie" (Sénac), 160–61

Pélégri, Jean, 170

Perez, Madame (Mokeddem character), 185

petits métiers, 400

Peyronnet, Jean-Claude, 417

Pham Dan Binh, 339–40n3

Pham Quynh, 364

Pham Van Ky, 360–64, 365n4

Phan, Elodie Hai-Duong Thanh, 339–40n3

photography, 400. *See also* Orientalist studio photography; postcards

Phuc, Kim, 327

Phuong Tran, 335–36

physiologie craze, 401

Piaf, Edith, 132, 133, 135

pied-noir culture: pieds noirs' pride in, 6–7; survival of, 5–6

pied-noir identity, nostalgia as component in, 221–22

pied-noir myth system: as effort to legitimize European control, 5; pan-Mediterraneanism in, xiii, 5–7. *See also* pan-Mediterranean civilization, myth of

"Pieds et poings liés" (Sénac), 158

pieds-noirs: defined, 262n37; migration

to Algeria, 5; public perception of, 106; repatriation settlement patterns, 6; resistance to social and political change, 4–5, 13; support for FLN, 168–74

"'Pieds-noirs,' mes frères" (Sénac), 156, 165, 167

"Les Pieds nus" (Lê), 330–34

The Pillar of Salt (Memmi), 273–74

Plan de Constantine (1958), 81

Pluyette, Jean, 54

Poèmes (Sénac), 150, 170

Poésies (Sénac), 156, 176

political correctness, Festival International des Théâtres Francophones en Limousin and, 424–25

Pommier, Jean, 12

Pompidou, Georges, 99

Ponsot, Henri, 35, 36–37

Le Portrait du Colonisé (Memmi), 250–51

Portrait of a Jew (Memmi), 264, 265

Portrait of Jacques Derrida (Cixous), 277–80

Ports of Call (Maalouf), 298–99

postcards: kinds of space in, 392; "scenes and types" genre, 400–401

"Pour que nos enfants cessent d'avoir honte de nous" (Eliakim), 6

"Premier (Ier) Novembre 1954" (Sénac), 158

Le Premier Homme (Camus), xiii, 9, 15–19, 20, 168

Le premier siècle après Béatrice. See The First Century after Beatrice (Maalouf)

Printemps inachevé (Ly Thu Ho), 358–60, 365n3

Prochaska, David, xxi, 10, 388, 389

"the proper," in Derrida, 280n8

provincial culture: juxtaposition of local and national in, 414; role in development of francophone culture, 414

transnational identity (*cont.*)
Juletane, 315–18; of Maalouf,
289–90, 299–300; of Maalouf char-
acters, 290, 291–92, 299; Maalouf
on modern need for, 290–91, 294,
297–98, 298–300
transnational youth counterculture:
Kassovitz's embracing of, 133–34,
142; in Kassovitz's films, 131–32
Le 13e convoi (Roseau and Fauque), 17
Trémois, Claude-Marie, 120
tribalism, Maalouf on consequences of,
295–97
Trinh Minh-ha, 327, 328–29, 332–33,
338–39
Trintignac commission, 84
Trintignac Report (1968), 85
Trouilloud, Lise-Hélène, 339–40n3
Troyansky, David G., xxii, 412
Truffaut, François, 120, 139
Truong sisters, 327
Truyên Kiều. See The Tale of Kiều
(Nguyễn Du)
Tu (Pham Van Ky character), 362–63
Tù-Hai (Nguyễn Du character), 353,
354, 355–56, 358, 363, 365n2
Tuoi (Ly Thu Ho character), 358, 365n3

"Under Western Eyes" (Mohanty), 377
Uniate Christians in Syria, Scouts de
France and, 42, 44, 45
United States immigration policy, racial
elements in, 54, 57
United States racism, French views on,
53–54
Université de Limoges, francophone cur-
riculum, 415, 425
Untitled Self-Portraits series (Bouziane):
Arab identity in, 402–8; as critique of
Orientalist studio photography, 389,
398–400; cross-dressing in, 398–400,
402, 403; exposure of constructed
nature of space in, 391–92, 393;
gender in, 389, 391, 408; identity in,

408–9; inspiration for, 388, 389–91;
juxtaposition and hybridity in,
407; "Untitled, Self Portrait," *390,
391–92*; "Untitled, Self Portrait 4,"
397, 398–400; "Untitled, Self Portrait 6," 405–8, *406*; "Untitled, Self
Portrait 8," *394, 395*; "Untitled, Self
Portrait 11," 403–5, *404*; "Untitled,
Self Portrait 12," 398, *399*, 401, *403*
urban youth riots of 2005: causes of,
117, 118; French public's reaction
to, 116, 118; *La Haine* as presage of,
116, 118; and resurgence of Republicanism, 143; as symptom of French
decline, 116–17, 118

Vacher de Lapouge, Georges, 54–55
Valéry, Paul, 6
Valmain, Frédéric, 12–13
Vân (Nguyễn Du character), 335, 365n2
Van Den Abbeele, Georges, xii, xx, 321
Van Peebles, Mario, 122
verbal nomadism, in Mokeddem, 193
Verheyen, Gunther, 297
Vernejoul, Robert de, 98, 108
Vichy State, organicist metaphors of
nationhood and, 64
Viêt-Kiêu: contradictory perceptions
of, 327; figurative exile of writers,
327–30, 335; heterogeneity of, 322,
339n3; importance of *The Tale of
Kiều* to, 327; loss of family ties, 326;
loss of place and home, 322, 325–26,
330–33; murdered inner self of, 329–
30, 333; names, changing of, 328;
number of, 321; return, complexity
of, 333–37; suffering of, 322, 324;
women's prominence among, 327
Viêt-Kiêu identity: loss of place and
home and, 332–33; multiplicity of,
329–30; reconstruction of, 326–27
Vietnam: introduction of Buddhism,
346–47; introduction of Confucianism, 345

Vietnam, French colonial: and Vietnamese liberal tradition, 356–57; and Vietnamese religion, 349–50
Vietnamese: diaspora, history of, 321–22; mixed-race, isolation of, 326; relationship to sea, 325; suffering of, 321, 322, 324
Vietnamese culture: Buddhism's role in, 347–50; Confucianism's role in, 345–46, 349–50, 357–58; importance of place, 322; national epic, 323; role of women in, 354–55, 362–64; Western influence on, 344
Vietnamese literature: compartmentalization by language, 339–40n3; and conundrum of situated multiplicity, 337; creative syncretism of, 341n12; Francophone, bibliography of, 339–40n3; French occupation and, 356–57; non-Western origins of liberal tradition in, 344–45, 356, 357–58, 364. See also *The Tale of Kiều* (Nguyễn Du)
Vietnamese living abroad. See Viêt-Ki u
The Vietnamese Novel in French (Yeager), 357
Vincendeau, Ginette, 118, 128
Vincent (Mokeddem character), 382–83
Vinz (Kassovitz character), 117–18, 126–27, 128, 129, 132
violence: in French-language literature of Algeria, 182; in *Les Hommes qui marchent* (Mokeddem), as effort to decolonize Algerian identity, 183–85, 188, 191, 195; violative, 188
visual artists, Western, revisioning the East, 388–89
La voyeuse interdite (Bouraoui), 377–81

Warner-Vieyra, Myriam, xx, 303–4, 315–18
Watenpaugh, Keith David, xiv, 24
Wazzan, Hasan al- (Maalouf character), 290, 291

Weil, Lucien, 62
Weltman-Aron, Brigitte, xix, 264
Western feminist paradigm: Algerian women writers' efforts to merge into, 373, 377–86, 384–85; Algerian women writers who avoid, 374–75; assumptions about Muslim women, 385–86; efforts to escape hegemony of, 376–77; imposition on Muslim women, 372–73, 376–77; reiteration of colonial paradigms in, 372, 376, 384–86
white race: assimilation and, 59–60, 62–63, 66; guilt of, in Bâ's *Un chant écarlate*, 309; history of concept, 56; preferential immigration policies for, 56–57, 61–62, 64–67; subdivisions within, 57–58, 60
Wide Sargasso Sea (Rhys), 304–5, 306–9
Wilder, Gary, xii
Wittig, Monique, 197n9
women: and colonial imposition of culture in Algeria, 189–90; central role in bidonville houses, 79–80; in *The Tale of Kiều* (Nguyễn Du), 354–56; and Viêt-Ki u experience, 327, 337–39. See also feminine as "other"; Muslim women
women, Algerian: and construction of Muslim femininity, 371–73; cultural role, 79–80; French reeducation of bidonville residents, 82–83, 84, 86; resistance to reeducation, 88
women artists, Western-based, revisioning the East, 388–89
women's oppression: in Bâ's *Un chant écarlate*, 309–15; and cultural hegemony, 306; literary metaphors of confinement, 304–6; in Rhys's *Wide Sargasso Sea*, 306–9; as ubiquitous cultural phenomenon, 318; in Warner-Vieyra's *Juletane*, 315–18
women's role: in Algerian culture,

women's role (*cont.*)
78–79; in Confucian culture, 354–55, 356, 361; in Judaism, 278; in Vietnamese culture, 354–55, 362–64
women writers, as figurative exiles, 328–30
women writers, Algerian: authentic voices among, 374–75; efforts to merge into Western feminist paradigm, 373, 377–86; feminist consciousness in, 373; imposition of Western feminist discourse on, 376–77, 379; Woodhull on, 381
Woo, John, 134
Woodhull, Winifred, 372, 381
worker productivity, and racist immigration policy, 59–60, 60–63
World Trade Organization, French fear of, 140
World War I, race-based grading of labor in, 60–61
writers in residence program, of Festival International des Théâtres Francophones en Limousin, 420
writing: of bisexuality in Mokeddem, 190–91; *écriture d'urgence*, 204–5; *écritures décentrées*, 135–36, 145n16; as exile, 327–30, 335; as exile and return, 335; Maalouf on goals of, 294
Writing French Algiers (Dunwoodie), 9, 10–12

written word, colonizers' supplanting of native identity with, 185–86

Xich-lo (Nguyên), 334–35
Xuân-Phuc, 325

Yacine (Mokeddem character), 382
Yacine, Kateb, 172, 176
Yaker, Layachi, 154
Yasmine (Mokeddem character), 195
Yeager, Jack, 357
Yédes, Ali, xx–xxi, 344
Yellow Nylon Rope (Bouziane), 389
Yiddish, and Jewish identity, 233
youth, construction of, Scouting and, 43–44, 44–45
youth, urban, riots of 2005: causes of, 117, 118; French public's reaction to, 116, 118; *La Haine* as presage of, 116, 118; and resurgence of Republicanism, 143; as symptom of French decline, 116–17, 118
youth counterculture, transnational: Kassovitz's embracing of, 133–34, 142; in Kassovitz's films, 131–32
Yvane, Jean, 244

Zap Mama, 135
Z brigades, 81–82
Zina, Aunt (Mokeddem character), 194
Zohra (Mokeddem character), 185, 190, 192, 193, 195

In the France Overseas series

To Hell and Back
The Life of Samira Bellil
Samira Bellil
Translated by Lucy R. McNair
Introduction by Alec G. Hargreaves

The French Navy and the Seven Years' War
Jonathan R. Dull

I, Nadia, Wife of a Terrorist
Baya Gacemi

Transnational Spaces and Identities in
the Francophone World
Edited by Hafid Gafaïti, Patricia M. E. Lorcin,
and David G. Troyansky

French Colonialism Unmasked
The Vichy Years in French West Africa
Ruth Ginio

Bourdieu in Algeria
Colonial Politics, Ethnographic Practices,
Theoretical Developments
Edited and with an introduction by
Jane E. Goodman and Paul A. Silverstein

Endgame 1758
The Promise, the Glory, and the Despair
of Louisbourg's Last Decade
A. J. B. Johnston

Making the Voyageur World
Travelers and Traders in the
North American Fur Trade
Carolyn Podruchny

A Workman Is Worthy of His Meat
Food and Colonialism in Gabon
Jeremy Rich

The Moroccan Soul
French Education, Colonial Ethnology,
and Muslim Resistance, 1912–1956
Spencer D. Segalla

Silence Is Death
The Life and Work of Tahar Djaout
Julija Šukys

Beyond Papillon
The French Overseas Penal Colonies, 1854–1952
Stephen A. Toth

Madah-Sartre
The Kidnapping, Trial, and Conver(sat/s)ion
of Jean-Paul Sartre and Simone de Beauvoir
Written and translated by Alek Baylee Toumi
With an introduction by James D. Le Sueur

To order or obtain more information on these
or other University of Nebraska Press titles,
visit www.nebraskapress.unl.edu.